QUEST FOR
ALL-WEATHER FLIGHT

QUEST FOR ALL-WEATHER FLIGHT

Tom Morrison

Airlife

Copyright © 2002 Tom Morrison

First published in the UK in 2002
by Airlife Publishing Ltd

British Library Cataloguing-in-Publication Data
A catalogue record for this book
is available from the British Library

ISBN 1 84037 259 1

Photographs used throughout this book are reproduced with
the kind permission of Philip Jarrett unless otherwise credited
on the caption.

Typeset by Rowland Phototypesetting Limited, Bury St
Edmunds, Suffolk
Printed in England by Bath Press Ltd, Bath

*Contact us for a free catalogue that describes the complete range
of Airlife books for pilots and aviation enthusiasts.*

Airlife Publishing Ltd
101 Longden Road, Shrewsbury, SY3 9EB, England
E-mail: sales@airlifebooks.com
Website: www.airlifebooks.com

Preface

This book owes its inception to Colonel Jack Kaiser, Royal Canadian Air Force (retired), long associated with the Victoria Flying Club, Victoria, British Columbia, as Chief Instructor and Manager, who instilled in his pupil his own fascination with instrument flying.

'Instrument flying' concerns the whole business of flying an aircraft blind through cloud or darkness without sight of the world outside the aircraft. Jack Kaiser taught me this skill at Victoria between 1984 and 1986. In those brief moments available for contemplation as I glared at the instruments from under the hood, or as we punched into any spare cloud that happened to be floating around, I wondered how all this came to be.

I discovered that very little had been published on the history of instrument flying and I decided to research the subject with the idea of remedying this deficiency. The major aviation historical collections were, however, too far away for me to gain access to them for any useful length of time while working at a full-time job. In early 1987, having moved to Vancouver, I happened to visit the University of British Columbia about some unrelated matter and, chancing upon the University Library, I found a large and diverse collection of published material on aviation, some of it dating back to the 1920s. With this valuable source near at hand, I was able to carry out the necessary research. This, and extensive reading in aviation literature, was the source of a suitcase full of notes and photocopies, accumulated between 1987 and 1991, from which this book was written. The notes had to be kept in a suitcase because most of the book was written in my spare time while living and working at remote, isolated mine sites in northern British Columbia and the Canadian Arctic. The draft manuscript was completed in the spring of 1996, nine years after its conception.

I am particularly indebted to the staff at the University of British Columbia Library for making available the material committed to their charge. Mr A. W. L. Nayler, one-time Librarian at the Royal Aeronautical Society in London and Mr F. Huntley, consulting archivist to British Airways, supplied valuable points of detail that could not have been obtained otherwise.

My special thanks go to the publishers, Airlife, especially to Peter Coles, Managing Editor, and his assistants for providing the illustratons. Many of these were highly obscure and much time and effort went into obtaining them. In particular, Messrs. P. Jarrett and L. Coombs were unstinting in their generosity with many photographs and other illustrative material in their possession. I am also grateful to Airlife for their meticulous scrutiny of the technical details of the text. In a book on a subject as complex and diffuse as this one, errors and omissions are unavoidable I ask for pardon for any that the reader may detect.

The project started off as a history of instrument flying, but it became apparent that instrument flying was only one aspect of a broader, and possibly more interesting, subject: the historical interaction between the development of aviation technology and the weather, in particular, the quest for the ability to fly in all weather conditions. Some authors have been dismissively glib on this subject: flying through cloud was impossible without gyroscopic instruments; gyroscopic instruments were invented in the 1920s so that pilots could fly through cloud; the first 'blind' flight was flown in 1929, and that was the problem solved. My researches showed that the real story was immeasurably more complicated than that, going back to the earliest days of aviation, and reaching a sort of *status quo* in the relatively recent past with the achievement of automatic blind landing in passenger service. In particular, the progress of all-weather flying has followed paths that are far from obvious. When an air traffic controller seated at a radar screen is about to steer a pilot in a series of unexpected directions, some of which may seem irrational, he or she gives warning with the words: 'Expect vectors.' In introducing the reader to this book, I can only do the same.

Tom Morrison
Vancouver, British Columbia, Canada

Foreword

From the vantage point of the year 2000 we look back on the twentieth century as stunned survivors, wondering what happened, trying to make sense of the maelstrom of events that has assaulted and overturned our most basic ideas and beliefs.

Current in 1900 was the belief that humans could not fly; only a few dreamers and crackpots thought otherwise. Yet, within a lifetime, not only did aircraft become a reality, they came to exert a pervasive influence on all of human society without exception. As a weapon, the aircraft became capable of exerting decisive influence in war and diplomacy. As a means of transport, it brought diverse people face to face and, by breaking down age-old barriers of ignorance and distrust, became a potent agent of world peace.

A small number of people, less than one in two thousand of the world's population, acquired the recondite skills to take these flying machines in their hands and cause them to fly, usually but not always in accordance with their wishes. A few of these pilots are known to history; the majority are the anonymous heroes of one of the greatest scientific revolutions the world has ever seen, yet for the most part unaware of their historic role. They were, and are, mariners in a strange ocean – 'strange' because three-dimensional, at first unfamiliar, always weird and to some extent unpredictable.

This revolution was led by just four countries: the United States of America, Britain, Germany and France. It was only ten years old at the outbreak of thirty years of war and revolution in Europe, followed by the forty-year arms race of the Cold War. Its course was symbiotic with these events, both driven by them and acquiring a driving force of its own. Less obviously, the aviation revolution was moulded by the climates and weather conditions of northern Europe, North America and the North Atlantic, a fact the more important because weather has always had a more limiting effect on the flight of aircraft than on the movement of any ship or land vehicle. The need to function through all the various weather conditions of these areas meant that an essential but sparsely acknowledged part of the aviation revolution was the quest for flight in spite of all weathers. In 1900–14 the Russians were beginning to display technical brilliance in aviation, but this ceased with the revolution of 1917 and, as far as these researches have shown, the USSR contributed nothing to the quest, for all-weather flight. Emigrants, such as Seversky and Sikorski, however, contributed greatly to aviation development elsewhere.

So much for the title and subtitle of this book. The quest took place, for the most part, between 1903 and 1982. On 17 December 1903, for the first time, a heavier-than-air craft took off under its own power and was controlled by a human pilot for the duration of its flight. Although this date has since become well known, 5 May 1982 passed almost unnoticed. On that date, for the first time, an airliner landed automatically in blind conditions of dense fog in normal passenger service. This event was not acknowledged by the aviation technical press, receiving only brief mention in a British Airways company newsletter.

In seventy-nine years a whole technology had come into being from nothing. Literally nothing, for it was conceived, designed, engineered and put into effect with no predecessor concept or technology. It reached maturity after accommodating itself to a set of economic and technical constraints which show no sign of being breached. The achievement of this extraordinary quest, the political events which drove it and were driven by it, the aircrew who made it happen and the acceptance of certain ultimate limitations are the theme of this book. Symbolically, the quest began and was completed on two quite small pieces of ground. It began with a take-off from the sands of Kitty Hawk in North Carolina and culminated with a landing at London Heathrow airport.

Contents

CHAPTER 1

That Day at Kitty Hawk

The Wright brothers' first sustained, powered, piloted flight on the dunes of the North Carolina coast would have taken place earlier than 17 December 1903, but for the weather. The brothers had been experimenting at Kitty Hawk since the summer of 1900, having selected the site both for its seclusion and for its windspeeds. They were delayed in starting their 1903 field season until late September and it was not by choice that they lingered in that bleak location until winter was upon them.

The Wrights' gliding experiments between 1900 and 1903 depended on just the right amount of wind for launching, not too much and not too little; the experimental glides were therefore flown as and when the weather permitted. The disassembled, crated Wright Flyer arrived at Kitty Hawk on 8 October 1903, but work on it was prevented by a four-day storm. Assembly of the machine, followed by unpowered glides to check the design, took up the balance of October. Breakages to the engine and the shipment of replacement parts between the site and the brothers' home town of Dayton, Ohio, went on until early December.

All was ready on 14 December. The machine did, in fact, make a flight that day, but the flight lasted only 3½ seconds and ended in a crash. The next day was spent repairing the damage. 16

The Wright brothers' first powered flight, 17 December 1903.

December was calm and no attempt was made. On the following day the wind was too strong for preference but, urged on by their desire to be home for Christmas and by the increasing cold and discomfort of their situation, the brothers made that celebrated first flight on 17 December 1903, at 10.35 a.m.[1]

Humans took to the sky in two very different types of vehicle: lighter-than-air and heavier-than-air. Lighter-than-air craft were the first to leave the ground and, in the early years of flight, seemed to be the more promising. They originated surprisingly far back in history in balloons filled with hot air, or with hydrogen when the gas could be produced in sufficient quantities.

On 1 June 1785: 'About 3 o'clock this Afternoon a violent tempest arose at Norwich in the North East, very loud Thunder with strong white Lightening with heavy rain – which lasted about an Hour – immediately after which Mr Decker's Balloon with Decker himself in a boat annexed to it, ascended from Quantrell's Gardens and very majestically … A vast Concourse of People was assembled to see it. It was rather unfortunate that the Weather proved so unfavourable – but added greatly to the Courage of Decker that he ascended so very soon after the Tempest.'[2]

It is not clear whether this was a hot air balloon or a hydrogen balloon. Nevertheless, the principle of these craft was simple. The contents of the gas bag was lighter than the volume of air that it displaced, with the result that the vessel floated in the air for the same reason that a cork floats in water. Altitude was controlled by jettisoning ballast or by releasing gas.

A balloon drifted with the wind and its speed and direction over the ground was that of the wind at its altitude, as some balloonists found to their cost. The same diarist as before records: 'Colin Roupe told us that the Balloon which Major Money went up in, went 7 Leagues on the Sea, and that Major Money was 5 Hours up to his Chin in the Sea before he was taken up, and then by chance, a Boat very providentially being returning by him.' This took place after another ascent from Norwich on 22 July 1785. Any usefulness as a vehicle was thus fortuitous.

Engines and propellers turned balloons into airships and enabled them to travel over the ground more or less in the direction that the crew wanted. Because of its bulk and limited power, an airship could force its way through the air only at low speeds and its progress over the earth's surface was

much susceptible to the wind. It was, however, inherently stable aloft, with no innate tendency to roll, pitch, or yaw, and it could remain aloft even if its engines were turned off.

Airships reached their apogee in the German Zeppelin and Schutte-Lanz airships of the First World War, and in those built by Great Britain and the US in the 1920s. Their hydrogen filling was dangerously inflammable and their huge structures were vulnerable to atmospheric turbulence. A series of disasters in the 1930s finished the airship as a practical vehicle. The powered rigid airships remain to this day as the largest artifacts ever to have left the ground.

The heavier-than-air machine was entirely different. First came the necessary belief that flight by this means was, in fact, possible, a radical idea propounded as long ago as 1647 by an Italian engineer, Tito Livio Burattini.[3] The first aeroplane to carry a human being in free flight was a glider built by the Englishman, Sir George Cayley.[4] The flight in question took place in 1853. Significantly, however, the human was a passive – and frightened – passenger exerting no control over the flight.

The Wrights were the first to understand the pilot's continuous active participation in controlling the aircraft. Once the craft was airborne, the problem of control was more complex and more dangerous than the problem of becoming airborne in the first place, so much so that a German balloon officer remarked in 1907: 'The Wright machine is more suitable for an acrobat than a soldier, as it carries only one man and he is far too busy looking after it to attend to matters of war.'[5]

An aeroplane in flight is subject to aerodynamic effects which are almost impossible to understand without having experienced them as a pilot. These effects are both static and dynamic and they interact in ways that are far from obvious. This is no place to discuss aerodynamics, but we need to be aware that the physics of heavier-than-air flight are far more complicated than the lighter-than-air variety. Its full complexity was not understood for several decades after 1903, and then only through the application of advanced mathematics. Aerodynamics research continues with even greater intensity today.

We need to be aware of a further important distinction: between manual and automatic flight. In manual flight the aircraft's control surfaces are extensions of the pilot's hands and feet just as a bird's flight feathers are extensions of its physical structure. The pilot controls the aircraft's attitude and direction by a continual series of small control pressures. In automatic flight the pilot detaches himself from the controls and substitutes a powered, mechanical feedback device – an autopilot.

In the early days a prolonged debate went on as to whether an aeroplane should be inherently stable in flight, needing little input from the pilot, or whether control should depend entirely and continuously on the pilot. Samuel P. Langley's powered model aeroplane of 1903, for example, flew in a straight line for 1,000 feet with only its own inherent stability to control it.[6] From this debate came the idea that an aeroplane could be unstable enough to be manoeuvrable, but that the pilot could augment its stability by engaging a device capable of detecting deviations from a desired attitude and direction of flight and producing compensating control pressures automatically. The idea of an autopilot as a mechanical copilot to relieve the pilot while flying long distances and, later, to follow prescribed tracks with superhuman precision, grew in response to problems that did not exist in the earliest days of flight.

Flight, by whatever means, would be sufficiently complex and demanding if the sky were always mild, calm and bright. Such is far from being the case. If flight was ever to be of any use, the aviator would have to contend with clouds, storms and darkness. Advances in aircraft construction would be futile without the ability to deal with such conditions.

Human flight entailed an immediate, close involvement with the weather. People had always been affected by the weather. Perhaps those most affected were mariners at sea, but they had voyaged on it since time immemorial and at least retained contact with the earth's surface. The aviators found that, whether they liked it or not, they were mariners in an ocean far stranger than the sea, capable of destructive violence and of other,

more insidious conditions in which a pilot could not fly and survive. It also beckoned them into a realm of illusion and sensory deprivation never before experienced by human beings.

As soon as an aircraft became a vehicle, rather than a curiosity, the need arose to navigate this ocean at the behest of commerce, war, or personal convenience, and not merely whenever the fickle weather was favourable. As aircraft became more capable, the demand intensified that they should fly from place to place at any time without regard to the weather. The development of aviation has been inseparably parallelled by a quest for the ability to fly in all weather conditions.

This quest for all-weather flight underlies a technology that developed from a mere hypothetical possibility in 1900 to maturity eighty years later and caused fundamental changes in human society. The literature of aviation history has neglected this aspect of flight almost completely. Hitherto there has been no compendious historical account of the quest for all-weather flight. The conventional history of flight deals with the development of airframes and engines, how aircraft have flown faster, farther and higher, and what they have done in commerce and war. The development of aviation could no more outpace its ability to deal with the weather than a child can outgrow its own shadow. Like many a quest, this one is richly imbued with triumph and tragedy, but few quests have come so far so fast, and few can have been so recondite, as this one pursued through the strange ocean of the sky.

---

1 Howard 1987, 136
2 Woodforde 1978, 250
3 Hart 1979, 269
4 Pritchard 1954, 701; Gibbs-Smith 1974, 125
5 *Flight*, 31 January 1935, 133
6 Howard 1987, 127

CHAPTER 2

Mariners in a Strange Ocean

For ten years after that momentous first flight the aeroplane showed few signs of what it would eventually achieve or become. It was an ungainly contraption of wood, wire and cloth. One, and sometimes two people rode on it, secured to crude seats only by gravity, unaware of the rapidity and ease with which the aeroplane could throw them off. The flying machine was a dangerous curiosity.

The challenge of heavier-than-air flight was nowhere tackled with more passionate enthusiasm than in France and the first performance records set there did in some way foreshadow things to come. On 31 December 1908, Wilbur Wright flew around a circuit for 2 hours and 20 minutes, covering 145 km (90 miles). On 26 July 1909, Louis Bleriot flew the 32 km (20 miles) across the Channel to England. In spite of claims that England was no longer an island, this visitor from France carried no payload and crashed on arrival. At the Reims air races in August 1909, the speed record around a 20 kilometre closed circuit was just 76 km/h (47 mph). In October 1910, a US alti-

The London to Manchester flight, 23 April 1910, Mr Claude Grahame-White leaving Rugby.

tude record was set at slightly above 2,135 metres (7,000 feet).

As a vehicle, the aeroplane was entirely at the mercy of wind and weather. In October 1910, during an International Aviation Tournament at Garden City, Long Island, two pilots, Hoxsey and Johnstone, on Wright aircraft, encountered such a strong wind at a height of 300 metres (1,000 feet) that, although flying into wind at full throttle, they were carried away downwind, flying backwards over the ground. One pilot landed 40 km (25 miles) away, the other 88 km (55 miles) downwind of his take-off point.[1]

Many aircraft in those days crashed with fatal results after being thrown out of control by wind and turbulence. Their performance resembled that of a present-day ultralight. Control of an ultralight is threatened by windspeeds above 9 km/h (5 knots), which robs it of any usefulness as a vehicle – precisely the problem facing the first aviators, except that the present-day ultralight pilot has a vast amount of aeronautical knowledge on which to draw. They had none.

In April 1910, a 296 km (184 mile) cross-country flight between London and Manchester in England showed what aeroplanes were capable of at that time, and what difficulties and hazards the weather imposed on their pilots.[2] The *Daily Mail* newspaper was offering an immense prize of £10,000 for the first flight to be completed between the two cities within a 24-hour period. The first serious contestant was Claude Grahame-White with a Farman biplane. The aircraft had no instrumentation of any kind. Grahame-White carried no maps, which would, in any case, have been difficult to use as the pilot was unprotected from the slipstream.

Grahame-White took off from London on 23 April at 5 a.m. He landed to refuel at Rugby, 134 km (83 miles) away, at 7.20 a.m. and took off again at 8.25 a.m. Gusty winds and engine trouble forced him to land an hour later, near Lichfield, having flown 182 km (113 miles). Unfortunately the aircraft was not tied down; a wind gust overturned it, causing severe damage, and it was taken back to London by train for repair.

By the time the machine was repaired, late on 26 April, a rival had appeared on the scene, the Frenchman, Louis Paulhan, with a Farman biplane of slightly different design. Both pilots were ready on 27 April but strong winds kept them on the ground. At 5.30 p.m. the more experienced Paulhan took off in spite of the wind. Grahame-White was elsewhere at the time, resting after working incessantly on his machine. Told of Paulhan's departure, he took off an hour behind the Frenchman. Both pilots landed with the onset of dusk at about 8 p.m., Paulhan at Lichfield 188 km (117 miles) *en route*, Grahame-White at Roade, only 97 km (60 miles) from London. Both pilots navigated by following the London and North Western Railway.

In desperation to catch up, Grahame-White took off again at 2.45 a.m. with the help of acetylene bicycle lamps and car headlights. His ground team of two men followed in a steam car. At one point they formed an extemporary navigation beacon by shining their lights on the whitewashed wall of an inn at a crossroads in the early hours of that morning. At dawn Grahame-White was flying in a hilly area near Lichfield in a rising wind. His heavy fuel load made it impossible to climb above the hills, but turbulence caused by the wind made control of his aircraft increasingly difficult. He landed at 4.15 a.m., just as Paulhan took off, only 16 km (10 miles) away, to complete his flight to Manchester. Paulhan landed at 5.30 a.m., completely exhausted by the struggle to control his aircraft in the turbulence, and won the prize.

The vast distances of North America offered correspondingly vast challenges. In August 1911, Harry Atwood flew a Wright Model B for 2,090 km (1,300 miles) from St Louis, Missouri, to New York in 12 days. In October 1911 Cal Rodgers left Sheepshead Bay, Long Island, on a Wright EX with a top speed of 88 km/h (55 mph). He reached Long Beach, California, 12 weeks later, after eleven major accidents; the aircraft had been so extensively repaired that little of the original material remained. That same winter Robert Fowler flew a Wright Model B from Los Angeles to Jacksonville, Florida. The journey took 112 days; he arrived on 8 February 1912.[3]

Calbraith P. Rogers's flight, an undertaking that his instructors, the Wrights, thought impossible, gave a daunting insight into some of the difficulty, danger and discomfort that the weather held in store for aviators,[4] In general Rogers did not fly in bad weather and remarked that:[5]

1 Performance records quoted in Howard 1987
2 Harper 1910
3 Howard 1987, 371–5
4 Stein 1985
5 Stein 1985, 299

The only obstacle I fear is the destruction of my airplane by a storm when it is not flying. [He did become entangled in one area of thunderstorms on the border between Indiana and Ohio on 1 October 1911, of which he wrote in his diary:] It was like flying through milky water. It was impossible to see a foot ahead of me … I didn't know what lightning might do to an aeroplane but I didn't like the idea … If you have ever been out in a hailstorm you will know how that rain cut my face. I had taken off my goggles for fear that I might be blinded by the water, and I took off my gloves and covered what I could of the vital points of the magneto. It was a cold and painful situation.

I looked for my engine to stop on me any minute and began searching for a place to alight. I couldn't find one because a big cloud had quickly rolled in under me and the earth had disappeared. It was lonesome. I might be a million miles up in space. I might be a hundred feet from earth. I breathed better when I sailed over the edge of the cloud and saw the misty land beneath me.

I expect to see the time when we are carrying passengers from New York to Los Angeles in three days. This will mean more than 100 mph, and the riders will have to be boxed in because the wind blasts one awful at that speed.

The capacity of the sky to blind and confuse the aviator was apparent at least as early as 1899.[6] In that year a balloon carrying one man was launched at the Crystal Palace in London. The balloonist expected that the easterly wind would carry him west over southern England. The balloon ascended through an overcast to float level in clear air at 900 metres (3,000 feet) for two hours. At the end of this time he expected to be near Reading, 80 km (50 miles) west of London. Descending through the cloud once more, he found himself, instead, over the sea. The wind then carried him to the east coast of England, far to the east of his launching point.

The answer to this riddle was that, while the balloon was drifting in the wind above a continuous cloud deck, the balloonist had no means of knowing where he was going. Launching in an easterly wind at ground level, he had ascended into an overrunning westerly wind aloft. This wind carried him far to the east so that, by the time he chose to descend, he was over the sea off the east coast of England. Below the wind shear once again, the

The London to Manchester flight. Paulhan and his Farman.

low-level easterly wind carried the balloon to shore.

At the Second International Congress of Aeronautics at Paris in 1900, 'The members interested themselves with the means to find the position of an aircraft within and above clouds'[7] This idea, sneaking into our tale as an intriguing speculation, will emerge as a central theme of this book.

One of the leading figures of the British aircraft industry for fifty years was Sir Geoffrey de Havilland. He built his own first aircraft in 1909 and taught himself to fly it. He was also an excellent writer and leaves us two vivid descriptions of his first involvement with flying in cloud.[8] Sir Geoffrey made his first attempt to fly through cloud in 1911. He took off beneath an overcast sky. Setting the aircraft in a straight, full-throttle climb, he penetrated the overcast and tried to rely on 'instinct and a sense of balance' to maintain a constant attitude. After a short time he broke out into 'a blinding world of billowing whiteness that stretched in every direction, magnificent, vast, and thrilling.' The wonder of that experience never left him.

A less pleasant experience befell him in 1913, flight-testing an RE-1 at Farnborough. One foggy early morning, he took off to inspect the weather and at once flew into fog so dense that he could not see enough to return to the airfield. After ten minutes dodging trees and houses, he realized that his only safe escape was to climb. Although terrified, he concentrated on keeping his aircraft in a straight climb. At 900 metres (3,000 feet) he emerged into a clear sky but had lost all contact with the ground and had no means of knowing where he was. Knowing that the country was more open to the west, he flew in that direction by his compass. Luckily he found a small hole in the fog and, spiralling down, he landed in the first field that he saw.

In 1911 a French navy lieutenant, Jean Conneau, was greatly confused when he tried to fly in cloud. 'Consulting my compass, I made straight north, yet I could not make out if I was following a straight line. I was caught in a whirlpool which made me face south, and was unable to understand this change of direction as I had not touched the rudder. I wondered if my compass was going mad …'[9] Some pilots claimed to have flown into 'magnetic clouds' that made the compass needle spin, unaware that the aircraft had been turning while the compass needle had been relatively still.[10]

Conneau was lucky to be no worse than confused, as he had been attacked by three phenomena about which nothing was known at that time: the lateral instability of his aircraft, the northerly turning error of the magnetic compass and sensory illusions.

An aeroplane may be stable longitudinally, yet unstable laterally. That is, it may tend to keep a constant attitude in the nose-up, nose-down direction without the pilot's intervention, but may roll and yaw in response to imbalance, control movements or turbulence if the pilot does not keep it constantly under control. Roll and yaw are coupled. Once a turn begins, one wing is flying faster than the other and generates more lift. As a result the aircraft banks. The more it banks, the faster it turns; the faster it turns, the more it banks. An aircraft in a turn loses altitude unless the pilot controls it. The result of an uncontrolled turn, therefore, is an ever-steepening downward spiral.

In cloud the pilot has no external references and can easily be unaware that the aircraft is turning. Other bodily senses are misleading. The magnetic compass cannot be relied upon because of 'northerly turning error'. The earth's magnetic field has a horizontal and a vertical component. The vertical component and the structure of the compass needle or card produce the northerly turning error. In an aircraft turning in the northerly arc of the compass, the compass card lags the turn, telling the pilot that the aircraft has turned less than it has. Indeed, when the turn is begun, the compass card indicates a turn in the opposite direction before beginning to follow the true turn. In the southerly arc, the compass leads the turn, indicating that the aircraft has turned more than is the case. These errors are most pronounced on north and south headings. The compass also swings if the aircraft accelerates or decelerates, even though its heading is constant. This swing is not constant in magnitude, but varies from a maximum on east-west headings to a minimum on north-south headings. Therefore the one instrument that has for centuries offered reliable directional guidance in the trackless places of the earth and sea was useless as a reference instrument in the ocean of the sky. Recognition of this prob-

6 Wright 1972, 28
7 Wright 1972, 19
8 de Havilland 1961, 66, 83
9 Wright 1972, 46
10 *Flight International*, 5 August 1971, 222

lem was slow, the analysis of its causes still more so.

The physical sensations that keep us upright and on course on the earth's surface are not only ineffective in an aircraft, but misleading. This has been intensively studied in response to the needs of aviation, but in Conneau's day nothing was known about it.

Conneau and many other pilots suffered from the combined effects of these phenomena, sometimes with fatal results, before they understood what they were. Sir Geoffrey de Havilland remarked that pilots often climbed through fog or cloud, but that they lived in a fool's paradise, unaware of the danger of what they were doing. He commented, however, that 'as long as we did not realize the danger all was well, but when it was realized, due to an increasing number of fatal accidents, no one could fly through cloud without apprehension of losing control'.[11]

Aircraft of that time had few instruments, if any, no electrical systems and no radio. The Wrights used three simple instruments to verify their design calculations, but not to control their aircraft.[12] These were an anemometer which measured the

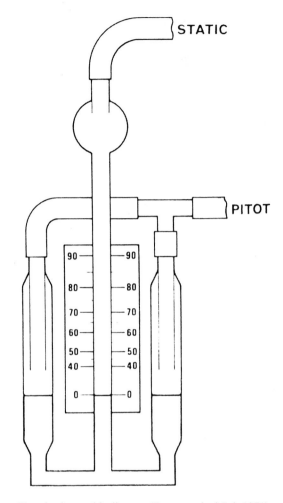

Short's airspeed indicator. (Aeronautical Jnl. 1971)

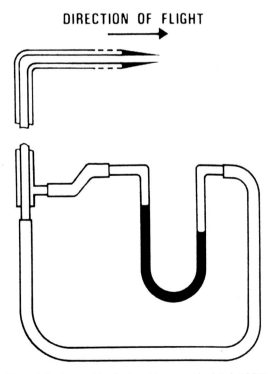

Darwin's airspeed indicator. (Aeronautical Jnl. 1971)

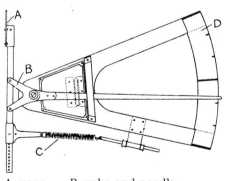

A: vane   B: yoke and needle
C: spring   D: calibrated dial

The Etève airspeed indicator.

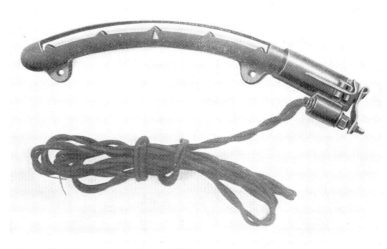

Above: Bubble-type cross level, 1920s.

Left: Fore and aft inclinometer, 1920s.

speed of the aircraft through the air, an engine revolution counter and a stopwatch. Most of the aircraft that flew during the next ten years had no instruments at all.

The first eight years of powered, heavier-than-air flight resulted in an awareness of the need to measure the aircraft's speed through the air, recognizing that airspeed was the source of lift and, hence, of controllable flight. The first airspeed indicators were activated by the pressure of the slipstream deflecting a vane against a spring or counterweight, causing a needle to move across a calibrated dial. One such instrument was invented by Etève in France in 1910. The vane airspeed indicator was subject to errors caused by manoeuvring of the aircraft and by the decreasing density of the air with increasing height.

Most subsequent air speed indicators have been based on the pitot-static principle, discovered in 1912–13. When an object moves, the dynamic pressure of the air against its front surfaces is greater than the static pressure of the undisturbed air. The pressure difference is proportional to the square of speed and can be calibrated in units of speed, such as knots or miles per hour. A pitot head, with its open end pointed in the direction of flight, senses the dynamic pressure. The static pressure is sensed through a static port in the side of the aircraft. The first instruments of this kind, such as Darwin's and Short's, used a U-tube partly filled with liquid (a manometer) to compare the pressures, but the inertia of the liquid caused unsteady, lagging readings.

An improved instrument was already being developed, in which the pitot and static pressures were applied to opposite sides of a diaphragm which moved an indicator needle through a mechanical linkage. This type of instrument is in almost universal use today.

The pitot-static principle was also used in a yaw indicator which compared the dynamic pressures at the aircraft's wingtips. The wingtip on the outside of the yaw would move faster than the wingtip on the inside, causing a pressure difference. This instrument was not used widely or for long. A similar instrument was a static-head turn indicator which measured the difference in static pressure between the aircraft's wingtips. In a bank one wing would be higher than the other, resulting in a slight difference in static pressure. Neither of these instruments was effective in blind flight.

An early attempt to measure rate of climb was based on a clockwork-operated valve allowing air into or out of a chamber at set intervals. If a change of altitude, and hence pressure, took place between openings of the valve, movement of air to or from the chamber was used as a measure of climb or descent.

Spirit levels were used as both lateral and fore-and-aft inclinometers. Although their use continued until the 1930s, manoeuvring of the aircraft

---

11 de Havilland 1961, 83
12 Chorley 1976, 323

caused such gross errors that these instruments were of little value in blind flying. Nevertheless, their use continued because they were the best that was available. Even today, in a Boeing 747-400, a bubble level is affixed to the back wall of the flight deck; in straight and level flight the aircraft can be levelled more precisely by this means than by any other. The most primitive of instruments thus continues in use in the most modern of aircraft.

Aneroid barometers calibrated in altitude had been used both in ballooning and as surveying instruments. Their use in aeroplanes soon followed. Several purpose-built aircraft altimeters came into service, capable of adjustment by the pilot to compensate for changes in ground-level barometric pressure. The instrument could not be reset in flight to compensate for changes in barometric pressure during the flight, or for differences in pressure between origin and destination, until there was a means to transmit this information to the pilot. Just because these instruments existed, it is by no means true that all, or even most, aircraft were fitted with them.

Surprisingly, autopilots were invented before there were aeroplanes for them to control and, consequently, before aeroplane stability and control could be understood. The complex mathematics of this question were first analysed by the Englishman, Professor G. H. Bryan, in 1911.[13] Before 1900 Sir Hiram Maxim invented an automatic stabilizer of which it was written in 1973:[14] '(Maxim's) whole autocontrol concept was far ahead of its time, and in detail his mechanical design is elegant to a degree which would be hard to match today.' Even in the earliest days of flying, crude automatic control systems were invented in the US, France and Germany. In 1909 a UK patent was issued to Dr

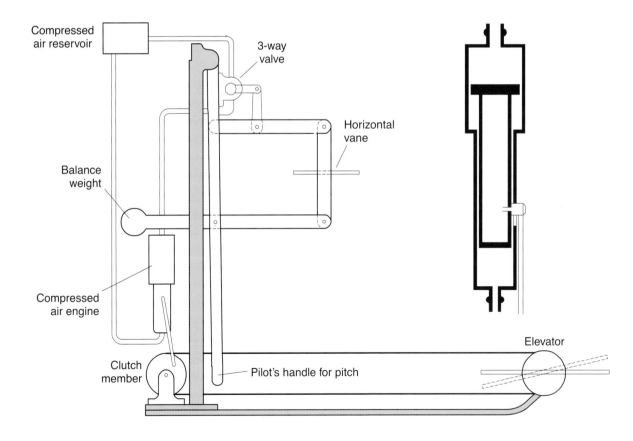

The Wright automatic aircraft stabilizer, 1909.

Ferranti (a famous name in British aviation) for a gyroscopic aircraft control.[15]

Although the debate over inherent versus automatic stability went on, in 1912 T. W. K. Clarke[16] made the prophetic remark: 'I look upon automatic apparatus as not so much a means of completely relieving the pilot of the responsibility of the (say) lateral control, as giving him something which can perform for him the greater portion of the physical effort involved, thus conserving his energy and leaving him more prepared to meet circumstances requiring steadiness of mind and body. Even with complete failure of the apparatus, such an automatically controlled machine becomes merely an ordinary hand operated one.'

Far ahead of the puny heavier-than-air machines were the rigid airships perfected in Germany. A colossal structure, filled with hydrogen, provided immense lifting power for engines, fuel, crew members, navigation equipment and the first heavy, bulky radios, not to mention passengers, freight or bombs. The lift force that can be generated by an aeroplane depends on the power of its engine(s) and the materials available for its construction. Airships were subject to no such limitations as they obeyed different physical laws.

The war that broke out in Europe in 1914 added a new dimension to the aviator's involvement with the weather. Aircraft were pressed into service for bombing and reconnaissance. An obvious advantage went to the side whose flights were least interrupted by the weather; cloud and darkness offered concealment. It is debatable whether aircraft had any detectable influence on the outcome of the war but this question is of no consequence to us compared with the fact that the sky itself became a battlefield.

13 Bryan 1911
14 Howard 1973, 533
15 de Ferranti 1970, 718
16 *Flight*, 6 July 1912, 622, quoted in Howard 1973, 538

CHAPTER 3

Battlefield in the Sky

The First World War broke out in Europe in August, 1914. In the next four years anything that would fly was pressed into military service for reconnaissance, interception, ground attack and, indeed, to strike at the enemy homeland itself. Military demands and spending forced the pace of aviation development with less consideration for cost and safety than would otherwise have been the case. As early as 1916 the British had a twin-engined bomber, the Handley Page 0/100, with a 30 metre (100 foot) wingspan and a gross weight of 7 tons, while the German Zeppelins had capabilities that aeroplanes would not match for decades. However, 90% of aircrew fatalities during the war resulted from pilot error, 8% from engine failure and only 2% from enemy action.[1]

The demands of war put the first military aircrew and their aircraft head-on against all the hostile weather conditions of northwest Europe. It was said that the British enjoyed an advantage in France because they were willing to fly in worse weather than the Germans, but the Germans developed more sophisticated equipment, in particular the first use of radio for navigation and the first gyroscopic instruments for aircraft.

The Royal Flying Corps (RFC) was established in 1912; the Royal Naval Air Service (RNAS) was formed from the RFC Naval Wing in 1914. Their first aircraft were current civilian types, although the development of military and naval aircraft soon began, both by civilian firms and by the Royal Aircraft Factory.

On 19 August 1914, a few days after the outbreak of war, Captain P. Joubert de la Ferté took off from Maubeuge in cloudy weather on the RFC's first war operation, to reconnoitre the Nivelles-Genappe area, 48 km (30 miles) to the northeast.[2] Flying through cloud, he tried to steer a compass course, but without success, and landed at Tournai, 48 km (30 miles) northwest of Maubeuge, to make enquiries. Taking off from Tournai, he became lost and landed at Courtrai, 24 km (15 miles) to the north. He finally returned to Maubeuge eight hours after his departure without having accomplished his mission.

For much of the war, and for most squadrons, flying was cancelled in bad weather – high winds, rain, snow, low cloud, poor visibility. In such conditions take-off and landing could be impossibly dangerous, formations would be separated, and pilots would be unable to navigate to their objectives or back to their bases. Fog was a particularly dangerous problem.

Cecil Lewis remembers from 1917:[3]

> About five I left (the Isle of Wight) for home. It developed into an awful journey. A heavy bank of fog came up and forced me lower and lower, so that at last I gave it up and climbed clear above it to eight thousand, trusting my compass to get me back to Rochford. I hoped that over the east coast it might break, but I was out of luck. As far as I could see in every direction was an unbroken floor, yellowish in the setting sun. Up here it was all right, a clean dome of blue, full of pale sunlight; but this vast tranquillity did not reassure me. I didn't like the colour of that floor. It was not cloud, it was fog; and how the devil was I going to get down?
>
> I flew on for a couple of hours. Petrol would be getting low. Better to come down while I had something in hand than to be forced down willy-nilly. I shut off and dropped into the fog, watching the altimeter like a cat. Here I should point out (for the benefit of the uninitiated) that the altimeter is really a barometer. To set it at zero before you leave the ground there is a thumb-screw beside the dial. But the ground at Rochford was not necessarily the same height as the ground I was at this moment dropping towards. I might come out over a hill, say two hundred feet higher than Rochford. My altime-

ter would still read two hundred feet; but I should hit the ground just the same.

When his altimeter read 150 metres (500 feet), Lewis opened the throttle to continue his descent as gently as possible. Even so, his first contact with the ground was the sight of a tree directly ahead, which he missed by a few feet. Dodging trees and hedgerows, and fearful of telegraph wires, he circled around a possible landing ground, struggling to keep it in sight through the dense fog. At last: 'The hedge passed underneath, the stubble was beneath me. She floated on for what seemed an eternity. At last I touched the ground. The opposite hedge loomed up. Should I stop in time? Should I run into it? The heavy stubble dragged at the wheels. The Pup came to rest nosing the hedge. Whew!' Lewis had no idea where he had landed and had to ask at a nearby house.

In daylight, even if cloud could be overflown, navigation remained problematical for the RFC and the RNAS, and later the RAF, throughout the war. On 29 June 1918, a Handley-Page 0/100 of 216 Squadron RAF, based at Nancy, flew to Mannheim above cloud in daylight, navigating by dead reckoning.[4] The crew made a blind descent through cloud at their estimated time of arrival, found and bombed Mannheim, and returned to France above cloud, navigating by dead reckoning as before. Anxious to avoid the cloud-covered hills around Nancy, they descended through cloud at an estimated time of arrival and landed 210 km (130 miles) from their base.

Contemporary accounts, however, leave us in no doubt that military pilots did fly in very poor weather, not always by accident, sometimes at night, and during the war experience accumulated on how to do this. Certain squadrons, such as 88 Squadron flying Bristol Fighters in 1918, specialized in bad-weather flying. Even so, pilots often lost control in cloud and relied on the cloud ceiling being high enough for them to recover after emerging into clear air in a spiral dive or a spin.

Darkness posed even worse problems than foul weather in daylight. The first night flight by an RFC pilot, as far as is known, was made by Lieutenant Cholmondeley of 3 Squadron on the night of 16–17 April 1913.[5] Pilots found that, when they were close to the ground, darkness obscured the horizon references which they needed in order to stay upright, and caused visual illusions. Consequently take-off and landing were particu-larly dangerous. A line of paraffin flares on the airfield were the first steps towards a solution.

Late in 1915 RFC artillery-spotting squadrons in France began to send single aircraft to bomb targets behind the German lines on bright moonlit nights.[6] These activities expanded in the following year and, early in 1917, 100 Squadron with FE-2bs was trained for night flying. Two more squadrons followed later that year and three more in 1918. Short flights on clear, moonlit nights progressed to longer flights in the darker periods of the moon and in weather previously considered unflyable. Casualties were extraordinarily low because of concealment in darkness; one night-flying squadron lost only five aircrew killed in more than a year of operations.

Pilots went to war with 30–40 hours of training at a flying school. An additional 10 hours of night flying was considered enough to produce a pilot capable of flying ground-attack sorties at night. One of the worst hazards of night flying was forced landing after an engine failure. One pilot wrote: 'I think it was the ever-present anxiety due to the danger of forced landings which made night flying a game which was trying to the nerves. Navigation at night, other than in good weather over lighted areas, was extremely difficult.' The same writer commented: 'The enclosed thickly wooded countryside of England is a bad land to fly over. Add to this the fact that mists and low clouds are frequent … It is easy to lose the way in rainy weather at night and difficult to compete with heavy rain.'

W. J. Harvey, flying as an observer in FE-2bs in France in the winter of 1917–18 recounted his experiences.[7] The FE-2b was a single-engined pusher biplane; the observer/gunner sat in an open position in the nose of the aircraft with the pilot behind him. They took off at 11 p.m. to strafe a German aircraft depot, although with instructions to return if the weather was bad. A snowstorm was forecast for midnight. The first part of the flight

1 Air Service Medical, UK, 1919, quoted in Journal of the Royal Aeronautical Society, 1949, 948
2 Norris, G. 1965, 54
3 Lewis, C. 1994, 223
4 Dead reckoning: a navigation method using an aircraft's compass heading and true airspeed, applying a correction for estimated windspeed, to deduce its position after a time elapsed from a known starting point.
5 Taylor, M. J. H., Mondey, D. 1983
6 Baker, C. 1920
7 Harvey, W. J. 1984, 86–92

was in a clear but dark sky. The observer was able to navigate by dimly visible landmarks and 'land lighthouses' or light beacons, flashing a Morse code identifying letter. These beacons were set up by the British and French air forces for night navigation.

Beneath, around and above us was one vast void of blackness: we could just see the dull reflection of our navigation lights, which in bad weather we generally kept switched on until we were nearing the enemy lines. I had to strain below and ahead for such lights and landmarks as I could pick up: a railway station, a bend in the river with some stray glint of starshine upon it, a peculiarly shaped blob of woodland, a land lighthouse flashing its recognition signal ...

A mile or so across the lines that night we flew into some of the thickest clouds I have seen in the whole of my flying experience – layer upon layer of dense, brutal stuff. We climbed to six thousand feet before we reached the 'ceiling' of the mist, then quite suddenly we found ourselves floating under a clear sky. Ahead of us loomed further banks of cloud looking for all the world like gently undulating foothills. Behind them, again, were great mountains of mist, holding the horizon, turrets and pinnacles, weird, fantastic needles standing out like white enamel against the intense black of the sky. We were now flying solely by compass. As we came towards these cloud mountains their outlines faded away imperceptibly; the snow patches and towering peaks seemed to melt together into a white haze, and for another thirty minutes we flew through a dense fog.

German gunners shot at the sound of their aircraft. Flying into clear air, Harvey spotted a town that he recognized, 15 km (9.5 miles) from the target. From there they were able to navigate to the target, which they attacked with bombs and machine-gun fire. That done, they turned west once more, and flew almost immediately into fog and rain.

Occasionally we caught a fleeting glimpse of the newly risen moon through scudding wracks of storm cloud. The temperature had gone down and the wind had both increased in velocity and changed in direction. For a short time we flew through blinding snow. During the snowstorm our compasses started to swing. We went on

blindly, hoping to get out of the clouds and pick up some landmark. After between two and three hours we caught a glimpse of what appeared to be moonshine on the sea. [Fuel shortage made it urgent that they land.] I glued my eyes earthwards through the mist. We were rapidly losing height. Presently I saw the lights of a town, and we flew towards them. Red and green signal lamps, steam from a locomotive showed us that we were over a railway station. We flew round once or twice at about a hundred feet, then my pilot 'chanced it' and put the bus down perfectly in a small field alongside the railway.

It was 4 a.m. Although the two men were unsure of their whereabouts, they had landed on the Allied side of the lines, about an hour's flying time from their base.

This crew survived through skill, experience and good luck. It is difficult for a modern pilot to imagine how this flight of five hours was carried out in almost continuous blind conditions at night in a primitive aeroplane with almost no instrumentation and no radio devices of any kind. On the other hand, the style of writing, dating from 1918, is too innocent to be anything other than authentic. Harvey, indeed, states plainly: 'During the later nights of the Amiens offensive we flew for the most part in mist and clouds.'[8]

Another FE-2b pilot had contrary memories:[9] 'Back in 1917 and 1918 we also welcomed bad weather! In bad weather we didn't fly! We not only didn't fly in bad weather; we didn't fly in anything but the best weather, with at least some moonlight. On black nights we didn't go up because we couldn't find any targets in the dark. And on rainy, foggy, or snowy moonlit nights, we didn't fly because the authorities knew we'd get lost, fail to find our target, and land all over France if we got back.'

It is clear, nevertheless, from various accounts[10] that by 1918 aircrew deliberately flew in cloud by day and by night, either for concealment or from force of circumstance, and that a body of experience had accumulated. One pilot recalled:[11] 'In 1918, when cloud flying was almost a routine operation, the turning indicator was a part of the standard equipment of certain aircraft. These instruments were of the static head type ...'

This experience showed that cloud flying was possible by paying close attention to the airspeed indicator and compass, assisted by lateral and longitudinal bubble levels. As long as the power set-

Cockpit and instrumentation of a Blackburn
monoplane, 1912/13.

In the effort to solve these problems much
thought was devoted to damping out the unstable
gyrations of the magnetic compass. S. Keith-Lucas
of the Royal Aircraft Establishment (RAE) at
Farnborough[12] studied the northerly turning error
experimentally, producing a mathematical analysis
in February 1917. The RAF (Royal Aircraft
Factory) Mark II Air Compass resulted from his
work. The compass card was suspended in a spherical glass bowl filled with liquid; its slow response
helped pilots to hold a straight course in blind conditions which also reduced the likelihood of loss of
control.

The following advice on the use of the magnetic
compass in blind conditions tells us much about
the status of blind flying in 1918.[13]

> [Because of northerly turning error] a cloud
> should, if possible, be entered flying in a
> southerly direction. The compass then correctly
> indicates small deviations from a straight course.
> If it is essential that a course in a northerly direc-
> tion should be followed, care should be taken to
> see that on entering a cloud the path of the
> machine is straight. The compass should then be
> closely watched, and small indications of the
> turn should be quickly and lightly checked by
> use of the rudder. [With an older, undamped
> compass]: the best course is to set the aeroplane
> on its compass course before entering a cloud,
> then leave it to itself, holding the rudder in the
> position for flying straight ahead. If the aero-
> plane is not deflected by bumps this will usually
> be effective. If the machine gets into difficulties,
> ... the best course is, on a stable aeroplane, to
> leave the controls completely, throttle down, and
> trim for gliding at a normal speed. The aeroplane
> will then take care of itself, and will ultimately
> emerge beneath the clouds when control can be
> taken again.

This advice represented the limit of the magnetic
compass as a blind flying instrument. Experience
showed clearly that some instrument capable of
providing the pilot with a constant reference in
blind conditions was essential. The potential value

ting was unchanged, a constant airspeed indicated
level flight or a steady climb or descent. A steady
compass showed that the aircraft was flying
straight. Thus, as long as the pilot kept airspeed
and compass heading steady, he could keep control
of the aircraft. Once either or both of these began
to fluctuate, however, the pilot, in trying to correct
them, could easily lose control. Control of an aircraft in blind conditions was tenuous at best; a
practised pilot could keep control of an inherently
stable aircraft, but only in straight flight.
Deliberate turns and any form of manoeuvring or
accurate course holding were impossible. Without
radio, the pilot in or above cloud was isolated from
the ground and could have only a vague idea of his
whereabouts.

8 Harvey, W. J. 1984, 143
9 Caldwell, C. quoted in *Flying*, September 1955, 67
10 Voss, V. 1977
11 Stewart, C. J. 1928
12 Melvill Jones, B. 1966
13 Fowler, K. 1918

of the gyroscope for this purpose was realized at an early date. In 1914 a writer in *Scientific American* wrote: 'Pilots will eagerly adopt a trustworthy gyroscopic indicator that will fulfil the difficult task of indicating the true horizontal. Once such an instrument is invented, flying will become 50% safer, and will be possible even in the dark.'[14] Construction of an instrument usable in aircraft was far from easy; neither the British, the French nor the Americans achieved this during the war. Their first application of the gyroscope to aircraft control was in automatic stabilization, harking back to the old argument about stability versus control.

The first scientific understanding of the gyroscope is attributed to Leon Foucault in the 1850s, although the principle had been known as a curiosity long before. The precision machining needed for the manufacture of a practical gyroscope was impossible until the first years of the twentieth century. As early as 1885, however, the French Admiral Fleuriais is said to have invented a sextant with a gyroscopic artificial horizon for use when the real horizon was obscured. The gyroscope was powered by a vacuum generated by a battery-driven air pump.[15] It is not known if this device ever entered service.

In the first decade of the twentieth century two inventors were at work on opposite sides of the Atlantic, putting the gyroscope to use in similar ways: Elmer Sperry of Flatbush, New York, and Hermann Anschütz of the German naval port of Kiel. They and others concentrated at first on marine applications, such as gyrostabilized compasses, autopilots, ship stabilizers and torpedo guidance mechanisms. The problem in adapting gyroscopes to aircraft use lay in making them light and compact enough to fit limitations of space and weight.

Through his work on gyroscopes, Elmer Sperry became involved in aircraft autostabilization. His son Lawrence, born in 1892, became an aviation enthusiast at an early age and, later, a pilot.[16] In 1912, after several years of development, the two Sperrys successfully flight-tested a gyroscopic stabilizer.[17] After two more years of development they won an Aero Club of France aeroplane safety prize of 400,000 francs with an autostabilized flight in a Curtiss flying boat near Paris on 18 June 1914. This device was later described[18] as a 'veritable supernova of engineering skill and practical accomplishment'. The stabilizer was ahead of its time and, although the French government bought

forty units in 1916, it did not come into general use. Development continued during the First World War, adapting it to a pilotless aircraft intended as a flying bomb. Equally far ahead of its time was the idea, expressed by Lawrence Sperry in December 1914, that flight through clouds and fog would demand automatic stability. His untimely death in 1923 robbed aviation of one of its finest brains.

Although the first Sperry autopilot was not widely used, it was the foundation of most subsequent automatic flight control. The system depended on a pair of gyroscopes that detected deviations from level flight. These activated mechanical switches that in turn operated pneumatic servomechanisms to move the elevators and ailerons. The basic principle has never changed since.

The first-ever air attack on Great Britain was made by a German aeroplane on 21 December 1914;[19] the last air attack on Britain of the First World War was made by a Zeppelin on 5 August 1918.[20] In the meantime 4,830 inhabitants of the island were killed or injured by bombing. Significant bomb tonnages were dropped by aircraft of three kinds: airships, Gothas and *Riesenflugzeuge* (giant aircraft).

The first Zeppelin made its maiden flight on 2 July 1900.[21] Between 1910 and 1914 the seven Zeppelins of Delag (Deutsche Luftschiffahrt AG) carried 34,000 passengers between various German cities without injury.[22] The Gothas were twin-engined biplane bombers named for their manufacturer, Gothaer Waggonfabrik, at Gotha in eastern Germany. They had the range and power to reach London from bases in Belgium, carrying a 300 kg (660 pound) bomb load at an altitude of 4,300 metres (14,000 feet). The *Riesenflugzeuge* were large multi-engined biplane bombers built in small numbers by several different manufacturers, each with their own design. Of these the Staaken R.VI, so called for its manufacturer, Zeppelin-Werke Staaken, at Staaken near Berlin, was the best known. The Staakens were the largest aircraft in wing span ever to raid the United Kingdom in either of the two World Wars.

The Zeppelin raids began in the spring of 1915; for concealment they were mostly timed to reach England at night. At 80–100 km/h (50–60 mph), sorties to England from bases in northwestern Germany could last 30–35 hours. Flying above 3,000 metres (10,000 feet), the Zeppelins were at first safe from both interceptor aeroplanes and

Zeppelin landing at Tempelhof in May 1931.

anti-aircraft fire. They could hide in or above cloud and were impervious to weather that was unflyable for the aircraft of that day and their pilots. At such altitudes, however, wind speeds could equal a Zeppelin's airspeed and blind conditions posed serious navigation problems.

On the night of 19–20 January 1915, Zeppelin L4 raided England in foggy weather.[23] The commander, Kapitänleutnant Magnus Graf von Platen Hallermund, knew where he had been only by reading English newspapers after the event. On the same night L3 under the command of Kapitänleutnant Fritz, having departed from Fuhlsbüttel in northern Germany, crossed the English coast 130 km (80 miles) off course because of winds over the North Sea.[24] Fritz identified his position by the light of a parachute flare and bombed Great Yarmouth. The weight of rain soaking the Zeppelin's envelope forced it down to 1,500 metres (5,000 feet); it returned to Fuhlsbüttel through freezing rain and fog. On 15 April 1915, two airships dropped their bombs on English towns and villages which they could not identify.[25] On 9 August 1915, four bombed four towns in England, every one of which they misidentified.[26] On 31 January 1916, nine attacked England on a night of fog, snow and freezing rain.[27] The radio direction-finding stations by which they tried to navigate were unreliable or useless. Bombs fell all over central England and no one on either side knew who was trying to bomb what. Sixteen British aircraft were launched into this appalling weather to intercept the raiders; two crashed into trees in the fog; no interceptions were made.

On 5–6 March 1916, the crew of L13 faced a northwesterly gale, hail, snow, icing and heavy rain. The weight of snow clinging to the envelope forced them to dump their bombs and 590 kg (1,300 pounds) of fuel to remain aloft.[28] That same spring of 1916, L20 tried to bomb England, but was blown so far off course that it force-landed near Stavanger in Norway, where it was wrecked.[29] No aeroplane in existence at that time could have flown in such weather. Even airships, however, were not immune to the turbulence and lightning of thunderstorms; L10 was destroyed by a thunderstorm near Neuwerk Island in September 1915.

The airship navigators depended mostly on dead reckoning. Because weather systems tend to approach northwest Europe from the west, their effects reach England before the European main-

14 *Scientific American*, 7 March 1914, p. 110, quoted in Chorley, R. A. 1976
15 Wright, M. D. 1972, 29
16 Davenport, W. W. 1978, 78
17 Howard, R. W. 1973, 538–9
18 Howard, R. W. 1973, 538–9
19 Norris, G. 1965, 84
20 Fredette, R. H. 1991, 212
21 Castle, H. G. 1982, 16
22 Davies, R. E. G. 1991, 4
23 Wright, M. D. 1972, 89
24 Castle, H. G. 1982, 45; Rimell, R. L. 1984, 33
25 Castle, H. G. 1982, 44
26 Castle, H. G. 1982, 77
27 Castle, H. G. 1982, 102
28 Rimell, R. L. 1984, 45
29 Rimell, R. L. 1984, 51

land. In both world wars, therefore, the Germans were at a disadvantage in forecasting the weather and winds aloft over England and this made the navigators' task more difficult. If they were above all clouds, celestial navigation could be used. One navigation aid specific to Zeppelins was a 'sub-cloud car'. A crew member could be lowered in a gondola on 1,500 metres (5,000 feet) of cable to check his position by looking at the ground. Airship crews also had the useful ability to stop to ascertain their position and, indeed, to turn off their engines and listen for noises from the ground.

Compared to the aeroplanes of the day, the lifting capacity of an airship was immense and was independent of its speed through the air. Bigger and faster airships were built during the war, ranging from LZ38, with a gas capacity of about 28,300 cubic metres (1 million cubic feet), four 156 kilowatt (210 hp) engines and a maximum speed of 88 km/h (55 mph)[30] to L70 built in 1917–18 with a gas capacity of 62,300 cubic metres (2.2 million cubic feet), seven engines and a top speed of 130 km/h (80 mph).

At a barometric pressure of 1,013 millibars, 60% relative humidity and a temperature of 0°C, hydrogen will lift 33 kg (72 pounds) per 28 cubic metres (1,000 cubic feet) of gas. L33, with a gas capacity of just under 56,635 cubic metres (2 million cubic feet) and a dead weight of 34,156 kg (75,300 pounds), thus had a useful lifting capacity in these conditions of 29,892 kg (65,900 pounds). This provided ample capacity for carrying, besides crew, fuel and bombs, the heavy and bulky radio transmitters and receivers of that time.[31] The German airships were the first users of radio for air navigation.

In 1899 Marconi transmitted a radio signal across the English Channel, followed by a signal across the Atlantic in 1901. The first airborne use of radio was in 1907[32] and artillery-spotting aircraft in France used radio signals during the subsequent war.

Early in the history of radio came the discovery that a loop antenna would transmit and receive most strongly in its own plane and weakest in a plane at right angles to it. By this means a signal could be transmitted with directional characteristics, or an operator could detect the direction from which a signal originated. In both cases, however, a 180° ambiguity existed which had to be resolved by other means.

By 1914 two radio direction-finding systems were being installed for marine use along the coasts of England, France and Germany. These were the Bellini-Tosi directional receiver and the Telefunken directional transmitter.[33] The Bellini-Tosi system had two concentric loop antennas set at 90° to each other in azimuth with a small rotatable loop inside them. The large antennas reradiated an incoming signal in a pattern related to the direction from which it originated. The small loop could be rotated to identify the weakest (null) signal and so determine the direction to the transmitter.

The Telefunken system was a transmitter with sixteen (later ninety) loop antennas aligned on the thirty-two points of the compass. A single non-directional signal was transmitted, followed by a signal from each of the sixteen directional antennas in sequence. The transmissions could be received on a normal receiving set. By timing the null of the directional signals after the non-directional signal, a radio operator could determine his bearing from the Telefunken transmitter. Both systems suffered from 180° ambiguity.

During the war the Germans set up Bellini-Tosi type stations at Sylt, Nordholz, Borkum and Bruges for the airships. At first the Zeppelins carried two transmitters of 1 kilowatt and 40 watt output and one receiver.[34] The navigator transmitted a request to two or more ground stations to take a bearing on his transmission and radio the results back to him; where the bearing lines from the ground stations crossed on his chart, there was his position – at least in theory. At that time, however, the distorting effects of dusk, dawn, shorelines and antenna positioning on the airship were unsuspected, and positions calculated from radio bearings could be seriously wrong. A salvo of bombs landing in the sea 105 km (65 miles) off Cromer on 5 August 1918 signified the futility of trying to bomb blind on radio bearings using the technology that was then available.

Transmissions from the airships became a source of danger to them, as they could be detected and plotted by the British to guide interceptor aircraft. In the last two years of the First World War, therefore, the Telefunken system was used instead of the Bellini-Tosi, with two ground stations at Cleve and Tondern, as this system required only a passive receiver in the aircraft. The ground stations transmitted every 30 minutes.

The horrendous problems of flying at night and in foul weather in small aircraft with minimal instrumentation and no radios were forced upon the RFC and RNAS in 1915–16 by the urgent need to intercept the airships, which cruised unopposed through the dark and cloudy skies. In October 1915, the RFC experimented with BE-2cs, a particularly stable aircraft, at Sutton's Farm to find out how best to guide pilots to a night landing. The result was two lines of paraffin flares laid out in the shape of an L. The long arm was 275 metres (900 feet) long, aligned with the wind; the short arm marked the upwind end of the landing field. A floodlight shone along the flarepath. The tactical value of electric lights, which could be switched on for only the shortest possible time needed for an aircraft to land, was recognized at an early date.[35] Pyrotechnics were used for signalling.[36] A pair of magnesium flares beneath the aircraft's wingtips with a burning time of one minute, ignited electrically from the cockpit, lit up the ground enough to help the pilot to land.[37] In the spring of 1916 the British planned to form eleven night fighter squadrons and to lay out thirty-three new airfields with flarepaths. The RFC used 19 Squadron at Hounslow to run night flying courses of about six weeks' duration.

Pilots relied on searchlights or anti-aircraft fire to indicate the position of an airship, or on occasional chance encounters. An object as large as an airship could sometimes be seen from great distances in clear weather at night, especially in moonlight. Many patrols, however, were both fruitless and extremely dangerous, flown in conditions that are incredible from the viewpoint of the present day.

Heroic efforts by interceptor pilots, improvements in aircraft performance, the growing skill and co-ordination of the home defence organization and the development of incendiary ammunition gradually destroyed the airship fleets and made attacks on England by this means practically suicidal, although attacks continued until August 1918. The airships were augmented by aeroplanes, first the Gothas and then the *Riesenflugzeuge*.

The Gothas were more vulnerable to bad weather than the airships; they were no better equipped for navigation and they had no radios. Greater speed allowed them to complete their sorties in less time – typically 4–5 hours from bases in Belgium. In these shorter periods weather forecasts were more likely to be accurate. On the other hand, the Gothas could remain aloft only for as long as fuel remained in their tanks, unlike the airships which could float motionless in the sky waiting, for instance, for morning fog to disperse from a land-ing ground. The Gothas were not intentionally launched into known foul weather, but that did not mean that adverse weather could be avoided. The first Gotha attack on Britain took place on 25 May 1917, but losses from British fighters in daylight forced the Gothas to fly over at night.

On the evening of 28 September 1917 twenty-five Gothas took off from Gontrode in Belgium to attack London under a clear moonlit sky.[38] Over the North Sea, however, they found cumulus clouds along the leading edge of a cloud deck, visible in the moonlight. Fifteen Gothas followed the advice of the squadron's weather officer and turned back, as did another with engine trouble. Although concealed from the anti-aircraft guns, and from the searchlights whose glow they could see through the cloud, the Germans were less sure of their position than they thought. Not a single bomb fell on London that night.

On the return journey the crews found that the cloud had moved east and they had to descend through it. A line of rain showers along the leading edge of the cloud added to their discomfort. One Gotha went into a spin and recovered only when the pilot caught sight of the sea at an uncomfortably low altitude. Guided by a light beacon on the Belgian coast, he managed to land safely. Darkness, low cloud and fuel shortage overcame the crews of six other Gothas which crashed with varying degrees of damage and injury.

Between 25 May 1917 and 20 May 1918, German aeroplanes (as distinct from airships) made twenty-seven attacks on England.[39] Three hundred and eighty-three Gotha sorties were dispatched; 297 (77.5%) attacked England. Sixty Gothas were lost to all causes – 15.6% of those dispatched. *Riesenflugzeuge* attacked England eleven times between 28 September 1917 and 20 May 1918, with thirty *Riesenflugzeuge* sorties dispatched, of which twenty-eight (93.3%) attacked. Only three *Riesenflugzeuge* were lost, 6.6% of those dispatched; and these were crashes on the approach to a fog-covered base in the early hours

---

30 Castle, H. G. 1982, 44
31 Rimell, R. L. 1984, 25
32 Oomen, P. 1955
33 Wright, M. D. 1972, 84
34 Rimell, R. L. 1984, 26
35 Baker, C. 1920, 631
36 Rimell, R. L. 1984, 57
37 Rimell, R. L. 1984, 76
38 Fredette, R. H. 1991, 139
39 Fredette, R. H. 1991, 266

of one morning. With four to six engines, wingspans up to 42 metres (138 feet) and bomb loads up to 2 tons, the *Riesenflugzeuge* were the most potent air weapons of the First World War.

The first squadron of *Riesenflugzeuge* was formed in Latvia in late 1915 and flew its first missions on the eastern front in August 1916.[40] By the time these aircraft began to attack England in the following year their crews had substantial experience in night flying and navigation. At the peak of their development in 1918 they were lavishly equipped with instruments and electrical equipment.

Standard equipment on the Staaken was a 1 kilowatt electric generator driven by a two-cylinder petrol engine.[41] This supplied power for a 10–30 MHz radio transceiver with a range of 595 km (370 miles), allowing the crews to receive weather, target and landing information and Telefunken navigation signals.

Flight instruments included dual airspeed indicators, an altimeter, a rate of climb indicator, a bubble inclinometer and, most significant of all, an artificial horizon. This instrument, manufactured by Anschütz, provided both pitch and bank information. Its gyroscope, however, was affected by centrifugal forces and the redesign needed to overcome this defect increased its weight to 40 kg (88 pounds). The gyroscope took ten to fifteen minutes to run up to speed. In November 1917 the Drexler bank indicator was introduced instead. Much simpler than the Anschütz instrument, it weighed only 5 kg (11 pounds). It was powered by electricity from a generator driven by a small propeller in the slipstream and took less than a minute to run up to speed.

A photograph of a Staaken cockpit shows an instrument face 150–200 mm (6–8 inches) in diameter with a double line, presumably indicative of biplane wings, to show bank and a pendulous, centre-index needle, presumably either to indicate rate and direction of turn or as a skid/slip indicator. This may have been the Drexler bank indicator. Some accounts refer to an artificial horizon in the form of a needle, kept vertical by a gyroscope, whose point moved within an inverted glass bowl. The position of the needle point in relation to index marks on the bowl showed the aircraft's attitude in pitch and bank. This may have been the Anschütz instrument.

The Drexler instrument was later licensed to,

and further developed by the Pioneer Instrument Co.,[42] formed by three Sperry employees to take over the manufacturing rights to the Sperry gyroscopic aircraft instruments after the death of Lawrence Sperry in 1923.

Notwithstanding their advanced equipment, the *Riesenflugzeuge* were still vulnerable to adverse weather. On 9 May 1918, four Staaken R-IVs took off at 8.05 p.m. from their base in Belgium to attack targets in the Calais–Dunkirk area. The weather forecast warned that fog might form over Belgium during the night. A warning was transmitted when the aircraft were over their target and conditions worsened while they were returning. Three Staakens crashed trying to land in the fog; the fourth landed safely through a chance patch of clear air. Three huge aircraft and their pilots, representing a degree of technical development that would not be surpassed for twenty years, had fallen victim to one of the most deadly combinations that would face the aviators in their quest for all-weather flight: fog, darkness, deficient ground facilities and a lack of proper procedures, or non-adherence to them.

Thus, within fifteen years of the Wright brothers' first flight, the Germans possessed a multi-engined heavy bomber with a range of 800 km (500 miles), equipped with radio, capable of blind flight and blind navigation and supported by ground-based dispatch services and radio navigation aids.

Four years of aerial warfare in the weather conditions of northwest Europe amply demonstrated the obstacles that the weather would place in the aviator's way. Military necessity produced some partial solutions that were usable or acceptable under wartime conditions but were not carried through into peacetime. Hopes for a lasting peace offered no incentive to develop military weather-flying capability and for the next twenty years the whole impetus towards all-weather capability would come from the civilian air transport industry. This, however, demanded far higher standards of safety than the military solutions reached during the war and progress in flying in bad weather lapsed for several years after the war ended.

40 Haddow, G. W., Grosz, P. M. 1962, 3
41 Haddow, G. W., Grosz, P. M. 1962, 231
42 Howard, R. W. 1973, 541

CHAPTER 4

Knights Without Armour

First World War aviation developments produced aeroplanes of substantial range and payload. The trouble was that, to keep their craft upright and on course, the pilots had to be able to see the earth's surface or, at the very least, the sun, moon, or stars. From the earliest days of aviation this requirement had proved difficult or impossible to reconcile with flying over any great distance or to any plan or schedule.

In 1919, only sixteen years after the Wright brothers' flight, aircraft crossed the Atlantic no less than four times: a US Navy Curtiss NC-4 flying boat in May and a Vickers Vimy in June, with a return trip by the British airship, R34, in July.

On 14 June 1919, a modified Vickers Vimy twin-engined biplane bomber took off from Newfoundland, bound for England, with Captain John Alcock as pilot and Lieutenant Arthur Whitten-Brown as navigator. Their navigation relied on celestial and dead reckoning methods, differing only slightly from current marine practice. They rejected radio direction-finding as too unreliable.[1]

Clear weather had been forecast, but less than an hour after their late-afternoon take-off Alcock and Brown flew between a fog bank and a cloud deck and this was followed by sixteen hours of flight in almost continuously obscured conditions of cloud or darkness at altitudes between 600 and 3,350 metres (2,000 and 11,000 feet), threatening the pilot's control of the aircraft and the navigator's ability to obtain drift sights on the sea or star shots. In addition, they encountered rain, hail, snow and airframe icing. They crossed the coast of Ireland at 8.25 a.m. Rather than risk hitting the cloud-covered hills, Alcock and Brown landed on what turned out, unfortunately, to be a bog. Captain Alcock had hand-flown an aircraft in an open cockpit, with no gyroscopic instruments, blind for much of the flight, on accurate compass headings, for just over sixteen hours.

Alcock's career came to a premature and tragic end on 18 December 1919. Flying a Vimy to Paris on a misty day, he crashed in northern France while trying to check his position, and was killed.[2]

Life was easier for the thirty-man crew of the RAF airship, R34, that left Scotland on 2 July 1919, bound for New York.[3] The airship needed less of the continuous control in three axes that was necessary for heavier-than-air craft, but it was navigated by the same means – dead reckoning and celestial. Blind flight was a problem only when it affected navigation. Cloud even made the airship's flight easier as it kept the gas bag cool, thus avoiding the venting and loss of gas.[4]

The airship commander, Major G. H. Scott, set course around the north side of a depression reported in the Atlantic to take advantage of the counter-clockwise wind circulation, one of the earliest known examples of pressure-pattern flying. This was only partly successful and R34 encountered headwinds over the western Atlantic which reduced its ground speed to nothing for a time over Nova Scotia. After four days in the air, fuel was low, but an airship had the options of being towed by a ship, or of mooring to a sea anchor and refuelling from a ship. R34 landed at New York 108 hours after leaving Scotland. It left New York on 10 July and landed near London 75 hours later. It is hardly surprising that Alcock and Brown commented on their Atlantic flight: '… it is evident that the future of transatlantic flight belongs to the airship.'

These were, however, experimental flights by military aircrew and equipment. What was acceptable in war was too dangerous for peacetime commercial flying; in particular, commercial flying was

1 Alcock, J., Whitten-Brown, A. 1969
2 Collinson, C., McDermott, F. 1934, 49
3 Casley, W. E. 1961, 748
4 Collinson, C., McDermott, F. 1934, 53

not even attempted at night. An RFC veteran[5] commented in 1920 that the development of night flying took place entirely on account of the use to which it would be put in war time. So much was this so that without the impulse of war's necessity it was doubtful whether its possibilities would have received very serious consideration. During the two years since the Armistice, there had been very little night flying done, and it is certain that next to nothing had been added to the experience gained during the war. A leader of British aviation, Sir Frederick Handley Page, commented, looking back from 1953:[6] 'Unfortunately it was not generally realized how much was lacking in the way of ground equipment, radio services, airfields and navigational aids.'

The full extent of this unawareness is clear from a 1919 lecture by Claude Grahame-White,[7] expressing all the naïve, but nonetheless prophetic, optimism that infected the visionary pioneers of civil aviation. He proclaimed:

When … we shall be able to dine in New York one evening and in London the next … the coming of this aerial age will do more for the world than any other invention or discovery man has ever made. [He went on:] … we shall eventually travel by air at a speed as great as 250 or 300 miles an hour. As to the comfort of passengers moving at such great speeds, and at very high altitudes, this can be assured by the use of specially-designed, totally-enclosed saloons, in which the air supply can be made independent of the changes in atmospheric pressure outside. [Of course:] It would be pleasant on the afternoon air service from Paris to London, or vice-versa, to serve tea say at mid-Channel; while on the morning services there is no doubt that a cocktail, some time during the flight, would be appreciated by many passengers. We must not forget the amenities of life, even when in the air.

The problems of operating scheduled air services in adverse weather were brushed aside. Nothing short of a hurricane would stop a commercial flight, not even fog.

Assuming we have the organization I shall describe, fog should not trouble us very much except at the moment of alighting after a flight. [Even then:] Round these [searchlight beams] he [the pilot] would then circle, reducing his altitude by degrees and estimating his height above ground level by means of his instruments. Then, when he had got low enough, he would turn in between any two searchlights and make his descent somewhere in the middle of the aerodrome – a manoeuvre he might accomplish quite safely, when he had become familiar with the general lie of the ground, without even having caught a glimpse of the actual surface on which he was alighting … This whole question of fog is, as a matter of fact, a fairly simple one.

As early as 20 October 1921, Captain R. H. McIntosh landed blind in fog at Croydon after making a timed descent from the Crystal palace, but this was not repeatable with any acceptable degree of safety.[7A]

This 'fairly simple question' would be pursued at immense cost for the next sixty years and remains unanswered for all but a minority of the world's aircraft and pilots.

In 1920 Professor B. Melvill Jones published an extensive discussion of weather flying in a paper[8] entitled *Flying Over Clouds in Relation to Commercial Aeronautics*. Among the opening remarks: 'Over-cloud flying can *only* be engaged in *commercially* with the assistance of organization on a large scale …' This came to be abundantly true. Equally true: 'The traffic controller at a large aerodrome would hold a very responsible position; he would be somewhat like a mixture between a railway signalman and a harbour master.'

The author went on to define the difficulties of flying below cloud in bad weather and the problems inherent in the alternative, listed as follows: (1) Difficulty of actual in-cloud flying; (2) Danger that the clouds may come to the ground whilst the aeroplane is in or above them; (3) Difficulty of navigation; (4) Difficulty of aerodrome finding at end of flight; (5) Danger of collision in the clouds; (6) Possibility of having to reach great heights to clear clouds; (7) Danger from storm clouds.

On the last item Melvill Jones opined that 'it is possible that storm clouds might form whilst an aeroplane is actually above clouds and that the electrical disturbances might interrupt communication with the ground'. This was seen as the worst threat offered by thunderstorms and shows how little was known about them in those days. The paper was prophetic in identifying most of the problems of flying during conditions of continuous, thick cloud cover. In 1920 the problems outnumbered the solutions and were insoluble with the equipment and organization available at the time.

Commercial air transport began before the First World War with the Delag Zeppelins in Germany and small scheduled aeroplane services in North America. Military aircraft were used to transport VIPs during and immediately after that war.

On 18 May 1918 Mr Winston Churchill was in Paris, attending the Inter-Allied Munitions Conference. On the following morning his work was finished and he wanted to return to London as quickly as possible. No regular air service existed between Britain and France. But Churchill went to Le Bourget aerodrome to see if there was anyone returning to England. A test pilot, Captain Patteson, was about to return to his base, No. 7 Aircraft Acceptance Park, at Kenley, from where new aeroplanes were tested and then flown to France. Patteson took Churchill back with him. While waiting for Churchill's official car to arrive and drive him back to Lullenden, Patteson entertained Churchill in his cottage close to the aerodrome.[9] Captain Patteson suggested that a passenger-carrying squadron be formed. The result was No. 1 Communication Squadron with Captain Patteson in command, equipped with DH-4s. His aircraft were put at the disposal of any senior politicians or service personnel whose official duties took them to France. Patteson himself offered to fly Churchill to France whenever necessary.

Not all were equally enthusiastic about this new mode of transport. T. E. Lawrence commented: 'For a year and a half I had been in motion, riding a thousand miles each month upon camels: with added nervous hours in crazy aeroplanes, or rushing across country in powerful cars.'[10]

Operating conditions differed profoundly between the US and Europe and gave rise to markedly different approaches to the problems of weather flying; these will appear and reappear in this narrative. The immense distances and political homogeneity of North America offered great scope for air transport, but sparse settlement and extremes of climate and terrain prevailed over much of the continent. Europe offered milder conditions of climate and terrain, but long periods of foul weather. Although much divided by political and linguistic boundaries, the area was densely settled and well provided with a sophisticated infrastructure. The presence of large bodies of water (the English Channel, the North Sea, the Mediterranean and the Baltic) would come to influence the development of aviation.

Civil aviation began in earnest on both sides of the Atlantic as soon as the war ended. The Hague Convention relating to air transport in Europe was signed on 13 October 1919 followed by the International Commission for Air Navigation, formed on 11 July 1922. In Great Britain the Directorate of Civil Aviation was formed in 1919 and the government-subsidized Imperial Airways came into being in 1924. In Germany the predecessors of Luft Hansa started up in 1923. In the US the Air Commerce Act took effect on 31 December 1926.[11]

Air transport made a better start in Europe than in the US. On 30 April 1919 Sir Frederick Sykes published the Air Navigation Regulations for Civil Flying in the United Kingdom. These governed every aspect of civil aviation, including standards for passenger aircraft. On 19 July 1919 a weekend service was opened from London to Brussels. On 25 August the world's first daily commercial service was begun. A single pilot and a single passenger set off from Hounslow to Le Bourget, with a cargo of newspapers, grouse and Devonshire cream. The journey took two and a half hours. By the end of September over 52,000 passengers had been carried in scheduled civil flights, operated by private companies, without government subsidy. Two hundred and fifty aeroplanes had been certificated as airworthy, and capable of passenger transport; 374 pilots had been given certificates; 300,000 miles had been flown. A regular cross-Channel mail service was started on 10 November. On 11 December the first England–Australia flight was completed in less than 30 days.[12]

In 1919 the US Post Office Department started an air mail service; of the forty pilots hired for this service in 1919, thirty-one had been killed in crashes by 1925.[13] Many of the crashes were due to the weather. In 1923 the first US airline went bankrupt; at that time thirty commercial flights crossed the English Channel each day (weather permitting). In 1925 all three US airline routes totalled

5   Baker, C. 1920, 627
6   Handley Page, F. 1953, 519
7   Grahame-White, C. 1919
7A *Flight International*, 9 March 1967, 361
8   Melvill Jones, B. 1920, 220
9   Churchill, R. S. and Gilbert M. 1975, vol. IV, 114
10 Lawrence, T. E. 1938, 502
11 Macmillan, N. 1930; Wronsky, M. 1930; *Flight*, 6 May 1937, 454
12 Churchill, R. S. and Gilbert M. 1975, vol. IV, 215
13 Serling, R. J. 1976, 4

480 km (300 miles). In that year Imperial Airways flew 15,000 passengers for 1,126,500 seat-km (700,000 seat-miles); a German airline carried 50,000 passengers, and French passenger air services linked Paris with London, Brussels, Berlin, Rotterdam, Warsaw, Constantinople and Casablanca.

The first US mail aircraft was the de Havilland DH-4, an open-cockpit biplane with a liquid-cooled, 300 kilowatt (400 horsepower) engine, a cruising speed of about 185 km/h (100 knots) and a range of 560 km (350 miles). With no blind-flying instruments or radio in the aircraft and no communication or navigation facilities on the ground, the pilots struggled through all weathers by day and night to get the mail to its destination. Many stories are told of flights successfully completed on winter nights in spite of violent winds, low clouds, bitter cold and snow, but crashes were frequent, many of them fatal. Sometimes, faced by dwindling fuel and low visibility, a pilot parachuted to the ground, leaving the aircraft to crash where it might, rather than risk almost certain death in a blind landing.

The pilots didn't take to the idea of night flying at first. E. Hamilton Lee said he'd try night flying when there were no more thrills left in daytime flying. Another pilot used to swear that each night of flying would be his last. He'd drive into a cloud bank or patch of fog, lose sight of everything; then he'd hit turbulence, and the engine would backfire and splutter. With everything black as the inside of a Barbary goat, he said his hair 'would be crawling around inside my helmet'. And then after a while he'd see a light, and then another light, and then the big searchlight at the field would show up, and then the field itself, with little jewels around its edge. Then he'd feel a little better about it and decide that most of it was imagination and that he'd try again.[14]

In 1921 ninety-eight aircraft were flying the US mail; forty were DH-4s. Radio communication was introduced in that year with seventeen ground

Croydon aerodrome, London, early 1920s.

stations. A decision to allow pilots, rather than ground superintendents, to make the final decision if the weather was flyable helped to reduce the fatality rate from 2.27 per million km (3.66 per million miles) flown in 1921 to 0.35 (0.57) in 1922. Night flying was cancelled for a time in 1921 but began again in 1922 with the help of light beacons on the ground.[15]

The first ground-based navigation aids in the US were bonfires, soon followed by gas and electric light beacons laid out to mark routes known as airways. In 1921 Army pilots experimented with a lighted airway 80 miles long between Columbus and Dayton, Ohio. The first lighted airway for civilian use was tested on 21 August 1923. On 1 July 1924, night transcontinental flights began, timed so that the night portion of the flight would be completed over the 3,035 km (1,886 miles) of lighted airway that was in place. By mid-1924 nearly 300 flashing gas beacons were in place between Chicago and Cheyenne, Wyoming. By 1935, 30,415 km (18,900 miles) of lighted airways were in use in the US and, even though radio navigation and blind flying were already well established, a further 5,630 km (3,500 miles) were under construction.[16] As part of the Post Office programme, lighted emergency landing strips were built every 40 km (25 miles) along airways, with revolving searchlights every 16 km (10 miles).

From 1919 to 1925 the air mail was operated by the US government. In 1925 the service was contracted out; some of the contractors were the forerunners of the airlines that we know today. The ground facilities installed for the benefit of the air mail were put to good use by the operators of subsequent freight and passenger services.

Examples from various parts of the world show how commercial air services of the 1920s dealt with bad weather in their own various ways, but progress was uneven, risky and in many cases, slight.

In February 1922, the British magazine *Flight*, in a column entitled 'London Terminal Aerodrome', commented:[17] 'This has been one of the worst weeks from a weather point of view for some time. Up to Saturday no machine had got through (between London and Paris) in either direction; in fact very little flying was attempted. The weather has been particularly bad in northern France, the district around Beauvais in particular having been very thick throughout the week.'

Pilots flying to and from England encountered foul weather in all its forms and 'those of us in England who began flying commercially made up our minds that we would win through in every case where it was humanly possible to do so'.[18] On one scheduled passenger service from Paris to London the pilot, Lieutenant H. Shaw, ran into gale-force winds, low cloud and continuous heavy rain. The London–Paris flight was cancelled because of impossible weather conditions, but a slight improvement in the weather at Paris prompted Shaw to take off in the opposite direction. At 600 metres (2,000 feet) over the English Channel peak wind gusts were estimated at 160 km/h (90 knots). Over England, clouds forced the pilot to fly lower and lower in deteriorating visibility. At one stage he was flying up a rain-swept valley, with the dim outline of hilltops higher than his wingtips on either side. After landing at Hounslow airport,[19] London, Shaw was so exhausted that he was barely able to leave the aircraft. Inability to fly blind kept pilots below the clouds in the worst of the turbulence near the ground.

Fog was a particular hazard; Captain G. P. Olley devised his own techniques for navigating above it. The heat and disturbance caused by express trains was sometimes enough to cut a track in shallow fog. A particular city might give its own distinctive tint to the fog, or the glow of smelters could be seen through it. Approaching Croydon aerodrome, London, above a fog bank on one occasion, Olley could see the top of the control tower and some buildings, so shallow was the fog.

> I crept down very cautiously, gliding in just over where I knew there was an unobstructed landing space. And when I entered the belt of fog I found I had been able to judge my position and height in such a way that, though the actual landing was a completely blind one, I managed to make my contact with the ground quite smoothly and in a perfectly normal way. After which perhaps the strangest thing of all happened, because as we dipped into the fog, just before touching ground, we lost sight of everything; and when I brought the machine to a standstill, we found ourselves engulfed in a fog so dense that one could hardly see one's hand in front of one's face.

14 Miller, E. M. 1966,
15 Smith, H. L. 1944, 72
16 *Aircraft Yearbook*, 1935, 207
17 *Flight*, 2 February 1922, p.74
18 Olley, G. P. 1934, 78
19 Close to the future site of Heathrow but not the same.

Night flying equipment, Croydon aerodrome, London, early 1920s.

An accomplished pilot might make such a landing in windless conditions in daylight in a stable aircraft with a low touchdown speed, landing through a shallow layer of ground fog onto a grass field, a chance perfect combination.

Deutsche Luft Hansa was an early leader in blind flying; a 1929 article[20] indicated that flights continued through blind conditions guided by radio bearings transmitted from the ground and non-directional radio beacons.

Pacific Air Transport, in California,[21] kept a car capable of 135 km/h (85 mph) to carry the mail from Los Angeles to Bakersfield if low clouds and fog covered the hills at night. The car would leave Los Angeles at midnight, reaching Bakersfield at 3 a.m. The airline operated its own light beacons on the ground, spaced not more than 16 km (10 miles) apart, and in rough country as close as 3–5 km (2–3 miles) apart. The dispatcher decided if weather conditions warranted the carriage of passengers. Rapid Air Lines of Rapid City, South Dakota,[22] admonished its pilots: 'Take no chances, do no stunting, when in doubt stay on the ground.'

The Ford Tri-motors of Transcontinental Air Transport[23] had 'landing lights for night flying in case darkness should overtake them in flight'. The article quoted contained a lengthy description of operating procedures, but not one mention of blind flying.

Sir Gordon Taylor[24] flew as a copilot in Fokker F-VII-3m tri-motors in scheduled passenger service over the Snowy Mountains of eastern Australia in 1928–9. The days of contact flying, of cancelling for weather, were gone forever. The Fokkers went out on time from Sydney airport and flew as the airlines fly today, climbing to altitude on course, levelling off and taking the weather as it came. But they had no radio and virtually no up-to-date knowledge of the weather either on the route or at the terminal. The aircraft had gyroscopic turn-and-bank indicators but no other gyroscopic instruments and no protection against airframe ice. There were also no ground-based radio navigation aids in Australia at that time. Navigation and the descent at the destination were by the pilot's mental dead reckoning. Taylor stated that this type of

Armstrong Whitworth Argosy passenger aircraft, 1920s.

flying 'could be undertaken only by freak pilots with a new and wider perception of flight, a relentless cunning, and a rugged ability to handle the aeroplane on primitive flight instruments in the most violent turbulence'. Even pilots such as these were not immune to disaster and the crash of a scheduled passenger aircraft in bad weather in the Snowy Mountains in March 1931 contributed to the failure of the company.

The airships cruised serenely above these endeavours. A few comments are appropriate here to put their commercial use into perspective. Between 1910 and 1914 small airships in Germany carried 17,000 passengers on 800 flights.[25] In 1919 the Zeppelin company used LZ120 on a scheduled service between Friedrichshafen and Berlin, carrying 2,450 passengers on 103 flights in three months before the service was stopped by the Inter-Allied Control Commission. In March 1932 the Zeppelin company began a summer scheduled service between Friedrichshafen (later Frankfurt) and Rio de Janeiro with LZ127 *Graf Zeppelin* and LZ129 *Hindenburg*. The 9,650-km (6,000-mile) flight lasted 80–120 hours. The *Graf Zeppelin* carried 13,310 passengers on 590 flights between 1932 and 1937 and the *Hindenburg* carried 3,088 passengers on 63 flights in 1936–7. Between them they made 181 Atlantic crossings between 1929 and 1937,

20 *Airway Age*, February, 1929, 51
21 *Airway Age*, February, 1929, 155
22 *Airway Age*, June, 1929, 846
23 *Airway Age*, July 1929, p.1027
24 Taylor, G. 1983, Chapter 4
25 Brooks, P. 1959, 780; the discrepancy with the figure quoted earlier may be due to recording differences between single and return trips.

Control deck of Zeppelin LZ127 *Graf Zeppelin*.

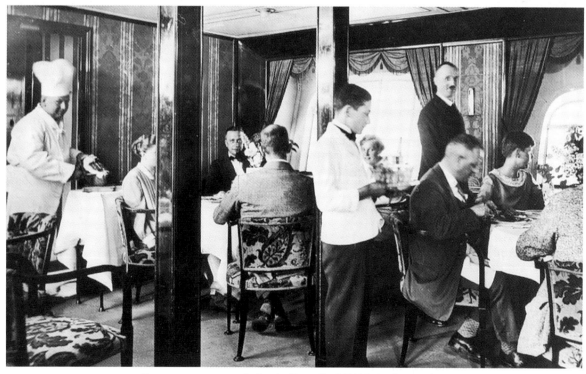

Passenger accommodation in Zeppelin LZ127 *Graf Zeppelin*.

Handley Page Hannibal airliner, 1920s.

carrying over 133,360 kg (294,000 pounds) of mail and freight and more than 16,000 passengers.[26] The *Graf Zeppelin* was used for proving flights across the North Atlantic and in 1936 the *Hindenburg* made ten scheduled return flights between Frankfurt and Lakehurst, New Jersey. The *Hindenburg* was destroyed at the end of its first crossing of the 1937 summer season. The airships were few and slow, but at the time no aeroplane could compete with them in range, payload or all-weather capability. Airships proved to be un-expectedly vulnerable to thunderstorms and turbulence. A number of gruesome accidents, cul-minating in the *Hindenburg* disaster, ended the career of the airship just when the full potential of the aeroplane was beginning to appear.

At the end of the 1920s European scheduled passenger air services extended all over Europe and to the Far East.[27] The first of these, about 1920, carried 'a couple of passengers, ... packed into one of these small aeroplanes like sardines in a tin', but by the end of the decade the four-engined, biplane, Handley Page Hannibal was coming into service with Imperial Airways, with forty passenger seats comparable in size to today's business class.

The ability of a fully equipped commercial air-craft to cope with bad weather had come a long way by 1930:[28]

26 Letter printed in *Flight International*, 27 April 1972, 597
27 Harper, H. 1930
28 Harper, H. 1930, 58

On one extremely unfavourable day, from a flying point of view, Captain Barnard was due to take one of the scheduled air expresses across to the Continent. It was raining hard and there were masses of heavy, low-lying clouds. Without hesitation, after ascending from Croydon, Captain Barnard went right up into clear air above the clouds, losing all sight of the earth below. Then he brought his wireless telephone into service, and kept in constant touch with the control tower. So he flew on, having obtained no glimpse of any landmark since ascending, until his wireless bearings and other calculations told him he should be at a point a little way inland on the other side of the Channel. Whereupon, the cloud bank below was not quite so dense, he called up the Croydon operator and said he was now going to descend through the clouds and check his position by a visual bearing. And a few minutes later Croydon heard his voice telling them that, thanks to the accuracy of their wireless work, he had found himself almost exactly at the point which he had expected, although until that moment, and from the time of leaving Croydon, he had been flying completely 'blind' from a visual point of view.

Ground-to-air radio could also be used to divert aircraft away from airfields that fogged in.[29]

Radio and the first blind-flying instruments

Handley Page Hannibal passenger accommodation.

Handley Page Hannibal flight deck.

were pointing the way to passing through bad weather or flying above it.[30] Inclinometers and turn indicators were helping pilots when navigating in cloud or fog, conditions which prevented them from seeing any horizon line from which to judge with their own eyes the attitude and inclination of their aircraft in relation to the ground below. In addition, by 1930, 'automatically, gyroscopically-operated control surfaces are … among the latest wonders of aerial science',[31]

It is surprising to us how much blind flying was done in the 1920s using only gyroscopic turn indicators, bubble levels and magnetic compasses. Even when gyroscopic artificial horizons and heading indicators did become available from 1929 onwards, their adoption was gradual, they were not particularly reliable and blind flying by 'needle, ball and airspeed' still went on. The early commercial pilots were knights without armour in their battles with the weather, battles that ultimately could not be won without better blind-flying instruments, better and more extensive radio navigation and a radical change to the way in which instrument flying was regarded.

29 Harper, H. 1930, 61
30 Harper, H. 1930, 49
31 Ibid.

CHAPTER 5

The Coming of Instrument Flight

As we have seen, one of the big problems facing aviation in the 1920s was the difficulty and danger of trying to fly an aircraft when cloud or darkness deprived the pilot of a horizon and landmarks visible outside the aircraft. Progress towards safe, regular commercial service was in direct proportion to this capability. Experience showed that aeroplanes could be flown in blind conditions only through the trained interpretation of instruments inside the aircraft; for that reason blind flying came to be known as instrument flying. In 1920 a few blind-flying instruments existed but little was understood about how to use them.[1] These were: the long-period compass, the static head turn indicator, the spinning top and the gyroscopic turn indicator. Blind flying also depended on a ground-based radio system transmitting various kinds of information and guidance. In 1920 these essential elements for blind flying hardly existed.

Keeping the aircraft flying in the right direction was recognized early on as the first essential of blind flying. Not only was this necessary for the aircraft to reach its destination, but the loss of directional control commonly preceded complete loss of control of the aircraft.

(The pilot's) first indication that something is wrong is, as a rule, either an increase or decrease of speed that is not counteracted by the accustomed movements of the controls. A period of wild suspense and utter bewilderment now follows, during which the pilot makes violent efforts to recover control, but without success. The next thing he realizes, if he realizes anything at all, is that he is either on his back or spinning, and the next thing he knows is that he is out of the clouds with the earth standing up at a ridiculous angle and spinning round like a drunken dinner plate. Happy is he that has plenty of air room under those circumstances ... Many a good pilot has had his last living view of the earth in this wildly gyrating form.[2]

The magnetic compass was useless for this purpose.

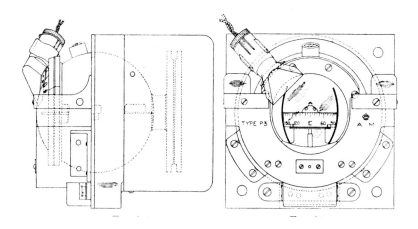

Aircraft compass, 1920s.

Once the violent accelerations attendant on an actual loss of control have started, the gyrations of the compass, as seen from the aeroplane, become something terrible, in a word, it appears to go quite mad, spinning and stopping again in a perfectly diabolical manner, so that the poor pilot who meets these phenomena for the first time is only confirmed in his belief that the laws of nature, as he is accustomed to them, are temporarily suspended.[3]

The long-period magnetic compass, discussed earlier, soon reached the limits of its very meagre potential as a blind flying instrument. The static head turn indicator, also mentioned earlier, was not an effective blind-flying instrument. The spinning top principle had been used as a horizon reference in the *Riesenflugzeuge*. A postwar version of this instrument was known as the Garnier spinning top.[4] It could be upset if the aircraft went outside a limited range of level flight attitudes and its usefulness was limited accordingly.

The instrument with the greatest potential for blind flying was the gyroscopic turn indicator. The Royal Aircraft Establishment in the UK developed a sturdy instrument with the important advantage that it could not be toppled by violent manoeuvres. It was derived from an invention dating back to 1908 by Professor J. B. Henderson of Greenwich

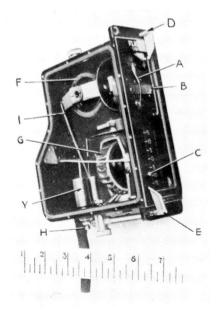

Pioneer pitch, bank and turn
indicator.

Royal Naval College for use in ships.[5] The gyroscope was driven by the aircraft's slipstream; its axis was horizontal and longitudinal to the aircraft, and it was free to precess in yaw against strong springs, driving a centre-zero needle on a dial through a mechanical linkage. The needle would deflect for as long as the aircraft was turning, but as soon as it resumed straight flight the pressure of the springs would realign the gyroscope axis with the aircraft's direction of flight and the needle would return to its central position. Because the gyroscope was restrained and thus could not be toppled, the instrument remained usable even in the most violent manoeuvres. Because the deflection of the needle was proportional to the rate of turn, the instrument could be used to turn accurately from one heading to another by means of a timed turn, using the magnetic compass to indicate the heading only at the start and finish of the turn. In America the Sperry company had developed a similar instrument. The gyroscopic turn indicator is the most basic of all blind-flying instruments and continues in use to the present time.

In the 1920s the American Pioneer company produced a device which incorporated a turn indicator and a fore-and-aft pitch indicator, each driven by its own gyroscope, both instruments mounted in the same instrument case. The pitch indicator indicated up to 17° above and below level flight. This must be regarded as one of the predecessors of the artificial horizon. The source consulted, however, states that the instrument is 'for use under conditions where the aeroplane must be held as closely as possible to an accurate level, both laterally and in pitch, as for example in aerial photography and surveying'. No mention is made of its possible use a a blind flying instrument.[5A]

An effective system of altimetry was essential for blind flying. The only altimeter available in 1920 was the aneroid instrument, mentioned earlier, adjustable for barometric pressure, and set to read zero on take-off. The instrument then read only altitude above the departure airfield, and that only for as long as the local barometric pressure stayed the same. If the pressure changed while the aircraft was flying, or if it flew to an area with different

1   Melvill Jones, B. 1920, 220
2   Ibid.
3   Ibid.
4   Ocker, W. C., Crane C. J. 1932, 48
5   Chorley, R. A. 1976, 323
5A Stewart, C. J. 1930, 162
6   Stewart, C. J. 1928

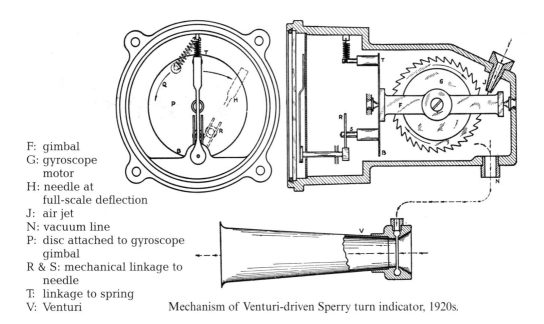

F: gimbal
G: gyroscope
   motor
H: needle at
   full-scale deflection
J: air jet
N: vacuum line
P: disc attached to gyroscope
   gimbal
R & S: mechanical linkage to
   needle
T: linkage to spring
V: Venturi

Mechanism of Venturi-driven Sperry turn indicator, 1920s.

pressure, or if the departure and destination airfields were at different elevations, the instrument reading would be either wrong or irrelevant. Internal friction caused the readings to lag in a long climb or descent (hysteresis error); this would be dangerous in a blind descent close to the ground. We see here two important, recurrent issues: the design and construction of the instrument itself, and the procedures for its use. In this case the usefulness of the aneroid altimeter was limited by the lack of procedures for pressure compensation, although in the 1920s pilots flying from London were issued with pressure compensation charts.[6] In most cases, the best advice available was: 'In foggy or misty weather it may be necessary to land by altimeter. In this case care should be taken to descend very gradually.'[7]

The immediate future of blind flying lay with the gyroscopic turn indicator. However, as late as 1928[8] there was still no standard turn indicator in use. One reason for this was that pilots held no definite opinions as to whether the turn indicator was useful or not. Also, the pilots of those days did not take kindly to new instruments. Even so, at that time six models of this instrument were in existence: the RAE, Royal Air Force Mark IV, Reid, and Schilovsky-Cooke in Britain, the Drexler in Germany and the Sperry in the US.

The Sperry turn indicator became the international standard instrument of its kind. Its principle of functioning is the same as the RAE instrument described above. The Sperry company developed the instrument during the First World War and obtained a US patent for it in 1922.[9] In its fully

Face of Sperry-type turn and bank indicator. Version at right has index marks for a Rate 1 turn.

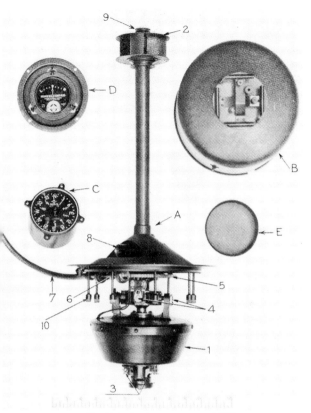

Earth inductor compass, 1920s.

An instrument panel containing a turn indicator, an airspeed indicator, an altimeter, an engine tachometer, a magnetic compass and a clock thus allowed a trained pilot to control the aircraft and navigate by dead reckoning in blind conditions, provided that he could see to take off and land. The turn indicator would function reliably in any attitude of the aircraft and could be used to regain control if control were lost in blind conditions. Needle, ball and airspeed remained as the basis of blind flying, even after artificial horizons became available. Even today, pilots are trained in this technique in case of failure of the artificial horizon.

Apart from its defects as a blind-flying instrument, the magnetic compass was ill-suited to aircraft use as it was affected by the magnetism of the aircraft's structure and electrical systems. Efforts to overcome these deficiencies led to the earth inductor compass, a north-sensing rather than a north-seeking device. The sensor was a rotor, driven by the slipstream, mounted in the tail as far as possible from magnetic interference. As the rotor turned, the earth's magnetic field generated a small alternating voltage, fluctuating in proportion to the angle that the coil made with the earth's field. The voltage was picked off by brushes whose orientation was controllable from the cockpit; it was thus possible to find the voltage null. The voltage was applied to a centre-zero voltmeter. Once the aircraft was on a selected heading, read off a conventional compass, the pilot could rotate the brushes until the needle centred. The meter would then indicate deviations from the set heading. The needle would centre on both the desired heading and its reciprocal, but on the reciprocal heading the needle indications would be reversed, so that a left turn produced a deflection to the right and vice versa.[11]

These instruments, and the ability to use them, allowed Charles A. Lindbergh to make his celebrated solo flight from New York to Paris in May 1927.[12] In the centre of Lindbergh's instrument panel[13] were the indicator of the earth inductor compass, the Sperry turn-and-bank indicator and a horizontal bubble inclinometer. These enabled

developed form it contained, in the same instrument face as the turn needle, a curved, liquid-filled glass tube containing a steel ball. Movement of the ball from its central position indicated a slip or skid. Deflection of the needle from its central position indicated the direction and rate of turn. This instrument enabled Lieutenant J. P. van Zandt to fly a DH-4 for 1½ hours in blind conditions from Moundsville, West Virginia, to Washington, DC, in 1921.[10]

The method of blind flying using a gyroscopic turn indicator became known as 'needle, ball and airspeed'. 'Needle and ball' referred to the Sperry turn indicator; as long as the needle and ball were centred, the aircraft was flying in a straight line. The pilot could put the aircraft into a turn and keep the rate of turn constant by reference to this instrument. As long as he kept the ball centred, which he could do by means of pressure on the rudder pedals, the aircraft was neither slipping nor skidding. Constant airspeed at a constant throttle setting meant that the aircraft was flying level or in a steady climb or descent.

7 Chorley, R. A. 1976, 330
8 Stewart, C. J. 1928, 425
9 Davenport, W. W. 1978, 134
10 Hallion, R. P. 1977, 102
11 Chorley, R. A. 1976, 333
12 Lindbergh, C. A. 1953
13 Lindbergh, C. A. 1953, Plate 10

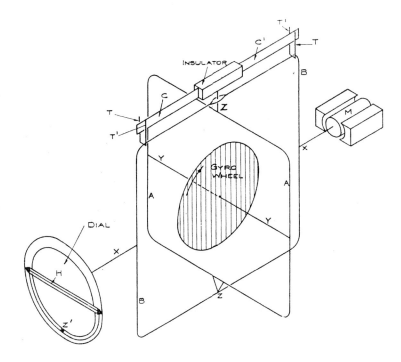

The Gyrorector: schematic.

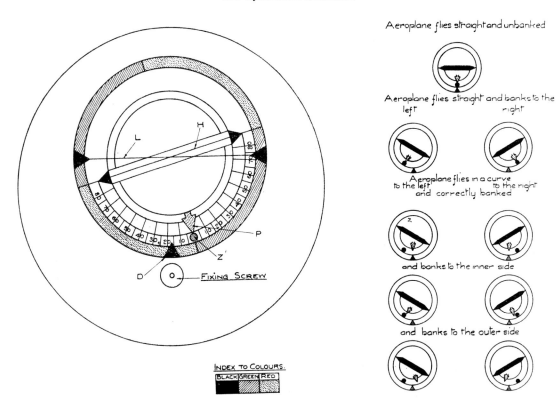

The Gyrorector: instrument face.

The Gyrorector: instrument indications.

him to fly straight and level for long periods blind in cloud and darkness. With no radio or autopilot, completely dependent on himself and his single-engined aircraft, Lindbergh was forced to take daylight and darkness, fair weather and foul as he found them during that 33½ hours of flight through the empty Atlantic sky.

Blind flying by needle, ball and airspeed was very tiring to the pilot because of the constant mental effort of deducing the aircraft's attitude from indirect, lagging instrument readings. At an early date the need for a true attitude indicator was recognized, showing the aircraft's attitude in all three axes continuously, instantaneously and reliably. An ideal instrument would indicate an aircraft's attitude throughout 360° of roll and pitch. This desirable feature was not achieved until after the Second World War.

Such devices already existed, as mentioned earlier. The Anschütz instrument was too heavy and too slow to run up to speed. The Drexler was lighter but indicated bank only. The Garnier spinning top was limited in its range of pitch and roll. The Sperry company worked on an artificial horizon during the First World War, but abandoned it in 1918 because it would not work satisfactorily in all attitudes of the aircraft.[14] This deficiency was later overcome by the combined use of an artificial horizon for normal flight with a gyroscopic turn indicator capable of functioning in all attitudes.

The next significant advance was the Gyrorector, manufactured by Gyrorector GmbH, Berlin.[15] In 1929 the German government presented an example of this instrument to the US Army Air Corps, who tested it at Crissy Field. It weighed 5.4 kg (12 pounds) and contained a gyroscope driven by a 110-volt AC electric motor at a rotor speed of 18,000 rpm. Complex electro-mechanical linkages and a small electric servomotor drove the instrument display. The Gyrorector indicated bank only; a movable face with an index line, controlled by the servomotor, represented the natural horizon. The pilot could compare this with a fixed line on the cover glass, representing the aircraft's transverse axis. A pendulous pointer, suspended from the centre of the instrument face, showed the direction of the resultant of gravitational and centrifugal forces and thus had the same function as the ball in the Sperry turn-and-bank indicator. Pitch information was provided by a fore-and-aft bubble inclinometer mounted beside the instrument.

A description of the Gyrorector presented to the Royal Aeronautical Society in 1927[16] drew the peevish comment:

> In the gyrorector we have a splendid example of what, I submit, an aeroplane instrument dial should not be. You have four pointers to watch – just little fingers that move about, and you have to determine what is happening by the relative positions of all these. I suggest it would all be rather difficult to follow, and that all the instrument does clearly is to show when you are flying level. Even so, the crossarm cants to port to show that the machine is canting to starboard, and vice versa. That seems a most undesirable complication to impose on a harassed pilot.

Reflection and experience would have shown the commentator that he was missing the point. The Gyrorector display was, in fact, simple to monitor for a pilot trained to do so. More important, in a turn in visual conditions a pilot's senses combine to tell him that he is sitting upright while the horizon has tilted. The Gyrorector imitated this sensation; in being true to life, it was easy to interpret and this made it easy for a pilot to become proficient in its use. Another comment was: '… whilst progress has been made in the design and perfecting of the actual instruments, little has been done with a view to grouping together the instruments and reducing their number to the minimum consistent with efficiency'. This discussion highlighted a nascent awareness that, if blind flying was to succeed, instrument presentations would have to provide an analogue of the outside world that the pilot could absorb continuously, accurately and without undue mental exertion. This became a major theme in the quest for all-weather flight.

Ability to fly blind produced a new problem: blind navigation. Radio direction-finding and the Bellini-Tosi and Telefunken radio navigation aids used by the airships have already been mentioned. German inventive genius produced another device, patented by Otto Scheller in 1907.[17] A transmitter on the ground was equipped with two crossed loop antennas. One transmitted a Morse code letter A (·-); the other transmitted a Morse N

14 Howard, R. W. 1973, 533
15 Stewart, C. J. 1928
16 Stewart, C. J. 1928
17 Hallion 1977, 103; Wright, M. D. 1972, 123; Williams, J. E. D. 1992, 187

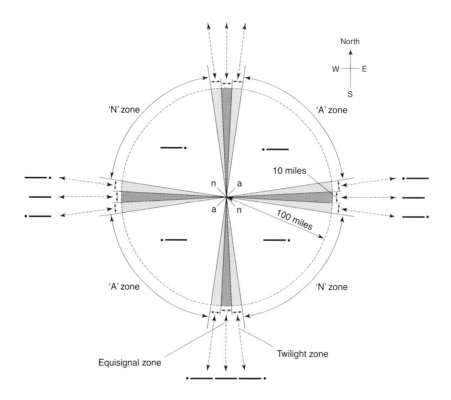

Radio range signal pattern.

(-·). The antennas radiated a signal pattern in the form of two lobes on opposite sides of each antenna. The lobes overlapped along four narrow sectors, separated by 90° in azimuth, where the Morse dots and dashes merged in a continuous tone or 'equisignal.' This formed a 'beam' or 'leg' which could be used for navigation.

Efforts to develop this device into a usable form were unsuccessful during the First World War, but it was brought to fruition during the 1920s in the US, where it was known as a radio range. In 1920 the US Bureau of Standards developed an aural receiver which allowed the pilot to hear the Morse code signals. In 1921 the Bureau of Standards set up an experimental radio range at Washington, DC. Tuning the As and Ns so that the equisignal was an exact monotone narrowed the beam width from 8° to 3°. The equipment was then moved to McCook Field at Dayton, Ohio. The system was further developed by Dr J. H. Dellinger of the Bureau of Standards over the next five years and by E. Donovan of the Ford Motor Company in 1926.[18]

The 1926 Air Commerce Act empowered the US Department of Commerce to construct radio navigation aids and in June of that year a conference was held to determine what types would be used. The Europeans were already using radio direction-finding. Aircrew transmitted a request for a bearing; operators at two ground stations took bearings on the transmission and radioed the results to the crew from which they deduced a position fix. The radio range, however, needed only an unmanned transmitter on the ground and a receiver in the aircraft. A pilot could track a range leg, using only the audio signal and a compass, with no air-to-ground communication and no need for help by other crew members. The Americans therefore selected the radio range as their standard.

In 1926–7 experimental radio ranges were set up at the US Army Air Corps (USAAC) experimental establishment at College Park, Maryland, and Bellefonte, Pennsylvania, transmitting on frequencies of 285–315 kHz. At the same time the Bureau of Standards Aeronautics Division developed a

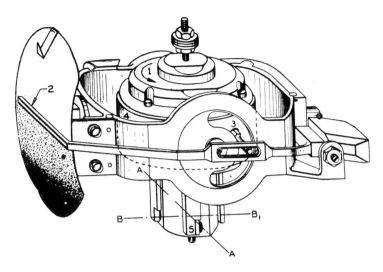

Mechanism of the Sperry artificial horizon.

visual cockpit indicator to display the equisignal. Two white metal reeds, side by side, vibrated with an amplitude proportional to the signal strength; equal amplitude indicated equal strength – the equisignal.

The radio ranges were originally intended as aids to night navigation, supplementing electric light beacons, but in 1929 the periodical, *Airway Age*,[19] made the prophetic remark: 'The moment the coolness of a cloud bank enfolds (the pilot), he is blind and lost unless some unseen hand is stretched forth to guide him. In a rolling sea of blinding vapour, radio direction keeps him on his course.'

The first radio range on an airway in the US went into service in 1928. So rapid was their construction thereafter that by February 1931, twenty-one ranges were in service between San Francisco and New York; by the summer of 1933 eighty-two range stations were in service and another twenty were under construction.

Morse combinations other than A and N were sometimes used. In 1929 a range at Cleveland, Ohio, transmitted -··· (B) and ···- (V). The Bellefonte range transmitted ··- (U) and -·· (D) in two irregularly shaped zones. Progress in radio range engineering made it possible to align the equisignals at angles other than 90° apart; radio ranges could thus be used to define continuous airways. Procedures were devised, using the A and N quadrants, for a pilot to orientate himself to a radio range and intercept an equisignal. Flying towards a range, he would hear the signal becoming stronger. A blank area of no signal existed directly above the transmitter and this so-called cone of silence told the pilot that the aircraft was over the range station. The cone of silence was, however, imprecise and could give a false position fix if the signal ceased for other reasons.[20] For greater certainty and as *en route* fixes, marker beacons were added to the system. A marker beacon transmitted a signal in a narrow cone vertically upwards, receivable only within 5–8 km (3–5 miles) of the beacon. Some marker beacons were designed to transmit weather or landing information, or coded signals to indicate local ceilings below 150 metres (500 feet) or visibilities less than 3 km (2 miles).

The groping, uncertain progress of the 1920s was changed forever by the Daniel Guggenheim Fund for the Promotion of Aeronautics. Founded in 1926 by the American millionaire,[21] the fund sponsored or managed several research projects for the technical advancement of aviation. In June 1928 the fund took on the problem of fog flying. It bought two single-engined biplanes, a Consolidated NY-2 and a Vought O2U-1, set up a Full

18 Mohler, S. R., Jackson, B. H. 1971, 47
19 *Airway Age*, June 1929, p.828
20 *Flight*, 6 March 1953, 291
21 Hallion, R. P. 1977; 1988, 97

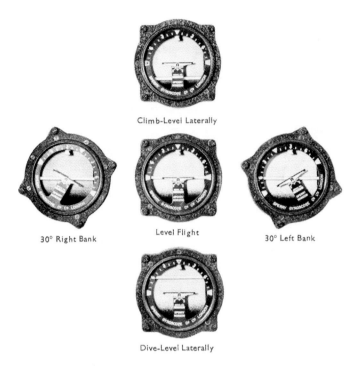

Climb-Level Laterally

30° Right Bank   Level Flight   30° Left Bank

Dive-Level Laterally

The Sperry artificial horizon and instrument indications.

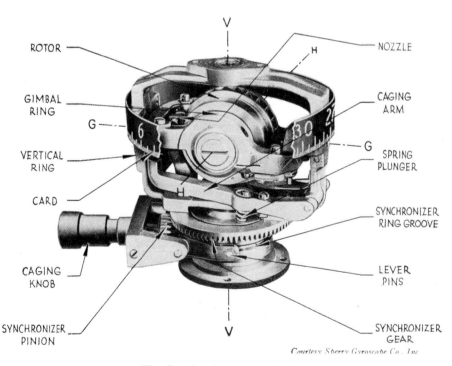

The directional gyro – mechanism.

The directional gyro – instrument face.

Flight Laboratory on Army land at Mitchel Field on Long Island, and engaged Major James Doolittle as a test pilot. Work on this project was extraordinarily vigorous, inventive and successful. In 1927 Dr Jerome C. Hunsaker stated: '… safe landing in fog is not today possible and no means are in sight to make it so', yet only two years later the 'impossible' was achieved. Several technologies were converging to make this possible, but what the Full Flight Laboratory achieved experimentally would not become a normal flight operation for another fifty years. This in no way detracts from the extraordinary progress made in so short a time.

The Full Flight Laboratory was ready to begin its work in early 1929. Three problems were identified immediately. First, none of the existing instruments provided a direct and reliable indication of attitude in pitch. Second, the combination of a turn indicator and the unstable magnetic compass did not provide a sufficiently precise and continuous readout of the aircraft's heading for a blind approach and landing. Third, the available altimeters were not accurate enough for safe manoeuvring in blind conditions close to the ground.

For the first two problems the Fund approached Elmer Sperry Sr. He delegated co-operation with the Fund to his son, Elmer Jr., who worked on both the design and the flight testing of the resulting new instruments. Within months Sperry Jr. and his design team had produced an attitude indicator capable of showing pitch and bank simultaneously throughout normal flight attitudes. An aircraft symbol was fixed in the instrument panel, while the gyro-controlled horizon bar indicated the position of the natural horizon relative to the aircraft's nose. The instrument display was thus true to life[22] and correspondingly easy to interpret. This instrument remains in use, substantially unchanged, to the present. It may be that the very rapid progress in 1929 resulted from the resurrection of the earlier work abandoned in 1918.

The gyroscope was vacuum-driven by a venturi on the outside of the fuselage. On startup it erected itself by reference to gravity. It is a fair question to ask how an instrument depending on gravity for its initial reference can be reliable in flight manoeuvres which can produce accelerations equivalent to gravity in any direction, whether aligned with gravity or not. However, accelerations in flight other than that due to gravity tend to be of short duration. If they are sufficiently prolonged, as during a continuous turn, the attitude gyroscope will gradually re-erect itself by reference to this false gravity. This was a minor problem compared with those which the artificial horizon solved.

The magnetic compass problem was solved by a gyrostabilized heading indicator. This instrument had no inherent north-seeking tendency, but was set manually by the pilot by reference to the magnetic compass whenever reliable readings could be obtained, such as before take-off or during straight and level flight. The gyroscope precessed at a rate depending on its quality and condition, causing the instrument reading to drift, so that for precise navigation it had to be reset every 15–20 minutes. In its original form the instrument displayed the side of a drum marked in degrees of azimuth. The drum rotated about a vertical axis under the control of the gyroscope. The modern version displays a complete compass card in plan view with a fixed aircraft symbol, but otherwise the instrument continues in use to the present day.

For the problem of altimetry the Bureau of Standards referred Doolittle to Paul Kollsman. Born in Freudenstadt, Germany, Kollsman founded the Kollsman Instrument Company in New York in 1928 and submitted an improved

22 Ocker, W. C., Crane, C. J. 1932, 50

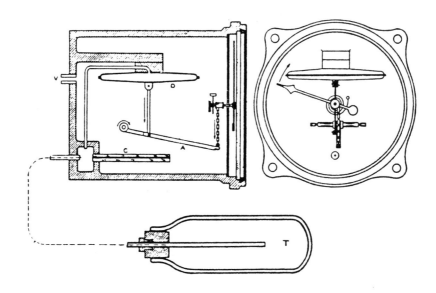

Vertical speed indicator – mechanism.

aneroid altimeter to the Bureau.[23] The first test flight with the Kollsman altimeter took place on 30 August 1929 in the Vought O2U-1 with Kollsman holding the altimeter in his lap. The instrument was accurate to within 1.5–3.0 metres (5–10 feet), instead of the 15–30-metre (50–100-foot) accuracy obtainable hitherto. Although publicized as the first 'sensitive' altimeter, the Kollsman instrument was preceded by a British (RAE) instrument with a scale of 600 metres (2,000 feet) for a single revolution of the needle, an error of less than 3 metres (10 feet) and a hysteresis error of only 1.4 metres (4.5 feet).[24]

The improved sensitivity of the Kollsman instrument resulted partly from a mechanism with less internal friction than previous designs and partly from an expanded scale, reading 300 metres (1,000 feet) per revolution of the needle instead of 6,100 metres (20,000 feet). The Consolidated NY-2 was the test aircraft; it was fitted with a normal altimeter for altitudes above 300 metres (1,000 feet) and a Kollsman altimeter (also known as a 'landing altimeter') for use in the approach and landing.

One instrument unmentioned hitherto is the vertical speed indicator. It contained a small chamber connected to the outside air by a capillary tube.[25] In level flight the pressures inside and out were the same. As soon as the aircraft changed altitude, the external static pressure differed from the static pressure trapped inside the chamber, the difference

being proportional to the rate of change. A needle mechanically linked to the chamber showed a climb or descent. When the aircraft levelled off, the pressures equalized through the capillary tube and the needle returned to its neutral position.

The work of the Full Flight Laboratory resulted in the six basic blind-flying instruments that continue in use to the present time, namely the artificial horizon, heading indicator, airspeed indicator, turn-and-bank indicator, altimeter and vertical speed indicator. These instruments allowed a trained pilot not only to control an aircraft in blind conditions, but to fly manoeuvres accurately enough to use the electronic navigation aids that were just beginning to come into service.

Mitchel Field already had a radio range that could be received 200 km (125 miles) away. Early in 1929 the Bureau of Standards installed a 'localizer' range on the east side of the field with the equisignal aligned across the field and a reception distance of only 24 km (15 miles). On the west side of the field a marker beacon was installed in line with the localizer equisignal. The plan was that Doolittle would approach from the west along the localizer and would use the marker beacon to begin his glide to touchdown. In practice he could also approach from the east, using the cone of silence over the localizer transmitter as the signal to begin his glide.

By September 1929 Doolittle and his fellow test

pilot, Kelsey, had perfected the technique of blind flying with the six instruments. The morning of 24 September dawned with Mitchel Field covered by thick fog. On the spur of the moment Doolittle had the NY-2 prepared for flight and the radio aids turned on. He took off into the dense fog, circled the field and landed blind ten minutes later. Later the same morning he repeated his performance for the benefit of the Guggenheim Fund executives, although by this time the fog was lifting and Doolittle flew under a hood with Kelsey in the front seat as safety pilot. In order to land, Doolittle flew the NY-2 at a steady airspeed and rate of descent from the marker beacon or the cone of silence until it touched down. This completely blind landing was possible only in a stable aircraft with a low touchdown speed in calm air or light winds. The problem of blind-landing full-sized commercial and military aircraft in all conditions would be a major preoccupation of the quest for all-weather flight for the next fifty years.

The flights of Lindbergh and Doolittle made a profound impact on the minds of an American public who regarded aviation as dangerous and impractical, and to whom pilots were only just distinguishable from tightrope walkers and trapeze artists. The gap between the potential of aviation and its actual capabilities was still large, but in 1929 it was remarked that:[26] 'Aviation has a great vogue in America, and upon all sides it is already a general and favourite topic for serious discussion.'

23 Hallion, R. P. 1977, 116
24 Stewart, C. J. 1928, 431
25 Ocker, W. C., Crane, C. J. 1932, 44
26 *Flight*, 24 January 1929, 67

CHAPTER 6

Blind Flying

The ten years between Doolittle's flight in September 1929, and the outbreak of war in Europe in September 1939, witnessed revolutionary advances in aviation. Ungainly, externally braced biplanes with fixed landing gear, uncowled engines and fixed-pitch propellers gave way to streamlined, all-metal, internally braced monoplanes with constant-speed propellers, retractable landing gear, flaps and ice protection. A comparable revolution took place in all-weather flying without which the advances in aircraft construction would have been less than worthwhile. Aircraft equipment was useless without pilots trained to use it. Pilots and aircraft could not use the available technology without a ground organization, the provision of which devolved increasingly on national governments.

Some further advances were made in flight instruments. Besides the six basic instruments discussed in the last chapter, various others were devised as aids to blind flying; some reached the prototype stage, others were merely fanciful.[1] Space does not permit them to be described here. The main progress of the decade was the introduc-

tion of blind flying into common service. Automatic flight control, which had previously languished for lack of need, gained importance. Instrument flying and complex new aircraft types demanded a profound shift in pilot attitudes, skills and training.

The brilliant success of Doolittle, Sperry and Kollsman is clear in retrospect, but at the time their work was only one set of experiments among many that were taking place in the US, England, France and Germany. Even the need for blind flying was still questioned. An article dating from 1930,[2] describing a new gyroscopic turn indicator, remarked: 'This type of instrument is undoubtedly a very great help when flying in cloud and particularly so for cabin machines. Whether or not a plain turn indicator justifies its expense or not is a highly controversial point ...' Pilots in open cockpits had a tenuous aid to blind flying in the wind on their faces, which was denied to pilots in enclosed cockpits, hence the reference to cabin machines.

New gyroscopic turn indicators appeared during the 1930s, such as the Mechanism (UK 1931),[3] the Schilovsky (UK 1934),[4] the Pullin (UK 1935)[5] and

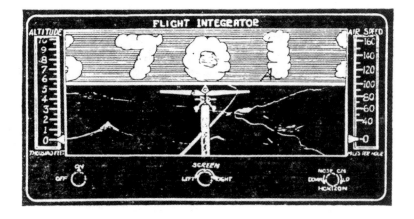

Ocker & Crane's flight integrator.

Early-type single-pointer altimeter with extended scale
and no barometric setting scale.

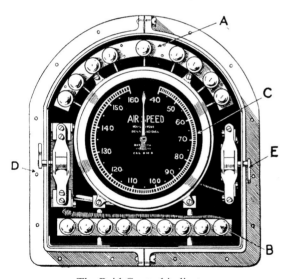

The Reid Control indicator.

1 Ocker, W. C., Crane, C. J. 1932, 59, 62; *Flight*, 5 December 1930, 1413
2 *Flight*, 5 December 1930, 1413
3 *Flight*, 4 December 1931, 1199
4 *Flight*, 10 January 1935, 45
5 *Flight*, 21 March 1935, 320
6 *Flight*, 11 April 1935, 406
7 *Flight*, 18 September 1931, 953; 13 October 1932, 971; 24 November 1932, 1127; 29 June 1933, 652
8 Chorley, R. A. 1976, 332
9 du Feu, A. N. 1968, 1066

the Brown Type V (UK 1935).[6] They did not, however, supplant either the Sperry turn and bank indicator or its British equivalent, the Reid & Sigrist.[7]

The Reid & Sigrist turn indicator was the brainchild of Squadron Leader G. H. Reid, who flew on bombing raids with the RFC during the First World War. He was particularly concerned with the problems of navigation when low cloud covered the route to the target. He was captured by the Germans and, while a prisoner of war, devised a gyroscopic turn indicator. Reid's first instrument was the Reid Control Indicator of the late 1920s. An airspeed indicator was placed in the centre of the instrument face. Grouped above and below it were electric lights indicating turn and bank. The turn lights were activated by a gyroscope; the bank lights were activated by a mercury switch.[8]

In the late 1920s Reid & Sigrist Ltd., located near London, developed a new instrument with the same functions as the Sperry turn and bank indicator in the US. The display consisted of two centre-zero needles with a common pivot in the centre of the instrument face. The top needle was driven by an air-damped pendulum and showed skid and slip. The bottom needle was driven by a gyroscope and showed rate of turn. The instrument was intended for use with a fore-and-aft bubble inclinometer to indicate pitch. The total weight was only 113 grams (4 ounces). Twenty-five prototypes were tested in various aircraft over a period of 2½ years, and the instrument was ready for service in the summer of 1931. By 1932 the Reid & Sigrist had been accepted in the UK as the standard instrument of its kind, both by the Royal Air Force and by civilian flying schools. It remained standard in British-built aircraft until the 1950s, when it was supplanted by the Sperry-type instrument.

As mentioned earlier, in the first altimeters a single needle traversed the dial; the altitude range so indicated varied according to the model of instrument. In some instruments a second, concentric scale, for a second revolution of the needle, extended its range. By 1930 instruments of this kind were available reading up to 12,200 metres (40,000 feet).[9] One of Kollsman's improvements was a pair of needles on a common pivot, one to read 300 metres (1,000 feet) per revolution, the second to read 3,000 metres (10,000 feet); the altitude was the sum of the two needle readings. In 1935 the three-pointer altimeter was introduced, with a third needle reading tens of thousands of feet. The problem of altimeter correction in flight had been

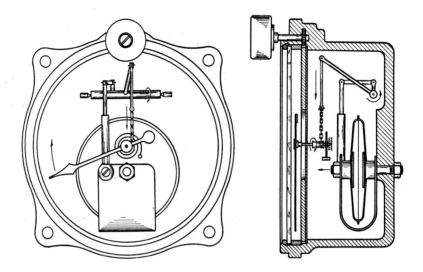

Single-pointer altimeter – mechanism.

Single-pointer altimeter with
barometric setting scale.

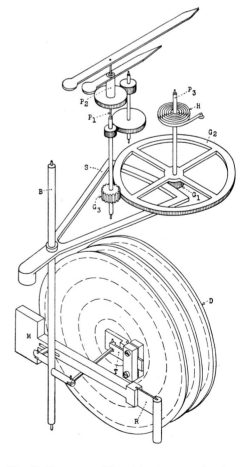

The Kollsman sensitive
altimeter – instrument face.

The Kollsman sensitive altimeter – mechanism.

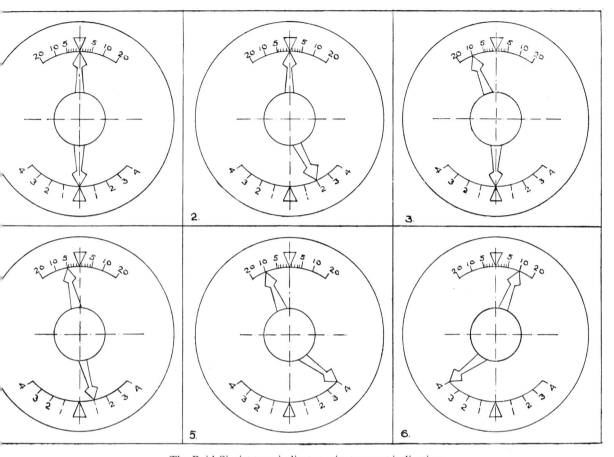

The Reid-Sigrist turn indicator – instrument indications.
1. Straight flying.
2. Correctly banked, turning right.
3. Sideslipping to left, no right turn.
4. Slow turn to right, little outside sideslip.
5. Spinning to right.
6. Spinning to left.

solved by 1931 by means of a subscale calibrated in barometric pressure[10] so that the pilot could set the altimeter according to a barometric pressure radioed from the ground. The manufacture of single-needle altimeters continued, incorporating the subscale,[11] while the new two- and three-needle instruments were designed with the subscale.

The search continued for an altimeter to give the aircraft's height above the ground directly. An Austrian engineer, Hans von Braun,[12] tried to use a sensitive gravimeter, seeking to use the fact that the earth's gravitational attraction varies in proportion to distance. Although Luft Hansa tested a prototype in 1931, nothing more was heard of it. Both

the French and the Americans experimented with acoustic altimeters,[13] but the experiments ultimately failed because of the unpredictable reflectivity of land and water. Of greater significance for the future, experimental radar altimeters began to appear.[14]

The external venturi used at first to drive the

10 Ocker, W. C., Crane, C. J. 1932, 106
11 Ocker, W. C., Crane, C. J. 1932, Fig.69
12 *Flight*, 23 October 1931, p.1063
13 *Flight*, 20 December 1934, 1363; Ocker, W. C., Crane, C. J. 1932, 105
14 *Flight*, 24 November 1938, 474

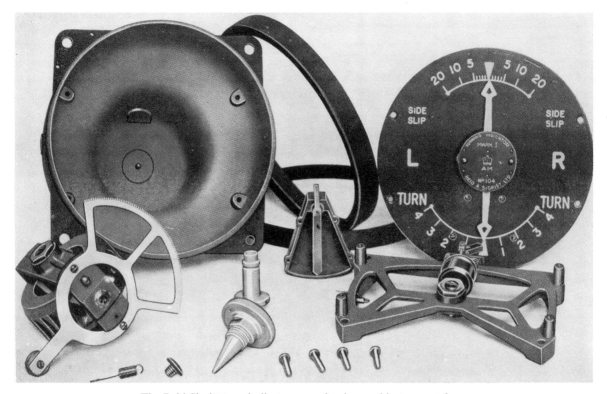

The Reid-Sigrist turn indicator – mechanism and instrument face.

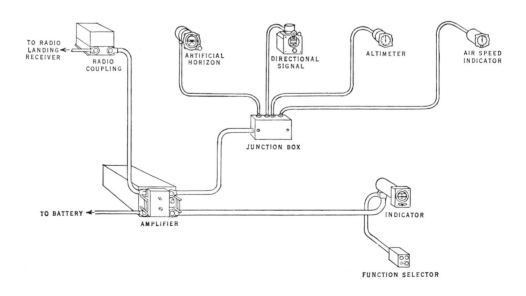

The Sperry Flight Ray – schematic.

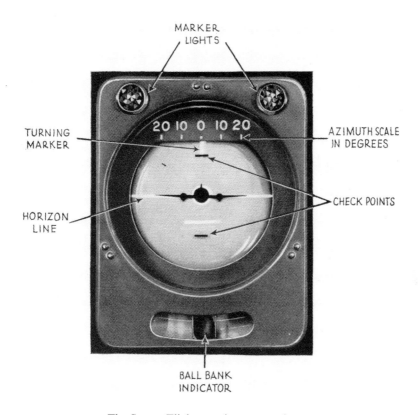

MARKER LIGHTS

TURNING MARKER

20 10 0 10 20

AZIMUTH SCALE IN DEGREES

HORIZON LINE

CHECK POINTS

BALL BANK INDICATOR

The Sperry Flightray – instrument face.

gyroscopes was not satisfactory because the gyroscopes could not be run up to speed until the aircraft took off. The pilot thus could not check their functioning until after take-off, which was unsafe for a departure into instrument conditions. The venturi also added drag and was liable to ice up. During the 1930s many American aircraft manufacturers went over to vacuum pumps driven directly by the engines; this spread to Great Britain in the course of the decade.[15]

Not until the late 1930s were blind-flying instruments set in a panel mounted exactly horizontally in the aircraft and protected from vibration by shock absorbers.[16] This design originated in the US and was adopted by the Royal Air Force in 1937. The RAF had already introduced a standard instrument layout in 1936 (The Basic Six).

In 1937 Sperry brought out the Gyro-Mag compass, a gyrostabilized magnetic compass eliminating the need for repeated resetting of the heading indicator. It entered experimental service with KLM and with airlines in America.[17] In 1938 Sperry brought out an extremely advanced instrument called the Flightray.[18] This combined the artificial horizon, heading indicator, turn-and-bank indicator, localizer, glideslope, stall warning and marker beacon lights in a single display. It was prophetic of the multifarious instrument displays still twenty years in the future.

The widespread introduction of artificial horizons was surprisingly slow. As late as 1936 it was written of Imperial Airways:[19] 'Most of our captains have learned their fog and cloud flying by the aid of the turn-and-bank indicator, and Imperial Airways were the first to standardize this type of instrument on all their aircraft. It is only during the last two years [1934–6] that those excellent instruments, the artificial horizon and directional gyro, have been added to our aircraft, and instrument flying has increased greatly in efficiency.'

15 *Flight*, 3 January 1935, 3
16 Williamson, G. W. 1937, 193
17 *Flight*, 15 July 1937, 71
18 *Flight*, 15 December 1938, 567
19 Brackley, H. G. 1936, 85

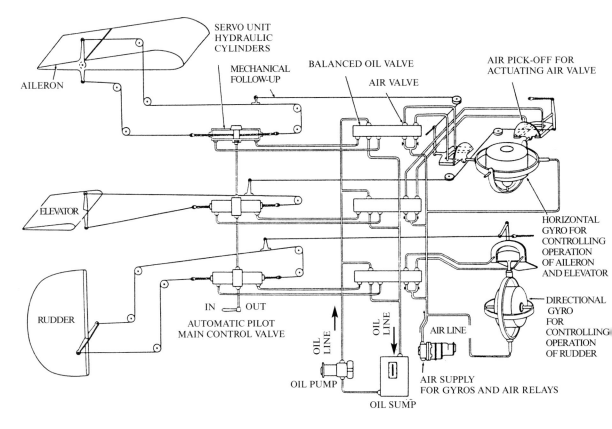

The Sperry autopilot.

'Mechanical Mike,' the Sperry Autopilot. The Sperry autopilot, used by Post during the 1933 solo world flight, incorporated two gyroscopes and operated upon compressed air and hydraulic pressure. It was a 'three-axis' autopilot, that is, one gyroscope sensed pitch changes and roll (bank) changes by the aircraft, and the other gyroscope sensed heading changes (yaw). The air compressor and the hydraulic pump were engine powered. The gyroscopes were driven by compressed air. Compressed air was also used to correct changes of aircraft attitudes in relation to pitch, bank, or yaw, through a system of small air ducts and semilunar plates. Attitude changes of the aircraft, produced pressure differentials in airflow in the ducts ending near the discs. The result was a proportional change in air valves that was transmitted to the appropriate hydraulic system which, in turn, moved the proper-control surface (elevator for pitch, aileron for bank, and rudder for yaw). The autopilot, which Post called 'Mechanical Mike,' required no electrical power and functioned very well. (Courtesy Sperry Gyroscope Company.)

Even the 1942 printing of Jordanoff's *Through the Overcast*, first published in 1938,[20] describes the artificial horizon as an instrument but does not mention it at all in the chapter on instrument flying technique.

At the beginning of 1935 the US Bureau of Air Commerce legislated that all airline aircraft be equipped with:[21] (a) a turn and bank indicator, (b) an instrument that would indicate the degree of bank and attitude during climb and descent (in effect, an artificial horizon), (c) an instrument that would indicate the amount of turn, (d) a rate of climb indicator, (e) at least one sensitive altimeter, (f) an electrically heated pitot tube, and (g) an outside air thermometer. Items (a), (b), and (e) were required to have two sources of power.

The First World War was fought without automatic flight control and little development followed its conclusion. The Americans already had their Sperry autopilot. In 1925 the RAE in the UK

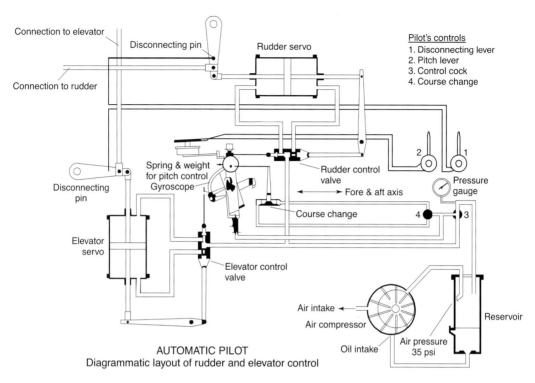

Connection to elevator
Disconnecting pin
Rudder servo

Pilot's controls
1. Disconnecting lever
2. Pitch lever
3. Control cock
4. Course change

Connection to rudder

Spring & weight
for pitch control
Gyroscope

Disconnecting
pin

Rudder control
valve

Fore & aft axis

2   1

Pressure
gauge

Course change

4   3

Elevator
servo

Elevator control
valve

Air intake
Air compressor

Reservoir

AUTOMATIC PILOT
Diagrammatic layout of rudder and elevator control

Oil intake

Air pressure
35 psi

British RAE/Smith's Mk I autopilot (rudder and elevator control), 1930.

started work on radio-controlled pilotless aircraft as anti-aircraft targets; the first British autopilots resulted from this work. In the 1920s the Germans began experiments to autocouple a magnetic compass to aircraft controls. This work was the start of a series of German course controllers linked to the aircraft's rudder. By the early 1930s the US, Great Britain and Germany had their own autopilots, respectively the Sperry, RAE/Smith and Askania.

The Sperry A1, A2 and A3 autopilots were connected to the gyroscopes of the Sperry blind-flying instruments. Economical though this system was, the pilot could not check the autopilot against the instruments. The Sperry system controlled the aircraft in all three axes with hydraulic control surface actuators.[22] The British system used two separate gyroscope packages, both separate from the flight instruments.[23] One package controlled the rudder and elevators; the other package controlled the ailerons. The actuators were pneumatic. In both the American and British systems the pilot could initiate simple manoeuvres by manipulating the autopilot; in essence commanding the autopilot to fly the manoeuvres.

The German autopilots were course controllers

with independent gyroscopes and pneumatic rudder actuation; hydraulic power was substituted later. In 1927 the German government asked the Siemens company to produce control devices for a pilotless target aircraft. In 1931–2 the company developed a three-axis autopilot, subsequently known as the Patin. Nevertheless, most Luftwaffe aircraft in the Second World War had single-axis autopilots controlling the rudder only.

In 1934 Siemens produced the sophisticated Mk D3 autopilot.[24] Although gyroscopes were used, they were not the only control input. A pitot-static system controlled the elevators and acted as a speed control. A pendulum controlled the ailerons and acted as a wing-leveller. A remote-sensing compass in the tail of the aircraft controlled the rudder. An altimeter statoscope controlled the throttles and acted as an altitude holding device. The autopilot thus responded to the aircraft's

20 Jordanoff, A. 1938
21 *Flight*, 31 January 1935, 133
22 See also Mohler, S. R, Jackson, B. H. 1971
23 See also Garratt, G. R. M. 1934, 766, 898
24 *Flight*, 10 January 1935, 41

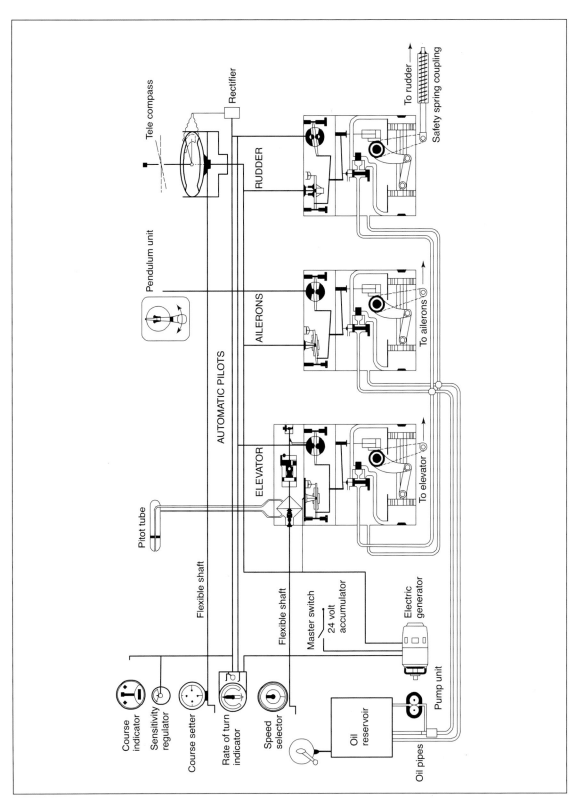

The Siemens D-3 autopilot, 1932.

external environment as well as relying on gyroscopes. In calm air the rudder control would hold a heading to ±2°; the elevator control held speed to ±3 km/h (1.9 mph); the autothrottles held altitude to ±12 metres (40 feet). The pilot could fly turns through the autopilot. The D3 weighed 117 kg (257 pounds) compared to 32 kg (70 pounds) for the Sperry A2.[25] Only five units were ever made; it did not progress beyond the experimental stage because it was more costly and more sophisticated than required by the German government at the time.[26]

Some noteworthy flights were made with automatic assistance. In 1935 a Martin bomber, equipped with a Sperry autopilot coupled to a Kreusi radio compass, was successfully flown automatically, using commercial radio stations at Dayton and Cincinnati as guidance.[27] On 23 August 1937 two US Army test pilots, Carl Crane and George Holloman and engineer Raymond Stout, flight-tested a Fokker monoplane with the autopilot coupled to the radio navigation equipment. The aircraft took off from Wright Field, was navigated automatically to Indianapolis and back to Dayton. The pilots tuned the blind approach aids at Wright Field and the aircraft is reported to have landed itself. The potential of an autopilot, coupled to ground-based radio navigation aids, to land an aircraft automatically was already recognized as the solution to landing in completely blind conditions. Both autopilots and radio aids, however, had a long way to go before they could be used for this purpose other than experimentally in ideal conditions.

The skills of all commercial and military pilots had to be upgraded to encompass this new branch of flying, which also became a new and demanding option for private pilots with suitably equipped aircraft. Both in the US and in Europe the airlines became the best equipped and most practised instrument flyers. Although military pilots in both countries were instrument trained, tactics and equipment current at the time did not reinforce training with adequate practice. In Germany Luft Hansa[28] trained future Luftwaffe pilots.

Since the earliest days of flying, pilots had been taught to fly by 'feel', using a wide range of sensory perceptions, and not by reference to what few instruments there were. Blind flying required the opposite. Pilots had to be taught that in blind conditions their senses were misleading, and therefore they should rely solely on instruments.

The beginnings of instrument flight training in

the Royal Air Force illustrates the scope of the problem.[29] The RFC's and the RNAS's First World War blind-flying experience was allowed to lapse after the war but work on blind-flying continued in France and it was to the French that the RAF turned in 1929. At that time RAF basic training included an hour of cloud flying, consisting of flight through broken cloud, but not of sustained blind flying. Flight Lieutenant W. E. P. Johnson, an instructor at the Central Flying School, was sent to a blind-flying course run by the Farman civilian flying school at Toussus-le-Noble. The training aircraft were equipped with gyroscopic turn indicators, liquid fore-and-aft inclinometers and airspeed indicators. The course consisted of eight hours of training in a hooded cockpit. Johnson, like every other RAF pilot, had been trained to believe that an aircraft could be flown by feel, even in blind conditions. This belief remained current in spite of the fact that a high proportion of fatal accidents was attributed to pilots losing control in cloud or fog and spinning into the ground.[30] The training that he received in France taught Johnson that, contrary to all existing doctrine, the senses were not only unreliable but misleading. On his return to the Central Flying School he had to report that one of the fundamental doctrines that had existed throughout the whole history of aviation was fallacious.

First Johnson had to convince his superiors of what he had found out. This was surprisingly easy, but it was then necessary to prove to other RAF pilots that they could not do something that they had always believed that they could. Next, Johnson and his colleagues had to analyse what was going wrong when pilots tried to fly blind without training. Next, a method of instruction had to be devised, for which the best available instruments had to be selected and obtained. Last, the new doctrine had to be spread through the whole RAF.

Tests on eighty pilots at the Central Flying School with 300 to 2,000 hours of experience showed that not one could maintain control of an aircraft under the hood for more than twelve minutes, even with instruments in front of them, if

25 Mohler, S. R., Jackson, B. H. 1971
26 Howard, R. W. 1973, 545
27 Taylor, H. A. 1935, 401
28 *Luft Hansa* (2 words) changed to *Lufthansa* (1 word) in 1933.
29 Johnson, W. E. P. 1951
30 Johnson, W. E. P. 1957, 199

Blind take-off by an Avro 504 at the RAF Central Flying School, Upavon, early 1930s, with no safety pilot.

they were not instrument-trained. Pilots flying in open cockpits had various cues that allowed them to keep control, such as the sounds and feel of airflow around the aircraft and glimpses of the sun, moon, cloud layers, or the ground. Johnson proved that, when they were completely deprived of all outside references, loss of control was only a matter of time. Johnson and his team met vigorous opposition when they travelled to spread the new doctrine to RAF squadrons. Many of the pilots had flown with the RFC and RNAS in the First World War and refused to believe that they could not fly blind without gyroscopic instruments and training. Of 250 such pilots only

RAF instrument panel, 1930s (Hawker Hart light bomber).

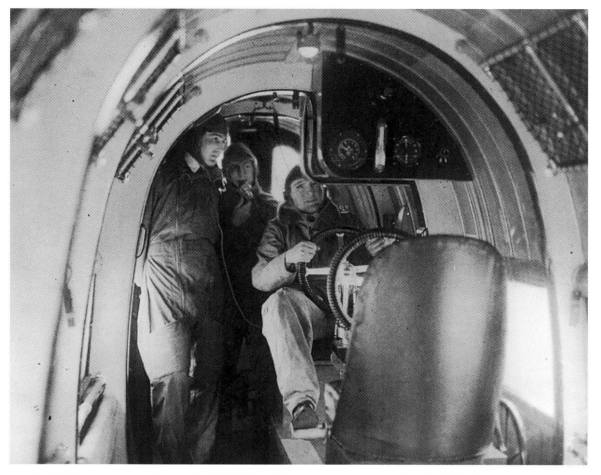

Blind flight training position inside RAF Vickers Victoria transport aircraft, early 1930s. Note two positions, facing forward and aft.

one was able to back up his assertion when tested under the hood; he was killed flying blind a year later.

The blind-flying team found that a standard sequence of events took place, sooner or later, when a pilot without instrument training tried to maintain control under the hood. The pilot invariably got the aircraft into a spin, sometimes without being aware that he had done so. If he did recognize his situation, recovery was usually followed by a second spin in the same direction as the first. A gyroscopic turn indicator that would function reliably in any attitude was an immediate, urgent priority.

In 1930 not a single RAF aircraft had a gyroscopic turn indicator installed. After extensive tests the blind-flying team selected the Reid & Sigrist type and then test-flew it in every type of RAF air-craft. For training they chose the Avro 504 single-engined biplane with a folding hood over the rear cockpit; the 504s had no radio. After the travelling courses put on by the Central Flying School team, RAF fatal accidents declined from eighty a year to forty. 'Within weeks of installing turn indicators in the Avros and giving instruction, the mysterious magnetic storms encountered in cloud that caused the compass to spin were practically a thing of the past.'[31]

The course given to RAF pilots included blind take-offs and spin recoveries. One of the tests was to fly a triangular course, blind, by dead reckoning, lasting about an hour, with the intention of arriving back over the starting point. This was rou-

31 *Journal of the Royal Aeronautical Society*, 1968, 540

RAF night bombing capability, early 1930s. A Vickers Virginia preparing for a night take-off at Worthy Down in 1932.

tinely achieved unless the winds aloft forecasts were wrong. By early 1932 fifty-nine RAF aircraft had been equipped for blind flying and 122 *ab initio* pilots had received training.[32] In 1932 a Vickers Victoria twin-engined transport was fitted up as a flying classroom with an aft-facing position for the student pilot completely enclosed inside the fuselage.[33] For his pioneering work Flight Lieutenant Johnson was awarded the Air Force Cross.[34]

In spite of this progress the situation in the RAF in 1933 was that[35] few pilots were trained in cloud flying, all bad-weather flying was discouraged and the attitude throughout the Service was 'if you can't see, stay on the ground'. In the 1933 annual exercises the RAF deployed no radio direction-finding equipment, so that, whatever the conditions of light and weather, pilots had no navigational guidance from the ground.

The civilian counterpart of the RAF training system was Air Service Training Ltd., a flying

British light aircraft instrument panel, 1930s. (de Havilland Leopard Moth)

school opened at Hamble, England, in 1931.[36] The school offered an instrument-flying course in addition to normal flight training, using Avro Tutors and Avro Avians with hooded rear cockpits. These aircraft were equipped with Reid & Sigrist turn indicators selected by the chief instructor, an ex-RAF pilot, after comparative tests with other models. The Air Service Training course was one of the first of its kind in the UK.[37] Fifty pupils took the course in 1932.[38] The trophy winner that year flew the 70 mile triangular blind-flying test course at an altitude of 600 metres (2,000 feet) in a 37 km/h (20 knot) wind and arrived within 400 metres (0.25 mile) of the airfield. Nine hours of flying sufficed for this training.

The pilot population adapted to blind flying only gradually. Crashes occurred then, as they still do, when a pilot with no instrument training flew into cloud deliberately or inadvertently and lost control. One pilot commented in 1935[39] that plenty of junior pilots could not fly straight, simply because they could not concentrate on their instruments. When they entered clouds, they became tense. An experienced pilot relaxed when flying by instruments. He also commented that airlines had difficulty finding instrument-qualified pilots, and that when new pilots joined the airlines they were usually surprised at the weather conditions in which the more experienced pilots were able to fly.

In 1937 British Airways established a Transport Pilots' School at Gatwick, near London.[40] The main focus of the school was instrument flying and navigation, but the advent of retractable landing gear, flaps, constant-speed propellers, mixture and exhaust gas analysers and de-icing made the technical section equally important. The school flew a Fokker F.8 and an F.12, both of which were fully equipped with radio for communication and navigation. The aircraft were also equipped for conventional navigation with a large chart table, a drift sight and a perspex blister for star shots. Students were trained in blind flying, with particular reference to blind approaches to airports in all weather conditions by day and by night.

British Airways aircraft for European operations carried two pilots and a radio operator. Aircraft for service outside Europe had to carry a specialist navigator as well. All of these crew members had to pass through the school. The increasing range, speed and complexity of airline aircraft placed ever-increasing demands on aircrew training. In 1937 it was emphasized that during the past two or three years the entire technique of transport flying had changed. There could be no return to the old methods. The commercial pilot would become primarily a scientific specialist.

Then, as now, the private pilot occupied an uncertain position on the fringes of these developments. By 1936 practically every club and school in the UK ran a standard instrument-flying course.[41] Most private aircraft, however, had no artificial horizons or directional gyros, and had nothing like the capacity needed for the heavy, bulky radios of the day. The radios were difficult for a solo pilot to operate while flying the aircraft. A turn indicator was regarded as a safety device for the pilot who inadvertently penetrated a patch of bad weather, or for brief periods of flying through cloud, but, in any case, 'Only a born idiot would set off into really thick weather with a single engine and no radio equipment ...'

Across the Atlantic training in instrument flying progressed along similar lines. As late as 1929 the USAAC was forced to avoid bad weather and to restrict night flying to clear periods, and then in assigned areas only, as the aircraft were not equipped for instrument flying and the pilots were not trained.[42] In June 1930 the US AAC added a blind-flying course to the curriculum of the Advanced Flying School at Kelly Field.[43] Instrument flight training in some cases developed on the initiative of individual unit commanders.[44] In 1933 the Office of the Chief of the Air Corps published the first training directive for instrument flying. All tactical pilots with low instrument proficiency had to take a ten-hour refresher course. Those who demonstrated proficiency or had taken the course were required to do only five hours of instrument flying a year. In October 1933 navigation schools opened for instrument training at Langley Field, Virginia, and Rockwell Field,

32 *Flight*, 4 March 1932, 198
33 *Flight*, 6 October 1932, 934; see also Baldwin, J. E. A. 1932, 945
34 *Journal of the Royal Aeronautical Society*, 1968, 540
35 Quill, J. K. 1985, 30
36 *Flight*, 3 July 1931, 636; 7 August 1931, 779
37 *Flight*, 15 January 1932, 56
38 *Flight*, 2 March 1933, 206
39 Brackley, H. G. 1936
40 *Flight*, 18 November 1937, 492
41 *Flight*, 23 April 1936, 443
42 Coffey, T. M. 1986, 213
43 Hallion, R. P. 1977, 125
44 Parton, J. 1986

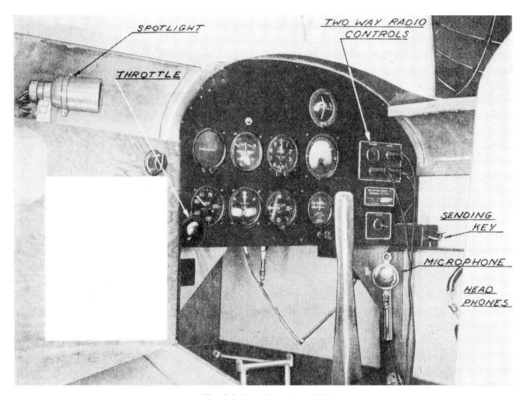

The Link trainer, late 1930s.

California. Only one class had graduated by February 1934.[45] The Air Corps was still dismally ill-equipped to handle the politically instigated air mail flying which began in that month.

In March 1934 the Office of the Chief of the Air Corps initiated a blind-landing course. The Army bought trucks and equipment for mobile instrument landing installations. From 1934 onwards all new military aircraft had radio transceivers and an extra 35 hours of instrument and navigation training was given to each military student pilot. In April 1935 the night flying requirement was increased from 15–20 hours to 25–42 hours a year and instrument time from 5–10 hours a year to 20–30 hours. Nevertheless, many Air Corps pilots took the view that, as pilots of both fighters and bombers had to see their targets to attack them, proficiency at blind flying was not important to their role as military pilots.

Airlines in the US developed their own rigorous and demanding training programmes including flight simulators.[46] The skills so imparted would be much sought after as the US became increasingly involved in the European war.

The idea of simulating flight for training dates far back in aviation history. Non-flying mockups for ground training are reported from the early histories of various air forces. The view outside the cockpit could not be simulated; this has become possible only recently through computerized virtual reality. When, however, the pilot's view was restricted to the interior of the cockpit and all relevant information could be displayed on instruments, simulation became practical. The operating cost of a simulator has always been lower than that of an aircraft and training is not interrupted by bad weather, take-offs and landings, or other traffic. Emergencies and equipment failures can be simulated that would be dangerous or impractical in an aircraft.

The founder of the instrument flight simulator industry was Edwin Link, born on 6 July 1904 in Huntington, Indiana,[47] son of the owner of a factory making pianos and organs. The idea of a non-flying simulator is said to have occurred to Link from the French air force method of training pilots by first letting them taxi on the ground. Link was a pilot himself and used his own instrument-equipped aircraft to commute between Newark, New Jersey, and Binghamton, New York.

The Link trainer, patented on 14 April 1929, was the first of a long and increasingly diverse series of instrument flight simulators. The first unit was produced at the Link Piano and Organ Co., although the company went into liquidation in December 1930.

The Link Aeronautical Co. was formed in 1931. Because of the sudden demand for instrument proficiency resulting from the Army air mail flights, the Air Corps took delivery of six Link trainers on 23 June 1934. Japan, Russia, France and Great Britain also bought Link trainers. The Model C of 1936 incorporated the six basic blind-flying instruments with a Morse key and other radio controls. A Model C cost $3,500–5,500, as much as some aircraft. The simulator consisted of a miniature aircraft fuselage on a pedestal. Bellows in the pedestal could move the fuselage through 360° of yaw and 50° of pitch or bank either side of the vertical. This range of motion even allowed the simulation of spins and spin recoveries.[48] Electromechanical linkages converted control movements into instrument readings. An instructor's control console beside the simulator with a chart table and a pen recorder completed the equipment. All procedures in relation to such navigation aids as radio ranges or Lorenz beacons could be simulated.

In 1937 Link tried to develop an instrument for blind flying which would combine all necessary information in one instrument. The Visualator was rejected by both the airlines and the military and was Link's first and last excursion into this field. By 1937 Link trainers were available with almost any range of instruments and European or American radio navigation aids that a customer might request. In 1937 Model Cs were bought by American Airlines, United Airlines, Pan American, Eastern Airlines, Australia National Airways and British Airways. The Models E and E Special of 1938–9 included crossed-pointer instrument landing system indicators, ADF and marker beacon indicators. By 1941 Link trainers were in service in thirty-five countries.

Whatever the efforts of the various training organizations, instrument flying was a matter of proficiency acquired through constant practice in real conditions of darkness and foul weather. On both sides of the Atlantic civilian transport pilots, striving to maintain their schedules, acquired a vastly greater experience of all-weather flying than did their military counterparts. Yet the war that was about to erupt in Europe would be fought out in a part of the world notorious for its foul weather.

45 Shiner, J. F. 1983
46 Gann, E. K. 1961, 1972
47 Kelly, L. L., Parke, R. B. 1970
48 *Flight*, 28 October 1937, 416

CHAPTER 7

Blind Navigation

The early aviators navigated in three ways: pilotage,[1] dead reckoning and celestial. For aircrew flying in cloud or between cloud layers, pilotage and celestial were unavailable, while dead reckoning was not accurate enough to allow a safe descent at the destination. The first systems for accurate blind navigation depended on radio transmitters at known, fixed locations on the ground. Different systems grew up on different sides of the Atlantic in response to differences in operating conditions.

Early radio equipment suffered from numerous problems from the point of view of aviation. Radios were heavy, bulky and unreliable. At the transmission frequencies that could be generated in the 1920s and 1930s, signals were subject to atmospheric interference and distortion; interference between stations and frequencies was difficult to avoid. Some on-board radios needed a specialist operator because of complicated tuning procedures. Other electrical systems in the aircraft tended to interfere with the radios. Nevertheless, the development of radio, both in the aircraft and on the ground, for communication and navigation was essential to the advances in all-weather flying that took place in the 1930s.

The American concept of blind navigation originated in the lines of bonfires and light beacons put in place to guide the early air mail pilots. The radio range, already described, embodied this concept in an electronic form. The development of the radio range and the construction of an airway system based on radio ranges and marker beacons has been described in an earlier chapter. The use of the airway between Chicago and Cleveland in 1930–1 serves as an example of the functioning of the radio range system.[2]

A pilot would leave Chicago with the Chicago range tuned on the aircraft's receiver, on 350 kHz, and would track the south-southeast range course.

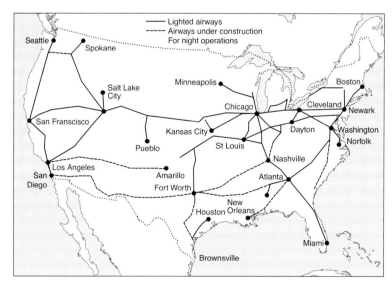

Map of US airways as at 1 December 1930.

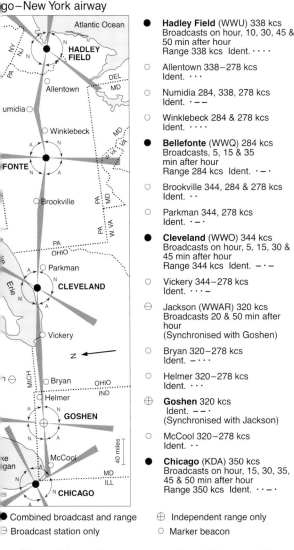

go—New York airway

● **Hadley Field** (WWU) 338 kcs
Broadcasts on hour, 10, 30, 45 &
50 min after hour
Range 338 kcs Ident. · · · ·

○ Allentown 338–278 kcs
Ident. · · ·

○ Numidia 284, 338, 278 kcs
Ident. · – –

○ Winklebeck 284 & 278 kcs
Ident. · · · ·

● **Bellefonte** (WWQ) 284 kcs
Broadcasts, 5, 15 & 35
min after hour
Range 284 kcs Ident. · – ·

○ Brookville 344, 284 & 278 kcs
Ident. · ·

○ Parkman 344, 278 kcs
Ident. · – ·

● **Cleveland** (WWO) 344 kcs
Broadcasts on hour, 5, 15, 30 &
45 min after hour
Range 344 kcs Ident. – · –

○ Vickery 344–278 kcs
Ident. · · · –

⊖ Jackson (WWAR) 320 kcs
Broadcasts 20 & 50 min after
hour
(Synchronised with Goshen)

○ Bryan 320–278 kcs
Ident. – · · · ·

○ Helmer 320–278 kcs
Ident. · · ·

⊕ **Goshen** 320 kcs
Ident. – – ·
(Synchronised with Jackson)

○ McCool 320–278 kcs
Ident. · ·

● **Chicago** (KDA) 350 kcs
Broadcasts on hour, 15, 30, 35,
45 & 50 min after hour
Range 350 kcs Ident. · · · –

● Combined broadcast and range   ⊕ Independent range only
⊖ Broadcast station only   ○ Marker beacon

Map of the radio range airway from Chicago to New
York, *c* 1930.

Every five seconds the Chicago identifier of · · · – (F)
would be superimposed on the Morse code A and
N sector signals. Six times an hour the range signals
would be replaced by voice weather broadcasts. At
an estimated time after departure the pilot would
tune the Goshen, Indiana, range on 320 kHz and
receive its A or N sector signals and its identifier of
– · (G). A marker beacon transmitting on 320 and
278 kHz at McCool, Indiana, marked the approximate point of intersection of the south-southeast
leg of the Chicago range and the west leg of the
Goshen range. The Goshen range broadcast its sig-

nals for a minute, followed by a minute of silence.
En route the pilot would also receive the marker
beacons at Helmer, Indiana, and Bryan, Ohio.
These transmitted on the same frequencies as the
McCool marker but with different identifiers:
McCool ·· (I); Helmer ··· (S); Bryan ···· (B). A
broadcasting station at Jackson, Michigan, transmitted weather information twice an hour on 320
kHz. Soon after crossing the Bryan marker, the
pilot would be able to receive the Cleveland radio
range on 344 kHz, identifier – · – (K). The Cleveland
range also broadcast weather information six times
an hour. The east leg of the Goshen range was continuous with the west leg of the Cleveland range. A
marker beacon at Vickery, Ohio, transmitting ····–
(V) on 344 and 278 kHz, marked the shoreline of
Lake Erie. This system of radio range airways was
extended during the 1930s to cover all the contigu-
ous 48 States.

The radio range was a major advance in blind
navigation and continued in use for nearly forty
years but it had serious limitations and defects.
The amount of aural information that the pilot
was expected to receive and interpret was a problem, especially as distortion hindered voice communication at the frequencies then available. The
equipment itself was often temperamental. Skill
and experience were essential to successful use of
the radio ranges, particularly to interpreting the
aural signals through static.

Once an aircraft deviated from the range
equisignal there was nothing to tell the pilot how
far off track he was,[3] nor was there any means of
homing to the range station other than along the
equisignals. This contributed to a mentality of following airways marked by range equisignals
regardless of other considerations, even though
one writer admonished: '… radio beams are an aid
to, never a substitute for, dead reckoning.'[4] Air
Vice-Marshal Bennett,[5] trained in British navigation methods, commented caustically on a ferry
flight in the US in 1940 or 1941:

> We went up through the States, sticking always
> strictly to airways, which added considerably to
> the distance and nothing to safety, in fact to the
> contrary. These two American pilots would not

1 Pilotage: navigation by landmarks and/or mapreading.
2 Ocker, W. C., Crane, C. J. 1932, 93
3 Denman, R. 1937
4 Jordanoff, A. 1938, 289
5 Bennett, D. C. T. 1958, 41

leave the beam for any reason whatever. Thus we unnecessarily went through heavy thunderstorms to our great discomfort, and remained in the thick of the airline traffic, to our considerable danger ...

The radio range itself had frustrating and dangerous defects. One range could interfere with another if the frequencies were too close together. Reflection from the ionosphere (skywave) could cause interference from distant stations transmitting on the same frequency. Mountains, large bodies of water, or mineral deposits could put a kink into a beam; a bend in a range course was confusing to a pilot trying to correct for wind drift. A clear equisignal could suddenly disappear, leaving an equally clear A or N. Some ranges sometimes produced multiple false beams indistinguishable from the true equisignal. The Salt Lake City range was notorious for this and several fatal crashes were attributed to it.[6] At sunrise or sunset a beam could oscillate by as much as 25° either side of its correct azimuth, or it could shift by 10–15°, remain on that azimuth for a time, and then return to its correct bearing.[7] Static electricity, caused by precipitation beating against the aircraft, could block reception altogether so that the range was often least reliable when it was most needed. Night effect, caused by reflection from the ionosphere, was so bad that some radio ranges, especially in mountainous areas, could not be used at distances greater than 50 km (30 miles). Sometimes the range signal would fade out completely, leaving the pilot to depend on dead reckoning and accurate course holding by reference to his directional gyro. Better antenna design alleviated some of these problems[8] but as early as 1933[9] the Americans were experimenting with an equisignal beacon transmitting on 34.6 MHz because at frequencies greater than 30 MHz radio waves did not reflect from the ionosphere.

Developments in radio range engineering added the Adcock range to the basic Loop version.[10] The Loop range signal was discontinuous, interrupted both by the Morse dots and dashes and by voice communication. The Adcock range, by contrast, transmitted a continuous signal and could therefore be used by an automatic direction finder (ADF) on board an aircraft. Voice could be transmitted in addition to, not instead of the navigation signals.

Even by the end of the 1930s instrument flying in general and range flying in particular were characteristic of the airlines and were little known to either private or military aviation. One navigation aid which was not available in the US at this time was the direction-finding (DF) steer or fix from ground stations. In Europe different operating conditions resulted in a different approach to blind navigation. In contrast to the American point-to-point concept, European blind navigation was based on position fixes provided by an international network of ground-based direction-finding (DF) stations.

When civil aviation began in Europe in 1919 RT/radio telephony (voice) was used on a single

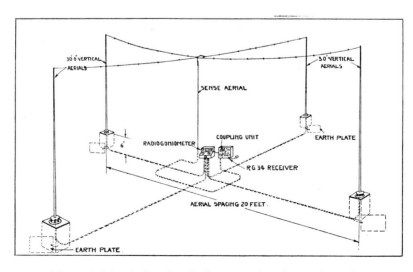

Marconi–Adcock direction-finding ground station – schematic.

Marconi–Adcock direction-finding ground station – radio equipment.

common frequency of 333 kHz, chosen as the best and most reliable frequency for both communication and DF.[11] Telegraphy (Morse) was soon substituted for voice because voice communication was a formidable problem in an area where many different languages were spoken, especially when heavily accented speech was subject to severe distortion. Telegraphy could overcome language differences by the use of an international code (Q code) adapted from marine practice. Air-ground communication is typically repetitive, conveying a narrow range of information; standard messages were suited to coded telegraphy. Thus: GED DE GEXYZ QTH BXL QAB BERCK QBH 1000 AR, transmitted in Morse, meant in English: 'Croydon Radio, this is aircraft G-EXYZ passing Bexhill, heading for Berck, altitude 1000 metres, below cloud, over', but was equally clear to an operator of whatever nationality who understood the code.

Other examples were: QDM: The course to me with no wind is ... degrees magnetic; QAH: My altitude is ... metres; QTF: Your position, according to DF bearings from stations which I control is ...; QFE: Field barometric pressure is ...; QFF: Sea level barometric pressure is ...; QBI: Poor-visibility rules are in force; QGO: Landing prohibited at ...; QAA: My estimated time of arrival at ... is ...; QBB: Base of the low cloud is ... metres; QFM: Fly at ... metres; QGP: You are number ... to land; QAI: Has any aircraft been signalled in my vicinity?; QTR: What is the correct time?; QGM: Do not enter the control zone; QBF: I am flying in

cloud at ... metres; QBG: I am flying above cloud at ... metres. A radio operator was an essential crew member under this system, especially on aircraft operating over long routes. Voice communication was slightly faster, message for message, but telegraphy was more effective, all conditions taken into account.[12]

Radio DF stations were set up in Europe and along some routes to Africa and the Far East. With experienced operators and communication between stations, bearings and triangulated positions could be given to several aircraft simultaneously. Highly skilled operators were needed to handle this traffic, all on 333 kHz; only about 15% of the operators at any one station had the necessary skill.[13] Transmissions on 333 kHz could be received up to about 290 km (180 miles) away by day. DF bearing accuracy was ±1°. Triangulation needed three stations to participate; an aircraft's position could be computed within a minute. At night DF suffered from serious errors at long distances, counteracted partly by the Marconi-Adcock antenna array and partly by using different frequencies. The Marconi-Adcock array,

6 Gann, E. K. 1962, 46
7 Jordanoff, A. 1938, 284
8 Diamond, H. 1933
9 Chinn, H. A. 1933
10 Deltour, B. V. 1960, 44
11 Samuelson, H. M. 1938
12 Crook, W. E. 1937
13 Oomen, P. 1955

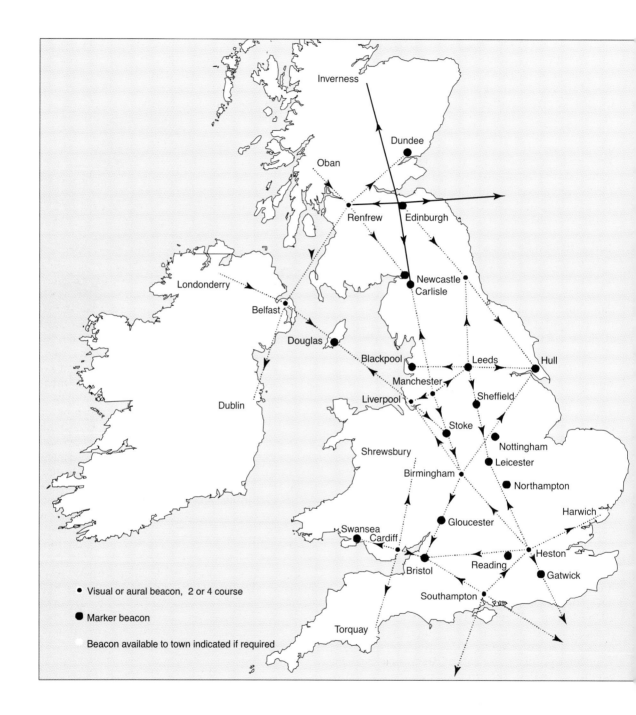

Map of Marconi proposal for a radio range airway system in the UK, 1936.

however, was so large that it was not installed at all stations. In 1932 only three DF stations were at work in Britain, but by 1936 this had increased to twenty-five. In 1932 these stations transmitted 1,032 position fixes and 2,065 bearings. In 1934 the DF station at Croydon alone transmitted 14,585 bearings[14] and positions to aircraft – forty per day. In 1936 the twenty-five DF stations transmitted 988 fixes and 54,340 bearings.[15]

Until the later 1930s only the medium-wave frequencies (100–1,500 kHz) could be used for DF. The characteristics of that frequency band restricted the range to 480 km (300 miles). In 1936–7 the introduction of equipment with a frequency range of 1,500 kHz to 20 MHz, made DF possible to distances as great as 3,220 km (2,000 miles).[16] Frequencies had to be adjusted to suit the distance and the time of day.

Although DF was not a part of blind navigation in the US, the Americans were not slow to make use of it where it was advantageous. Thus, in 1937, Pan American Airways used their own version of the Marconi-Adcock antenna at their DF station at Honolulu and claimed accuracies better than 2° at distances of more than 1,600 km (1,000 miles).[17]

In 1931 two radio ranges were installed in Europe, at Croydon, UK, and Abbeville, France. The Croydon range was described[18] as 'the latest means of assisting aerial navigation by wireless, and it will act as an automatic guide to aircraft approaching and leaving the aerodrome on the Continental route'. The Abbeville range was placed so that its equisignal joined Paris and Dover.[19] It transmitted on 311.2 kHz between 8 a.m. and 5 p.m. only, with a reception distance of 130 km (80 miles). Instead of A and N, the two quadrant letters were F (··−·) and L (·−··). In 1937 a new radio range, transmitting on 355 kHz, went into service at Croydon[20] to relieve the frequency congestion caused by the transmission of DF bearings. In Europe radio ranges were used as isolated navigation fixes, but not as continuous airways. In 1936 Marconi's Wireless Telegraph Co. Ltd[21] proposed a network of ten radio ranges and fifteen marker beacons covering most of Great Britain. The worst problem was to find frequencies which would not suffer from mutual interference with European frequencies. A further problem was that the density of air routes in northwest Europe would entail an excessive number of different frequencies if interference between radio ranges was to be avoided.[22] For these reasons the proposal was never implemented.

On both sides of the Atlantic during the 1930s it became increasingly necessary for a pilot to be able to home to a radio beacon using nothing more than the equipment on board. In Europe the increasing speed and density of air traffic made the transmission of bearings more and more impractical due to frequency congestion. In America the only means of homing to a radio range was to find and follow one of its four equisignals. The 1930s, therefore, saw the development of what is now known as the Automatic Direction Finder (ADF).

The forerunner of the ADF was an airborne version of the Bellini-Tosi system mentioned earlier. As modified for airborne use, the two loop antennas were fixed to the wings and fuselage on the aircraft's transverse and longitudinal axes. It was suitable for large aircraft with a radio operator on board whose duties allowed him the time and working space to take bearings and plot them on a chart. In 1930–1 the Marconi company in England was manufacturing the AD-16 aircraft directionfinder, Bellini-Tosi system.[23] The system was still in use in 1935.[24] The next development was a loop antenna wrapped around the fuselage. When the aircraft was pointed at the beacon, the loop antenna would be in the null orientation and no signal would be generated in the aircraft's direction-finding receiver. Heading error would generate a signal in the loop antenna. The direction of the error could be determined by connecting the loop and trailing antennas, but in two opposite combinations of circuitry. A comparison of signal strengths allowed the radio operator to determine the direction of the heading error.[25] By this means an aircraft could home to a transmitter, such as a public broadcasting station, without depending on DF from the ground. In 1933 Imperial Airways reported being able to home on transmitters from 400 km (250 miles) away.[26]

It was not long before the loop antenna was made smaller, rotatable and set on top of the

14 Furnival, J. M. 1936, 174
15 Denman, R. 1937
16 *Flight*, 8 July 1937, 61
17 Samuelson, H. M. 1938, 90
18 *Flight*, 27 November 1931, 1177
19 *Flight*, 10 April 1931, 324
20 *Flight*, 26 August 1937
21 Furnival, J. M. 1936, 159
22 Denman, R. 1937, 54
23 *Flight*, 17 April 1931, 347
24 *Flight*, 14 March 1935, 277
25 *Flight*, 18 May 1933, 482
26 *Flight*, 30 November 1933, 1205

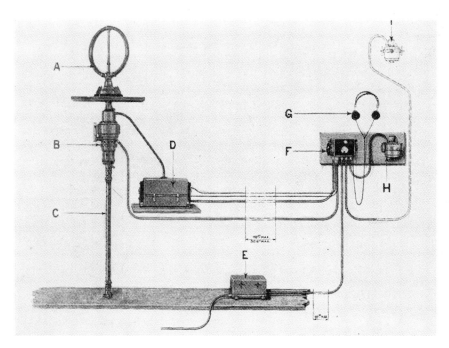

A. The rotating loop
B. The motor unit
C. Supporting tube
D. The radio receiver
E. Rotary transformer
   for high tension
   supply
F. Remote control unit
G. Telephones
H. "Navigator"
   indicator
I. "Pilot" indicator

Airborne Direction-Finder with rotatable loop – equipment layout.

fuselage so that a crew member could turn it and obtain the null.[27] This made it possible to take bearings on radio stations on either side of the aircraft's track without turning the aircraft towards the station. In Europe this early airborne DF equipment used public broadcasting stations and coastal marine beacons before beacons were built for aviation use.

In the US in 1931 G. R. Fisher and G. G. Kreusi, both employed by Western Air Express, developed an 'automatic radio compass'. The cockpit instrument was a centre-zero heading deviation indicator and the device was thus not the true radio compass that it would eventually become. A developed form of this device, with circuitry patented by Kreusi, was fitted in Wiley Post's aircraft for his 1933 solo flight around the world.[28] The Kreusi equipment was manufactured by the Fairchild Aerial Camera Corporation.[29] A small loop antenna was set above the fuselage, either fixed or rotatable. With a fixed loop the aircraft was steered until a null was obtained. With a loop rotatable by hand inside the aircraft, the loop bearing could be read off a scale. The Kreusi radio compass, like its British equivalent, could be used either for homing or for position-finding by cross-bearings. The 180° ambiguity could be resolved by making a deliberate turn and comparing the direction of the turn with the move-

ment of the indicator needle. The receiver could be tuned within a frequency band of 150–1,500 kHz. Bearings were obtainable at 480 km (300 miles) over land or 1,125 km (700 miles) over water. The receiver alone weighed 20 kg (45 pounds).

The Standard RC-5 equipment in Britain was an improvement with a bearing indicator in the form of a compass card from which the bearing of the manually rotated loop could be read directly rather than by way of the centre-zero null indicator of the Kreusi equipment. The card could be used as a backup turn indicator. At the end of 1935, with twenty-six broadcasting stations in Europe and coastal marine beacons, the radio compass was considered to be 'a very valuable aid to air navigation'.[30]

By 1937 frequency congestion in Europe was becoming so severe that an alternative to DF steers had to be found.[31] In January 1938 a beacon was set up to serve Croydon airport, but only the most modern transport aircraft carried the necessary equipment to make use of a transmitter of this kind.[32] These beacons were known as 'omnidirectional' because their signals radiated in all directions. Today such beacons are called non-directional beacons (NDB) because they provide no track guidance. By the summer of 1938 omnidirectional beacons were in service at

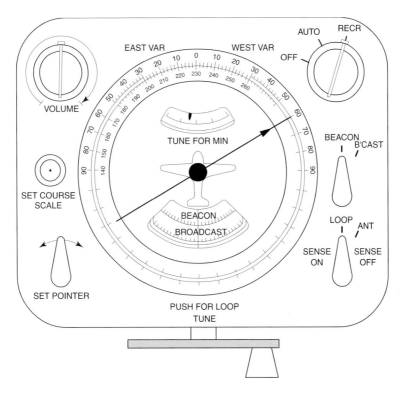

Sperry-RCA ADF – instrument face and controls.

Amsterdam, Paris Le Bourget and Croydon, all transmitting on 263 kHz.[33] In America, because of the defects of the radio range, it became compulsory on 1 January 1938 for commercial aircraft to carry DF equipment.

The final development in airborne DF was the automatic direction finder (ADF), giving the pilot an immediate, direct and continuous indication of the bearing to a selected beacon. This breakthrough occurred in 1938 on both sides of the Atlantic, with the Roberts-McGillivray direction-finder in Great Britain and the Sperry-RCA ADF in the US.[34] The signal generated in the loop, when it did not face the transmitter, drove a servomotor that returned the loop to the null position. The cockpit installation of the Sperry-RCA ADF looked like an ADF of today. An important benefit of this device was that a pilot could track to or from a beacon in a straight line, flying a heading that compensated for wind drift. This was difficult or impossible with the earlier equipment.

Because the 333 kHz frequency became too crowded with transmissions, the 1934 Warsaw Conference allocated a frequency band of 319.8–365.0 kHz to aviation use in Europe. This band was suited to both communication and DF, but it was subject to atmospheric interference, while reflection from the ionosphere at night caused severe DF errors (night effect). Although reduced by better antenna design, night effect remained a problem with medium wave DF, causing errors as great as 16°–18° at sunrise and sunset.[35]

In contrast to the Europeans, the Americans used the medium wave band for radio ranges and a different band, 3–6 MHz, for air–ground communication which was entirely by voice. This had advantages and disadvantages. In Europe a radio operator often had to be carried but one radio set

27 *Flight*, 24 May 1934, 524; 14 March 1935, 274
28 Mohler, S. R., Jackson, B. H. 1971
29 *Flight*, 11 April 1935, 400
30 *Flight*, 19 December 1935, 650
31 Denman, R. 1937
32 Taylor, H. A. 1938, 52
33 *Flight*, 7 July 1938, 15
34 *Flight*, 27 October 1938, 377; 17 November 1938, 445
35 Taylor, H. A. 1936, 120

sufficed for navigation and communication. In America the pilot and copilot could do all that was necessary to operate the radios, but separate navigation and communication radios were required.[36] Airborne radios were heavy and bulky by modern standards; a radio and its accessories weighed as much as a crew member. The Marconi AD-41A/42A transmitter and receiver of the early 1930s weighed together 45 kg (99 pounds).[37] It could be used for voice or Morse; a trailing antenna was reeled out to stream behind the aircraft in flight. Power was supplied from a generator driven by a small windmill mounted on the exterior of the fuselage. Windmills current in 1931 were available in several sizes, generating 100–500 watts.[38]

In the mid-1930s radio transmitters and receivers were separate sets. In Great Britain the use of receivers was unrestricted but 'Since the safety of all aircraft in the air during conditions of bad visibility depends to such a large extent on radio, it is obviously impossible to permit uncontrolled and promiscuous transmission from the air. The use of transmitters is therefore, confined to aircraft on scheduled air lines, and to those of certain responsible charter pilots and taxi operators.' Then, as now, private pilots complained that they were being excluded from the air traffic system.

With increasing traffic density and more flying in low visibility, air–ground communication and position-reporting became more and more essential. On both sides of the Atlantic control zones were established to guide the flow of traffic near major airports.[39] As early as 1935 traffic congestion, especially in cloudy or foggy conditions, was already a problem in Britain[40] and in 1936 the US Bureau of Air Commerce introduced Air Route Traffic Control. In Britain four control zones had been established by 1938.[41] Aircraft were not allowed to fly in these zones when visibility was less than 900 metres (3,000 feet) horizontally or 300 metres (1,000 feet) vertically without permission from the Air Traffic Control Service, a branch of the Air Ministry. Conditions of lower visibility were known by their Q-code title: QBI. Flight planning requirements came into force in Britain and the US during the late 1930s. Airline pilots had to file flight plans before departure stating estimated times of departure and arrival and intended routes and altitudes.[42]

In 1937 'Advances in air navigation instruments, engine dependability, and flying techniques have made it possible for aircraft to undertake blind flying on an extensive scale. Cancellations are necessary nowadays for aircraft with full radio and instrument equipment only when conditions are zero-zero, or nearly so, at airports where take-offs and landings have to be made. Bringing about a greater adherence to schedules, with benefits to the industry and the flying public, blind flying as a routine operation also has brought new difficulties. The pilot flying in the clouds cannot see other aircraft, and there is the possibility under such conditions that aircraft may get too close to each other for safety.'[43] A connection appeared between blind navigation and air traffic control which would become closer with the passage of time.

The American navigation system was more effective for traffic control than the European system because routes could be more clearly described. The detailed routings by reference to radio ranges, range legs, leg intersections and marker beacons, confirmed by air–ground radio, that came into use in the US during the late 1930s, were not possible with the European system.[44] Both systems were equally effective for *en route* navigation but the European system provided no fixes near airports for use in blind conditions. Morse became increasingly inadequate to handle the volume and complexity of air–ground communications. During a blind approach a Q-code message received by a radio operator and passed verbally or in writing to a busy pilot in a noisy cockpit was no substitute for direct voice communication between a pilot and air traffic control. The American blind navigation and air traffic control system was able to continue its 1930s development undisturbed by the war which broke out in Europe in 1939. The European system, already inadequate by the end of the 1930s, was completely disrupted by the war. Its post-war reconstruction was complicated by many factors which came into play in the meantime, as will be described in a later chapter.

36 *Flight*, 21 May 1936, 540
37 *Flight*, 22 December 1932, 1219; 19 April 1934, 393
38 *Flight*, 17 April 1931, 347
39 *Flight*, 14 March 1935, 274
40 *Flight*, 29 August 1935, 217
41 Taylor, H. A. 1938, 52
42 *Flight*, 15 December 1938, 567
43 *Aircraft Year Book*, 1937, 96
44 Yuill, G. F. 1939, 270c; Gann E. K. 1962

CHAPTER 8

Blind Approach and Landing

Pilots recognized early on that, when the clouds were low, with visibility beneath obscured by such conditions as fog, rain, snow or darkness, taking off was easier than finding the destination airport and making a safe approach and landing. The demand for the solution to this problem came from civil aviation, which had to compete with trains and ships in safety and reliability of service if it was to make headway.

Landing in dense fog was the most obvious and extreme form of this problem. Although achieved experimentally, this ultimate goal of all-weather flight remained elusive. Concentration on completely blind landings may have diverted research from equipment and procedures that would enable a pilot to fly a blind approach low enough and close enough to the destination airport to catch sight of it and land visually.[1] Such capability would permit reliable service in most weather conditions. Even today, true blind landings are rare and the aircraft and crews certificated to fly them are few compared with blind approaches followed by visual landings.

The problem of blind approach and landing was tackled in Europe and America with similar concepts but different results. The Europeans and the Americans both refined their *en route* blind navigation systems to provide approach guidance. Both recognized that this idea had limitations. The Americans developed the greater number of different radio approach guidance systems, none of which progressed beyond the experimental stage during the 1930s, but all contributed to defining the solution. The German Lorenz blind approach system not only entered commercial service, but rapidly became the European standard and was installed at several major airports. The British and French made almost no progress in this field at all.

The first American blind approach system was developed by the Bureau of Standards in 1919.[2]

Based on a 0.5 kilowatt, approximately 300 kHz spark transmitter, it was intended for use with a direction finder in the aircraft as an aid to finding an airfield in poor visibility. There was no further progress for nearly ten years.

In 1928 the Bureau of Standards devised a blind landing system for the Aeronautics Branch of the Department of Commerce. A radio range was placed near the airfield with one equisignal aligned with the landing direction, known as the 'localizer'. This provided the final approach track. One or more marker beacons told the pilot when he could safely descend, and when to begin the final descent to land. The Guggenheim Fund used this system, with one marker beacon, in 1929. In theory, the pilot could begin his glide to land on crossing the marker beacon closest to the airfield, knowing that a glide at a known airspeed and rate of descent would result in a touchdown in the right place. In practice, however, different aircraft had different gliding performances and wind would lengthen or shorten the glide.

In 1933 the Airways Division of the Department of Commerce installed a similar experimental system at Newark, New Jersey, with a radio range about two miles from the airfield and a marker beacon about 300 metres (1,000 feet) from the airport boundary. The pilot needed only a radio receiver and a Kollsman altimeter. The marker beacon transmitted on a frequency only 1 kHz different from the radio range; its distinctive aural signal could be received on the aircraft's radio. The best accuracy that could be maintained reliably in Kollsman altimeters was ±12 metres (40 feet), a figure that remains in effect today. This was safe enough for a blind approach using the radio ranges, but not a blind landing. A variation on this system was installed at Washington, DC, in 1933

1 Blucke, R. S. 1938, 483
2 Jackson, W. E. 1938, 681

with a radio range 4 km (2.5 miles) from the airport and two marker beacons on the opposite side of the airfield to the radio range, so that the aircraft flew towards the range station along a progressively narrower and stronger equisignal.

The US airlines of the 1930s developed a standard radio range approach procedure. An inbound aircraft would navigate to the radio range, crossing it 600–900 metres (2,000–3,000 feet) above the ground. On crossing the range station, as indicated by the cone of silence or by a marker beacon, the pilot would turn onto the range leg pointing away from the airfield. Established on this leg, he would descend to 450–600 metres (1,500–2,000 feet) above ground level, tracking outbound for long enough to give himself space to make a similar descent inbound. He would then fly a 'procedure turn' to reverse track. After completing the turn, and being sure that he was on the range course inbound, the pilot would descend to 200–300 metres (700–1,000) feet. On crossing the range station for the second time, he could descend to 75–90 metres (250–300 feet) above ground level, holding his course towards the airfield. If he did not see the airfield after a certain elapsed time from the range station, he would climb away and either make another attempt or fly to another airport. The range leg azimuths, layout of beacons and altitudes for the initial approach, procedure turn and final descent

were specified for each airport where such a procedure was available and were published on charts. The first such charts were developed from notebooks kept by Elrey Jeppesen while flying for Varney Airlines. Some airlines printed their own charts but found that his were better.[3] The Jeppesen company has been synonymous with instrument approach charts ever since.

An accurately flown radio range procedure allowed safe landings to be made under cloud ceilings as low as 90 metres (300 feet) and in visibilities less than a mile. The benefit of this procedure was enormous because it allowed blind approaches to be flown to successful landings in most weather conditions. The only equipment needed in the aircraft was the radio receiver used for *en route* navigation. Although marker and non-directional beacons were useful additions, the procedure could be flown using only a single radio range. Nevertheless, ceiling and visibility could at times be below what was needed for a radio range approach. Lower landing minima and, in particular, blind landing in fog needed some form of electronic vertical guidance, known as a 'glideslope'. The first glideslope was invented by H. Diamond and F. W. Dunmore of the US Bureau of Standards in 1929; an experimental installation was built at College Park, Maryland. The localizer transmitted on 278 kHz, the marker beacons on 3,105 kHz and the glideslope on 90.8 MHz. The

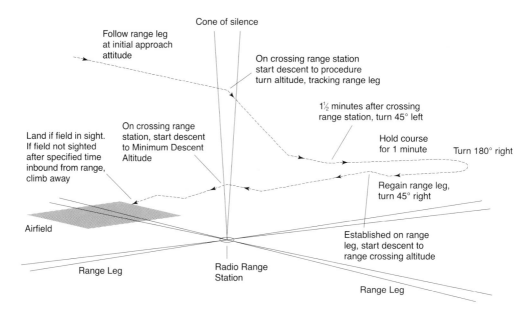

Radio range approach layout.

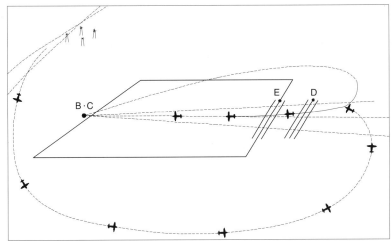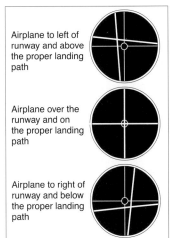

Airplane to left of runway and above the proper landing path

Airplane over the runway and on the proper landing path

Airplane to right of runway and below the proper landing path

US Bureau of Standards blind approach system, 1929: layout and instrument indications.

Left: Aeroplane landing by means of radio system for blind landing. A indicates the location of the main radio range beacon, B and C the runway localising beacon and landing beam, and D and E the marker beacons. On the right, the dial of the combined instrument used in landing by radio.

first blind landing using this system was made by M. S. Boggs on 5 September 1931. The Bureau of Standards built a second installation at Newark, New Jersey, in 1933, where over a hundred blind landings were made, and a third at Oakland, California, in 1934.

This and other glideslopes of the 1930s required the pilot to intercept and follow a line of equal field strength in a lobate signal pattern.[4] The glideslope was, therefore, not at a constant inclination but flattened progressively from first interception onwards. With the radio frequencies that could be transmitted at the time, ground interference prevented the transmission of a glideslope using the equisignal principle because the ground interfered with the lower of the two signal patterns. The Bureau of Standards work included a crossed-pointer instrument with a vertical needle for the localizer and a horizontal needle on the same instrument face for the glideslope on the same instrument face.[5] This principle continues in use today. In the original instrument, however, the needles showed the position of the aircraft relative to the correct flight path. For example, a left deflection of the localizer needle meant that the aircraft was to the left of the localizer, requiring a correction to the right. Consequently, the pilot had to fly 'away from' the needles, rather than 'towards' them as in modern instruments.

United Airlines and Transcontinental and Western Air aircraft and pilots experimented with the Newark installation and its variations during 1933–4. Experimenters discovered that railway lines, power lines and other ground features caused bends in the localizer course. In 1933 the Washington Institute of Technology further developed the Bureau of Standards system. This new system, built in 1935, consisted of a 278 kHz localizer, a 93 MHz glideslope and an aural marker beacon on the localizer frequency. The equipment was mobile and could be set up to suit any wind direction. The power output of the localizer and glideslope was 400 watts each, giving a range of 24 km (15 miles); heavy static could reduce this to 3 km (2 miles). The localizer suffered from the same inherent defects as other radio ranges.

The major disadvantage with this system and all other systems using runway localizers operating on relatively low radio frequencies was the fact that the use of these frequencies was apt to give numerous bends and multiple courses which made it difficult, if not impossible, for the pilot to land on an

3 *Flying*, February 1997, 30
4 Ocker, W. C., Crane, C. J. 1932, Fig. 57, p. 100
5 Jackson, W. E. 1938, 683; Ocker, W. C., Crane, C. J. 1932, Fig. 60

airport consistently under blind conditions.[6] Aviators were beginning to be aware that a blind landing was not merely an extension of a blind approach, but a different and vastly more demanding field of endeavour.

Difficulties continued. In 1935 Transcontinental and Western Air set up a localizer and glideslope at Kansas City using a frequency of 85 MHz. However, considerable difficulty was encountered because of variations in the altitude of the glide path when crossing over a river and a dike near the river's edge. The discontinuity in the path was considered to be a serious objection and it was not until later that it was determined that the vertical polarisation of the beams was responsible.[7] The localizer at Newark suffered from multiple and bent courses, but a similar installation on the same frequency at Indianapolis suffered from no such distortions. In 1935 the Bureau of Air Commerce of the Department of Commerce experimented further at Newark with a 227 kHz localizer and a 93 MHz glideslope, but the use of this equipment was aborted because of design faults.

The Bureau of Standards equipment at Oakland was transferred to United Airlines in 1934 and the Bendix Radio Corporation agreed to work on it with United; Transcontinental and Western Air joined the venture in 1936. A VHF[8] localizer was substituted, localizer and glideslope both transmitting on 91 MHz. Progress was made with using an autopilot to fly the approach; the pilot manipulated the autopilot and throttles to keep the aircraft on localizer and glideslope until it touched down and then closed the throttles. In 1936 and 1937 airline, Army, Navy and Bureau of Air Commerce pilots flew about 3,000 landings with no exterior vision in a Boeing 247 and a DC-3 equipped for the tests.

This project also started to develop approach lighting. Lights on the ground to help the pilot to orientate himself to the runway when it appeared out of the obscurity would become more and more important in the years to come. Indeed much work would focus on the problems of a pilot breaking out of a low ceiling and making a visual landing, as well as on the ultimate goal of completely blind landings.

This work did not result in an acceptable localizer and glideslope by 1940, and the radio range approach continued as the standard American means of blind approach. It did, however, establish the requirements for an 'instrument landing system'; the resulting device became the international

standard and continues in use to the present time. It was established that the localizer should transmit on 92–96 MHz, or 108–112 MHz if used without a glideslope. (The 108–112 MHz band is still in use for localizers.) The localizer should be straight, free from distortion and receivable 32 km (20 miles) away at 900 metres (3,000 feet) above ground level. The glideslope should transmit on 92–96 MHz; it should be free from distortion and adjustable as to angle. Marker beacons should transmit on 75 MHz with aural and visual indication in the cockpit (as today). The outer marker should be located at the intersection of the glideslope with the initial approach altitude. The inner marker should be located at the airport boundary. The marker signal should be receivable within 200 metres (700 feet) of the localizer on each side and for 90 metres (300 feet) along the localizer, up to an altitude of 600 metres (2,000 feet). A low-powered NDB (non-directional beacon) for homing should also be a component of the system. Other, more detailed requirements were also arrived at, in particular the need for fully automatic landing and for a glideslope at a constant inclination.

A separate line of development was the US Army Hegenberger system developed at Wright Field in 1932–3. The Hegenberger approach procedure was based on two NDBs, using the aircraft's ADF. The outer beacon was 3 km (2 miles) from the airport boundary, the inner beacon 450 metres (1,500 feet) distant. In 1934 a USAAC Ford Tri-Motor made more than 150 blind landings using the Hegenberger system.[9] The Bureau of Commerce adopted the system and began installing it at thirty-six US airports, but the airlines rejected it for lack of precision and the programme was abandoned.

In 1937 the USAAC achieved a semi-automatic blind landing,[10] using a Fairchild radio compass connected to a Sperry autopilot. The ground layout consisted of three to five low-powered NDBs transmitting on 200–400 kHz, each with a VHF marker beacon. Passage over each beacon told the

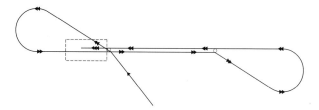

Hegenberger blind approach system layout.

pilot he could safely descend to a new, lower altitude. The pilot tuned the beacon receiver and used the throttles to control the descent rate. The final landing glide was maintained to touchdown; compression of the landing gear strut closed the throttles and applied the brakes automatically.

Two other systems were experimented with in America during the 1930s. I. Metcalf of the Bureau of Air Commerce experimented with three lights, two on posts either side of the runway, and one embedded in the centre of the runway at the touchdown point. On the correct glideslope the pilot would see all three lights in a horizontal line, equally spaced if he was on the centreline of the runway. With new methods of generating radio frequencies as high as 600 MHz, it was hoped that this concept could be reproduced electronically.[11] In 1939 the US Navy experimented with signal cables along the ground (known as leader cables) to transmit a guidance signal to an inbound aircraft, with a trial installation at Lakehurst, New Jersey.[12]

In spite of these advances, Messrs. Lyman and Moseley of the Sperry Gyroscope Company commented in 1938:

> It is paradoxical that though the modern transport airliner can fly through nearly any type of weather with perfect safety, it can land only where the weather is suitable. This is a situation which we all know will not long endure, and yet it is one which has defeated all attempts to remedy it through a period of nineteen years. It is true that the first instrument landing occurred nine years ago, but it is equally true that no reputable airline would consider, even at the present date, actually landing a load of passengers on a completely fog-bound airport.[13]

American blind approach and landing development was able to continue after 1940, unaffected by war.

The increasing use of radio ranges revealed dangerous shortcomings; a series of weather-related accidents in 1936–7 resulted in a critical review.[14]

> The conclusion was arrived at that the USA might avail itself of the progressive development of European ground organization. The Department of Commerce granted large sums for improving the flying safety in the US. American air lines carried out exhaustive tests at Indianapolis with the German Lorenz ultra-

short-wave blind landing system; Eastern Air Lines and Transcontinental and Western Air took part in the experiments. According to a comment in *Les Ailes* the experiments demonstrated the superiority of the German system over that put forward by the Air Corps and the Department of Commerce.

In Europe the Germans led the field in blind approach and landing. In spite of their legendary bad weather, the British concentrated on the (in hindsight) astonishingly impractical idea of using a tethered balloon as an airport marker.[15] This was usable only in shallow ground fog with clear air above and calm winds. On 18 June 1930, an RAF pilot made five successful blind landings in an Avro 504. This idea dates back even further to work with a Vimy at Farnborough in 1923.[19] A weight was trailed beneath the aircraft which lit a cockpit lamp when it struck the ground, whereupon the pilot closed the throttle. It was proposed that a man-carrying balloon be sent up to ensure that the marker balloon was above the fog.[16] Blind approach research in France favoured leader cables. The French were working on this idea at least as early as 1929.[17]

Just as American radio range technology extended naturally into their ideas for blind approach, so did the European system of radio DF. An aircraft could be guided blind by DF steers on predetermined, unobstructed final approach tracks and could then be advised when to make a descent below cloud.[18] If the cloud base was 100 metres (330 feet) or more above any obstructions around the airport, DF bearings guided the air-

6 Jackson, W. E. 1938, 689
7 Ibid.
8 For clarity this frequency band is referred to by its present-day title. At the time it was described as 'ultra-high-frequency' or 'ultra-short-wave'.
9 *Flight*, 20 December 1934, 1367
10 *Inter Avia*, #484, 26 October 1937, 1–2. Abstract in *Journal of the Royal Aeronautical Society*, 1937, p.1160
11 *Flight*, 15 September 1938, 233
12 *Flight*, 27 July 1939, 86d
13 *Aircraft Year Book*, 1939, 243
14 *Inter Avia*, #433/4, 22 May 1937, 9; *Les Ailes*, #838, 8 July 1937, 9. Abstract in *Journal of the Royal Aeronautical Society*, 1937, 742
15 *Flight*, 27 June 1930, 721
16 Meredith, F. W. 1930, 1226
17 Franck, P. 1929, 930
18 Brent, F. 1939, a
19 *Flight*, 9 March 1967, 361

craft to a position above the airport at an altitude not less than 150 metres (500 feet) above any local obstructions. When the aircraft's engines were heard overhead, the airport radio operator transmitted QFG in Morse. The pilot then flew a heading 30° off the reciprocal of the final approach track for two minutes and turned through 210° onto the final approach heading, descending to the minimum safe altitude. If he did not have the airfield in sight 1.5 minutes after completing the turn, he climbed away on a published heading known to be free of obstructions.

A refinement of this system, introduced in 1930[19] and said to have been devised by air mail pilots flying to Paris Le Bourget,[20] was known as the ZZ procedure. On initial radio contact, the airport radio operator would transmit the field barometric pressure and the approach sector according to wind direction and would then tell the pilot when the aircraft was heard over the airfield. The pilot would turn onto the outbound heading and fly it for eight minutes. He would then reverse course and be guided back to the airport by DF, progressively descending to the minimum safe altitude. When it was clear beyond doubt to the ground staff that the aircraft could make its final descent safely, ZZ was transmitted in Morse, or JJ if landing was not safe. For clarity the aircraft's registration letters could be inserted between the two letters.

At some airfields DF stations were placed on the approach paths to steer aircraft to the runway threshold. DF stations beside the approach path provided cross-bearings and determined the aircraft's distance to touchdown. A refinement was for the aircraft to transmit continuously on one frequency while the DF operator gave continuous directions to the pilot by voice on a different frequency. It was also found that a DF operator could take bearings on the radio-frequency signal emitted by an aircraft's generator.

The ZZ procedure was difficult to use and was at first regarded as an improvisation for dire necessity. Nevertheless, between October 1933 and February 1934, it was used forty-eight times on the Berlin–London night mail and freight service. In the course of time it was used satisfactorily with cloud ceilings down to 75–90 metres (250–300 feet). With practice, complete familiarity with the aerodrome and its surroundings, and skilful air and ground radio operators in close co-operation, a pilot could complete blind approaches by this system consistently and safely with ceilings down

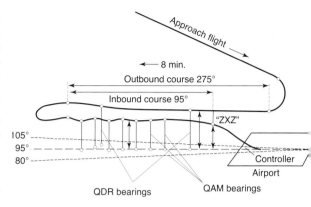

ZZ procedure layout.

to as low as 45 metres (150 feet), and in visibility as short as 365 metres (1,200 feet).[21] Accidents did occur. One aircraft landed safely after hitting a radio mast; another landed short of the airfield. DF could not provide the continuous and precise horizontal and vertical guidance that was needed for a safe blind approach.

The German Bureau of Flight Safety (Reichsamt für Flugsicherung) pressed for a solution to this problem; C. Lorenz AG and Telefunken undertook the work, supported by the German Aviation Experimental Institute (Deutsche Versuchsanstalt für Luftfahrt). The resulting Lorenz VHF equisignal beacon was tested at Berlin Tempelhof in the winter of 1932–3.

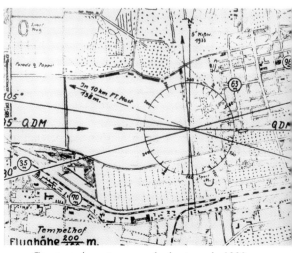

German airport approach chart, early 1930s.
(*Royal Aeronautical Society Library*)

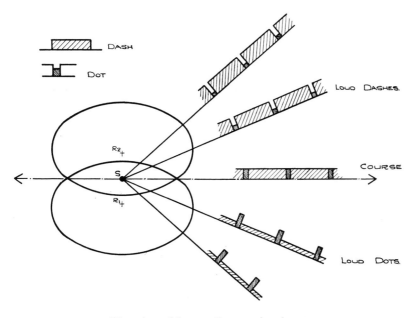

Plan view of Lorenz Beacon signal pattern.

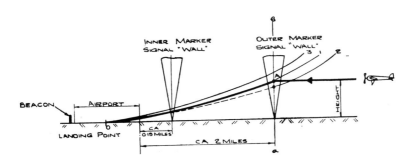

Side view of Lorenz glideslope and marker beacon.

The Lorenz beacon transmitted 300 watts on 33 MHz; the equisignal was 6° wide. The absence of skywave propagation and the short range of the signal, compared with the signal range at lower frequencies, meant that many different Lorenz beacons could use the same frequency without mutual interference. This frequency also meant that the Tempelhof antenna array needed to be no more than 10 metres (33 feet) high. The localizer was defined by an equisignal with aural dots on one side of the course, dashes on the other and 38 MHz marker beacons.[22] The localizer beacon was sited on the airport boundary opposite the approach direction, with the equisignal aligned across the airfield, so that the aircraft was always flying towards the beacon during the approach and landing. Two marker beacons were installed on the line of the equisignal under the approach path, one close to the airport boundary, one farther away. The system also transmitted a glideslope; like contemporary American systems, the pilot was intended to follow a line of equal field strength which was curved because of the signal propagation.[23] Like a radio range, the beacon emitted two equisignals in opposite directions. The front course and back course were both usable but there was no

19 *Flight*, 4 October 1934, 1042
20 *Flight*, 13 September 1934, 961
21 Brent, F. 1939, a
22 Taylor, H. A. 1935, 175
23 Stüssel, R. 1934, 825

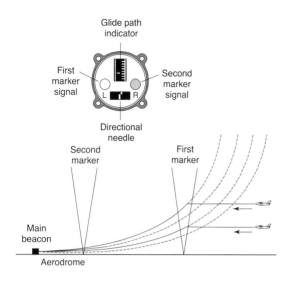

Side view of Lorenz glideslope signal pattern.

This sketch gives a diagrammatical 'section' through the main beam and indicates how machines, which enter at different heights, will reach the aerodrome boundary at the same height if the glide path needle shown in instrument above, is held in a constant position.

glideslope on the back course and the localizer needle indications were reversed in the cockpit instrument.

The Tempelhof experiments were successful and in 1934 Lorenz beacons were installed at Königsberg, Munich and Frankfurt.[24] New installations followed at Paris Le Bourget, Zurich, Vienna, Stuttgart, Amsterdam Schiphol and other major cities in the course of the 1930s.[25] A Lorenz approach system was installed at London Heston in 1935.[26] Soon after it was installed, a Lufthansa pilot landed a Ju-52/3m in 365 metres (1,200 feet) visibility. The same pilot demonstrated a Lorenz approach in even worse conditions at dusk on the same day, when the ground was invisible from an altitude of 30 metres (100 feet).[27]

American and German advances were not matched in Britain.[28] While Lorenz beacons were already in service in Germany by the end of 1934, British progress consisted of placing 7.5 cubic metres (10 cubic yards) of chalk in a trench 736 metres (2,415 feet) long at London Heston as a guideline for take-off in fog.[29] Pilots were able to take off in low visibility but not to land; consequently traffic was completely disrupted by fog. One writer reported that[30] 'A Deutsche Luft Hansa

pilot approached Berlin flying high and found his windscreen frozen up solid and with visibility through it about equal to that through a frosted-glass bathroom window. Rather than hang about waiting for the ice to melt, he landed perfectly by the Lorenz system. At Croydon the equivalent system would consist of lowering the First Officer on a rope to look at the chalk lines.' Although a Lorenz beacon was installed at Heston at the end of 1935, the busier airport at Croydon was not equipped[31] until the following year.[32] The Croydon beacon was first used in airline service in December 1936, when two Swissair Douglas airliners landed without difficulty at night. One of the pilots said that landings could be made with ceilings as low as 40 metres (130 feet).[33]

In January 1936, not one British aircraft or pilot was equipped or trained to use Lorenz equipment[34] and, even a year later, the approach beacons (of various kinds) in the UK outnumbered the British aircraft equipped to use them.[35] This was partly due to a lack of progress in screening aero-engine ignition systems which produced radio-frequency emissions. The UK manufacturing rights for Lorenz ground equipment were licensed to Standard Telephone and Cable Ltd.; the airborne equipment was handled by Smith's Aircraft Instruments Ltd.[36] The first British aircraft to carry Lorenz receivers were de Havilland DH-86As with British Continental Airways.[37] Including ignition-shielding, the equipment weighed 54 kg (120 pounds).

Localizer and marker beacon indications were aural and visual. Unlike the American crossed-pointer instrument, the Lorenz cockpit indicator had localizer and glideslope needles on separate scales. One indicator light was provided for each marker beacon. The localizer needle kicked to indicate the direction towards the equisignal. The use of this equipment was easily learned by a proficient instrument pilot.[38] The beacon was typically first received 56 km (35 miles) away at 1,220 metres (4,000 feet) above ground level. The pilot positioned the aircraft outside the outer marker at 600 metres (2,000 feet) above ground level and turned inbound on the equisignal. He began his descent on crossing the outer marker, 2.4–3.2 km (1.5–2 miles) from the airport boundary. Because the glideslope was curved, the pilot could either fly a progressively flattening descent to keep the needle position constant or fly a constant descent, allowing the glideslope needle to fall, knowing that it would recentre as the descent progressed. On cross-

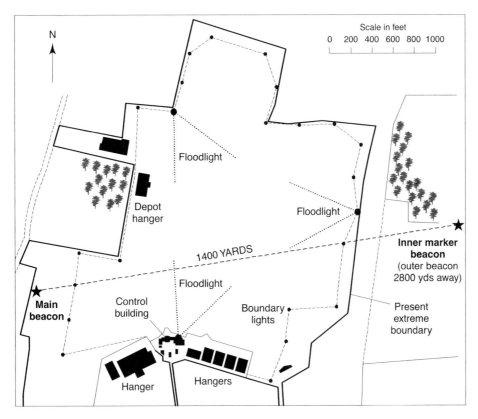

Airport layout for use with Lorenz. (Heston, 1935)

ing the inner marker he could throttle back and land. The glideslope was found to be unreliable and was a suspected cause in the crash of a KLM DC-3 on final approach in low cloud and drizzle at Schiphol on 14 November 1938. The aircraft crashed short of the runway; the captain, three aircrew and two of the fourteen passengers were killed.[39] After 1938 Lorenz was more commonly used for track guidance only; pilots flew a stepped descent, using the marker beacons and a Kollsman altimeter.[40]

By the end of the 1930s four blind approach procedures were in use in Germany:[41] DF to break cloud, the ZZ procedure, the QGH procedure which was based on a series of timed turns near an NDB, and the QGG procedure based on a Lorenz beacon. To use the QGH procedure the pilot homed onto an NDB, using an ADF in the aircraft. After crossing the beacon, the pilot followed a procedure, based on exact turns at 180° per minute and stopwatch timing. Strong winds could distort the flight path and bring the aircraft dangerously close to obstructions near the airport.

Much more reliable than the QGH procedure was the QGG procedure, based on Lorenz and developed by Lufthansa. In 1938–9 Lufthansa placed NDBs on some of the Lorenz localizers in Germany, 12–15 km (7.5–9 miles) from the airport.

24 *Flight*, 6 September 1934, 913
25 Hoffman, K. O. 1965, Vol.I, 119; Taylor, H. A. 1938, 134a
26 *Flight*, 9 January 1936, 46
27 *Flight*, 5 March 1936, 265
28 *Flight*, 6 September 1934, 913
29 *Flight*, 27 December 1934, 1389
30 *Flight*, 12 December 1935, 624; *Flight*, 2 January 1936, 22
31 *Flight*, 31 October 1935, 409; *Flight*, 12 December 1935, 624
32 *Flight*, 5 March 1936, 263
33 *Flight*, 31 December 1936, 699; *Flight*, 7 January 1937, 17
34 *Flight*, 23 January 1936, 94
35 Denman, R. 1937, 54
36 *Flight*, 27 February 1936, 240
37 *Flight*, 28 May 1936, 587
38 *Flight*, 14 February 1935, 175; Taylor, H. A. 1936, 587; Taylor, H. A. 1936b, 648; *Flight*, 17 September 1936, 28
39 *Flight*, 24 November 1938, 474a, 469
40 *Flight*, 2 February 1939, 109
41 von Handel, P. 1938–9; von Gablenz, C. A., 1941–2

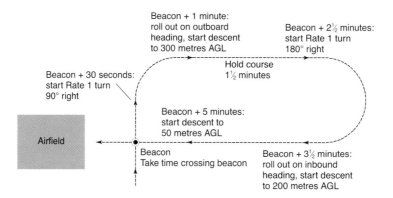

Layout of QGH procedure.

The NDB transmitted on 345 kHz, with a 38 MHz fan marker (so-called because of the shape of its signal field) at the same site; this combination was known as the approach beacon (*Ansteuerungsfunkfeuer*). An inbound pilot could home to the NDB, and use it as a holding fix in times of dense traffic. After an initial approach at an altitude not less than 150 metres (500 feet) above the highest obstruction in the approach sector within 30 km (18 miles) of the airport, the aircraft descended in a racetrack holding pattern, using the NDB and the Lorenz equisignal, to a published minimum safe altitude. The pilot maintained this altitude, tracking inbound along the localizer, until crossing the middle marker (*Voreinflugzeichen*), another 38 MHz fan marker 3 km (2 miles) from the airport. There the aircraft descended again to a final descent altitude maintained until crossing the inner

marker (*Haupteinflugzeichen*) 300 metres (985 feet) from the airport boundary. The inner marker was the signal to make the final descent to land. Skilled pilots were able to use this procedure to land in very low visibility.

A variety of MF and HF equisignal-type approach beacons was in service in Europe at that time, although the sources consulted are not specific as to their details. For example, in 1935 a beacon of this type with two marker beacons, made by Marconi and transmitting on 355 kHz, was installed at Liverpool Speke.[42] These beacons had the advantage that they could be used by aural indications alone, with no separate cockpit instrumentation, but at those frequencies, as in the US, distortion and splitting of courses was a problem.

In 1936 the French developed a blind approach system with both vertical and horizontal guid-

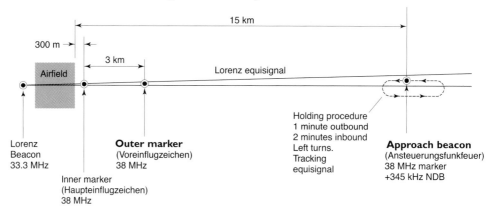

Layout of Lorenz QGG procedure.

ance.[43] Two radio beams were transmitted on 37.5 and 42.8 MHz. The aircraft had two receivers, one for each frequency, connected to the horizontal and vertical plates of a cathode ray oscilloscope. When the aircraft was on localizer and glideslope, the oscilloscope trace was a circle, changing to an ellipse if the aircraft strayed from either one. Nevertheless, the glideslope functioned on the same unsatisfactory principle of following a line of equal signal strength.

Increasing attention was paid to runway and approach lighting to help the pilot to see the runway on final approach at night or in low visibility.[44] In particular an approach lighting layout with lights on poles to indicate a safe glide path was devised in Britain. In England, France and Germany major airports were equipped with lights set into the ground as fog lines for take-off and landing guidance in fog. In 1939 the fog line at Paris Le Bourget was extended for 4 km (2.5 miles) from the airport. Airport lighting would become an increasingly important adjunct to blind approach radio equipment.

Both in Europe and in North America the concept of a blind approach followed by a visual landing became firmly established in the course of the 1930s. By the end of the decade true blind landings, manual and semi-automatic, had been achieved experimentally, but such landings would not become a part of normal operations for another forty years, and then only under carefully controlled conditions. The blind approach to a visual landing remains standard practice today.

42 *Flight*, 21 March 1935, 318; 30 December 1937, 645
43 Chïreïx, M. H. 1936. Abstract in *Journal of the Royal Aeronautical Society*, 1936, 733
44 *Flight*, 26 January 1939, 89; Vulliamy, A. T. 1939, 102f

CHAPTER 9

The Airlines Lead the Way

During the 1930s commercial flying on both sides of the Atlantic took on a recognizable resemblance to airline flying today. Airlines in Europe were at first more numerous than in the US and the Europeans were the first to produce large, multi-engined airliners, but as early as 1933 American scheduled air services flew more miles at night than the rest of the world's scheduled services by day and night combined.[1] From the mid-1930s onwards, sophisticated transport aircraft from Boeing, Lockheed and Douglas established an American dominance of this industry. Military flying, by contrast, made little progress in all-weather capability in Britain, France or the US; in the US in particular this lack of capability was embarrassingly displayed. Germany, however, used its commercial and sport aviation to develop a new air force and became a mare's nest of sinister and secret developments.

Airlines bore heavy fixed costs in equipment and staff, yet at the beginning of the 1930s flights were still grounded by bad weather so often that winter services were reduced or shut down, and little flying was done at night. The fixed costs had thus to be supported by a few revenue flying hours. Bad weather could cause financial disaster; Northern Air Lines Ltd., for example, based at Manchester, UK, went into receivership in the winter of 1931–2 due partly to this cause.[2] Airlines on both sides of the Atlantic were not commercially viable at that time and could not become so until bigger aircraft became available in the late 1940s, together with almost total all-weather capability. They were therefore shaped by government subsidies and air mail in Europe and by air mail contracts in the US. Throughout the 1930s the whole impetus towards all-weather flying came from civil aviation. In particular, the air mail pilots pioneered night flying and forced their way through weather of all descriptions.

In America the heroic efforts of the air mail pilots and aviation entrepreneurs of the 1920s grew into a vigorous airline system which was still, nevertheless, supported by government mail contracts. In the early 1930s, however, the contracts came under such unfavourable political scrutiny that President Franklin D. Roosevelt cancelled them and assigned the air mail to the US Army Air Corps on 20 February 1934. The US Army Air Corps claimed that it could do the job, but the generals were naïve and, in the event, nothing could have given more blatant publicity to the Air Corps' lack of all-weather capability.

On 16 February 1934, General Benjamin D. Foulois, officer in command of the US Army Air Corps, testified:[3] 'We have had a great deal of experience in flying at night, and in flying in fogs and bad weather, in blind flying, and in flying under all other conditions.' He also asserted: 'The hazards involved in carrying the Air Mail are not, in my belief, as great as those normally encountered by the Army combat pilots in the normal performance of their duties.' Bravery and hazard were, however, becoming obsolete concepts compared to a level of training and technology which the airlines had but the USAAC did not.

There were ominous warnings. In September 1933 seven Army aircraft based at Mitchel Field, Long Island, encountered fog one evening. Three crews bailed out; two made emergency landings at civilian airfields; two landed at their base. In February 1934 the Air Corps owned 274 directional gyros and 460 artificial horizons, few of which were installed in aircraft; once installed, the instruments became useless without vibration-damped mountings. The Air Corps owned 172 radio transceivers which were not channel-tuned and had a range of 50 km (30 miles) compared with the channel-tuned sets in commercial aircraft with a 150 km (90 mile) range. Although the Air Corps had done some work on blind flying, funding shortages had relegated night and instrument flying to a low priority. Commercial pilots flew an average of 900 hours a year over routes that they came to know well; Army pilots averaged 200 hours a year over no fixed routes. Finally, the typical Army aircraft of the time was an open-cockpit biplane with a payload of 45–225 kg (100–500 pounds) compared with the multi-engined monoplanes in airline service with payloads of 800–900 kg (1,800–2,000 pounds).

Warning voices went unnoticed. The 14 February 1934 *Washington Post* quoted Department of Commerce officials as saying: 'Lack of pilot experience and instruments for night and blind flying, both highly important factors in handling the air mail, may prevent the Army from ever successfully carrying the mail to the point of efficiency maintained by the commercial airlines.' Captain Eddie Rickenbacker, of Transcontinental and Western Air, stated bluntly: 'Either they are going to pile up ships all across the continent or they are not going to fly the mail on schedule.'

The last mail-carrying airline flight before the Army took over was on 18 February 1934,[4] when Captains Rickenbacker and Frye flew a DC-1 with twelve passengers and mail from Los Angeles to New York. Considering that little more than four years had elapsed since Doolittle's flight in 1929, the advance in equipment and all-weather capability achieved by the American airlines in that time is astonishing. Equally astonishing to us now, accustomed as we are to military leadership in technology, is the degree to which military flying lagged behind civilian capability.

The flight from Los Angeles to Albuquerque took 3 hours 15 minutes, crossing the Rockies at 4,270 metres (14,000 feet) in clear weather.[5] On the next leg to Kansas City the pilots were warned by radio of stormy weather over Missouri, but they were able to overtop the storm at 3,660 metres (12,000 feet). The Sperry autopilot was much used. Columbus reported a ceiling of 300 metres (1,000 feet) with a storm closing in on the airport; the instrument approach and landing were uneventful. The DC-1 was refuelled in 15 minutes and climbed on its way through a snowstorm. Rickenbacker and Frye were able to climb to 5,940 metres (19,500 feet) which took them into the sunlight above the clouds; the passengers were provided with oxygen. The temperature outside the aircraft was –29°C (–20°F) but steam heat kept the cabin warm. The pilots reached Newark after nightfall, made an instrument approach and landed, completing the 4,270-km (2,653-mile) flight in 13 hours

4 minutes, at an average speed of 330 km/h (205 mph), including fuel stops. This achievement, both the flight itself and the state of the art that it represented, was consolidated during the late 1930s, particularly by the DC-3, one of the most successful aircraft in the history of aviation.

The Army had nothing to match this capability and the start of US Army air mail service, with 148 aircraft,[6] coincided with the worst of the seasonal weather. On 11 February 1934, General Foulois ordered Army mail flights to comply with peacetime military take-off minima of 150 metres (500 feet) cloud ceiling by day or 450 metres (1,500 feet) by night. Even so, fatal accidents began in training before the start of the service with two crashes on the night of 16 February. Lieutenants J. D. Grenier and E. D. White were killed in an A-12 attack aircraft in a snowstorm between Cheyenne and Salt Lake City. Lieutenant J. Y. Eastman was killed in a B-7 bomber in an emergency landing at Jerome, Idaho. All three pilots had less than a year's experience.

The Army mail flights were a disaster; ten pilots were killed in the first month, a period of sustained and widespread foul weather. On the night of 22–3 February four aircraft were lost. One pilot crashed fatally in fog at Deshler, Ohio, after straying 80 km (50 miles) off course. Another crashed in fog between Newark and Richmond. While recovering from his injuries he said that he had been 'afraid to rely on his flight instruments'. Another pilot lost his way in a snowstorm and bailed out near Fremont, Ohio. Another made a successful emergency landing at Woodland, Pennsylvania.

On 24 February General Foulois issued orders attempting to limit duty hours and to inhibit flying at night and in bad weather, but if the early air mail pilots had followed such instructions the service would never have continued. The result was a temporary relief from crashes but in the last week of February and the first week of March the Army cancelled more mail flights than it flew. Even so, in the early morning of 9 March both engines failed on a B-6 bomber and a crewman was killed in the ensuing forced landing at Daytona Beach, Florida. The same night near Cleveland, Ohio, a pilot was

1 *Flight*, 7 December 1933, 1224
2 *Flight*, 4 December 1931, 1196
3 Shiner, J. F. 1983
4 *Aircraft Year Book*, 1935, 135; *Flight*, 1 March 1934, 191
5 Smith, H. L. 1944, 251
6 Smith, H. L. 1944, 253

killed when he flew into the ground in a snow-storm, and two pilots were killed in separate crashes on take-off at Cheyenne, Wyoming. The following night one aircraft crash-landed in bad weather in Iowa, another in South Carolina and a third in Pennsylvania.

Improving weather in late March resulted in safer and more regular operations and the Army increased instrument training. The mail service was so disastrous, however, that on 28 March the government advertised for bids from civilian contractors. In May the airlines took over the mail routes once more. The Army flights cost sixty-five crashes and twelve fatalities; the airline industry took four years to recover. US domestic airline flying in the late 1930s is evocatively and comprehensively described in the first chapters of E. K. Gann's book, *Fate is the Hunter,*[7] one of the great works of aviation literature.

The European night air mails began later than those in the US and with more advanced equipment at a time coincident with the coming of instrument flying. The first of these was Luft Hansa in 1926, followed by the Compagnie Internationale de Navigation Aerienne of France (CIDNA) in 1928 and by the Belgian Sabena and the Swedish Aerotransport in 1930.[8]

The Germans led European all-weather flying. Lufthansa was also a covert school for Luftwaffe aircrew; abundant technical and procedural developments were put to military uses. Deutsche Luft Hansa was formed on 6 January 1926, by merging

a network of air carriers covering much of northern and eastern Europe that moved 40% of the total airline traffic of the world.[9] The merger involved 162 aircraft of nineteen types. Such were the difficulties of night flying that, before the merger, only proving flights had been flown at night in the period 1924–5. The Berlin–Moscow air service, for instance, included an overnight train journey between Berlin and Königsberg. Aircraft utilization, averaged over the year, was only one hour per day. Advances in weather flying increased this to three hours per day by the mid-1930s.

On 1 May 1926, Luft Hansa began a regular night service from Berlin to Königsberg, using a Junkers G-24 and airway beacon lights; 503 trips were flown during the year. The service was flown only in summer until 1933, when year-round service began. Junkers Ju-52/3ms replaced the G-24s in 1931.

The reliability of Luft Hansa service gradually increased, as did the number of routes flown. Instrument flying was introduced in 1927; pilot instrument qualification became mandatory in 1929.[10] In the 1928 season from 23 April to 29 September reliability was 90.5%, improving to 98.9% between 1 January and 31 October 1934. Reliability in ten months of 1934 was better than in five summer months of 1928;[11] some of this at least was due to better weather-flying capability.

In common with the rest of Europe, blind navigation was by radio DF, transmitted in Morse. In 1929 Luft Hansa aircraft obtained 1,610 bearings.

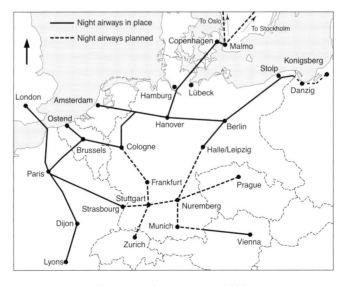

European airway system, 1930.

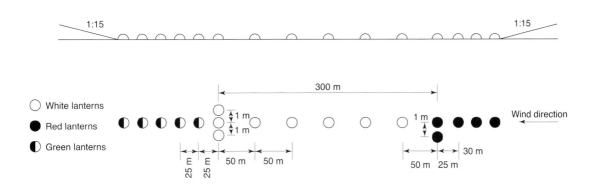

Landing direction lights, German system, 1932.

By 1933 this figure had increased to 32,550.[12] Telefunken developed an ADF to ease the burden on the ground services, which were operated by the airline. Luft Hansa aircraft radio logs[13] showed the percentage of flights that flew blind for long enough to need radio navigation. Between October 1933 and February 1934 this ranged from 40% on the Munich–Venice day service in January 1934 to 100% on the Vienna–Salonika day service in December 1933. In the same period the percentage of flights that were unable to reach their destinations because of bad weather ranged from nil on some routes up to 37.5% on the Berlin–London night mail and freight service in December 1933. Luft Hansa's operations remained free of serious accidents, although icing caused several forced landings. On one occasion an aircraft was damaged on take-off because of a swerve on snow-covered ground. On another occasion, 'starting in driving snow, great quantities of snow were accumulated on the wings which apparently influenced the steering properties of the aeroplane to such an extent that it was impossible to avoid collision with an obstruction'.[14]

In 1931 Captain Carl Florman, manager of Aerotransport, commented on the needs of commercial air services in Europe.[15] Instrument pilots were in short supply and prolonged night flying made extreme mental and physical demands on them. Inherently stable aircraft were needed to make their task easier. Ground facilities were rudimentary and light beacons were still the only available route markers. Floodlighting the airport surface was still seen as the best aid to night take-offs and landings. The radio frequency congestion that became such a problem in Europe was already foreseen.

In this still-tentative stage of instrument flying it was remarked that:[16] 'If the atmospheric visibility diminishes to less than a distance of between three quarters of a mile and one mile, it is in the interest of safe flying not to fly by the (light) beacons but to fly blind at an altitude which excludes any collision with the ground or with the highest points in the neighbourhood of the air route. The aircraft can be steered to its destination with the help of the compass and direction-finding much more safely than can be done with the help of beacons. Even so, light beacons give the pilot relief from instrument flying, however brief, and a chance of strengthening his trust in his instruments, which will fortify his moral power and endurance for worse weather conditions.'

Between 1929 and 1931, 813 km (505 miles) of lighted airways were installed in Germany, but in 1932 night flying was still rare.[17] Effective airport lighting was seen as essential for the development of commercial air services,[18] as was an efficient meteorological service, but in 1934 the needs of an all-weather airline service still far exceeded what was available.

As late as 1935 British domestic air services were

7 Gann, E. K. 1961, 1962
8 Florman, C. 1931
9 Davies, R. E. G. 1991, 19
10 Davies, R. E. G. 1991, 22
11 *Flight*, 24 January 1935, 109
12 Stüssel, R. 1934, 807
13 Stüssel, R. 1934, 812
14 Stüssel, R. 1934, 815
15 Florman, C. 1931; *Flight*, 11 September 1931, 925
16 Benkendorff, R. 1932
17 *Flight*, 24 June 1932, 572
18 Ward, C. E. 1933, 1224

German airways system, 1938.

so far behind the US and Germany that[19] 'Although internal services have, on occasion, completed journeys in the dark, there has not yet been a service so scheduled that the arrival must be made by floodlight.' Britain lagged far behind Germany in ground facilities and procedures.[20] British airports were still grass fields with only parking areas paved. White fog lines were used to guide take-off and landing in low visibility, but only a few airports had even this primitive aid. Obstructions were marked with flags. Several airports were tight for take-off in certain wind conditions. Radio approach aids were too few to be used for practice. Air traffic control was also becoming

a problem in low visibility. Weather information was often transmitted by unqualified staff, sometimes with serious results. So few radio frequencies were available that congestion was a menace. Pilot qualifications were questionable. Airline operators employed pilots of a few hours' experience to fly on routes in England which, from the point of view of weather and lack of facilities, were admitted to be among the most dangerous in the world. In the political climate of the 1930s, Britain's technical lag behind Germany had terrifying military implications.

In spite of primitive conditions, weather-related air carrier accidents were relatively few. On 30

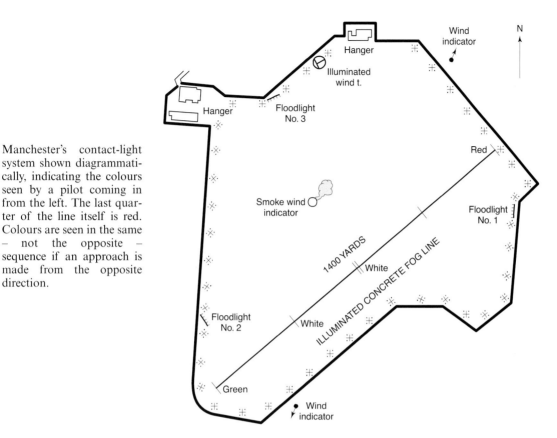

Manchester's contact-light system shown diagrammatically, indicating the colours seen by a pilot coming in from the left. The last quarter of the line itself is red. Colours are seen in the same – not the opposite – sequence if an approach is made from the opposite direction.

Lighting layout at Manchester airport, late 1930s.

December 1933 an Imperial Airways Avro 10, flying from Brussels to London on a foggy afternoon, hit a radio mast at Ruysselede in Belgium and crashed, killing all aboard.[21] On the night of 15 January 1934 a French Dewoitine carrying three crew and seven passengers from Saigon to Paris broke up in flight in severe turbulence over the Morvan Mountains.[22] On 31 May 1934 an Air France aircraft, leaving Croydon at 5 a.m. on a foggy morning, crashed into a radio beacon mast which was almost directly in line with the take-off direction.[23] On 2 October 1934, a de Havilland Dragon Six flew into the sea off the English coast while making a descent in low visibility. In spite of the pilot's overall experience, this accident was attributed to a lack of instrument-flying skill.[24]

A more amusing outcome befell Wing Commander N. J. Capper, pilot of an Imperial Airways DH-86 en route from Budapest to London on 22 October 1935.[25] He had been flying the route for eight months, after five years in the RAF,

including three years of intensive cloud flying. He claimed: 'I probably knew as much as anyone at that time about flying in cloud and the effects of ice accretion; but on that October day I was to learn a lot more.' After leaving Vienna, the DH-86 was flying at 1,980 metres (6,500 feet) between two cloud layers. Suddenly the two layers merged and the aircraft began to collect ice rapidly. The external venturi and pitot system iced up, disabling the airspeed indicator, heading indicator and artificial horizon, leaving only the turn indicator, compass and bubble inclinometer. 'This was no great problem, as I had done many years of cloud flying with

19 *Flight*, 3 October 1935, 370
20 *Flight*, 25 March 1937, 310
21 *Flight*, 4 January 1937, 17
22 *Flight*, 18 January 1934, 56; *Flight*, 1 February 1934, 100
23 *Flight*, 7 June 1934, A2
24 *Flight*, 10 January 1935, 57
25 Capper, N. J. 1964

Controls and instrument panel of de Havilland Dragon Rapide.

these alone.' Wing Commander Capper turned back towards the lower ground and warmer air near Vienna, but the icing was so severe that the aircraft could not maintain altitude. By the greatest good fortune he was able to crash-land in a snow-covered clearing which appeared out of the mist; he estimated the visibility as less than 60 metres (200 feet).

He commented that:

> There were moments of dread until I found that the passengers were all right, and then I felt like a million dollars at being so unexpectedly alive. My next feeling was that I owed them some kind of apology, but all I could think of was 'I'm terribly sorry' – which in the circumstances seemed a little inadequate.
>
> My passengers might have been hand-picked; they were a doctor, a nurse, and an insurance man! The nurse produced some brandy, and the doctor – who was most appropriately dressed in plus-fours, thick stockings and heavy climbing boots – asked if he could help. I told him I was not sure whether we were in Austria or Czechoslovakia, and he said it didn't matter anyway, because he could speak both languages; so I packed him off to see if he could find a tele-

phone and let the people in Vienna know that we were down and all alive.

Eventually he returned with a huge cart drawn by two powerful but very slow horses handled by a dwarf. He had found the north Austrian village of Zwettl, about four miles away. The warmth, hospitality and local wine at the inn in Zwettl soon put us right.

Later that autumn a Sabena aircraft crashed in England at Tatsfield. The suspected cause was ice accretion.[26] In the autumn of 1936 a British Airways Fokker F-12 crashed at 3.40 a.m. on a circling approach after being brought in to London Gatwick on radio bearings.[27] A similar accident took place at Paris Le Bourget at 5 a.m. on 22 February 1938.[28] This type of accident would be repeated again and again. Only precise lateral and vertical guidance to the runway threshold and strict adherence to carefully devised approach procedures would reduce the number of accidents such as these. The problem of exhausted pilots faced with instrument approaches in bad weather in the early morning remained long after technically advanced aircraft were introduced, indeed they made it worse.

On 9 December 1936 a KLM DC-2 crashed into buildings near Croydon after taking off in daylight, using a fog line, in visibility of 45 metres (150 feet). Fourteen people were killed.[29] On 26 November 1937 a Lufthansa aircraft flew into a hangar at Croydon after taking off at night in fog so thick that even the fog line was invisible.[30] Captain Pelly, who took off in a similar machine soon afterwards, said that the visibility was so bad that it was impossible to follow the white line and that he chose to start his run from the tarmac end (the airport parking area) so that he would know exactly where he was. Croydon was a grass field with neither paved runways nor guidance lights. The astonishing comment was made: 'It is, perhaps, necessary to say that there was no reason why the machine should not have taken off in the prevailing circumstances, for only a few minutes later a British Airways machine went away.'[31] Seasonal restrictions on some services, cancellation of

26 *Flight*, 19 December 1935, 658
27 *Flight*, 26 November 1936, 590
28 *Flight*, 10 March 1938, 227
29 *Flight*, 17 December 1936, 663
30 *Flight*, 13 January 1938, 44
31 *Flight*, 2 December 1937, 540

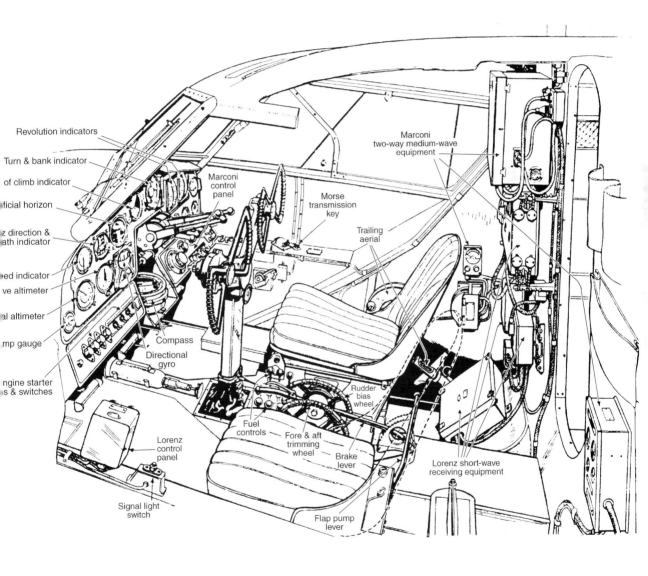

Revolution indicators

Turn & bank indicator

of climb indicator

ficial horizon

z direction &
ath indicator

ed indicator

ve altimeter

al altimeter

mp gauge

ngine starter
s & switches

Marconi
control
panel

Compass

Directional
gyro

Lorenz
control
panel

Signal light
switch

Fuel
controls

Fore & aft
trimming
wheel

Rudder
bias
wheel

Brake
lever

Flap pump
lever

Morse
transmission
key

Trailing
aerial

Marconi
two-way medium-wave
equipment

Lorenz short-wave
receiving equipment

British commercial aircraft cockpit, 1930s.

Controls and instrument panel of de Havilland DH-86 airliner. Note the three 'primary' blind-flying instruments in centre and artificial horizon and directional gyro to left.

flights and the extreme skill of civilian transport pilots kept the weather-related accident rate during the 1930s to within acceptable limits.

Air mail pilots routinely pushed their way through weather conditions that were unacceptable for passenger flights. '... The job of the early morning newspaper pilot (between London and Paris) is no sinecure. Although (Mr Pugh) has been on this job for a very considerable length of time, he still looks on it as one with immense and unplumbed abominable characteristics.'[32] Weather reports were often obsolete, wrong, or both. He was under heavy pressure to land at Le Bourget, whatever the weather. One wet morning in 1934,[33] he took off from Croydon in a de Havilland Dragon at 5 a.m. by floodlight, setting course by compass. He maintained his course at 1,460 metres (4,800 feet) through cloud by means of the Reid &

Sigrist turn indicator, airspeed indicator, altimeter, compass and inclinometer. Sighting the French coast, he descended to keep the ground in sight and flew on in rain and patchy cloud a few hundred feet above the ground until Paris came into sight. No radio contact with Le Bourget could be obtained until the aircraft was over the city. As mentioned, the air mail pilots devised their own instrument approach system for Le Bourget, later known as the ZZ procedure, but sometimes radio frequency congestion and fuel shortage led to forced landings.

The Americans had their problems too; mountains, radio ranges and bad weather were a lethal combination. Of nine weather-related Boeing 247 crashes in 1934–7, eight took place in the mountainous states of Washington, Oregon, California and Utah; three were near Salt Lake City.[34]

Controls and instrument panel of Boeing 247.

The new American monoplane transports, equipped from the outset for instrument flying, swept the board in airline purchasing on both sides of the Atlantic, although in Europe the Junkers Ju-52/3m, a fixed-undercarriage monoplane based on a 1920s design, held its own. The Ju-52/3m prototype flew in May 1932. The much more advanced Boeing 247 flew for the first time in February 1933, but was eclipsed by the Douglas DC-2, which entered service at almost the same time, and the DC-3, which first flew on 17 December 1935. Lufthansa flew some Boeing 247s, but the DC-2 and DC-3 soon joined the airlines in Great Britain,

Switzerland and Holland. Lockheed competed successfully with the smaller but faster L.10 (1934), L.12 Electra (1936) and L.14 Super Electra (1937).[35] These aircraft were built with flaps, retractable landing gear, constant-speed propellers, de-icing gear, engine instrumentation for fuel economy, full panels of blind-flying instruments and whatever radio equipment the customer specified.

32 *Flight*, 18 July 1935, 87
33 *Flight*, 13 September 1934, 961
34 Van der Linden, F. R. 1991, Appendix B
35 *Jane's Encyclopedia of Aviation*, 173, 336, 338, 538, 595

Controls and instrument panel of Douglas DC-2. Note Sperry combined artificial horizon, directional gyro and autopilot in centre.

Douglas DC-2.

At the end of 1935 five new DC-2s enabled Swissair to start year-round non-stop service between London and Zurich.[36] The DC-2s had Sperry blind-flying instruments and autopilots, Telefunken HF communication radios with fixed and trailing antennas, a Telefunken ADF and a Lorenz receiver. The autopilot could hold a course more accurately than a human pilot and was used even during a Lorenz blind approach, being disconnected only on crossing the inner marker. Zurich Dubendorf was fully equipped with Lorenz, NDBs and DF stations; Swissair pilots used all three as cross-checks.

An account of a flight from England to Germany, Denmark and Sweden in a British Airways Lockheed L.10A in the autumn of 1937 shows the advanced state of all-weather flying that had been reached in Europe during the late 1930s and illustrates the procedures in use.[37] The aircraft left Croydon under a 200 metre (650 foot) overcast,

36 Taylor, H. A. 1936; *Flight*, 12 August 1937, 169
37 Taylor, H. A. 1937; *Flight*, 7 December 1933, 1224

Lockheed Electra.

Lockheed 14.

Junkers Ju 52/3m.

Douglas DC-3.

Lockheed Electra instrument panel, late 1930s. Note two altimeters on right side of panel, single-pointer and Kollsman type.

climbing to 2,400 metres (7,900 feet) above cloud. Captain Pelly flew across the North Sea on dead reckoning, out of sight of land or sea, correcting his course by radio bearings from stations in Holland. A mapboard covered by a 1:1,000,000 scale chart was carried on board. Each DF station was marked by a press stud surrounded by a compass rose. By snapping transparent celluloid rulers to the press studs and laying them on the chart according to the DF bearings, the aircraft's position could be read off the chart where the rulers intersected. Radio bearings were an essential check on dead reckoning in obscured conditions because the weather services could not provide accurate reports of winds aloft.

The aircraft flew first to Hamburg, then to Copenhagen and Malmö, returning to London

via Hamburg the next day. Fog and ceilings of 300 metres (1,000 feet) or lower prevailed throughout. At each destination DF bearings guided the aircraft to the Lorenz beam, followed by an instrument approach. At Hamburg the beam was cut for about 400 metres (0.25 mile) by a factory with a metal roof, necessitating a 360° turn and DF bearings from the airport to return the aircraft to the beam. British Airways allowed mail and freight flights to fly approaches down to 40 metre (130 foot) ceilings. As well as DF steers, altimeter settings and flight altitudes for traffic avoidance were transmitted by radio.

On the flight from Hamburg to London the weather on the route was considered extremely good for the time of the year. As dusk fell, the ground was in view for more than 10 minutes near Amsterdam. The barometric pressure difference between Hamburg and London was equivalent to 182 metres (600 feet) on the altimeter, showing the importance of correct settings. The Electra reached Croydon at night in heavy rain and sleet. Although precipitation static in the all-metal aeroplane interfered with radio reception just when it was most needed, the capability of pilots and aircraft had advanced so far that even in those conditions a safe arrival was assured.

By 1937 it was becoming clear to many that war with Germany was inevitable. The RAF would have to fight in the weather conditions just described against an aggressive, well-trained and technically sophisticated enemy. In training and equipment it was ill-prepared to do so. Even as the threat of war grew in Europe, however, proving flights were in progress with the aim of starting scheduled passenger service across the Atlantic.

CHAPTER 10

The Challenge of the North Atlantic

By 1930 several successful flights had been made across the Atlantic, indeed it had come to be regarded by some as a stunt, entailing risk and expense with no compensating benefits to science.[1] Few transatlantic flights were made in the mid-1930s but, following the Ottawa Conference of 1935, both Imperial and Pan American Airways began proving flights in the summer of 1937, with a view to scheduled passenger service within the next few years.[2] This new series of flights used the biggest aircraft of the day, the four-engined monoplane flying boats. Flying boats had the advantage of being able to operate from any large area of calm water, whereas few airfields could handle landplanes of that weight.

Because of expanding British Empire passenger and mail traffic in the mid-1930s, Imperial Airways ordered twenty-eight four-engined flying boats off the drawing board from Short Brothers, the leading British manufacturer of this type of aircraft. The first flew in July 1936.[3] Three were equipped for the Atlantic flights.[4] Fuel and oil tankage was increased from 2,250 kg (4,960 pounds) in the standard version to 8,505 kg (18,750 pounds), giving a range of 4,020 km (2,170 nm) at 260 km/h (140 knots) against a 65 km/h (35 knot) headwind. Even so, a gross take-off weight of 20,412 kg (45,000 pounds), with a crew of four, left a payload of only 363 kg (800 pounds). Contributing largely to the 658 kg (1,450 pounds) of special equipment were five radio sets: three transmitters and two receivers for American and European domestic frequencies, long-range communication and DF.

On 5 July 1937 *Caledonia* took off westbound from Foynes in Ireland, on the first of the proving flights; at almost exactly the same time *Clipper III*, a Pan American Airways Sikorsky S-42B, took off from Botwood, Newfoundland. The British aircraft flew at 450–1,500 metres (1,500–5,000 feet) to minimize the effect of headwinds and landed at Botwood 15 hours later before going on to Montreal and New York. The Sikorsky took 12½ hours at an average altitude of 3,050 metres (10,000 feet), landing at Foynes before going on to Southampton.

The British aircraft carried two pilots, a navigator and a radio operator. The American crew comprised a commander, first officer, second officer/navigator, two flight engineers and a radio operator. In both aircraft the radio operator's duty was to obtain DF bearings for the navigator as well as communication. The navigators relied on dead reckoning, celestial and radio DF. Dead reckoning depended on winds-aloft forecasts which could be wrong and on drift sights on the sea which could be obscured. Star shots could be impossible because of cloud. Radio bearings from Ireland or Newfoundland could only provide the aircraft's position across track; they could not provide position information along track. Medium wave DF from stations in Europe and North America had a range of about 640 km (345 nm), leaving a gap of 1,930 km (1,042 nm) or more. Short wave DF was possible over greater ranges, but its accuracy was inconsistent. Radio bearings from ships could provide cross-bearings but their crews were not necessarily sure of their own position.[5]

The key to regular transatlantic service lay with the weather.[6] For six months before the proving flights a British Air Ministry meteorologist travelled back and forth in a merchant ship, making observations so that winds aloft could be forecast reliably. Accurate forecasts were vital, both for dead reckoning and to ensure that the aircraft would have enough fuel, but at the same time were

1 *Flight*, 4 July 1930, 757; Lovel, M. S. 1989, 177
2 *Flight*, 11 July 1946, 29
3 *Jane's Encyclopedia of Aviation*, 802
4 Taylor, H. A. 1937; *Flight*, 15 July 1937, 68
5 Taylor H. A. 1939; *Flight*, 13 April 1939, 370
6 Taylor, H. A. 1937

Boeing 314 Clipper flying boat, late 1930s.

Boeing 314 controls and instrument panel.

Short Empire flying boat, late 1930s.

difficult to provide.[7] The long ocean flight involved a great risk of the aircraft being blown off course by unforecast winds, while knowledge of the whereabouts of weather systems was essential to avoid turbulence and icing and to make the best of the wind. Should the flight encounter unexpected bad weather or headwinds, no intermediate airports existed and a new concept in navigation was the ominously named point of no return.

Besides the direction and strength of the wind, its variability from season to season and the probability of abnormal headwinds were equally important. Westbound flights against the prevailing wind were especially vulnerable. If an aircraft carried enough fuel to reach its destination regardless of headwinds, it could carry no payload. Alternatively, slender fuel reserves and unanticipated headwinds could cause the aircraft to run out of fuel short of its destination. Weather studies showed that a westbound aircraft had to carry enough fuel to allow for a 35-knot headwind. This fuel and tankage weighed 2 tons. As a result, the 'headwind allowance', therefore, made the difference between a revenue and loss, but the risk of flying without it was unacceptable.

Three routes were available: the northern route via Iceland, Greenland and Labrador, the direct route from Ireland to Newfoundland and the southern route via the Azores and Bermuda. The direct and southern routes both included 3,200 km (1,728 nm) stretches over water; the northern route included no single stage longer than 1,450 km (783 nm). The northern route faced the most continuously hostile weather: fog, low cloud, icing, strong winds and, in winter, low visibility on the ground in blowing snow and flying-boat bases clogged with ice. The northern route was, however, best for avoiding headwinds while westbound, because it lay to the north of the tracks followed by most of the depressions that crossed the Atlantic.

On the direct route wind speeds were the most variable and least predictable, and weather observations the sparsest. Over the 3,200 km (1,728 nm) of open ocean between Ireland and Newfoundland at 240 km/h (130 knot) an aircraft's time of passage could vary between 11 hours, with an 85 km/h (45 knot) tailwind, and more than 25 hours against a 90 km/h (50 knot) headwind, if its fuel lasted that long. The direct route crossed all the weather systems in all seasons, forcing aircraft to pass through extensive areas of continuous, deep cloud cover with prolonged instrument flying, turbulence and icing. Weather observations in the interior of Newfoundland beginning in 1935 showed fog to be less common in the interior than on the coast.

7 Entwistle, F. 1939

Focke-Wulf Fw-200 Condor.

Consequently a transatlantic air terminal was built at a place that would become known to every pilot who crossed the North Atlantic – Gander.

The southern route offered the best weather, although threatened at times by strong winds and thunderstorms, but was longer than the other two. In 1937 there was no airport on the Azores; wind and ocean swell made a permanent flying-boat base problematical. At the end of the 1930s, only the southern route was feasible for year-round service, but by flying boats only. Weather on the northern route was too hostile, both for flying and for the construction and maintenance of airports, conditions that would be overcome only by the demands of war and unlimited military spending. A scheduled summer service appeared possible on the direct route; winter service was problematical because of weather.

By 1937 a network of weather stations on both sides of the Atlantic, each making eight observations a day, was amplified by observations from ships. Information was exchanged twice daily between Europe and North America by radio stations at Arlington, Virginia and Rugby, UK. Weather charts covering North America, the Atlantic and western Europe were drawn twice a day. The transatlantic aircrews strongly advocated a stationary weather ship in the North Atlantic, similar to the French *Carimaré* stationed between the Azores and Bermuda for two trial periods in 1937 and 1938. Such a ship would not only provide a navigation fix but might also be able to give warning of sudden and unexpected weather devel-

opments. The two bases at Botwood in Newfoundland and Foynes in Ireland were in radio contact with each other. When a flight was scheduled, an exchange of weather reports and forecasts began which continued at regular intervals until the flight was completed. The captain's briefing enabled him to decide on track and altitudes and to estimate the flight time. Aircraft in flight were in radio contact with both ends of their route and could receive weather updates while in the air.

The two British flying boats *Caledonia* and *Cambria* made a total of five round-trip flights across the Atlantic in the summer of 1937; the Pan American Airways Sikorsky made three round trips, two by the direct route, one by the southern route.[8] The summer of 1938 was a hiatus with no American flights and only one trip by the British piggy-back aircraft *Mercury* and *Maia*. Underlining the absence of British or American flights, in August the Germans scored a brilliant success, with no advance notice, which made the British and American efforts seem plodding by comparison. July 1937 saw the first flight of the prototype Focke-Wulf 200 Condor,[9] a four-engined, 26-seat airliner with a normal range of 1,600 km (864 nm). Two Condors entered Lufthansa service in 1937, followed by three in 1938, and five in the following year.[10]

At 7.30 p.m. on 10 August 1938, the Condor *Brandenburg* took off from Berlin, crossed Scotland, continued over the Atlantic, and landed at New York 25 hours after leaving Berlin, having flown just under 6,400 km (2,160 nm). The crew

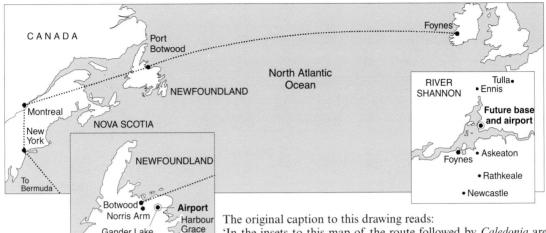

The original caption to this drawing reads:
'In the insets to this map of the route followed by *Caledonia* are shown the two major terminal points concerned. The Irish base is at present at Foynes, but the final base will be at Kilconry, where an airport is also to be laid out by the Irish Free State. In Newfoundland the main flying boat base will be at Botwood, with an auxiliary alighting place at Gander Lake, a mile or so from the new airport. Norris Arm is the location of the meteorological station.'

The North Atlantic air route, 1939, map of facilities.

consisted of two pilots, a radio operator and a flight engineer. The aircraft was equipped for normal Lufthansa service, except for an increased fuel capacity of nearly 9,100 litres (2,000 gallons).[11] The news broke with a radio message announcing landfall over Newfoundland. The aircraft had crossed the British Isles undetected, a bad omen for a country on the brink of war with Germany, and completed its flight without using the facilities so laboriously set up by the British and Americans for their own transatlantic flights. The arrival of the *Brandenburg* in America, smoothed by an astute diplomatic manoeuvre, symbolized the fast-growing technical, and ultimately military, ascendancy of Nazi Germany. The return flight to Berlin was completed in just under 20 hours, also non-stop.

This flight was no isolated feat. It was preceded by a 5,800 km (1,950 nm) non-stop flight by a twin-engined Junkers Ju-86 from Germany to West Africa in 1936 and was followed by a flight by the *Brandenburg* from Berlin to Tokyo in 48 hours in November 1938 with only three stops, at Basra, Karachi, and Hanoi. The *Brandenburg*'s career came to an unfortunate end when it ditched in Manila Bay in January 1939 while returning to Germany from Japan.

In 1939 the British flying boats *Cabot* and *Caribou* made eight round trips with in-flight refuelling. Pan American began a scheduled passenger service with one round trip each week on the direct and southern routes, using Boeing 314 flying boats. Service on the direct route was suspended in October because of weather hazards, although the Americans planned to continue the southern service.

Extraordinary advances in Atlantic flying had taken place in ten years. The heroic, and sometimes foolhardy, feats of privately funded pioneers had become highly organized efforts backed by national governments. The war effort built on these advances and forced the pace of transatlantic flying to such an extent that scheduled passenger services would be crossing the ocean before 1950. Essential to this effort, and in many ways more important to this than to other branches of aviation, were advances in the science of meteorology, leading to an understanding of global weather processes and greatly improved and expanded weather forecasting.

8 Christie, C. A. 1995, 21–23
9 *Jane's Encyclopedia of Aviation*, 397
10 Davies, R. E. G. 1991, 56
11 *Flight*, 18 August 1938, 148

The New Science of Meteorology

Predicting the weather is one of humanity's oldest endeavours. Clay tablets have been preserved from as long ago as 650 BC with inscriptions on weather forecasting in cuneiform script.[1] Systematic observations began in the sixteenth century. Measurement became possible with the invention of the thermometer in about 1600 and the barometer in 1643. Observers became aware that weather could be different at the same time in different places; the first recorded simultaneous observations were made in France and Sweden in 1649–51. In 1653–7 the Italians developed the idea of a common reporting format, including pressure, temperature, humidity, wind direction and sky condition. By the time the reports could be compared, however, they were weeks old, as were the weather conditions that they might have been used to predict.

This changed suddenly with the nineteenth-century invention of the telegraph. For the first time data could be assembled from wide areas almost as soon as the observations were made. Reporting networks were established in the US and Great Britain. Public weather forecasting began on both sides of the Atlantic, printed in daily newspapers. Synoptic charts, isobars and wind symbols came into use at this time.

The First World War brought with it an unprecedented demand for accurate weather information. No longer could the weather be ignored as a factor in warfare.[2] A pilot could not wisely take off without considering the prospects of finding suitable weather for landing. The German armed forces had aviation weather services organized and in place before the outbreak of war, and before the British and French even realized that they were necessary. British soldiers, it was said, did not go into action carrying umbrellas.

The weather forecasting of the day was based on accumulated records; theoretical studies were only just beginning. As early as 1883 Ralph Abercromby produced the idea of a depression, an area of low barometric pressure and its associated weather,[3] further developed in 1906–11 by W. N. Shaw.[4] At about the same time, the Austrian meteorologist, Max Margules, hypothesized that a linear discontinuity could form when air masses of differing characteristics met. In 1911 Wilhelm Schmidt produced the theory of a line squall. In 1915 Julius Hann described cyclonic weather in a German meteorological textbook.[5] Powered flight began to open a window on the three-dimensional structure of the atmosphere and as early as 1910 unmanned weather balloons had led to the discovery of the stratosphere. The science of meteorology advanced rapidly and radically between 1918 and 1922 through the work of the Norwegian physicist Vilhelm Bjerknes.[6]

In 1901–2, while working in Stockholm, Bjerknes realized that his theoretical work on the mechanics of unconstrained fluids might be applicable to weather forecasting, as existing methods relied on empirical signs or statistical regularities without incorporating physical theory.[7] In 1913 he became Director at the Leipzig Geophysical Institute in Germany where he continued his work on meteorology, but, because of difficulties caused by the war, he accepted a professorship at the new geophysical institute at Bergen, Norway, in 1917. Among the ideas brought back to Norway from Leipzig was the understanding that surface winds could converge along lines hundreds of miles long, causing clouds and rain.

In October 1918 Jakob Bjerknes, Vilhelm's son, wrote one of the most important papers ever to appear on the subject of meteorology: *On the structure of moving cyclones* which remains the origin of our understanding of frontal depressions. The Bergen school not only developed a new, three-dimensional model of the frontal depression, including the structure of warm and cold fronts, but showed that fronts and depressions were integral parts of each other, and used that theory to forecast the weather in the temperate latitudes. The final amendment to the Bergen cyclone model was the understanding of occlusion and the infilling of depressions. Primarily the work of Tor Bergeron, this was developed between 1920 and 1922 and published in 1922 as a paper by J. Bjerknes and H. Solberg entitled: *Life cycle of cyclones and the polar front theory.*

During the 1930s national governments began to organize weather reconnaissance flying units. One example was the Royal Air Force Meteorological Flight at Duxford in eastern England.[8] In 1933 the 'Met Flight' was equipped with Armstrong Whitworth Siskin fighters. Using oxygen and electrically heated flight suits, the pilots climbed to 7,600 metres (25,000 feet) twice a day, measuring temperature, humidity, and the types and heights of clouds. They carried no radio because in those days there were few direction-finding stations on the ground so R/T was not usable for navigation or as a let-down aid. The pilots preferred to dispense with the weight of radio sets and once airborne they were very much on their own. In thick fog they took off along a chalk line set into the grass airfield, having been told of fog-free airfields where they could land. There was usually no wind in the zero-zero conditions so the pilot positioned the aircraft at the inner end of the fog line, leant his head out of the side of the cockpit, opened the throttle and followed the line. To start with the Reid & Sigrist instrument, being Venturi-driven, was inoperative but as the aircraft reached flying speed it began to come to life.

The Met Flight pilots were often in cloud and icing from ground level to the top of their climb. One remembered 'collecting fantastic amounts of ice on wing leading edges, struts, flying wires and windscreen and it used to break off in great chunks every so often. It caused a great deal of vibration but never once do I remember being seriously bothered by lift or control problems. It certainly looked very daunting at times but one learned to keep one's spirits up and not worry about it.' In one period of thirteen months the Met Flight did not miss a single flight.

In the 1930s, for the first time, small balloons were released from the ground, carrying instruments to measure certain characteristics of the atmosphere at different levels and transmit them by radio back to the ground. Much ingenuity was devoted to tracking the balloon and producing a cheap, expendable set of instruments and

transmitters, later known as a radiosonde, but ultimate success was not achieved during the decade.[9]

The idea of dispersing fog rather than trying to land through it dates back at least to 1929, attributed to an American gravel pit operator who noticed that the heat from a kiln for drying gravel would cause fog to disperse. At the time of Doolittle's flight at Mitchel Field, E. C. Reader was there also, experimenting with a blowtorch.[10] In England ten years later, the same idea led to the wartime FIDO (Fog Investigation and Dispersal Operation) system.[11]

Increased flying in all weathers brought aircraft into closer contact with thunderstorms. Severe turbulence gave every incentive to avoid such storms, but this was easier said than done. Airline traffic had to penetrate areas or lines of convective cells too extensive to circumvent, while in certain weather conditions storms were hidden in masses of cloud so that a pilot could easily fly into one unawares. Lightning striking the aircraft was thought at first to be the worst hazard. Although unnerving to those on board, experience showed that lightning-strikes usually caused only minor damage, unless a trailing antenna was in use.[12] Aviators were slow to become aware of the true danger of thunderstorms, believing that bigger aircraft of higher performance would pass unscathed through the violent interior of a storm. A long series of fatal crashes proved that this was untrue.

Flight through extensive areas of cloud brought the hazard of ice accretion on airframes and propellers. The basic causes, characteristics and effects of ice accretion, and the feasible methods of prevention, were all known in principle as early

1 Hardy, R., Wright, P., Kington, J., Gribbin, J. 1982
2 Shaw, W. N. 1919
3 Abercromby, R. 1883
4 Shaw, W. N. 1911; Ludlum, F. H. 1966
5 Hann, J. 1915
6 Most of the following information is taken from Friedman, R. M. 1989
7 Friedman, R. M. 1989, 53
8 Quill, J. K. 1985, Chap.3
9 Feige, R. 1935; H. M. Stationery Office 1937; Anon., 'Radio Meteorograph System,' abstract in *JRAS*, 41, 1937, 504; Thomas, H. A. 1938; Diamond, H., Hinman, W. S., Dunmore, F. W. 1938
10 Hallion, R. P. 1988, 102
11 *Flight*, 22 June 1939, 640
12 Brintzinger, W., Viehmann, H. 1934; NACA Technical Note #94, March, 1934; Anon. 1934 Researches on Lightning Discharges Striking Aeroplanes; *Flight*, 16 December 1937, 611

as 1935.[13] Although the empirical facts were known, the processes behind them are still acknowledged to be complex. An aircraft flying in cloud, rain, and sometimes snow, in temperatures below freezing is likely to accumulate ice on the leading edges of wings, propeller blades, antennas and other parts. The highest rates of accretion occur in freezing rain and in cumulonimbus clouds. Otherwise icing may be expected in cloud in temperatures between 0°C (32°F) and –20°C (–4°F) to extremes of +3°C (37°F) to –40°C (–40°F). The occurrence of icing cannot be predicted with certainty, even today.

Ice impairs the aerodynamics of wings and propellers. Ice on propellers unbalances them, causing dangerous vibration. Icing also increases the total drag of the aircraft; the weight of the ice is less significant. Severe icing can force an aircraft to the ground or render it uncontrollable. Much depends on the rate of accretion and the performance of the aircraft. Ice can form and sublime or melt as the aircraft flies into and out of icing conditions. A powerful aircraft – over the years some aircraft have developed better reputations for carrying ice than others – flying in light icing may be unaffected after an hour or more. Yet in rare and extreme conditions aircraft have been rendered uncontrollable in a few minutes. The hazard of icing has always been indefinite. In the 1930s icing was recognized as a problem, not only because of increased flying in cloud but also because thick monoplane wings accumulated ice more readily than did the comparatively thin, externally braced wings of biplanes.[14]

Three principles were devised to prevent icing: thermal, mechanical and chemical. In the mid-1930s it was thought that, for thermal de-icing to be effective, the whole wing would have to be heated, as ice melting off a hot leading edge would only refreeze farther back on the wing.[15] This was a problem in terms of ducting, heat transfer and the effects of heat on the wing structure and fuel tanks.

Icing could be prevented mechanically by means of a rubber skin (boot) fixed to the wing leading-edge with tubes beneath it inflatable by compressed air. Once ice had accumulated, inflation of the tubes would break it up, causing it to blow away in the slipstream. This method of ice prevention continues in use on propeller-driven aircraft to the present. It is not, however, effective in all conditions of icing.

Certain chemicals were found to inhibit ice accretion. The active ingredient lowered the freezing point of the water droplets hitting the wing leading-edge, so maintaining a liquid boundary layer. Ice would build up but, being prevented from adhering to the wing, would break off and blow away before it could accumulate to any dangerous extent. Various mixtures were experimented with in the search for a durable anti-icing dope. Wind tunnel experiments at the RAE demonstrated the usefulness of anti-ice mixtures consisting of glue, treacle, Castile soap, and sodium chloride.[16] Heavy rain could wash the dope off before it could be useful but for the next ten years the British tended to rely on anti-icing dope rather than on the de-icing boots favoured by American aircraft manufacturers. Methods of exuding chemicals through a porous leading edge were considered, but the search for the right combination of materials continues today. The problem with this system lay in the cost and weight of tankage, pumps and ducting, especially in a large aircraft, and in the fact that, once the de-icing fluid was exhausted, the aircraft was defenceless. Chemical de-icing was, however, applicable to propellers; alcohol could be exuded at the blade root and distributed along the blade by centrifugal force.

A 1937 article by two German authors[17] shows not only an advanced understanding of the three-dimensional nature of weather systems but also an appreciation of their potential for icing. On the other hand, one British source[18] pointed out that icing was so variable and so hard to predict that the Meteorological Office was reluctant to issue ice warnings for fear of losing credibility. A related hazard was snow and frost on the wings of parked aircraft. Accidents occurred when pilots tried to take off with snow or frost on the wings, an insidious hazard, not always obvious, which continues to the present.[19] Encounters with icing and thunderstorms are graphically described in Gann's *Fate is the Hunter*.[20]

The quest for all-weather flight not only made ever-increasing demands on the science of meteorology but also made it possible to study the atmosphere as never before in all three dimensions by

---

13 Lockspeiser, B. 1936
14 *Flight*, 3 May 1934, 447
15 Lockspeiser, B. 1936
16 Lockspeiser, B. 1936, 5
17 Noth, H., Polte, W. 1937
18 Simpson, G .S. 1937
19 *Flight*, 15 September 1938, p. 233
20 Gann, E. K. 1961

direct observation. The new theoretical science of meteorology expounded by Vilhelm and Jakob Bjerknes and by the Bergen school was indivisibly linked to the development of modern aviation. These and other peaceful developments of aviation were disrupted, distorted and changed forever by the outbreak of war in Europe in September 1939.

It would be neither useful nor interesting to try to analyse the interaction between aviation and the weather throughout the full spectrum of wartime flying that covered unprecedented portions of the globe. Instead we will pick out some subjects that pushed the quest for all-weather flight to its limits and profoundly influenced the development of weather-flying equipment and techniques. They are: the German attack against Great Britain of 1939–41, the British bombing offensive against Germany of 1939–45, and four notable airlifts: the Stalingrad airlift in 1942–3; the North Atlantic ferry service of 1940–5, the 'Hump' route between India and China of 1941–5 and the Berlin airlift of 1948. Much historical material has been published about all of these, but relatively little in the context of the airman's struggle with the weather.

Wir Fahren Gegen England

On the outbreak of war in 1939 the Luftwaffe possessed the most powerful and most technically advanced bomber force in the world, equipped with secret devices to attack through cloud and darkness years before the Royal Air Force even realized that such devices were necessary. Even in 1938 the Luftwaffe had an all-weather capability that would not be matched by the RAF until 1943.

In Britain and Germany secret preparations for war began as early as 1933–4. In Germany fertile minds realized that, with more powerful transmitters and more sensitive receivers, a Lorenz equisignal could be used for navigation over much greater distances than the approach to an airfield. If two transmitters could be set far apart, with the equisignals intersecting at a wide angle, the result could be a device of extraordinary precision to bomb a target without ever seeing it.

As early as 1904 Christian Hülsmeyer proved that a metal object produced a measurable disturbance in an electromagnetic field by using this principle to detect a ship from a bridge over the Rhine. The idea became dormant for lack of either military or commercial interest.[1] In England in 1933 Arnold Wilkins, working at the National Physical Laboratory Radio Research Station, noticed that a passing aircraft interfered with an experimental VHF radio-telephone link.[2] Wilkins calculated that at certain frequencies a metal aircraft would absorb radio energy and re-radiate a signal. A resulting report by Robert Watson Watt, dated 12 February 1935, titled *Detection and Location of Aircraft by Radio Methods,* suggested not only a device that would give the range, bearing and elevation of an aircraft, but also a device in the aircraft to transmit a coded return; the paper also suggested the possibility of automatic tracking.

Almost at once, on 26 February 1935, a demonstration was arranged for the Air Ministry. Flight-Lieutenant Blucke, at the RAE, Farnborough, was briefed to fly a Handley Page Heyford at an altitude of 1,830 metres (6,000 feet) between Daventry and Weedon. Daventry was the site of a powerful British Broadcasting Corporation transmitter. A receiver was set up at Weedon, about 8 km (5 miles) away, with a cathode ray oscilloscope to compare the direct signal from Daventry with any signal that might be re-radiated from the bomber. The bomber was detected with a signal frequency of 6 MHz.

With Air Ministry backing, progress was rapid. In May 1935, a secret experimental station was set up at an isolated site at Orfordness on the east coast of England. By September aircraft were being tracked in range and elevation at 24–32 km (15–20 miles). The station transmitted pulsed signals, using an oscilloscope to compare the outgoing signal with that returned by a target. The problem of finding a target's bearing was solved in January 1936. The new device was given the cover title of 'Radio Direction Finding.' This may, intentionally or otherwise, have been the perfect cover, as radio direction finding, although in a different form, was an integral part of pre-war European air navigation. The Americans later gave it its present title Radar (Radio Detection and Ranging).

A second experimental station was built in 1936 and by the outbreak of war twenty stations guarded the whole southern and eastern coast of England, capable of detecting an aircraft at 1,500 metres (5,000 feet) 64 km (40 miles) away, increasing to 225 km (140 miles) for an aircraft flying at 9,100 metres (30,000 feet), far beyond human sight and regardless of darkness or cloud cover. The radar sets transmitted through stationary antenna towers on 20–30 MHz. This frequency provided wide but imprecise coverage. Interference from the earth's surface prevented it from detecting ships or low-flying aircraft. These deficiencies were remedied by a set transmitting on 200 MHz through a smaller, steerable antenna in the manner of a searchlight, compared to the floodlight effect of the lower-frequency set.

The Germans were not far behind the British. In early 1939 they became aware of the radar sites in the UK but did not know what they were for. In May 1939, one of the last flights by a Zeppelin was one of the first flights ever made for electronic intelligence. LZ130, *Graf Zeppelin*, was returned to service and equipped with radio receivers believed to be suitable. The airship left Frankfurt and cruised along the English coast, out of sight of land. British radar detected the Zeppelin, but the radio operators on the airship did not detect the British radar transmissions. The Germans searched only in the 225–600 MHz band that they themselves were using and not the 20–30 MHz band. Another flight in August 1939 had the same result. The Germans consequently underestimated the British radar system and made few attempts to destroy it. Although the RAF developed procedures for directing fighters from the ground by radar and radio, their fighter capability was reduced by bad weather and was non-existent at night.

Contrary to expectations, the outbreak of war in September 1939 did not lead to an immediate deluge of bombs on the UK. For eight months German flights over Britain were limited to reconnaissance and small bombing attacks.[3] The Blitzkrieg broke out in the spring of 1940. The British Army was evacuated from France at Dunkirk between 26 May and 4 June, leaving the RAF and the Luftwaffe facing each other across the English Channel. The famous Battle of Britain went on from 13 August to 23 September, when the invasion of England was postponed indefinitely. The Luftwaffe night offensive began on 28 August 1940, with four attacks on Liverpool, each by about 160 aircraft.[4] Night attacks on London began on 7 September 1940, and continued for the next fifty-seven nights, leaving 13,000 people dead and 16,000 injured by year-end. At night England was almost defenceless and London was an easy target to find.

The Germans had three equisignal-type blind navigation and bombing aids: *Knickebein*, *X-Gerät*,[5] and *Y-Gerät*. The occupation of France gave them territory surrounding Britain on the east and south and these devices were used to attack Britain as soon as transmitters could be set up. Information from various sources alerted the British to the possibility of such devices, but their intelligence service was confused by the existence of three similar devices and by internal disagreement as to whether they were technically possible.

Developed by Telefunken, *Knickebein*[6] was based on two Lorenz equisignals intersecting over a target. By the end of 1939 three *Knickebein* transmitters were in operation in western Germany, transmitting on the three standard Lorenz frequencies of 30.0, 31.5, and 33.3 MHz. An aircraft flying at 6,400 metres (21,000 feet) could receive *Knickebein* signals at up to 435 km (270 miles). Refinement of the equisignal to a width of 0.30° gave a potential accuracy of 1.6 km (1 mile) at 290 km (180 miles) from the transmitter. No additional equipment was needed in the aircraft, except that the Lorenz receiver had to be more sensitive than necessary for blind approach. Bomber pilots would navigate along one equisignal, re-tuning the Lorenz receiver to the frequency of the intersecting equisignal as they approached the target. Reception of the dots or dashes of the intersecting beam would warn the pilots that they were close to the target. Reception of the equisignal itself was the signal to release the bombs. The accuracy of the intersection depended on the angle at which the beams intersected; the occupation of France thus improved the geometry of *Knickebein* beams intersecting over Britain. Targets in the Midlands were harder to find than London and the Germans depended more on *Knickebein* when attacking them.

The British became aware of *Knickebein* during the summer of 1940. Navigation notes found in a German bomber shot down over England in March 1940 suggested a blind navigation or bombing aid, although no special equipment was found in the aircraft until an astute investigator noticed that the Lorenz receiver was more sensitive than necessary for its normal purpose. Prisoners-of-war were subtly interrogated. A Luftwaffe radio message intercepted and decoded in June 1940 showed that a German aircraft known to have been over England on the night of 5 June 1940 had been on a calibration flight.

---

1 Williams, J. E. D. 1992, 202
2 Johnson, B. 1979, 78
3 Bowyer, C. 1981, 40
4 Hecks, K. 1990, 97
5 To be correct *Gerät* referred to the airborne equipment whereas the whole system was termed '*Verfahren*' (Wakefield 1981). For simplicity and convenience the one term: *Gerät* is used here.
6 Price, A. 1977; Johnson, B. 1979

Heinkel 111.

In June 1940, based on accumulated evidence, an Avro Anson of the Blind Landing Development Flight at Boscombe Down was equipped with a sensitive civilian VHF receiver; the RAF had only the standard Lorenz blind-approach sets of normal sensitivity. On the night of 21 June the crew of this aircraft detected both *Knickebein* equisignals, intersecting over the Rolls-Royce factory at Derby. No raid took place that night, leaving unanswered the question of why the system was switched on at all. Signals were also picked up on the ground along the English coast and VHF receivers were placed in radar stations to give warning when the transmitters were turned on. Specially equipped aircraft would then take off to search for the equisignals. Detection was helped by the fact that the Germans left the transmitters turned on for extended periods even when no raids were in progress.

The first British countermeasure was to transmit noise on the *Knickebein* frequencies to blot out the aural dots, dashes and equisignal. A more subtle countermeasure (Aspirin) simulated the *Knickebein* dashes. Over England the Aspirin transmitters were strong enough to superimpose their dashes on the equisignal, leading the German pilot to believe that he had drifted off track. Whatever course correction he applied, however, he would continue to receive the dashes. Another planned countermeasure was to receive *Knickebein* dots with a ground receiver and send them by telephone line to be re-transmitted beneath the area covered by the dashes, producing a false equisignal with no directional properties. This was not put into service. Not only was *Knickebein* jammed, but the nature of the jamming was distorted by rumour which added to its psychological effect.

The British also jammed the German NDBs and radio DF. The Luftwaffe continued to use the pre-war network of about eighty NDBs all over Europe, transmitting on 200–500 kHz. Their signals could be received on the ground in England. The British picked up the signals and sent them over telephone lines to transmitters which re-radiated them as false beacons. This countermeasure, known as Meaconing, was put into effect in August 1940. Ground stations in England picked up German requests for DF bearings and re-transmitted them from false positions elsewhere. As a result the German DF operators either gave wrong bearings or were so confused that they refused to give any bearings at all. German-speaking radio operators in England contributed false information.[7]

In those days all radio equipment was temperamental and any countermeasure could magnify a natural mistrust. Experienced instrument pilots could discriminate between *Knickebein* and Aspirin signals but inexperienced pilots could be so confused that they became lost or even panicked and parachuted from their aircraft. German bombers carried no specialist navigator and, once deprived of electronic guidance, their navigation was much impaired. In July 1940, a Ju-88 landed in England after its crew had been confused by countermeasures. In October 1940, a Do-217, returning from a patrol over the Atlantic, blown off track by unforecast winds, landed in England after the crew had homed on British meacons simulating beacons in France. A similar fate awaited an He-111 that November.[8]

In September 1940, the British suspected a new blind navigation device. They were at first confused by the existence of two separate, but similar devices. Dr Hans Plendl had started work on another Lorenz derivative as early as 1933. The result was known as *X-Gerät*. The Luftwaffe set up a flight test unit in 1938, but did not use it against England until transmitters could be built in France in the autumn of 1940. Even then it was entrusted to a special bomber unit, KG 100, with the task of finding targets and marking them with incendiary bombs.

X-Gerät was similar in principle to *Knickebein* but, instead of one cross-beam, three were used on frequencies of 66–74 MHz. The navigation beam consisted of a coarse equisignal as a guide to the fine equisignal which was aligned over the target. A cockpit visual indicator replaced the *Knickebein* audio equipment. The cross-beams were received on a separate radio set operated by the navigator. The first of these crossed the navigation beam 30 km (19 miles) from the bomb-release point and warned the crew that they were approaching the target. Twenty kilometres (12 miles) from the bomb-release point the bomber crossed the second cross-beam and the observer started the first of two hands on a stop-clock. Crossing the third cross-beam 5 km (3 miles) from the target, the navigator stopped the first hand of the clock and started a second. When this hand caught up with the first an electric circuit released the bombs. This time ratio compensated automatically for the effect of wind on the aircraft's ground speed or on the flight of the bombs. During a test in Germany in June 1936, bombs were dropped into a 300-metre × 300-metre (1,000-foot × 1,000-foot) area 300 km (187 miles) from the transmitter.[9]

X-Gerät was first used operationally in the first-ever blind bombing attack carried out successfully with electronic guidance, against a munitions plant near Warsaw on 1 September 1939, by KG 100 with He-111s and was used several times during the Polish campaign. Eight transmitters were in service by September 1939; two in southern Germany, three in Austria, two in eastern Germany on the northern frontier of Czechoslovakia, and one in East Prussia.[10] By December 1939, another six transmitters had been built in western Germany. KG 100 flew tests over England in December 1939, but early in 1940 the equipment was removed from the aircraft for security reasons, to be held for a major offensive.[11] The use of *X-Gerät* was resumed on 13 August 1940, by which time there were three transmitters in France. Each one radiated a fan of seven equisignals with a total spread of about 100°. Rotating the antenna rotated the whole array. Any pair of transmitters therefore radiated a grid-like pattern of intersecting equisignals, available for *en route* navigation.[12]

This advanced equipment was by no means trouble-free. On the evening of 13 August 1940, the crews of KG 100 were briefed to attack Birmingham. From their base at Vannes in Brittany they were to fly to an NDB at St Malo and intercept the *X-Gerät* signals over the English Channel. Otherwise they were to use dead reckoning, NDBs and DF. *Feldwebel* H. Schmidt's crew could not receive the first *X-Gerät* signal over the Channel but identified the English coast visually. They used *X-Gerät* to bomb but saw no effects. On the return flight the autopilot and gyro-compass system failed. 'We could have been anywhere in the darkness of that night, wandering around and looking at the direct-reading compass now and then.' Over Brittany the approach of dawn affected the NDB signals and 'QDMs were most inaccurate, too, and we missed the airfield several times, but at last we got down, dog-tired, apathetic, dead-beat.'[13] The same night other KG 100 aircraft bombed an aircraft factory at Castle Bromwich, causing some damage. But time was to reveal that only rarely did KG 100 repeat even this mediocre success.[14]

7 Wakefield, K. 1992 ed., 169
8 Price, A. 1977, 41, 50
9 Wakefield, K. 1992 ed., 26
10 Wakefield, K. 1992 ed., 30, 34
11 Hecks, K. 1990, p.67
12 Wakefield, K. 1992 ed., 81
13 H. Schmidt quoted in Wakefield, K. 1992 ed., 80
14 Wakefield, K. 1992 ed., 86

Between August 1940 and June 1941, KG 100 made 144 attacks on Great Britain. *X-Gerät* was an aid for both navigation and bombing; bombs were aimed visually when visibility permitted. If the equipment failed or if, as became increasingly frequent, the British jammed the signals, they had to use *Knickebein* or dead reckoning.[15] For both devices, the beams were weaker and less precise on northerly targets, such as Liverpool and Manchester, than on targets closer to the transmitters.

The British discovered *X-Gerät* similarly to their discovery of *Knickebein*, but it was harder to jam. The first attempt (Bromide) failed because the modulation frequency of the false dashes was wrong by 500 Hz; the receivers carried in the bombers had bandpass filters with a bandwidth of only 100 Hz. *X-Gerät* was never as effectively jammed as *Knickebein*.

In spite of these sophisticated devices, of the 54,000 tons of bombs dropped on Britain in 1940–1 40,000 tons fell on open country.[16] The memories of one KG 100 crewman show how confusing a night raid could be:

> I began to take radio bearings and finally told Gebauer to transmit the position report we were supposed to make just short of the French coast. Dawn was close as I obtained a 330° relative bearing to Brest. We turned 30° left and obtained another bearing. The same, and then – ah, the bearings are changing! We were flying only a few hundred metres above the ground when the searchlights came on. I immediately answered by firing the recognition signal, and the lights went out. We continued and started to turn when again the searchlights came on. I fired the recognition signals once more but this time the searchlights did not go out. I was getting angry and fired another signal. This time they went out so I set about getting some bearings – 060°, 040°, 025°, 000°! Christ! We're not flying backwards are we? Filled with doubts I said, 'I think we're over England!'

Another KG 100 crew, trying to attack Birmingham in November 1940, were so baffled by bad weather and equipment failure that, after wandering about until they ran out of fuel, they landed on what they thought was the north coast of Spain, only to find that they had landed on the south coast of England.

By the end of 1940 a third device was ready for use, also invented by Dr Plendl, known as *Y-Gerät*

or *Wotan*. *Y-Gerät* used only a single transmitter and frequencies of 42–48 MHz. It transmitted a complex equisignal which was displayed on a cockpit instrument and to which an autopilot could be coupled. Whereas *Knickebein* and *X-Gerät* used intersecting beams to provide a position fix, *Y-Gerät* transmitted a ranging signal to a transponder in the aircraft which replied on a slightly different frequency. The ground station calculated the distance to the aircraft from the phase difference between the outgoing and returning signals. *Y-Gerät* gave an accuracy of 90 metres (300 feet) at 400 km (250 miles), but only one aircraft could use it at a time. *Y-Gerät* transmitters in northern France were operational by October 1940.[17]

Y-Gerät was surprisingly easily jammed using a disused television station, transmitting on 45 MHz. The ranging signal sent by the aircraft was picked up by a receiver in London, sent by telephone line to the TV transmitter and re-radiated. A special bomber unit, KG 26 with He-111s, was the first to use *Y-Gerät*. The first use of the countermeasure coincided with their first operation and the crews distrusted the device immediately without realizing that it had been jammed. In any event, as soon as an aircraft carrying the device was shot down, a specimen of the new equipment was examined and other, simpler jamming methods were devised.

The pre-war *Lufthansa* pilots had acquired the skills needed to fly a bomber at night over blacked-out territory in bad weather from thousands of hours of airline flying. Such skills were not instantly transferrable to the new pilots of an expanding Luftwaffe and, once lost to the frontline squadrons through combat losses, accidents and the demands of the training system, were irreplaceable. Weather and accidents caused more casualties than the British defences. Countermeasures might combine with cloud and darkness to foil or disperse German raids, but initially the British defences were ineffective and forces of up to 500 bombers caused terrible damage and loss of life. From November 1940 to February 1941, the Luftwaffe flew about 12,000 night sorties over England for the loss of seventy-five aircraft – 0.6%. From August 1940 to May 1941 German air raids killed 44,000 British civilians and injured another 103,000.[18]

Like the RFC and RNAS twenty-five years before, the RAF was at first unprepared to meet bombing attacks at night. Although instrument-equipped, Hurricanes and Spitfires were too unsta-

Bristol Beaufighter.

ble to make good aircraft for the instrument flying that was an inescapable part of night fighting. Their endurance was limited; they had no blind navigation equipment; their pilots had little night- or instrument-flying experience. The use of day interceptors at night was a costly failure, especially as the pilots could not see the enemy bombers. Bristol Blenheim light bombers were pressed into service as night fighters, but they were no better able to make contact with their intended prey.

For the night fighter crews the winter of 1939–40 was a struggle to survive and: 'Our pilots fought a war that was far from phoney against an enemy that was much deadlier than the Luftwaffe.'[19] The same air gunner commented: 'Up to this time only a few of the pilots had done any appreciable amount of night flying and even that had been in slow and stable aircraft in clear weather, flying from one brightly lighted town to another. Now that we were at war it was all very different. All the familiar landmarks were swallowed up in the blackout, and winter had come to cast its shroud over the comforting horizon, bringing with it an increasing blindness.'[20]

Returning to their bases, night fighter crews had other problems to contend with:

We had no homing beacons and there was no system of blind approach, no way in which we could be talked down to a safe landing. Our radio was feeble and short-range, and the blind-flying instruments were astonishingly temperamental. Night after night our crews launched

15 Wakefield, K. 1992 ed., Appendix 2
16 Hecks, K. 1990, 124
17 Hecks, K. 1990, 69
18 Johnson, B., Cozens, H. I. 1984, 162
19 Rawnsley, C. F., Wright, R. 1957, 25
20 Rawnsley, C. F., Wright, R. 1957, 24

themselves hopefully into the unfriendly darkness. Night after night we chased around after rumours and found nothing, and then had to grope our way back through the weather, which, that winter, was horrible. It was with sighs of relief that we bumped down on those small grass airfields dimly lit with paraffin flares and primitive floodlights.[21]

Most of the numerous RAF night fighter casualties that winter were caused by weather-related accidents.

One pilot reminisced:[22]

It really is very hard to realize just how difficult it was to try to operate aircraft at night during that period. At that stage of the war the chief task confronting anybody who took off at night was to try and get himself and his aircraft back safely on the ground. The accident rate was extremely high. Many people got lost and had to spend most of their time in the air trying to find out where they were. [Of his first night patrol in southern England, in a single-engined Boulton Paul Defiant, in October 1940, he remembered:] I took off with the aid of the six glim-lamps, which were immediately extinguished as I went into the air. The airfield was being bombed at the time. I was shot at by the airfield defences as I took off, coned by searchlights soon after and then got lost in cloud, only to find that my radio had packed up!

Radar development quickly progressed from large ground-based transmitters to smaller sets with higher frequencies and greater directional accuracy. The first airborne sets were installed in Blenheims in November 1939. So temperamental were the sets and so great were the difficulties of developing procedures for night interception that another eight months passed before the first successful night interception took place. On 22 July 1940 a Blenheim from an experimental unit shot down a Do-17.[23] Successes were few, however, during the slow and difficult introduction of radar

into squadron service during the remainder of 1940. The early airborne radar sets were unreliable and difficult to adjust. Training, practice and natural aptitude were needed on the part of the specialist aircrew operator to interpret the signals on the oscilloscope screens and give directions to the pilot.

The early ground radar could not position a fighter closer than 8–9.5 km (5–6 miles) to a bomber; the Mark 4 Airborne Interception radar had a range of only 5–6.5 km (3–4 miles). This problem was solved only when Ground Controlled Interception radar stations were built in the winter of 1940–1, enabling a controller to vector a fighter to within 1.5–3 km (1–2 miles) of a bomber.[24] This was complemented in the air by the Bristol Beaufighter, the first purpose-built night fighter with radar, a radar operator and a heavy armament, which entered service in the autumn of 1940. The first successful night interception by a Beaufighter followed on 20 November 1940.[25]

Improving weather in the spring of 1941 brought increased Luftwaffe activity,[26] but by April 1941, the British had seventeen Bromide transmitters in service and the interrogation of captured German airmen showed that this countermeasure was beginning to take effect. The Luftwaffe failed to maintain their initial technical ascendancy and the British defences became more and more successful. Accidents and increasing combat losses took their toll of the bombers flying against England, imparting a growing sense of doom to their crews. The German offensive against Great Britain was much reduced from May 1941 onwards, as most Luftwaffe units were moved east for the attack on Russia which began on 27 June 1941.

21 Rawnsley, C. F., Wright, R., 1957, 25
22 J. G. Benson quoted in Brandon, L. 1992 ed., 45
23 Hecks, K. 1990, 98
24 Rawnsley, C. F., Wright, R. 1957, 82; Brandon, L. 1992 ed., 40
25 Rawnsley, C. F., Wright, R. 1957, 66
26 Wakefield, K. 1992 ed., 141–142

CHAPTER 13

To Pulverize the Entire Industry and Economic Life of the Enemy

Within an hour of the declaration of war on 3 September 1939, a Royal Air Force Blenheim took off to reconnoitre the German naval base at Wilhelmshaven. The crew completed their mission unopposed at an altitude of 7,300 metres (24,000 feet); they could not report back to base while in flight because the radio was frozen. An attacking force of Blenheims that took off that day met severe thunderstorms over the North Sea and turned back. That night ten Whitleys took off to drop propaganda leaflets on Hamburg, Bremen and the Ruhr industrial area. Leaflets landing in Holland, Belgium and Denmark indicated the difficulties of navigation at night in wartime conditions. Within twenty-four hours of the outbreak of war the difficulties that would face Bomber Command for the next five years from natural phenomena alone were revealed.

RAF bombers attacking German warships along the North Sea coast of Germany in late 1939 suffered such disastrous losses to fighters that daylight bombing without fighter escort was realized to be impossible. No RAF fighter had the range to accompany the bombers and these raids barely penetrated enemy airspace. By contrast, bombers flying at night ranged all over Germany with impunity. The stage was thus set for the long, tragic and appallingly destructive night bombing campaign waged by RAF Bomber Command with increasing ferocity for the next five years.

The first British night bombing raid on German soil took place on 19 March 1940, when fifty bombers attacked an air base on the island of Sylt.[1] Photo-reconnaissance the next day revealed an embarrassing and complete absence of damage to the target.[2] Bombing by both sides escalated during the summer and autumn of 1940. Night raids ranging deep into Germany made a mockery of

Goering's boast that no RAF aircraft would ever enter German airspace but achieved little else. Bomber Command was unprepared for this type of operation; at first the problems were immense and the results insignificant. The biggest problem was navigation. The Ruhr was 480–640 km (300–400 miles) from RAF bases; Berlin and Munich were twice as far. All except the first 320 km (200 miles) had to be flown over hostile territory. Although an RAF bomber crew included a navigator, the methods available in 1939 were pilotage, dead reckoning and celestial navigation. Over the distances involved, and especially over the Ruhr, continuous good visibility was rare. From the mainland coast onwards good navigation fixes plainly visible at night were few, as Germany consists of large expanses of uniform terrain. Winds aloft over the European mainland could not be predicted reliably. Star shots depended on clear skies and their accuracy depended on straight and level flight in smooth air.

RAF aircrew of 1939 had little night-flying experience. One pilot, after two years as a cadet and six as a pilot, had 1,000 hours of flying time.[3] Of that only 21 hours had been as pilot-in-command at night. Current attitudes in the squadrons were summed up as: 'Only owls and bloody fools fly at night.' This was not a promising basis for a night offensive against Germany.

In the winter of 1940–1 aircrew reports were vague, yet tersely descriptive of confusion, deadly hazard and minimal results. 'Wenzendorf aircraft works, target not located. Intense AA fire over

1 Hecks, K. 1990
2 Babington-Smith, C., 1958, 88–93
3 Sawyer, T. 1982, 15

Handley Page Hampdens.

Armstrong-Whitworth Whitley.

Bremen, both engines holed.' 'Jettisoned bombs over Emmerich owing to ice accretion. Intense electrical storm.' 'Düsseldorf. 10/10ths cloud all the way. Saw nothing. Brought bombs back.' 'Kiel. 70 miles off course because of deficient gyro. Saw bombs fall between warehouses at Bremerhaven and near aerodrome.' 'Emden. Target located and attacked through gap in clouds. Bursts not observed, but believed near oil plant.'[4]

An air gunner wrote in a letter in 1941: 'Yes, I like flying. Aeroplanes have a fascination that is quite astonishing. Of course they are quite impractical. They are good for nothing except war and their utility in that can well be exaggerated.'[5] Fifty years later, he wrote: 'We were always more or less lost when grinding about in the darkness for about the first half of the war before sophisticated navigational devices were introduced.'[6] That was the problem. How could a bomber hit its target if the crew could not find it? After one attack in early 1941, aimed at the Skoda works at Pilsen in Czechoslovakia, local intelligence revealed that the nearest bomb had fallen 80 km (50 miles) away.[7]

Once airborne, each crew was on its own.[8] Flame floats dropped over the North Sea could provide drift readings to correct for wind. The crew hoped to see landmarks for the navigator to update his dead-reckoning plot, but this was possible only if the air below was clear. If the aircraft was in cloud at its cruising altitude of 1,500–3,000 metres (5,000–10,000 feet), all such navigation aids were cut off. The crew could only continue on their way, flying as constant a heading and airspeed as possible. If the winds aloft were not as forecast, the errors after several hours – and some operations lasted as long as 8–10 hours, could be enormous. In cloudy conditions crews dropped their bombs at an estimated time of arrival or aimed them at lights, fires, ground features, anti-aircraft fire, or searchlights, thinking that it was their target, or any target. Subsequent research found that at that time only 5% of bombers bombed within 8 km (5 miles) of their targets.[9] One crew bombed an airfield in East Anglia, thinking that it was their target in Holland. This was the means available to carry out Winston Churchill's intention 'to pulverize the entire industry and scientific effort on which the war effort and economic life of the enemy depend'.[10]

En route the pilots had to face prolonged instrument flying, sometimes in turbulence, thunderstorms or icing. Many aircraft disappeared without trace.[11] One night, in December, 1940:

On leaving the Suffolk coast at about 3,000 feet and starting a climb for the Dutch coast, we ran into a gentle misty drizzle – which had not been forecast, needless to say – and were soon engulfed in thin wet cloud. It was very cold, and the drizzle froze into ice the moment it touched the aeroplane,[12] giving a coating of crystal-clear glazing on the front of the wings and cockpit. We had switched on the pulsators from the first, but as we climbed higher pure ice was piling up on the leading edges and spreading slowly backwards down the wings, the de-icers becoming completely overloaded and useless. Forcing a side window open, we could see it all from the glare of the exhausts of our Merlin engines. We struggled to 8,000 feet hoping to clear the cloud and wet, but could get no higher ... because the deposit had altered the shape of the wing ... and therefore the flying characteristics.

The aircraft was as soggy as a wet brick and becoming difficult to handle, and great chunks of ice were being thrown off the airscrews and thumping ominously against the sides. It was time I tried to get down to warmer air, so I put the nose down and dived gently to escape, noticing immediately that there was no increase in the airspeed. This could mean only one thing, which was that the 'pitot' head itself had been gummed up with ice ...

So now I could only guess at our airspeed by keeping the rev counters and boost gauges at normal, and by the feel of the aeroplane, all of which was somewhat difficult with the heavy coating of ice gumming everything up. We got down to 1,000 feet – still on course and probably over Holland by then – and with the amount of ice we were carrying slowly increasing and creating great difficulty in the handling of the controls, I regretfully decided that we must turn for home, making a wide careful turn on to the necessary course. The ice started to come off at five hundred feet, with much banging and cracking. The navigator had coded up a signal to Group

---

4 Logbook of Wing Commander E. A. Morrison, the author's father.
5 Letter E. A. Morrison to I. J. Morrison, 29 March 1941
6 Letter E. A. Morrison to T. A. Morrison, 25 June 1992
7 Johnson, B. Cozens, H. I. 1984, 173
8 Sawyer, T. 1982
9 Richardson, F. C., quoted in Williams, J. E. D. 1992, 241
10 Johnson, B., Cozens, H. I. 1984, 167
11 Sawyer, T. 1982, 43
12 An Armstrong-Whitworth Whitley twin-engined bomber.

Vickers Wellington.

and we got back home after more than five hours of instrument flying under tiring and somewhat nerve-racking circumstances.[13]

Even having braved everything that the weather and the enemy could throw at them, the returning crews, short of fuel and sometimes with battle damage and wounded crewmen, had to navigate back to their bases. In bad weather they had to make a blind descent, perhaps with DF bearings, perhaps not, followed by a night approach and landing at a dimly lit airfield. At the worst a crew might have flown for five hours or more by dead reckoning without a visual, celestial or radio fix at any time. Some returning crews overflew the whole width of England without knowing it and ran out of fuel over the Irish Sea.[14]

During the first two winters of the war the only electronic guidance was radio DF, and that was not always reliable. In these days of continuous, reliable air-to-ground contact it is difficult to understand just how weak, intermittent, unreliable and temperamental communications with valved, HF radios were. Crews had no option but to make a descent on estimated time of arrival at their base and hope that they broke out of cloud at a safe height above the ground. Over the flat country of

East Anglia and Lincolnshire this was less of a problem than over the more northerly bomber bases in Yorkshire with hills rising to between 450 and 600 metres (1,500 and 2,000 feet) not far distant.

Bases were marked by light beacons flashing a Morse-code identifier and these helped navigation once the aircraft was clear of cloud. Beacon lights, however, could also be used by the Luftwaffe, so the codes were changed frequently and in East Anglia the lights were hooded so that they were visible from one direction only. Runways were marked with paraffin flares or dim electric lights.

The worst hazard of all was fog, which could form quickly over wide areas in the small hours of the morning. If an aircraft did not have enough fuel to divert to a fog-free airfield, the crew could either try to land through the fog or bail out, leaving the aircraft to crash. Crashes were common throughout the war as bombers tried to return to their bases at night and in bad weather.

Although the British had the elements of a system for air traffic control and blind approach in the form of radar, transponders (known then as Identification Friend or Foe (IFF)), NDBs and Lorenz (known as Standard Beam Approach (SBA)) these were too immature to be integrated

Instrument panel of the Short Stirling. Note Sperry-type turn and bank indicator rather than Reid-Sigrist, Lorenz glideslope indicator and blind-flying instruments in vibration-damped panel.

into a unified system to benefit Bomber Command. In the early years of the war the equipment and trained users were too few. Later, when as many as a thousand aircraft might arrive in an area a hundred miles long and fifty miles wide in 1–2 hours, no air traffic control system, even with today's technology, could handle that volume of traffic. An instrument approach using Lorenz entailed 10–15 minutes of manoeuvring by the inbound aircraft, four to five aircraft per hour, whereas up to thirty-five bombers could arrive over a base within a short space of time, all short of fuel. Many pilots' post-war memoirs refer to training in the use of SBA, few to using it in operational flying. An interesting comment was made in 1947:[15] 'SBA during the war ... failed just as much because the psychology of the business was overlooked as for any other reason.'

By early 1941, the accumulated evidence of bomb-release photographs, photo-reconaissance and intelligence proved that the RAF offensive was having no worthwhile effect. All the work put into bigger bombers, and the training of their bigger crews, was wasted if the crews could not find their targets. The Butt Report, issued on 18 August 1941,[16] stated that, although 67% of crews

dispatched believed they had attacked their targets, only 20% bombed within 8 km (5 miles) of the target, only 7% on Ruhr targets because of strong defences and haze. Post-war research showed that even these figures were optimistic. Recognition of this state of affairs at the highest levels of the RAF and the British government had two main results: the accelerated development of electronic navigation aids and the formation of an elite Pathfinder Force to mark targets with pyrotechnics, so providing an aiming point for the main bomber force. The British spent the winter of 1941–2 building up their bomber force with new aircraft, crews and electronic aids.

The official history of the Bomber Command offensive[17] states plainly that 'During the Second World War no radar device was evolved which, for long-range flights, formed a complete substitute for dead-reckoning navigation. Nor was any radar method of blind bombing as accurate as visual

13 Sawyer, T. 1982, 56
14 Sawyer, T. 1982, 47
15 *Flight*, 1 May 1947, 393
16 Hecks, K. 1990, 125
17 Webster, C., Frankland, N. 1961, Annex I

Short Stirling.

aiming when the target could clearly be seen. But as an aid to dead-reckoning navigation and as a means of bomb aiming when the target was obscured, radar was fundamental to the success of Bomber Command.' 'Radar' here encompasses all forms of electronic guidance.

The first of the new devices was codenamed Gee. The concept originated with R. J. Dippy of the British Telecommunications Research Establishment in 1937–8 as a civil aviation blind approach aid, but without immediate results. A prototype was demonstrated to Bomber Command officers in October 1940, but it was a long road from a prototype to an equipped and trained bomber force. The first trial over Germany, and that by only two aircraft, followed ten months later on 11 August 1941; the first use in a major raid (on Essen) followed on 8 March 1942, nearly eighteen months after the prototype demonstration.[18]

Gee used three transmitters in England on a line 200 miles long: the A, or Master, station and the B and C, or Slave, stations, transmitting on 20–80 MHz. Each signal from B and C was sequenced to a signal from A, producing a signal pattern which can be imagined as the expanding and overlapping rings of ripples formed by three pebbles thrown into a pond. The aircraft's receiver compared the time differences between the A signals and the B and C signals and displayed them on a cathode-ray tube. The navigator used a chart overprinted with

the signal lattice to obtain two position lines and, hence, a fix. A good navigator could get a Gee fix in less than a minute, accurate to 1–8 km (0.5–5 miles), depending on signal geometry. Accuracy depended on the angles of intersection of the signals. The farther the aircraft was from the transmitters, the more oblique the angle and the lower the accuracy. The maximum range was 650 km (400 miles), covering Germany as far east as the Ruhr; at that distance the accuracy was about 8 km (5 miles). The Germans discovered Gee almost at once and began to jam it in August 1942, rendering it unusable beyond the mainland coast. Even so, it was a great step forward, as dead reckoning could be started from a fix on the eastern side of the North Sea. The navigation of returning aircraft became easier and the dangers of an instrument let-down over England were reduced. This alone was ample justification.

It was hoped that Gee would permit accurate blind bombing but, like blind landing, this remained elusive. At the same time the British developed an imitation of *Knickebein*, which they codenamed J, the two words Gee and Jay sounding similar. J was leaked to German intelligence to induce them to jam it rather than Gee. Not only did this ploy delay the jamming of Gee, but when the Germans discovered that J was a hoax, they stopped jamming it and J continued in use as a navigation aid for the rest of the war.[19]

Handley Page Halifax.

The second device was codenamed Oboe, inspired by the German *X-Gerät*. Prototype trials began in December 1941; Oboe Mark I began operational service in December 1942. Oboe used two transmitters 160 km (100 miles) apart, transmitting on 200 MHz; a transponder in the aircraft returned their signals. The station known as Cat measured the distance to the aircraft and transmitted dots or dashes to indicate deviation from a preset range. The equisignal was only 15.5 metres (51 feet) wide,[20] forming an arc passing over the target, although at normal ranges this arc was nearly a straight line. Secondary, concentric equisignals, identified aurally by X, Y and Z in Morse, were spaced 8, 16 and 24 km (5, 10 and 15 miles) on either side of the main equisignal. The station known as Mouse used a similar ranging process to measure the aircraft's progress along the arc. By this means, and taking into account the ballistics of the bomb to be dropped, a time of release was calculated and signalled to the aircraft.

The pilot concentrated on following the Cat arc while the navigator received the bomb release signals through his headphones. Ten minutes from the target he heard four Morse As, followed by a low note for two minutes. Eight minutes from the target he heard four Bs, at 5 minutes four Cs, at 3 minutes four Ds. After this he heard a continuous note until five seconds from bomb release, when five dots were heard over a 2.5-second period, followed by a 2.5-second dash at the end of which the navigator pressed the bomb release button.[21]

Oboe demanded extremely precise flying. One pilot recalled: 'One had to navigate to an exact point in space and be there within about 30 seconds of a stated time ... The bombs were dropped on receipt of a signal and when one returned home one was told how much off the target the bomb had been. We averaged about 100 yards error on Ruhr targets.'[22] The reception distance increased with increasing altitude to a maximum of 435 km (270 miles) for an aircraft at 8,530 metres (28,000 feet), covering the Ruhr from the English coast. Although Oboe was a blind-bombing aid of extraordinary precision, it had no other function; other means were needed to navigate to the Cat arc. Each pair of Oboe stations could serve only one aircraft at a time. Its best application was therefore to high-flying de Havilland Mosquitos, which dropped marker bombs. The Germans tried to jam Oboe, but never completely succeeded. Improved versions followed the Mark I, using different frequencies.

18 Hecks, K. 1990, 137
19 Hecks, K. 1990, 108, although rarely mentioned elsewhere.
20 *Flight*, 6 September 1945, 253
21 Ibid.
22 Boyd, H. C., quoted in Middlebrook, M. 1973, 2nd ed. 1980, 18

Avro Lancaster.

The third of the new devices was ground-mapping radar. As early as 1936–7 the British had discovered that a downward-looking airborne radar set could distinguish between land and water, built-up areas and open country.[23] The RAF saw its potential for blind navigation as early as 1938, but little more was achieved until the Butt Report gave it a new priority and smaller, higher-frequency radar sets became available. As with other such devices, years elapsed before H2S, as it was known, entered service. In particular, satisfactory definition depended on high power generation at extremely high frequencies. This was first achieved by the secret magnetron oscillator valve, invented by J. R. Randall and H. R. H. Boot at Birmingham University, UK, while working on microwave transmission for the Admiralty in early 1940. Magnetron-valve radar was first used in maritime reconnaissance aircraft and night fighters which did not fly over Germany and so did not expose the magnetron valve to the risk of discovery. The use of H2S, which incorporated the magnetron, over the European mainland was delayed until the benefits outweighed the certainty of discovery.

H2S was first used operationally on the night of 30–31 January 1943, in a raid on Hamburg. Even at the end of May 1943, maximum availability was still only eighteen aircraft, but this soon increased.

H2S Mark I transmitted at 3,000 MHz; H2S Mark III, with better definition because of its 10,000 MHz radiation frequency, entered service in November 1943.

Because H2S was self-contained, it was usable wherever the aircraft flew. The navigator still had to know his approximate position, as H2S was by no means a moving map. Interpretation took skill and experience; features that were plain on a chart did not necessarily show up clearly on H2S and vice versa. Some targets had a clear H2S image; others did not. If a target was recognizable on H2S, or if a timed run could be made from a clear fix, the device could be used for blind bombing. The method was not proof against ambiguities. On the night of 2–3 December 1943,[24] the H2S-equipped Pathfinders were supposed to approach Berlin by following the images of three towns in a line; Stendal, Rathenow and Nauen. Mistaken wind forecasts drifted some aircraft south, where they found similar images of the three towns of Genthin, Brandenburg and Potsdam. Those aircraft dropped their markers 24 km (15 miles) south of the aiming point, causing scattered bombing. On the other hand, on two consecutive nights in November 1943, RAF crews dropped 3,900 tons of bombs on Berlin without ever seeing their target.[25] H2S became dangerous to its users, however, when

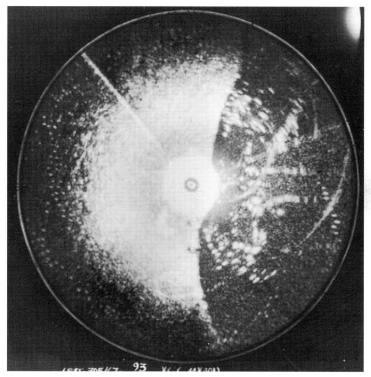

H2S image. Note difficulty of interpretation.

the Germans developed a device that enabled night fighters to home onto its transmissions.

The most accurate of all the British Second World War blind navigation aids was Gee-H; Gee and an aid called H could be used separately or in combination. Little has been published about Gee-H and it remained secret for many years after the war. Described as Oboe in reverse, it could be used by a hundred aircraft at one time. A radio transceiver in the aircraft interrogated two ground stations. Their bearings and distances, measured by the return pulse on the aircraft's Gee set,[26] provided an extremely accurate position fix. H was as accurate as Oboe, but the procedure to obtain a fix was complicated. The Air Ministry Research Establishment advocated H as early as June 1940, but Gee was given priority because unlimited numbers of aircraft could use it at the same time. Interest in H grew as the limitations of Gee, Oboe and H2S became apparent; development was resumed in July 1942. The first blind Gee-H attack was made on 7 October 1943, on Aachen, but another year passed before the device could enter widespread service in Bomber Command. Considering how long these sophisticated devices took to develop, it

speaks volumes for the German rearmament of the 1930s that the Luftwaffe had equivalents ready for use in 1938.

The first Pathfinder attack was against Flensburg on 18 August 1942. Gee-equipped aircraft marked the target with flares and incendiaries as an aiming point for the main force. Pyrotechnic target indicator bombs were introduced in January 1943. Target indicator bombs, aimed visually or by H2S, could be seen at night through haze and thin or scattered cloud; if the target was completely cloud-covered, parachute flares were dropped as 'sky markers' at which the main force aimed their bombs. In strong winds, however, the parachutes drifted, reducing the accuracy of the bombing. If cloud cover was deep and continuous, the sky markers disappeared into it and were useless. The crew briefing included the marking techniques to be used, based on forecast weather over the target at the estimated time of arrival.

23 Webster, C., Frankland, N. 1961, Annex I
24 Middlebrook, M. 1988, 134
25 Middlebrook, M. 1988, 112–122
26 Hecks, K. 1990, 174

The new Bomber Command tactics from 1942 onwards demanded precise navigation and timing, both to penetrate darkness and bad weather and to saturate the defences with dense swarms of aircraft. In spite of these advances, bombs were still being dropped as far as 50 km (30 miles) from their targets.[27] The weather remained a potent factor in the success or failure of an attack.

On the night of 2 August 1943, Bomber Command, albeit unintentionally, made the biggest mass penetration of an area of thunderstorms in the history of aviation.[28] An attack on Hamburg, planned for the night of 31 July–1 August, was cancelled as thunderstorms and heavy rain moved eastward across England. This same persistent weather system dissuaded Bomber Command once more on the following night. On 2 August the thundery conditions were thought to have abated enough for an attack to be launched. A weather reconnaissance Mosquito, flying over north-western Germany in the early evening, reported cumulonimbus development south-west of Oldenburg with tops to 9,100 metres (30,000 feet). The last Meteorological Office forecast for Hamburg sent to Bomber Command before take-off read: 'Patches of medium cloud between 10,000 and 20,000 feet. Total amounts of cloud below 18,000 feet probably less than 5/10ths but slight risk of 10/10ths cumulonimbus, tops 30,000 feet.'[29] In England it was an evening of gusty winds, low clouds and rain showers. More than 700 aircraft took off for Hamburg at about 11 p.m.

The bombers climbed over the North Sea through cloud which topped at 2,400 metres (8,000 feet), so that at cruising altitude they were above it. Directly ahead of them, however, was a sight to terrify any pilot, an area of intense thunderstorms 130 km (80 miles) across with so much lightning that at first many pilots did not know what it was. The whole bomber force plunged into this witch's cauldron of violent vertical currents, extreme turbulence, lightning, St Elmo's Fire and severe icing.

> The ends of my guns had blue streaks flashing off them like a 'witch's broom' about fifty feet long.[30]

> It was my first raid and I couldn't be sure what was Flak and what was lightning. The cu-nimbus cloud seemed to be exploding. It was only on my second raid that I realized what real Flak was.[31]

> We were tossed about almost out of control.[32]

> I have never been as scared in my life and never will be again… Suddenly we started icing up. The wings of the kite were a white sheet. Great chunks of ice were flying from the propellers and hitting the fuselage like machine-gun fire. Then the port wing went down and we started dropping like a stone.[33]

> A 115 Squadron Lancaster blew up, probably when struck by lightning, and scattered its wreckage and dead crew members over three German parishes.[34]

One crew member remarked: 'Thunderstorms and aircraft don't mix well at the best of times but fill the storm with flak, tracer, and searchlights – everything but the kitchen sink – and it sure was one hell of an experience.' But another recalled it as 'an exhilarating experience … like an inferno in the clouds.' Of the 727 aircraft that took off to attack Hamburg, 102 jettisoned their bombs in the sea, 107 jettisoned their bombs over Germany, 80 bombed alternative targets, four or five were known to have been destroyed in the storms. Four hundred got through, but their attack was scattered. The survivors all remembered the Night of the Storm.

The Americans based in England had their own problems with their daylight operations.[35]

> Bombers did not just fly over from America and go into action. The crews had first to be trained in the special problems of formation flying in appalling weather and against opposition not found in any other war theater. And they had to be educated in the new techniques and technology, mostly British, of long-distance navigation and, quite often, bombing through overcast at targets discernible only through such devices as H2X[36] and Oboe.

Through the autumn and winter of 1943–4 the Americans attacked targets through cloud, sometimes flying as high as 9,100 metres (30,000 feet) to get above it, but the results were inconclusive and 'Control of the air … belonged to the clouds.'

RAF Bomber Command's struggle with darkness and the weather culminated in the Battle of Berlin in the winter of 1943–4. An attack on Berlin on the night of 18–19 November 1943 was a foretaste of things to come. Cloud cover over Germany was thicker than forecast and the wind forecast was wrong, which changed the time of arrival over the target. Most of the aircraft that were supposed to mark the target using H2S could not do so, either because their sets failed or because their crews could not identify Brandenburg which was their H2S fix for a timed run. Marker bombs disappeared into the clouds which reached 3,000–3,700 metres (10,000–12,000 feet) and bombs were scattered all over Berlin.[37]

Fog forming over the bomber bases at night was a deadly hazard of winter. A forecast serious risk of fog could cancel an attack but, if raids had been cancelled on every forecast of bad weather, Bomber Command would never have left the ground. Each night's operations were a vast, shrewdly calculated gamble.

On the evening of 26 November 1943, 443 Lancasters took off for Berlin.[38] Fog formed over East Anglia in their absence so that only the aircraft of 6 Group, based in Yorkshire, were able to land at their own bases. Three hundred and fifty aircraft, low on fuel, were left trying to land in other parts of England. Those without enough fuel to divert had to try to land in the fog and darkness. Twenty to thirty Lancasters crash-landed in England; fifteen were wrecked, killing thirty-nine aircrew and two civilians. By 1943, two landing aids were available: SBA (mentioned earlier) and FIDO (Fog Investigation and Dispersal Operation), an array of petrol burners paralleling the runway. The heat evaporated the fog, leaving clear air over the runway. FIDO saved many lives during the war.[39]

The worst disaster caused by fog that winter was on the night of 16–17 December 1943, when the survivors of an attack on Berlin by 483 Lancasters were returning to England. The bombers had taken off at 4 p.m. and were returning at midnight. A layer of very low cloud formed all over southern and eastern England; the only clear airfields in the country were out of range of the returning bombers.

One crew flew to a FIDO-equipped airfield but, on contacting the control tower by radio, they were told that they were number thirty-six to land and were instructed to hold at the radio beacon at 18,000 feet; thirty-five other aircraft were holding at the same beacon at 500-foot vertical intervals, with the bottom aircraft of the stack making an approach. This crew had enough fuel to hold until their turn came to land. Another crew reported:

The FIDO at Ludford was operational, I think, but flying control could handle only a limited number of kites coming in on SBA and, being well down the field on return, I was diverted to Leconfield. *En route* thither, with barely enough juice left to fill a lighter, my bomb-aimer spotted circuit lights through a hole in the murk and, on the 'bird-in-the-hand' principle, I let down over the glow of the lights, broke cloud at something like 250 feet, saw the circuit clear and lobbed down. It turned out to be Grimsby. The final approach was well lit by the burning remains of a Lanc that didn't quite make it.

One pilot's diary entry on this same raid gives a terse summary of how things often worked in practice.[40]

Ten tenths cloud over target. W/T and Gee packed up on way home, so homed across North Sea on D/F loop, which luckily was not jammed. Homed onto base on SBA beam, breaking cloud at 250 feet to find fog, rain and visibility about 300 yards and deteriorating. R/T then packed up, so after circling for ten minutes at 200 feet, landed without permission in appalling conditions. Six other aircraft landed at base, three landed away, three crews baled out when they ran out of fuel, four crashed when trying to land, and one was missing.

Mistaken altimeter settings had fatal consequences in such conditions. The rear gunner of another crew making an approach[41] 'saw the glow of fires beneath the fog and knew that aircraft were going into the deck.' They would have done so themselves, had the rear gunner not seen the ground in time. They had been given a wrong altimeter setting; they landed safely after it was corrected. That night twenty-eight Lancasters

27 Middlebrook, M. 1988, 269
28 Middlebrook, M. 1980, 109
29 Ibid., 303
30 Pascoe, G. H., quoted in Middlebrook, M. 1980, 309
31 McLaughlan, J. G., quoted in Middlebrook, M. 1980, 309
32 Ibid., 310
33 Ibid.
34 Middlebrook, M. 1980, 311
35 Parton, J. 1986, 156, 306, 324, 328
36 American name for H2S.
37 Middlebrook, M. 1988, 107
38 Ibid., 131
39 Hecks, K. 1990, 223
40 Owen, C. B. quoted in Hastings, M. 1979, 278
41 Flight-Sergeant R. S. Buck quoted in Middlebrook, M. 1988, 186

crashed while trying to land; another four were destroyed when their crews baled out rather than attempt a landing; 127 aircrew were killed in these accidents and thirty-four injured.

In December 1943, 'windfinding' was added to navigation methods. Selected, experienced navigators calculated windspeeds aloft from Gee, H2S, visual fixes and dead reckoning, and transmitted them to Group Headquarters in England. The reports were averaged and broadcast every half hour for the other navigators.[42] This was not proof against error. On the evening of 19 February 1944, 832 bombers took off to attack Leipzig. The attack was timed to allow for a forecast strong wind from the east. The actual wind was light from the north. Some navigators detected this and delayed their arrival at the target to meet the time assigned. Others did not and their aircraft arrived early. The bomber stream was scattered; marking and bombing were disrupted, resulting in a failed attack and heavy losses.[43]

Winter weather, the nature and distance of the target and the German defences proved too strong for Bomber Command; the Battle of Berlin failed in its stated aim, which was to end the war. Nevertheless, 811 aircraft made one final attack on 24 March 1944, with results as disastrous as any hitherto.[44]

The winds were forecast from the north at 33 km/h (18 knots) over the North Sea, increasing to 70 km/h (38 knots) over Denmark. When outbound aircraft began crossing the mainland coast 50 km (30 miles) south of track the navigators at first doubted their own skills but, when they recalculated the wind speeds with their new fixes, the results showed winds from the north at 209 km/h (113 knots). In disbelief, wind reports were transmitted with reduced wind speeds; for the same reason, wind speeds were reduced still further in the broadcasts that followed. As a result the necessary heading corrections were never made and the bombers scattered as each navigator made his own assumptions. The final approach to Berlin was from the northwest. Aircraft whose navigators did not correct for the true wind arrived early and west of Berlin. The defences at first remained quiet and many aircraft flew past the city unawares. As a

result, bombing was scattered. The return route had been planned to run north of the Ruhr, but the wind drifted the bombers to the south, exposing them to the Ruhr defences and further loss. Although Berlin had been covered by low-lying thin cloud, the sky was clear at the bombers' altitude and the scattered bomber stream, now 210 km (130 miles) wide, gave ample opportunity to the German night fighters. The result was one of the heaviest RAF losses of the war.

Bad as these setbacks were, Bomber Command continued to grow in strength and proficiency. The procedures developed for blind bombing at night were applied to bombing through overcast by day, first by the Americans in their daylight offensive and, in the closing months of the war, on daylight raids by the RAF. The same air gunner who recorded the danger and frustration of the early raids also recorded some of the last Bomber Command operations. They were very different from those early raids on which crews were 'always more or less lost'. 'Wiesbaden. Bombed on Gee through cloud. Bright moon. No flak.' 'Dortmund – coking plant. Bombed on special equipment through 10/10ths cloud.' 'Bremen. Focke-Wulf tank works where Germans were dug in. British troops only three miles away. Target accurately bombed on G.H., confirmed by bombsight. 7/10ths cloud. Flak heavy.' It was his stated ambition to drop the last bomb on Germany; he nearly did.

In 1939 RAF Bomber Command was a technically primitive force with less than a hundred bombers capable of reaching Germany, sustained by a naïve overestimate of the effects of bombing and incapable of penetrating German airspace by day or of finding their targets by night. By 1945 it had evolved into an all-weather bomber force capable of converting entire cities into rubble and craters in a matter of hours, and of doing so by day or night in any weather in which an aircraft could survive.

42 Middlebrook, M. 1988, 190
43 Ibid., 271
44 Ibid., 276

CHAPTER 14

Air Transport Comes of Age

The Second World War produced sudden, unprecedented and insatiable demands for the rapid movement of large quantities of passengers and freight; cost and safety took on a sharply reduced importance. These demands, with incalculable political and military consequences at stake, brought aircrew into collision with the worst obstructions that the weather could put in their paths. At the same time, aircraft of vastly greater range and payload than anything hitherto came into service. As a result, between 1940 and 1950 air transport suddenly came of age as an efficient, commercially viable means of long-distance transport rivalling surface methods.

It is unprofitable to pursue the question of what, technically, was the first airlift. Probably the first attempt to keep an army supplied solely by air, with the intention of continuing to do so indefinitely, was the Stalingrad airlift in the winter of 1942–3.[1] This was a disastrous failure for several reasons which are clear in retrospect.[2]

In the autumn of 1942 Field Marshal Goering's promise that the Luftwaffe would keep General Paulus's Sixth Army supplied was one reason for Hitler's decision to order his troops to hold Stalingrad, even though they were about to be surrounded by the Russians. Dissenting voices within the Luftwaffe were ignored.[3] The Russian encirclement was completed on 23 November 1942. At the end of the year the two airfields nearest to Stalingrad still in German hands were 210 and 260 km (130 and 160 miles) away, but in January 1943 the Russian advance forced the transport base back to airfields more than 320 km (200 miles) from Stalingrad, thus increasing the fuel needed for each flight and, hence, reducing the payload. The most numerous aircraft available were Ju-52/3ms, with a capacity of 2 tons, and He-111 bombers with a payload of 1.5 tons. A few Ju-86s, Fw-200s and Ju-90s were also available. Too few and too late were the few prototype Ju-290s, four-engined aircraft capable of carrying 10 tons. To supply the troops with a bare minimum of 500 tons a day needed 300 flights a day, one landing every five minutes around the clock.

The ground organization was completely insufficient to maintain and operate the aircraft fleet in the Russian winter. A senior Luftwaffe officer visiting one of the supply bases found 106 Ju-52s on the field, many of them buried in snowdrifts and frozen solid; forty-two were damaged. The wind was blowing at 83 km/h (45 knots) with a temperature of –25°C (–13°F); there was no shelter of any kind.

By mid-January 1943 the airlift had delivered only 5,300 tons of supplies in total, instead of the 30,000 tons needed, and that in the face of disastrous losses caused by bad weather and Russian opposition. In mid-month only fifteen Ju-52s out of 140 were serviceable, forty-one out of 140 He-111s, and one out of twenty Fw-200s. Instead of the 300 flights a day needed, on 16 January 1943 only seven Ju-52s and eleven He-111s were scheduled to fly to Stalingrad. Of the two airfields within the Stalingrad pocket, one was overrun by the Russians on 14 January; the other was in poor condition and was not equipped for night landings. On 15 January 1943, Field Marshal Erhard Milch was put in command but, in spite of immense and, at last, properly directed efforts, the military situation was irreparable and German resistance ceased on 2 February 1943. In seventy-two days the Luftwaffe had flown 8,350 tons of supplies to Stalingrad, less than a quarter of the bare minimum needed, at a cost of 488 aircraft and 1,000 aircrew. The Stalingrad airlift failed in its purpose, attempting against extreme weather conditions

---

1 Irving, D. 1973, 183–196
2 Hoyt, E. P. 1993, 210, 213
3 Hoyt, E. P. 1993, 210, 213

Junkers Ju-90.

Curtiss-Wright C-46.

Consolidated C-87.

something that had never been tried on that scale before.

If any single operation proved the ability of air transport to rival surface means, it was the airlift between India and China, known as The Hump. In the 3½ years from December 1941 to August 1945, 167,685 trips were flown across the Hump, transporting 721,700 tons of freight, more than was moved along the Burma and Ledo Roads combined. More than 600 aircraft and more than 1,000 aircrew were lost.

In 1936 the Japanese invaded China and blockaded its ports; as a result the Burma Road was built from India across the mountains into western China, and opened in December 1938.[4] Clandestine American support for the Chinese began in the autumn of 1941 with the mobilization of General Claire Chennault's American Volunteer Group. When the Japanese declared war against the Allies with the attack on Pearl Harbor on 7 December 1941, support for the Chinese suddenly became important because of the potential of the war in China to absorb Japanese troops. In March 1942, the Japanese overran Burma, cutting the Burma Road. From then until the opening of the Ledo Road in January 1945, and the retreat of the Japanese from Burma, the American Volunteer Group, later the US 14th Air Force, depended on resupply by air and the Chinese forces could not have stayed in the war otherwise.

The risk of interception forced the transport aircraft to fly far to the north, over mountains rising to 4,500–6,000 metres (15,000–20,000 feet). This area receives the heaviest rainfall in the world from violent convective storms. Strong winds aloft, enormous thunderstorms with extreme turbulence, hail and icing, sparse navigation aids, hypoxia, mechanical failure and overworked crews flying overloaded aircraft across high terrain produced 800 km (500 miles) of the most dangerous air transport route in the world. Although clouds concealed the unarmed transports from interception, the Hump was, above all, a battle against the weather. 'Young inexperienced flight crews

4 Spencer, O. C. 1992. Unless otherwise noted most of the material on the Hump is drawn from this source.

were flying heavy planes through constant bad weather, day-after-day bad weather – weather never before encountered in any flight operations in the world.'[5]

China National Aviation Corporation DC-3s, flown by American crews, made the first flights, augmented in 1942 by DC-3s and C-47s of the USAAF Ferrying Command, renamed Air Transport Command in June 1942, which took control of the Hump route in October. Between August and December 1942, the CNAC flew 873 round trips, carrying 2,000 short tons of supplies eastbound and 1,800 short tons of equipment and 7,000 Chinese troops westbound for training in India. In December 1942, 1,226 short tons were carried over the Hump. At first only DC-3s and C-47s were available, but in January 1943 three C-87s arrived, increasing to fourteen in July, joined in February 1943, by C-109s. The C-87s and C-109s had a service ceiling of 11,000 metres (36,000 feet), a range of 5,300 km (3,300 miles), and a payload of 7 short tons. Possibly the most significant new type to join the fleet in 1943 was the Curtiss-Wright C-46. Carrying a 7.5 short ton payload to 7,300 metres (24,000 feet), the C-46 'tamed the Hump, flew through any weather the Rockpile offered, and kept China in the war against Japan. Many C-46s went down and many crews died, and its path across the Hump was called 'the aluminum trail,' but old Dumbo prevailed.'[6]

The Hump made sudden, unprecedented demands on instrument-flying skills. The following are typical:

'It was rare in flight school to get actual experience in real weather. We flew when the weather was good and stayed on the ground when it was bad. Many pilots came to the Hump with no actual instrument time. But in the CBI, over the Hump, we flew when the birds were walking.'

'Flying weather on instruments continued to be the most threatening ordeal for Hump pilots. Piloting a plane through the angry limbo of clouds was strange and frightening – flying twenty-five tons of metal, gasoline, high explosives, and humanity at 250 miles per hour through an unknown sky. 'Flying instruments' sounded   simple – so precise and scientific. In actual flight, instrument flying in bad weather was the most stressful and agonizing part of a mission.'

'On many flights, within seconds after a heavy, sluggish take-off in India, the plane disappeared into a world of visual nothingness. Climbing, flying, navigating, fighting turbulence, winds, ice – all completely by instruments – with no reference to the ground. Long hours later, at the end of the flight, a tiny pointer on the instrument panel spins from zero to 180 degrees and tells the pilot, if he is lucky, that he has crossed the beacon. His landing field is somewhere below. Nosing down through the clouds to the landing approach; down, down, down, the plane suddenly breaks into the clear and the pilot sees the runway in China less than a minute before touchdown.'

'For 2–3 months at Lal-Hat[7] it never stopped raining, day or night, and the ceiling was 50–100 feet much of the time. We used to fly a rectangular let-down pattern coming over the radio at 400 feet, descending and hoping to break out in time to make a landing. If we missed the runway, we would fly a box pattern at 100 feet, going out 90° for 30 seconds, turn parallel for one minute, another 90° for 30 seconds, and turn onto final approach. This usually worked out all right if you didn't get too low and clip the trees on the turn. One plane with passengers did clip the trees and we lost them all.'

Goaded by incessant demands from Chennault and Chiang Kai Shek for increased tonnage, in the summer of 1943 President Roosevelt sent Captain Eddie Rickenbacker and General George Stratemeyer to investigate the airlift. They found crude airport facilities and a shortage of maintenance personnel, spare parts and radio navigation aids. Colonel Thomas O. Hardin was appointed forthwith to take charge.

Hitherto many flights had been cancelled because of bad weather and no flying was done at night because of the lack of radio aids. Hardin declared: 'There is no weather over the Hump,' and night flying started in August 1943. Hardin was no mere desk pilot and flew his share of missions. Tonnage increased sharply, from 2,300 short tons in June 1943, to 12,590 short tons that December. So did the accident rate. Between June and December 1943, 168 aircrew were killed in 155 accidents. Fatigue and hypoxia were among the probable causes of otherwise unexplained accidents. Returning aircraft were allowed to carry only the minimum of fuel theoretically needed to return to India; fuel exhaustion contributed to the accident rate.

> Three commanders before Hardin had failed to bring the airlift up to Washington's expectations. Colonel Hardin was the first commander to make the Hump work. He flew the Hump himself and knew what pilots and planes could do. His successes cost men and aircraft and lowered morale, but the airlift came into its own under Hardin. He created an efficient, around-the-clock operation that was beginning to change the direction of the war in that region. Day and night, ignoring the weather, the C-46s averaged two round trips a day over the Himalayas.

By the end of 1943, 178 aircraft, C-47s, C-87s and C-46s, were flying the Hump. Air force crews from Britain, Canada, Australia and New Zealand augmented the American effort. In November 1943, RAAF C-47s hauled 7,500 short tons, more than the Americans themselves.

An American system of air traffic control for instrument flight was established at both ends of the route, based on NDBs and VHF radio. Mountain effect, night effect, thunderstorms and Japanese jamming made the NDBs unreliable, but they were the only radio aid available. The crews included a radio operator, but no navigator; navigation was by dead reckoning. With little information on winds aloft, especially at high altitudes over the mountains, this was imprecise until an aircraft flew within range of an NDB. 'We were at 18,500 feet and the overcast had abruptly begun to thin. The next instant we were in the clear and heading directly for a snow-capped mountain peak that rose to a good 19,000 feet.'[8] The situation improved somewhat with the introduction of Loran;[9] the C-46s carried Loran receivers. The extreme physical and weather conditions, however, affected all forms of radio navigation.

The one unchanging feature of the Hump was the appalling weather. An updraft took a C-46, flying at 6,100 metres (20,000 feet), and threw it out through the top of the clouds at 8,800 metres (29,000 feet). The clouds were part of a thunderstorm 320 km (200 miles) across that destroyed another C-46 in flight and twisted the fuselage and warped the wings of a C-54. Another thunderstorm took a C-54, flying at 5,800 metres (19,000 feet), turned it upside down, and threw it into a spiral dive. Centrifugal forces prevented the crew

from baling out. According to the pilot, the aircraft reached 965 km/h (600 miles per hour) in a split-S and righted itself at 1,200 metres (4,000 feet). The crew managed to land the aircraft which by then had buckled wings, torn rivets and shredded de-icer boots; the pilot went to hospital with a nervous breakdown. On 6–7 January 1945, the storms were so bad that CNAC cancelled all flights after losing three aircraft and nine crewmen. That night the storms destroyed eighteen aircraft and killed forty-two aircrew and passengers.

In August 1944, the capture of Myitkyina in Burma by Allied forces provided a staging point on a more southerly, lower-altitude route. The same month Colonel Hardin handed over to General William H. Tunner. He, like Hardin, believed in leadership from the front and began his command by taking an unfamiliar aircraft over the Hump. He was appointed to build on Hardin's achievements by improving safety and morale. Hardin's decree was replaced by Tunner's: 'Weather is a factor which every operations officer will consider in dispatching aircraft', but the attitudes instilled by Hardin persisted until the end of the war.

Under Hardin crews flew 650 hours and then returned to the US, some flying as many as 165 hours a month which, in the conditions of Hump flying, led to extreme fatigue and accidents. Tunner increased the tour to 750 hours but added a minimum duration of one year. He also improved food, accommodation, maintenance and air traffic control. By the end of the war the SCS-51 Instrument Landing System had been installed at some of the Hump bases. In October 1944, the first C-54s arrived. The C-54 was the first aircraft to deliver more aviation fuel over the Hump than it burned *en route*. Carrying 13,000 litres (3,450 US gallons), a C-54 could fly to China, leave 3,800 litres (1,000 US gallons) from its own tanks, and fly back to India in addition to carrying a payload three times that of a DC-3.

The Hump was an extraordinary demonstration of the new capabilities of transport aircraft. The monthly tonnage increased from 12,590 short tons in December 1943, to 34,914 short tons in November 1944, and to 71,042 short tons in July

5 Spencer, O. C. 1992, 12
6 Spencer, O. C. 1992, 100. Several C-46s are 'alive and well' at the time of writing, flying freight in the Canadian Arctic and Alaska.
7 D. S. Dennis quoted in Spencer, 1992, 71
8 Genovese, J. G. 1945
9 Loran: a radio navigation aid similar in principle to Gee.

Douglas C-54 of the USAF All Weather Flying Centre in 1947.

1945. The Ledo Road was opened in January 1945, but no more than 6,000 short tons per month reached China by road. Road maintenance needed twenty engineering battalions; airfield maintenance needed two. An aircraft could cross the Hump in 5–6 hours; a truck took a week with a smaller load. In 1945 the Hump airlift was operating with 400 aircraft and 3,026 pilots from ten bases in India and twelve in China.

The demand for supplies from the Allied forces in China was insatiable. The Hump crews celebrated Armed Forces Day on 1 August 1945 with a maximum effort; General Tunner flew two trips. One C-54 flew three trips and was airborne for 22.25 hours in the twenty-four. A total of 1,118 trips moved 5,327 short tons of supplies: one aircraft over the Hump every 72 seconds, moving freight at 4 short tons per minute. Of the total tonnage carried between December 1942 and August 1945, 76% was flown in the last eight months. After the war ended the repatriation of servicemen began and in August and September 1945 47,000 troops were flown from China back to India. The last flight of the Hump airlift was flown on 31 December 1945.

The demands of war turned the transatlantic proving flights of the late 1930s into a regular service for military passengers and freight, with civilian services beginning soon after the war. In the early

years of the war the British began to buy aircraft from the Americans, in particular the Lockheed Hudson light bomber, the Consolidated Catalina/Canso/PBY maritime reconnaissance flying boat, and the Consolidated B-24 and Boeing B-17 bombers. It was quicker, safer and more practical to fly these aircraft to Britain than to send them across on ships. The basic organization for a transatlantic air service was in place in 1939. This included airfields and flying-boat bases in the British Isles and Canada, a meteorological service with intercontinental radio links and a small number of experienced aircrew. The first aircraft flown across was a PBY, crossing via Bermuda in October 1940.[10]

The next crossing was by twenty-one Hudsons in November 1940. They assembled at Gander and flew to Belfast in Northern Ireland. The Hudsons had no de-icing boots, but the wing leading-edges were painted with an ice-inhibiting paste trade-named Kilfrost. Because of a lack of navigators, they flew in three flights of seven, each led by an experienced captain. Each flight leader planned the headings, altitudes, airspeeds and engine settings to be followed by the other crews, should the formation be dispersed by cloud and darkness.

First was Captain D. C. T. Bennett, an Australian-born former RAF and Imperial Airways pilot, one of the pioneers of the North Atlantic route, and subsequently commander of the RAF Pathfinder Force. He commented: 'Never before had the Atlantic been attempted so late as the middle of November, and, indeed, all previous attempts made later than September had ended catastrophically.' The formations took off from Gander after nightfall on 10 November 1940. Partway across the Atlantic they ran into frontal cloud and separated. Moderate icing was encountered and Bennett's aircraft was still in cloud at 6,700 metres (22,000 feet). They broke cloud at low altitude over the sea the next morning, made a landfall on the coasts of Scotland and Ireland, and landed safely; the aircrew returned to Canada by sea. During the first eleven months of the Atlantic Ferry only one aircraft was lost *en route*, a Hudson forced down in Canada by icing and engine failure: only the pilot survived.

As the B-24s came into service in early 1941, crews could be flown back to Canada instead of going by sea. On 8 May 1941, a B-24 made the first flight by a landplane from the UK direct to Montreal, taking just under 17 hours. The British Overseas Airways Corporation (BOAC) began its Return Ferry Service across the Atlantic with six converted B-24s on 24 September 1941.[11]

Sir Gordon Taylor, airline pilot in Australia in 1928–9 and pioneer of long-range flying over the Pacific, brings us this description of an eastbound crossing in a B-24.[12] After conversion training on the B-24 at Montreal in the spring of 1942 he was sent to fly an aircraft to England with a copilot, a navigator and a radio operator. In addition to the normal equipment, this aircraft had a radar altimeter.

They left Montreal in daylight under a 150 metre (500 foot) overcast, breaking out into clear air at 2,400 metres (8,000 feet) to cruise at 2,700 metres (9,000 feet). Navigation was by dead reckoning; the cloud broke up over Nova Scotia, allowing them to fix their position from landmarks. The radio operator took the latest weather report from Gander: ceiling 550 metres (1,800 feet), wind 18 km/h (10 knots) from the southeast, visibility 13 km (8 miles). They descended over the Cabot Strait through broken cloud based at 760 metres (2,500 feet), expecting to continue to Gander in visual conditions and make an approach under a lower ceiling than would be permissible using the radio range. 'But I really wanted to skate low over Newfoundland, discover this new, dark land, holding the aeroplane in my hands, and feel the thunder of her engines in the hills, roar her over the uplands, and pour her down the valleys.'

Twenty miles from Gander the clouds came down to the hills and Taylor climbed into the cloud to fly on instruments at a safe height of 1,200 metres (4,000 feet). The ADF was unserviceable. They discovered by radio that Gander weather had deteriorated to a raining 120 metre (400 foot) overcast with more cloud at 60 metres (200 feet). Taylor flew the published radio range approach which specified an altitude of 600 metres (2,000 feet) crossing the range station inbound, with a minimum altitude of 383 metres (1,256 feet) – 243 metres (796 feet) above ground level as the airport elevation was 140 metres (460 feet).

At the B-24's approach speed the airport was 1.5 minutes from the range station:

A minute to go. Round us must be the hills; straight ahead and close below, the invisible airport. With us there was nothing but the rumble of the motors, the flight instruments, and the sounds in the earphones. I glanced out an instant, searching down for the earth we knew was there. There was only the dark closeness of the cloud and rain streaming in, tearing harshly at the screen. There was tight suspense in the invisible closeness of the earth as I held the instruments with my eyes and felt their readings through my hands and feet on the controls. Forty seconds to go. Eighteen hundred feet. No sign of the earth. I let her go down, brought up the rate of descent to go quickly to the minimum, then if there still were nothing I could ease her a shade below it approaching the runway.

Fourteen, thirteen, twelve-fifty. Twenty seconds. Cloud; no sign of the earth.

'Stand by for the gear.'

Twelve hundred. Eleven-fifty. Eleven. Nothing. Blind rain and cloud smoking over the nose. A climax reached up, rushing in on us. No future in this.

'Gear up', I pressed forward the throttles and lifted her out. Get clear of the earth. The motors hauled her away, up from the invisible hills.

Taylor diverted to Stephenville, where the weather was better, and landed. The next day they obtained their Atlantic clearance, flew to Gander,

10 Bennett, D. C. T. 1958, 1988 ed., 79–101
11 Bennett, D. C. T. 1958, 1988 ed., 98–9; *Flight*, 27 September 1945, p.329
12 Taylor, G. 1983, 126–140

and took off eastbound into a dark night with a low overcast. After climbing through the cloud they broke out into clear air at 2,700 metres (9,000 feet) and continued to their cruising altitude of 3,350 metres (11,000 feet) where Taylor turned on the autopilot. He wrote: 'I didn't particularly want to know anything about our position for at least two hours. There was every kind of aid to navigation on the Atlantic.' The navigators fixed their position by star shots, which was one reason for crossing the Atlantic at night. 'Always at night over the ocean there is a sense of complete detachment from the earth.' 'We ran through a light warm front about an hour out and then came out to night so clear and still and black that the airplane seemed motionless in the heavens.'

Other aircrew were less fortunate that night. At about 4 a.m. Taylor's radio operator received an SOS from a B-17 with engine trouble. The Fortress and its crew disappeared without trace. As dawn broke, Taylor and his crew were flying above a continuous deck of cloud. Not long before, the navigator had taken a star shot, confirmed by a DF bearing from Iceland and another from southeastern England. A sun shot would be their final position fix before using radio navigation to penetrate the higher and thicker cloud over Ireland and Scotland. The Germans were also known to jam the radio beacons and DF from time to time, and in daylight over the eastern Atlantic they ran some risk of interception by Fw-200s.

At 7 a.m. they tuned the Derrynacross radio range on 225 kHz. 'It was there all right; just a faint N in the on course signal persisting through a lot of intermittent crackling and the faraway squeak of the double identification.' Over the Irish coast they flew into dense convective cloud and the aircraft 'began to bounce around, stabbing into the rough air and shaking the springy wing in a way that made her feel uncomfortable to me, too mechanical on the autopilot. I switched it off and flew her through the weather. I heard her cut through the north leg of the Derrynacross Range, the radio screaming and crackling through the great mountains of cloud and rain that lie over the hills of Northern Ireland.' Abruptly they flew into clear air and landed on a bright morning at Prestwick.

In June 1942, BOAC made twenty-nine crossings. While BOAC carried passengers, the RAF 45 Atlantic Transport Group organized the ferrying of military aircraft. The BOAC service was the first to cross the Atlantic in winter; American services began in 1943. It was inevitable that the vast extent of the Atlantic, its vicious weather, human error and mechanical failure would cause tragic mishaps. Conditions improved as airfields, weather stations and radio beacons were built in Labrador and Greenland, but the 10,000 aircraft delivered by RAF Ferry Command and its predecessors between 1941 and 1945 cost the lives of more than 500 aircrew and passengers and 151 aircraft, of which forty-nine disappeared without trace.[13]

By the later years of the war a constant flow of air traffic crossed the North Atlantic: USAAF, RAF, BOAC and ferry flights of every one of the thousands of multi-engined aircraft built in North America and sent to Europe. At one time the USAAF Air Transport Command was flying twenty crossings in each direction each day.[14] In four years BOAC made 1,750 Atlantic crossings and carried 20,000 priority passengers, 635,000 kg (1.4 million pounds) of freight and 1,043,280 kg (2.3 million pounds) of mail. In 1945 twelve Liberators provided this service, crossing the Atlantic eleven times a week, with a crew of five and space for sixteen passengers.[15] The journey between the UK and Montreal took about seventeen hours westbound and thirteen hours eastbound. It remained for post-war pressurized aircraft, such as the DC-6, Constellation and Stratocruiser, to make regular passenger service between Europe and North America a reality.

Under the 1945 partition of Germany for military occupation, the Russian zone extended well to the west of Berlin. The western powers, however, held an enclave in the west of the city to which the Russians allowed access along specified road, rail and air corridors. In April and May 1948, the Russians began to restrict surface access from West Germany to Berlin,[16] followed by a complete ban on 24 June. They could not, however, prevent air access without provoking a war and the British and Americans decided to supply the city by air. The population of West Berlin was 2.4 million; they needed 12,000 short tons of freight every day, although the Allied authorities estimated the bare minimum necessary for survival as 4,500 short tons per day. On 29 July 1948, General William Tunner was appointed to command the American effort to

---

13 Christie, C. A. 1995, Appendix B
14 Taylor, M. J. H. 1989, 341
15 *Flight*, 27 September 1945, 330
16 Merer, J. W. F. 1950

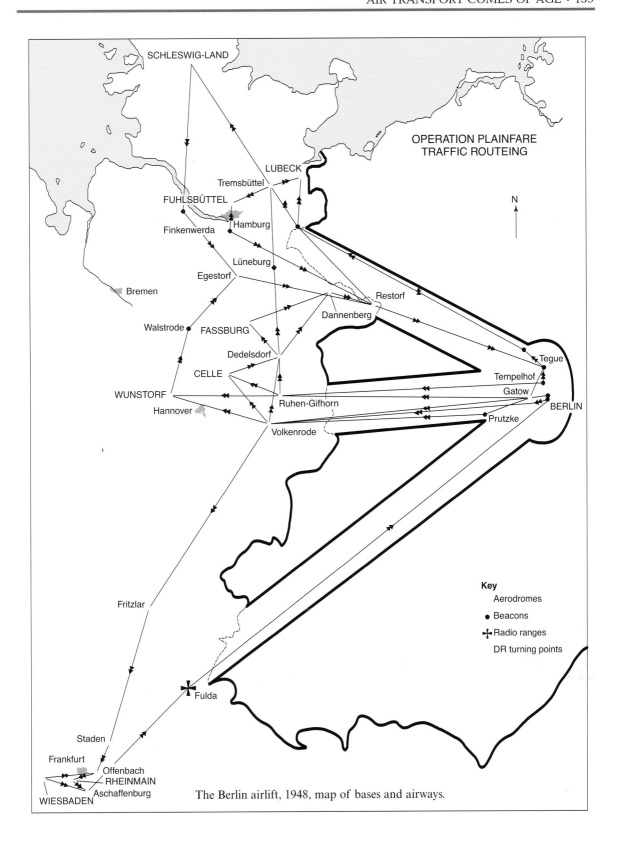

OPERATION PLAINFARE
TRAFFIC ROUTEING

N

SCHLESWIG-LAND

LUBECK

Tremsbüttel

FUHLSBÜTTEL

Finkenwerda

Hamburg

Lüneburg

Egestorf

Restorf

Bremen

Dannenberg

Walstrode

FASSBURG

Dedelsdorf

Tegue

CELLE

Tempelhof

Gatow

WUNSTORF

Ruhen-Gifhorn

BERLIN

Hannover

Prutzke

Volkenrode

Key

Aerodromes

• Beacons

⊹ Radio ranges

DR turning points

Fritzlar

Fulda

Staden

Frankfurt

Offenbach

RHEINMAIN

Aschaffenburg

WIESBADEN

The Berlin airlift, 1948, map of bases and airways.

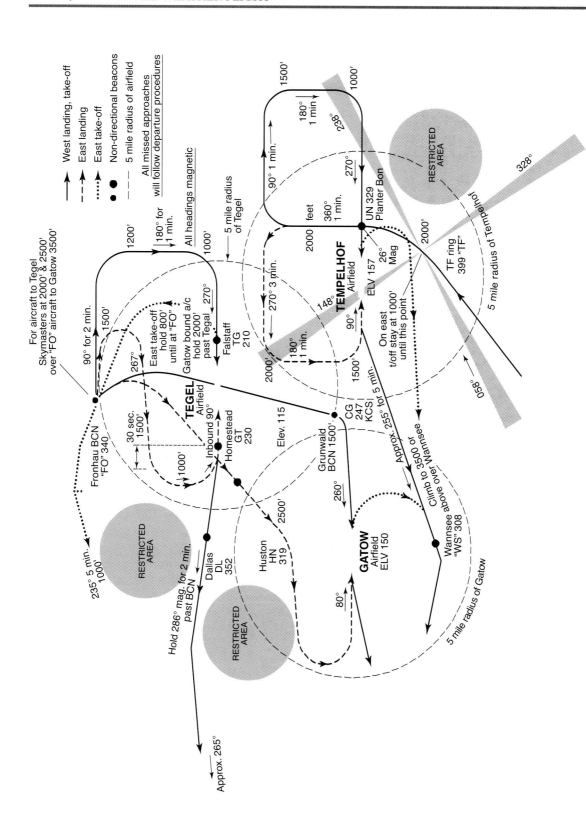

The Berlin airlift, 1948, Berlin area traffic procedure.

Berlin and on 14 October the British and American forces were combined under his command.[17]

Under the 1945 agreement with the Russians, flights to Berlin were restricted to three corridors, each 32 km (20 miles) wide, extending from ground level to 3,000 metres (10,000 feet), converging on Berlin from Hamburg (corridor 152 km (95 miles) long), Hannover (188 km (117 miles)), and Frankfurt (348 km (216 miles)). The three corridors met in the Berlin Control Zone, a circular area 32 km (20 miles) in radius except for restricted areas of 3-kilometre (2-mile) radius centred on the seven Russian military airfields surrounding Berlin. At the start of the airlift there were two airfields in West Berlin, Tempelhof and Gatow, but US Army Engineers built a third, Tegel, in three months which was opened on 1 December 1948. Nine airlift bases were established in West Germany. Apart from British Sunderland and Hythe flying boats, flying between Hamburg and a lake in West Berlin in the summer and autumn of 1948, the aircraft were all landplanes.

The aircraft were operated by the USAF, the RAF and by twenty-three civilian charter companies. DC-3s and the USAF's C-54s and C-82s were accompanied by RAF or civilian-operated Yorks, Haltons, Lancastrians, Tudors, Vikings, Hastings, Lincolns and Bristol Freighters. A Douglas C-74 Globemaster I made a few flights to Berlin but was too heavy for the runways; wear and tear and runway bearing strength were among the critical factors during the airlift.

The airlift added impetus to the change from tailwheel landing gear to tricycle gear. Gatow, Tegel and two bases in West Germany had only one runway each. Tailwheel aircraft could not operate safely in crosswinds stronger than 22–28 km/h (12–15 knots), whereas the C-54s had little difficulty in crosswinds up to 56 km/h (30 knots).

A continuous, dense flow of traffic along narrow corridors with aircraft of varying performance made rigorous traffic control essential; aircraft were assigned closely specified altitudes and tracks. This meant that aircrew had to cope with whatever the weather threw at them with no opportunity for deviation except in an emergency, for which an altitude of 900 metres (3,000 feet) was designated. Close monitoring of the weather allowed traffic to be kept at its maximum safe density. Ground-Controlled Approach radar (GCA) and the British Blind Approach Beacon System (BABS) were installed as instrument-approach aids. Weather

minima were 60 metres (200 feet) ceiling and 730 metres (2,400 feet) visibility. Flights were particularly disrupted by high winds and fog in November and December 1948. On one occasion 241 GCA approaches were made at Gatow in 24 hours. The Americans were not equipped or trained for BABS; the SCS-51 Instrument Landing System was not available; they therefore depended solely on GCA. Centreline and horizon-bar approach lights were installed at Gatow and Wunstorf in October 1948.

The high traffic density required precise navigation. The available radar was not accurate enough for traffic control, although early in 1949 an American CPS-5 search radar with a range of 80 km (50 miles) was installed at Tempelhof. In this respect the British had an advantage; their aircraft carried a navigator and Gee, ADF and radar which provided range and bearing from Eureka beacons on the ground. American air navigation, based on radio ranges and NDBs, suffered from the fact that no marker beacons could be installed in the Russian-occupied territory beneath the air corridors. American aircraft therefore had no indication, other than time, of their progress along the corridors. Time and altitude blocks were therefore allocated to categories of aircraft according to their navigation capabilities.

A single set of routes and procedures covered all three airports, incorporating eight NDBs and one radio range. All possible measures were taken to ensure a steady flow of traffic. No holds were allowed and any aircrew missing their approach returned to West Germany with no second attempt to land in Berlin. By the end of September 1948, 250 aircraft were flying to Berlin; landings averaged 380 at Gatow and 220 at Tempelhof every 24 hours. By April 1949, 868 flights went to Berlin every 24 hours. On 16 April a maximum effort was made to test the air traffic control system. The three Berlin airports handled 2,796 landings and take-offs in 24 hours, one every 31 seconds, moving just under 13,000 short tons of freight.

Much was learned from the airlift. The C-54, with its 10 short ton payload, emerged as the real workhorse; it demonstrated the immense gains in efficiency obtainable with large aircraft. The care and accommodation of crews was as important as the mechanical condition of the aircraft. It was found by experience that the maximum sustained

17 Collier, R. 1978, 177, 181

intensity of flying which could be expected of a crew without loss of efficiency was about 70 hours a month and two consecutive sorties in a 24-hour period; it was found that the working day should be limited as nearly as possible to eight hours.[18] At that time the British Ministry of Civil Aviation imposed a limit of 125 hours a month on civilian pilots.[19] Decades would pass before North American operators imposed any such restrictions. Sixteen fatal crashes occurred on the airlift from all causes between June 1948 and May 1949, resulting in the deaths of fifty-seven aircrew and seven passengers.

The airlift became a highly organized system, functioning by day or night in almost all weathers, interrupted only by dense fog, strong crosswinds on the airfields, thunderstorms and severe icing – specific hazards of limited duration. The incessant drone of aero-engines convinced the Russians of the futility of trying to starve the western Allies out of West Berlin; on 12 May 1949 the surface corridors were reopened and the airlift was run down. At that time 95 RAF, 200 USAF and 45 chartered civilian aircraft were flying 8,000 short tons of supplies into the city every day and were returning with outbound passengers and manufactured goods. By the end of July 1949, 2.2 million short tons of supplies had been flown in, 0.5 million short tons by the British (70% RAF, 30% charter), the balance by the Americans, an average of 5,579 short tons per day. Any means of transport that was capable of supplying a whole city for a year had clearly come of age.

---

18 Merer, J. W. F. 1950, 523
19 James, J. W. G. 1949; Irving, D. 1973, 183–196

CHAPTER 15

A 'Plethora of Imperfect Electronic Riches'

The 1940s were a turning point in the development of air navigation. The methods and equipment used previously were either adapted from maritime practices or traced their origins to bonfires and light beacons. From then on, however, air navigation systems were, almost by definition, systems for blind navigation. As J. E. D. Williams put it succinctly:[1] 'The plethora of imperfect electronic riches which was the Second World War's legacy to navigation offered a confusing choice to civil aviation.'

In the 1920s and 1930s, as mentioned earlier, two different concepts of blind navigation evolved on opposite sides of the Atlantic: track guidance in America, area navigation in Europe. The American system had the advantages that a specialist navigator was not needed and the tracks and fixes helped with air traffic control. It depended, however, on a dense, costly and maintenance-intensive network of ground beacons, well suited to the US, but less suited, if at all, to other parts of the world. The European concept was not limited by seas or frontiers but depended on a navigator in the aircraft. Although it allowed more flexible routings than the American system, it was ill suited to air traffic control. The two concepts collided when intercontinental commercial flying made international standards essential.

Beginning in the late 1930s, a new series of radio aids was devised, known as 'hyperbolic' systems; signals from two or more transmitters on the ground produced a signal field of wide extent from which a navigator could obtain fixes at will. These were Gee, Decca, *Sonne*, and Loran. All were developed during the Second World War for military purposes.

The development of Gee has already been described; it continued in use after the war. Freed from jamming, it covered much of northwest Europe. Originally the transmitters had to be synchronized by skilled operators; this was now automated. The new Mark III airborne set was smaller and lighter than earlier sets and the position-fixing process was partly automated. A left/right indicator in the cockpit allowed the pilot to follow one of the lines of the signal lattice. In 1945 three chains of Gee stations were in service in England. In 1947–8 they were relocated for better coverage and a fourth chain was built in Scotland,[2] the only Gee chain ever built for civilian use.[3] BEA (British European Airways) used Gee during the 1950s; RAF use continued until 1969. By that time civilian and military users had turned to other systems and the Scottish chain was the last to be closed down.

Decca was invented by the Chicago-born William J. O'Brien in 1937.[4] Unable to arouse any interest in the US, in August 1939 O'Brien wrote to a friend, Harvey Schwartz, who was working for the Decca Gramophone Company in England. In April 1942, Decca offered the system to the British Admiralty and a chain of transmitters was built in southern England in time for the Normandy invasion in 1944. As soon as the war was over Decca was advertised for civilian shipping and aviation, where it gained wide acceptance.[5]

The first Decca receiver built for aircraft use weighed 12 kg (27 pounds). Two indicators showed the aircraft's position along two intersecting lattice

---

1 Williams, J. E. D. 1992, 190
2 *Flight*, 16 October 1947, 450
3 *Flight International*, 17 July 1969, 104
4 Williams, J. E. D. 1992, 226; *Flight International*, 19 March 1970, 430
5 *Flight*, 5 December 1946, 629; 20 March 1947, 243

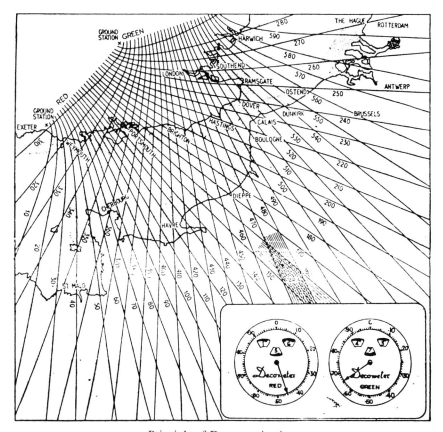

Principle of Decca navigation.

A small-scale typical chart on which only every ten signal paths are shown. Readings on the dials give a fix, as shown, above Paris. On actual charts every signal line is shown.

lines. The intersection of the two lines on a chart overprinted with the lattice was the aircraft's position. This simplicity of output was an advance over Gee, which needed a navigator to use it. The original system had a maximum range of 2,400 km (1,500 miles); the best accuracy was 90 metres (300 feet), obtainable at up to 480 km (300 miles). Accuracy declined farther from the transmitters as the lattice lines crossed at increasingly obtuse angles.

A chain of Decca stations was built in southern England for trial aviation use in 1945–6,[6] using the 70–130 kHz band. In 1945 the French built a chain to cover France and French North Africa;[7] at the end of 1947 Air France began to use Decca in three DC-3s flying between London and Paris.[8] In 1947 the Danish Ministry of Marine contracted for a chain of four stations in Denmark, covering a 480 km (300 mile) radius from Copenhagen.[9] This, with the English chain and a proposed Scottish

chain, would cover a large part of north-west Europe. The Americans experimented with Decca in 1947 and used it as a subsidiary navigation system.[10] Decca was also supplied to Sweden for marine use.[11]

Sonne was a wartime German system[12] developed by the Lorenz company for navigation over the Atlantic. The U-boat campaign depended on the precise navigation provided by *Sonne* for both submarines and aircraft but the British discovered it and used it themselves. Transmitters on the European mainland, using the 300 kHz band, covered the north-eastern Atlantic to ranges of 1,930 km (1,200 miles) by day and 2,400 km (1,500 miles) by night. *Sonne* resembled Gee in that a chart with the signal lattice printed over geographic co-ordinates was needed to obtain a fix. Unlike Gee, however, only a communications receiver was needed; the navigator obtained a fix by counting audible signals. When the Allies captured *Sonne* stations late in the war, they recognized its potential for airline use. Further developed by Marconi in the UK, the system was renamed Consol.[13] New stations were still being built in 1970, but it was eventually made obsolete by more advanced systems, such as Loran and Omega, that provided an automatic position readout.

The Americans were well aware of the benefits of hyperbolic systems. Loran was an American invention for long-range coverage over oceans or sparsely settled areas; the first experiments took place in 1942.[14] At frequencies of 1,700–2,000 kHz, Loran had a range over water of about 1,370 km (850 miles) by day and 2,570 km (1,600 miles) by night, but performance over land was found to be poor. With the equipment available in 1947 a navigator could obtain a position line in about a minute and a fix in 2–5 minutes. Low-frequency Loran, using 180 kHz, was under development in 1947 and was expected to be available over the Atlantic within two years with ranges of 2,400–3,200 km (1,500–2,000 miles).

The British pointed out that hyperbolic systems could cover wider areas more cheaply, more reliably and more accurately than track guidance systems. Apart from the fact that the Americans dominated post-war civil aviation, air traffic control using hyperbolic systems was, however, relatively difficult. Decca tried to solve this problem, but unsuccessfully, with the Decca Track Control Unit,[15] which used fixes pre-recorded on film strips to define a track. Hyperbolic systems did not come into their own until microcomputers became available which could convert hyperbolic signals into rectangular co-ordinates and provide bearing, distance, and time with push-button ease and speed. Meanwhile, radio ranges were installed in Europe for American aircraft, and were also used by some British civilian aircraft.[16]

The British developed a short-range homing and distance measuring system during the war, code-named Rebecca/Eureka. Rebecca was the airborne equipment which provided bearing and distance from the Eureka ground beacon. The Eureka beacon was portable and could be used to guide supply-dropping aircraft. The concept of Rebecca/Eureka was developed into Distance Measuring Equipment (DME), using an airborne transmitter to interrogate a ground transponder. The reply time gave the distance from aircraft to transponder. The introduction of DME into service was delayed by disagreements as to its usefulness and by political wrangling between the proponents of incompatible systems.

The limitations and defects of the radio range led the American CAA to think about replacing it as early as 1936.[17] Any replacement for the radio range had to meet three requirements. First, the beacon had to transmit on frequencies less subject to distortion and mutual interference than those used by the radio range. Second, the beacon had to provide bearing and distance information that was not limited to the four legs of the radio range; the radio provided no distance information at all. Third, the information had to be provided to the pilot visually rather than aurally. The result was a ground beacon, similar in concept to the First World War Telefunken navigation aid which, itself, harked back to earlier coastal light beacons, known as the VHF Omnidirectional Radio Range, VOR or Omni. It was developed during the 1940s through the Radio Technical Committee for Aeronautics, a joint body set up by the aviation industry and the US Government.[18]

The VOR beacon, using the 112–118 MHz band, transmitted a non-directional signal at a regular interval and a directional signal rotating like the beam of a lighthouse. There was thus a distinctive time relationship between the non-directional and directional signals on any given bearing from the beacon. The airborne receiver timed this difference and displayed the aircraft's bearing from the beacon. The pilot first tuned the beacon on the receiver, according to frequency and identifier information published on charts, and then tuned a bearing line from the beacon, known as a radial. A left/right course deviation needle in the cockpit instrument centred either when the pilot tuned the radial on which the aircraft happened to be (regardless of its heading) or when the aircraft intercepted the radial that he had tuned. The cockpit instrument showed the azimuth of the radial.

6 *Flight*, 1 August 1946, 113
7 *Flight*, 20 December 1945, 664
8 *Flight*, 12 February 1948, 187
9 *Flight*, 13 March 1947, 223
10 *Flight*, 3 April 1947, 286
11 *Flight*, 21 August 1947, 199
12 Williams, J. E. D. 1992, 224
13 *Flight*, 27 April 1956, 495
14 *Flight*, 20 March 1947, 244; Spencer, O. C. 1992, 105
15 *Flight*, 19 September 1946, 315
16 *Flight*, 23 January 1947, 96
17 Williams, J. E. D. 1992, 190
18 *Flying*, June 1955, 66

By using the aircraft's compass or heading indicator, the pilot could turn the aircraft onto the radial and track it by flying a heading that kept the needle centred. This did not tell the pilot whether he was flying towards the beacon or away from it. He could, for example, be flying east, tracking the 090° radial with nothing to show whether he was east or west of the beacon; a to/from indicator resolved this ambiguity.

The standard VOR beacon of the early 1950s[19] had a power output of 200 watts, giving a range of 80 km (50 miles). VORs on the same frequency needed to be at least 640 km (400 miles) apart to avoid all risk of interference at their theoretical maximum range of 290 km (180 miles) for an aircraft flying at 22,860 metres (75,000 feet).[20] Pre-certification tests by the Airborne Instruments Laboratory found that errors were within 4.5°, depending on terrain, providing a track less than 5.5 km (3.5 miles) wide at 80 km (50 miles) from the VOR. VORs of 50 watt power were installed to fill gaps in coverage and were used as approach aids near small airports where the cost of an ILS was not justified. The VOR did not provide homing information directly, but in the mid-1950s even this minor problem was solved by the Radio Magnetic Indicator (RMI).[21] A compass card, rotating beneath a lubber line and driven by a remote compass, gave the aircraft's magnetic heading. Two centre-pivoted needles indicated the magnetic heading to two NDBs, a VOR and an NDB, or two VORs as selected by the pilot. An RMI thus functioned both as a heading indicator and as an ADF equally capable of using VOR signals.

Intermediate between the radio range and the VOR was the Visual-Aural Range (VAR).[22] Derived from the SCS-51 Instrument Landing System, it came into use in the US during the 1940s and was used in Australia and north-west Europe, but was made obsolete by the VOR. A VAR beacon was, in effect, a VHF four-course radio range transmitting, additionally, an SCS-51 localizer in two reciprocal directions. Continuous air routes could be defined by 200 watt beacons at 160 km (100 mile) intervals. Transmitting on the same VHF frequency band as SCS-51, VAR signals could be received both aurally and on an ILS set. The VAR was replaced by the much more flexible VOR, with which its name is sometimes confused. The biggest users of VAR were the Australians, who had a continental network in service by June 1950. They also used the 33 MHz VHF radio range which had been only experimental in the USA.[23]

Although VOR signals differed from both VAR and ILS localizer signals, the same course deviation indicator could be used for all three navigation aids. Various manufacturers produced a variety of instruments and tuning devices, differing in detail, for selecting and displaying VOR, VAR and ILS signals.

The most advanced of the pre-war blind approach systems was the German Lorenz equipment, adopted by the British and used by the RAF as the Standard Beam Approach (SBA).[24] Most SBA-equipped airfields had radio DF and this or other means brought an inbound aircraft within the zone of 'strong signal strength', defined as the zone within which the signals could just be heard with the volume turned down to minimum. The azimuth of the equisignal was published and the pilot could tell from the dots or dashes which sector he was in; he could therefore intercept it. Beyond that, however, orientation along the beam and positioning the aircraft to make a landing was a complicated procedure, involving turns back and forth across the equisignal and procedure turns to reverse course and regain the beam, requiring much mental agility. The minimum descent altitude until crossing the outer marker inbound on final approach was 180 metres (600 feet) above ground level. On crossing the outer marker, the pilot descended to 30 metres (100 feet), which he maintained until crossing the inner marker. From there a landing could be made unless conditions of wind and visibility were especially bad. If the wind prevented a landing in the normal direction, the procedure could be reversed, using the main beacon as a marker. In this case the pilot, on regaining the beam on final approach, descended to 60 metres (200 feet) which he maintained until crossing the main beacon, from which point he landed or missed the approach.

Even with DF, the full procedure was unlikely to take less than 20 minutes from entering the zone of strong signal strength, during which time no other aircraft could safely occupy the approach area. SBA was thus not satisfactory for large numbers of bombers returning from a raid, but was usable by individual aircraft if weather conditions so demanded. The RAF procedure was based on the use of Lorenz equipment alone; where other navaids could be used as well, the procedure time could be reduced.

It can well be imagined that to fly a heavy aircraft, blind, down to 30 metres (100 feet) above ground level, level out, and then maintain that

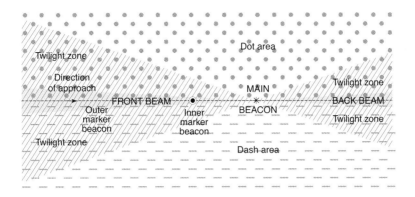

RAF Standard Beam Approach – signal pattern.

altitude while tracking an aural signal was a potentially hazardous procedure requiring a high degree of instrument flying skill. A minority of RAF test pilots and instructors became highly proficient with SBA and could make full use of its possibilities. The average bomber pilot, although trained in its use, did not fly for long enough to become proficient and did not use SBA as a routine. One pilot recorded 'Lorenz practice' in his log book, but fifty years later could not remember what it was.[25] SBA was superseded by the American SCS-51 Instrument Landing System.

Another RAF Second World War blind landing aid was the Beam Approach Beacon System (BABS)[26] using the 208–232 MHz band. A transmitter in the aircraft triggered a transponder at the far end of the landing runway. The transponder used two transmitters to radiate an equisignal and distance information. A cathode-ray tube in the cockpit provided left/right commands and distance to touchdown. Ranging was accurate to within 150 metres (500 feet). Although BABS had no glideslope, the continuous distance information allowed a final approach descent to be flown using the aircraft's altimeter. Approach minima were 90 metres (300 feet) above ground level with a slant visibility of 900 metres (3,000 feet). An aircraft 300 metres (1,000 feet) above the ground could receive signals up to 32 km (20 miles) away.[27] The on-board equipment weighed 54 kg (120 pounds). Up to fifty aircraft could use one BABS at a time. It was made obsolete by other developments, but it was used at some airfields as an alternative to SBA. (See page 151)

The American experiments with instrument landing systems during the 1930s resulted in a clear definition of the requirements. This enabled the CAA to develop a workable system by 1942. The original version was truck-mounted for rapid deployment and was called SCS-51. The USAAF was the first user; B-25 pilots were being trained in its use at Barksdale, Louisiana, in December 1942, and the system was installed at some of the Hump bases towards the end of the war.[28] In 1944 it was still only at the demonstration stage with the USAAF in Britain and did not play a significant part in the bomber offensive there.

The problem still unsolved in 1940 was the glideslope. Vertical guidance using lines of equal field strength in a single radiation pattern had been tried, both with the CAA system and with Lorenz, but was not successful. The first attempts at an equisignal glideslope in the 1930s did not succeed because, at the radio frequencies which could be generated at that time, the ground interfered with the signal pattern. The problem was solved with the invention of the klystron valve by Sigurd and Russell Varian at Stanford University in 1937;[29] one of its first applications was to generate a UHF equisignal glideslope.

19 *Flight*, 6 March 1953, 291
20 Deltour, B. V. 1960, 44
21 *Flight*, 12 April 1957, 497
22 *Flight*, 6 March 1953; 11 March 1955, 332
23 *Flight*, 30 March 1950, 399
24 Air Ministry Publication 1732b, 242–261
25 A. Foord, personal communication, 1995.
26 Pritchard, H. C., 1946
27 *Flight*, 16 May 1958, 676
28 Spencer, O. C. 1992, 9, 191
29 *Encyclopedia Americana*, 1991 ed., vol. 16, 502

Method of entering the beam when homing by D.F.

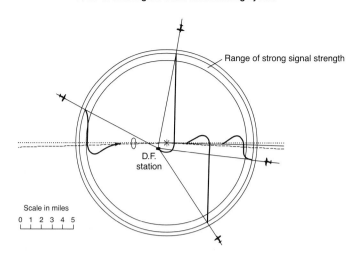

Range of strong signal strength

D.F. station

Scale in miles
0 1 2 3 4 5

Timing the beam

Fly at right angles to the beam

Turn 120 in the direction of the kicker

Turn in direction of shorter timing run

0 1 2 3 4 5
Scale in miles

Short figure of eight

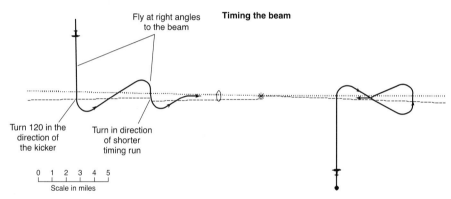

Count same number of dots as you counted dashes

Note: If drift has been assessed, read QDMD for QDM and QDMD for QDR

Then Rate 1 turn onto

Beam on QDM

Outer marker beacon

Inner marker beacon

Main beacon

Rate 1 turn onto

QDR + 30°

Count dashes to the beam

0 1 2
Scale in miles

Long figure of eight

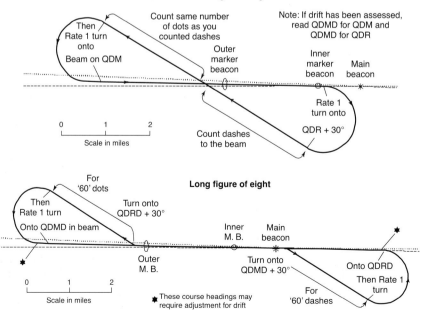

For '60' dots

Turn onto QDRD + 30°

Then Rate 1 turn

Onto QDMD in beam

Inner M. B.

Main beacon

Outer M. B.

Turn onto QDMD + 30°

Onto QDRD

Then Rate 1 turn

For '60' dashes

0 1 2
Scale in miles

★ These course headings may require adjustment for drift

RAF Standard Beam Approach – orientation procedures.

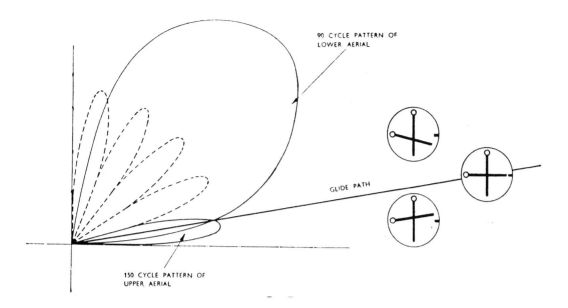

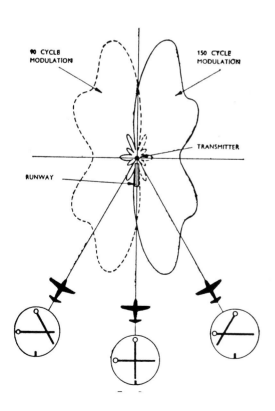

SCS-51 Instrument Landing System – signal pattern.

The ILS localizer and glideslope were both formed by the equisignals of pairs of lobate radiation patterns. One pattern was modulated at 90 Hz, the other at 150 kHz. The airborne equipment compared their signals electronically and displayed the result on a centre-zero micro-ammeter in the cockpit, the equisignal being represented by zero current. Full-scale deflection occurred at 3° off the localizer centreline, beyond which the relationship between angular error and current through the micro-ammeter became non-linear. Localizers transmitted on 108–111 MHz; adjacent localizers were assigned frequencies within this band which avoided mutual interference. All glideslopes transmitted on 335 MHz with the same modulation frequencies and readout as the localizer. One frequency sufficed for all glideslopes because the directional and attenuation properties of that frequency prevented interference between nearby glideslopes. Full-scale needle deflection occurred 0.6° above and 0.3° below the glideslope. The angle of the glideslope could be varied between 2° and 5°, 3° being the most common.

The localizer and glideslope readouts were combined in a crossed-pointer instrument. This idea dated back to the 1930s but, unlike the original version, the needles indicated the position of the localizer and glideslope relative to the aircraft rather than vice versa. For example, a deflection of the localizer needle to the right meant that the pilot needed to fly to the right to regain track, thus flying 'towards' the needle rather than 'away' from it. The ILS airborne equipment weighed 29 kg (65 pounds). Marker beacons were installed under the localizer course 60 metres (200 feet) (inner marker), 1,460 metres (4,800 feet) (middle marker), and 7 km (4.5 miles) (outer marker) from the runway threshold. Each marker transmitted a fan-shaped signal on 75 MHz, longer across the localizer than along it, and was consequently known as a fan marker. A marker beacon receiver in the aircraft indicated passage over each marker by lighting one of three lamps in the instrument panel and producing audio signals. The outer marker aural signal was two dashes per second at 400 Hz; the middle marker aural signal was six dots per second at 1,300 Hz; the inner marker transmitted a continuous tone at 3,000 Hz. The aural signals thus conveyed a sense of increasing urgency as the pilot approached the runway. The marker beacons indicated distance to touchdown at only three points in the approach but when, later, DME was paired with ILS, this minor deficiency would be overcome. Significant for the future, the SCS-51 receiver produced electric currents proportional to divergence from the localizer or glideslope which could be used as input to an autopilot. The biggest problem for this concept was distortion caused by signal reflection from objects on the ground.

After 1945 civilian use of ILS spread rapidly. The CAA planned to have it in service at ninety-eight domestic airports in the USA by the end of October 1947; fifty of these were operational by summer.[30] By year-end twelve American airlines were authorized to use ILS at forty-three airports, with more being approved. The minimum ceiling at which an approach was allowed was 90 metres (300 feet) at most sites. A CAA subcommittee, convened in the winter of 1946–7, recommended ILS and High-Intensity Approach Lighting for a new total of 106 airports[31] and the International Civil Aviation Organization called for ILS to be installed at all international airports.[32] By mid-1947 SCS-51 had been installed in Europe at Prestwick, Brussels, Geneva, Amsterdam, Stockholm, Paris and Copenhagen, with an installation on the island of Jersey in 1948[33] and another at Dublin in 1949.[34]

In 1949 the CAA planned to have a complete blind navigation system, based on VOR, DME, ILS and GCA, covering the USA within five years. By 1949 300 VOR stations were in service with another 100 to be built, but there were only two DME installations in the country.[35]

Once the war was over, radar was taken off the secret list and was applied to civil aviation in various ways, some immediately useful, others promising, others abortive. Wartime radar technology designed to detect enemy aircraft had immediate potential for air traffic control in areas of high traffic density around airports. Approach control radar sets, transmitting on 3,000 and 10,000 MHz, had a range of 48 km (30 miles) horizontally and 1,500 metres (5,000 feet) vertically.[36] It was found that rain clouds and ground features appeared on the screen as 'clutter,' although this could be minimized by using Doppler shift.[37] Although the early radars of this type used unmodified aircraft returns, the use of a 'secondary' radar was foreseen which would display only returns from transponders, thus providing a picture free of clutter. The information was displayed in plan view on a cathode-ray tube known as a Plan Position Indicator (PPI). A refinement of this idea developed as Ground Controlled Approach (GCA).

In 1940 the Massachusetts Institute of Technology discovered that centimetric radar was precise enough to guide an aircraft's blind approach to an airfield.[38] By 1945 this had been developed into the system known as Ground Controlled Approach (GCA). GCA radar sets were mounted in vehicles and could be set up in 30 minutes, usually a mile from the touchdown point and 90–120 metres (300–400 feet) to one side of the runway centreline. A GCA installation was manned by a crew of five.

A 3,000 MHz radar was used for the 'search system,' covering an area of 24 km (15 miles) radius and up to 1,200 metres (4,000 feet) above ground level. The radar picture was displayed on two Plan Position Indicator cathode-ray tubes. Two directors handled inbound traffic, vectoring aircraft to final approach or issuing holding instructions. When the inbound aircraft was 460 metres (1,500 feet) above ground level, 11 km (7 miles) from touchdown and within 600 metres (2,000 feet) laterally of the final approach track, it was passed to the Controller.

A 10,000 MHz set was used for the 'approach system'. The information from this radar was presented on two cathode-ray tubes; one showed a plan view of the final approach, the other a side view of the glideslope. A crewman known as an Azimuth Tracker followed the aircraft's echo on the plan view screen with an illuminated cursor which drove a meter measuring divergence from the

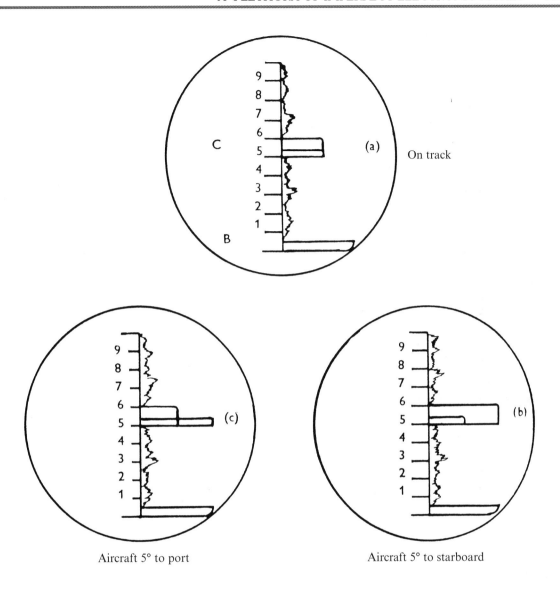

(a) On track

(b) Aircraft 5° to starboard

(c) Aircraft 5° to port

RAF Beam Approach Beacon System – instrument indications.

centreline. An Elevation Tracker did the same for the screen showing the glideslope. The Controller read the elevation and azimuth meters and radioed corrections to the pilot. The azimuth meter was accurate to within 15 metres (50 feet), the elevation meter to within 6 metres (20 feet). GCA could handle up to fifteen aircraft at the same time, with a landing every 3–4 minutes. Minima in Britain were 60 metres (200 feet) ceiling and 800 metres (0.5 mile) visibility, but the system was so easy to use by a proficient instrument pilot that landings were made in conditions of zero visibility by

30 *Flight*, 21 August 1947, 199
31 *Flight*, 25 December 1947, 727
32 *Flight*, 13 May 1948, 527
33 Ibid.
34 *Flight*, 10 March 1949, 281
35 *Flight*, 21 July 1949, 66
36 *Flight*, 20 March 1947, 244
37 Doppler effect: relative movement between a signal source and a receiver causes a difference in frequency between the emitted and received signals. In this case an aircraft would have a Doppler shift which a cloud would not.
38 *Flight*, 11 July 1946, 47

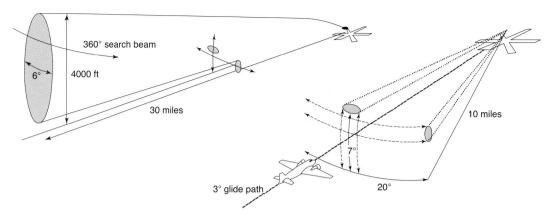

Diagrammatic representations of the sections of the radar beams used in the G.C.A. system Above is the search 'lobe' for which two plan position indicator tubes are used to give a 360 degree picture of the area within thirty miles of the air field. On the right is a detail diagram of the 'precision' part of the system, which is used to bring the aircraft in onto the runway.

Quest for All-Weather Flight Fig 119

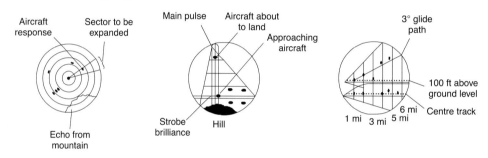

G.C.A. displays. (Left) Search display. (Centre) Azimuth precision display.
(Right) Composite precision display – a recently evolved improvement.

Ground Control Approach – layout and radar screen indications.

pilots who had had no previous training and, indeed, had never previously heard of the system.

By 1946 GCA was in extensive use in various parts of the world and in Britain nine RAF airfields were equipped by mid-year. Early in 1947 Airfield Control Radar and GCA were installed at London's new Heathrow airport.[39] GCA was planned for two airports in Ireland, Belfast Nutt's Corner and Shannon, in 1947.[40] GCA was seen as an effective interim measure, pending international standardization on new blind approach systems, especially as no extra equipment was needed in the aircraft.

In the first two weeks of January 1947, low cloud, snow, fog and icing covered large areas of the USA.[41] A number of fatal accidents resulted. The Army and Navy, however, operated in these conditions with impunity using GCA; Army transport aircraft were brought safely into east coast airports with ceilings of 60–120 metres (200–400 feet) and visibilities from 400 metres (0.25 mile) to almost zero. It was thought that civilian pilots did not make use of military GCA in such conditions because they did not know of its existence, were not familiar with it and distrusted giving up control of the aircraft.

The CAA arranged with the USAAF to provide GCA for civilian use at New York, Washington and Chicago, with tests to begin in 1947[42] and the CAA subcommittee convened in the winter of 1946–7 recommended that thirty to forty airports be equipped.[43] The success of GCA at New York and Chicago led to its immediate installation at four other airports.[44] At Gander, Newfoundland, a search radar with a range of 240 km (150 miles) was added to the existing GCA equipment.[45]

Early in 1947 RAF equipment and crews were loaned to the Ministry of Civil Aviation to train civilian crews on the London Heathrow GCA; they began using the equipment operationally in May and the Ministry took over from the RAF in July. Between 1 July and 2 December 1947, the unit handled 1,012 approaches, some in bad weather, some for practice. Pilots were enthusiastic and airlines in other European countries sent aircraft and crews for training. Approaches could be made down to 60 metres (200 feet) ceiling and 180 metres (600 feet) visibility. A GCA approach took 10 minutes compared with 15 minutes using SCS-51 or eight minutes using SBA. By the end of 1947 the London Heathrow GCA was judged a great success.[46] After a year in service 2,148 GCAs had been flown, half in blind conditions, half for practice.[47] Bad weather in November 1949 resulted in 343 ground-controlled approaches at Heathrow alone. Other UK civilian installations were at Prestwick, Aldermaston, Liverpool Speke, Bovingdon and London Northolt.[48]

During the war radar sets of three different kinds had been carried in aircraft, specifically designed to detect other aircraft (Airborne Interception, AI), to detect ships (Air to Surface Vessel, ASV) and for navigation by ground mapping (H2S). AI and ASV could also obtain range and bearing from Eureka transponder beacons on the ground. The twelve Short Solent flying boats built for BOAC in 1946–7 carried ASV Mk.II radar for homing to Eureka beacons.[49] Avro Tudors were to be similarly equipped. The radar carried by Boeing Stratocruisers was intended to detect turbulence, icing and high ground, to map coastlines for navigation and to use transponder beacons as an approach aid. The connection between turbulence and precipitation was already recognized; precipitation could be detected by radar.[50] Proponents hoped that airborne radar would become an all-seeing eye for blind conditions, able to detect high ground, turbulent clouds and other aircraft, but of all these potential uses, only the detection of turbulent clouds continues to the present.

Some other ideas were abortive. A combination of radar and radio DF, known as Condar, was designed to plot the range and bearing of an aircraft's VHF radio transmission automatically on a cathode-ray tube. Teleran was an idea so far ahead of its time that it never came to fruition. An approach control radar was to display aircraft echoes on a screen with navigation and weather information superimposed on a transparent sheet. A television camera was to view the composite plan and transmit it to a TV receiver in an aircraft, providing the crew with weather, navigation and traffic information on one screen. Teleran was also be adapted for approach guidance. The objectives of Teleran have never yet been combined into a single device.

One of the many tasks facing the post-war civil aviation community was to impose order and worldwide standards on this 'plethora of electronic riches'. On 7 December 1944, following a conference at Chicago in November,[51] fifty nations signed the International Civil Aviation Organization Convention, resulting in the formation of the International Civil Aviation Organization (ICAO).

The North Atlantic Air Route Service Conference,[52] held in Dublin in March 1946, recommended Consol and Loran for *en route* navigation, supported by HF radio DF. Loran was to cover the North Atlantic by January 1949, followed by Southeast Asia, Australasia, the Pacific, Africa and the South Atlantic in 1951. Thirty transatlantic terminal airports were listed; each was to have ILS. Numerous upper-air observation stations were needed in northeastern Canada, Greenland, Iceland and Norway, and thirteen weather ships in the Atlantic. A search-and-rescue organization was to be put in place.

In November 1946, the Radio Technical Division of the Provisional ICAO (PICAO) con-

39 *Flight*, 21 November 1946, 573
40 *Flight*, 17 July 1947, 61; 21 August 1947, 199
41 *Flight*, 13 February 1947, 163
42 *Flight*, 5 December 1946, 630
43 *Flight*, 25 December 1947, 727
44 *Flight*, 21 August 1947, 199
45 *Flight*, 25 September 1947, 369
46 *Flight*, 18 December 1947, 698
47 *Flight*, 22 July 1948, 101
48 *Flight*, 12 February 1948, 172
49 *Flight*, 10 April 1947, 321
50 Jones, F. E. 1949, 433
51 *Flight*, 15 December 1949, 760
52 *Flight*, 4 April 1946, 347

cluded its discussions in Montreal.[53] The SCS-51 Instrument Landing System came through as the best available blind approach system and was recommended for all international airports by the end of 1950, with radar and a means for precise distance measuring to be added.

The solution was less clear for short-range navigation, where existing American and European systems were in conflict, and PICAO hesitated to make a recommendation. VOR/DME was the most promising of the available systems and was recommended for international routes at least until 1955. Radio ranges were to be retained for use near airports. The debate between voice and Morse for air-ground communication went on for a surprisingly long time. This was less surprising when considered from the viewpoint of a polyglot Europe. The PICAO came down in favour of voice as the primary means of air-ground communication. The ICAO would be much abused for ineffectiveness, indecision and political partiality in several long, hard-fought disputes in the coming years.

53 *Flight*, 5 December 1946, 629

CHAPTER 16

The Problem of Landing in Fog

In spite of the technical developments just described, the problem of landing in fog, especially at night, remained dangerous and intractable. In North America only a few cities were affected; fog-free airports were seldom far away. In northwest Europe fog, especially when mixed with industrial pollution, covered large areas for long periods. The problem was tackled in three ways. Attempts to disperse fog were short-lived. Runway lighting and devices in the cockpit helped pilots to land manually in progressively lower visibilities. The ultimate solution was achieved when the aircraft landed itself.

As the RAF offensive against Germany intensified in 1941–2 so did the problem of fog forming over the bombers' bases in their absence. A solution was demanded at the highest levels of the British government.[1] Blind landing, whether manual or automatic, was not possible at that time, nor was there any immediate prospect of its becoming so. Efforts therefore turned to fog dispersal, hence the acronym: FIDO (Fog Investigation and Dispersal Operation).[2] Every conceivable method was considered: supersonic waves, large electrical discharges, chemical absorption, refrigeration, bulk conditioning of the air, aero-engines blowing warm air across an airfield. The scientists working on the project agreed that fog could be evaporated if enough heat could be generated. This idea was not new and earlier studies that had been abandoned in 1939 were taken up anew in September 1942, involving several major British companies: Imperial Chemical Industries, General Electric Company, the Gas Light and Coal Company and the London Midland and Scottish Railway.

The result consisted of a line of pipes and petrol burners along each side of a runway to evaporate the fog and provide a clear area over the runway. Air Vice-Marshal D. C. T. Bennett, commanding 8 (Pathfinder) Group, Bomber Command, enthusiastically endorsed this idea.[3] The first trial installation was built at RAF Graveley in January 1943, with a second at Downham Market, both Pathfinder bases. Perversely, fog thick enough for a test did not occur until 17 July 1943; FIDO increased visibility from 90 metres (300 feet) in the fog to 1,190 metres (3,900 feet) over the runway. An aircraft took off and landed four times. The first operational users were four Halifaxes on 19 November 1943. Six other FIDOs were built in August and September 1943, ready for the winter of 1943–4.

One flight test report describes not only FIDO but also the British weather that this and other blind landing systems would have to deal with. Wing Commander J. Wooldridge reported that:

> The fog over Downham Market had lain for three days and considerable amounts of cloud had drifted in above. This cloud was giving a percentage of precipitation which implied that FIDO had to deal with moisture 70% beyond its capacity.[4]

> At 1600 on November 21 (1943) the test aircraft (an Airspeed Oxford) took off from RAF Station Feltwell and set course for RAF Station Downham Market, where a specimen landing was to be attempted.

> The ground was obscured immediately after take-off and the fog bank eventually cleared between 300–400 feet. A cloud layer was then seen to be lying 300 feet above the aircraft and there were additional indications of cloud extending in further layers up to 15,000 feet. The

---

1 *Flight*, 21 November 1946, 573; 6 March 1947, 193; West, W. 1957, 26
2 FIDO is fully documented in Williams, G. *Flying Through Fire: FIDO – The Fogbuster of World War Two*, Allan Sutton Publishing Ltd., UK, 1995.
3 Bennett, D. C. T. 1958; 1988 ed., 180
4 Quoted in *Flight*, 6 March 1947, 194

A FIDO burn.

windscreen of the aircraft was misted over with moisture throughout. The aircraft set course for Downham, flying solely on instruments, and the Downham beam was picked up successfully shortly after take-off. So bad were general conditions, however, that the lighted burners were not sighted until the aircraft was flying at 1,500 feet across the aerodrome, and they first appeared as a considerable diffused red glow. By the time we were directly overhead the plan of the burners could be seen quite clearly through the intervening mist and low cloud.

Normal beam approach procedure was carried out, with the aircraft again flying in completely blind conditions until it reached a point almost 1,000 yards from the beginning of the runway. From that point on, the burners became progressively more visible and the pilot was able to line up his aircraft by looking out ahead and a satisfactory landing was carried out. Local met. informed us that the cloud base was below 100 feet with moderately heavy rain.

The glow of a FIDO burn was also a navigation beacon, sometimes visible from 80 km (50 miles)

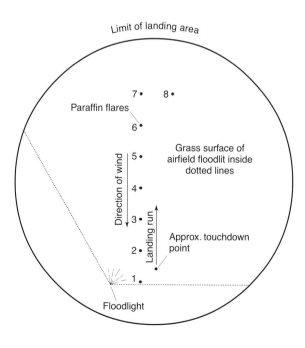

Earliest RAF airfield lighting.

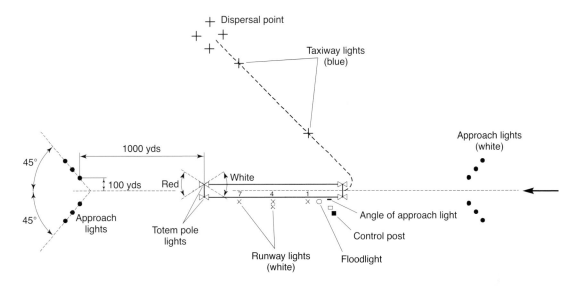

Lighting equipment at Drem Aerodrome

Approach lights – 60 watt lamps in bulkhead fittings. Visible all round.
Runway lights – 15 watt lamps. Visible 15° above horizontal and 30° azimuth.
Totem poles – 5 lights arranged as vertical bar. Same lamps and cut-off as runway lights.
Floodlight – Consumption 4 kW. maximum intensity 1,000,000 candles. Horizontal divergance 100°.
Angle of approach light – Yellow upper sector, green middle sector, red lower sector.

RAF 'Drem' airfield lighting system.

away. Fuel consumption was astronomical: 341,000 litres (75,000 gallons) per hour at a normal FIDO, while the big units at the three outsized emergency runways at Woodbridge, Carnaby and Manston could burn 18,200 litres (4,000 gallons) per minute. By 1945 fifteen FIDOs were available in the UK; 2,500 landings had been made using FIDO, involving 10,000 aircrew.

When the war ended only the Manston FIDO was retained for emergencies, although another was built at London Blackbushe in 1947.[5] FIDO was not planned for Heathrow because of improving radar and approach aids and because it could disperse fog only in still air.[6] A FIDO was installed at Arcata, California, in 1947 and another, using diesel oil, at Los Angeles in 1949. The Los Angeles system was designed to increase the ceiling in the approach area from 23 metres (75 feet) to 90 metres (300 feet) and visibility from 550 metres (1,800 feet) to 1,190 metres (3,900 feet) in two minutes at a cost of $200. The Manston FIDO was still in service in 1957. An attempt to disperse fog at Paris Orly by releasing atomized propane worked only when the temperature of the fog was below freezing.[7] United Airlines tried to disperse fog by

seeding it with dry ice at eighteen airports in 1967 and more trials followed in California in 1968.[8] Other experiments were made in Norway and at London Heathrow.[9] FIDO was doomed by its operating costs and the whole concept of fog dispersal died out during the 1960s as advances in low-visibility landing finally made such attempts obsolete.

The conversion to night operations forced on RAF Bomber Command early in the Second World War increased the attention paid to airfield lighting.[10] Pre-war British military airfields were grass-surfaced. For night flying a line of paraffin flares indicated the wind direction and a floodlight illuminated the approach end of the field. Aircraft landed away from the floodlight and to the right of the flares. Wartime conditions and paved runways

5 *Flight,* 23 October 1947, 478; 6 November 1947, 527
6 *Flight,* 7 February 1946, 145
7 *Flight International,* 7 March 1963
8 *Flight International,* 2 November 1967, 718; 30 May 1968, 820
9 *Flight International,* 19 December 1968, 1019
10 Calvert, E. S. 1948

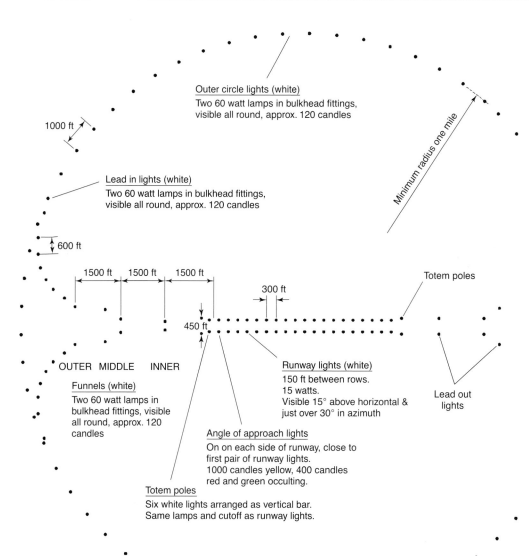

Outer circle lights (white)
Two 60 watt lamps in bulkhead fittings,
visible all round, approx. 120 candles

Minimum radius one mile

1000 ft

Lead in lights (white)
Two 60 watt lamps in bulkhead fittings,
visible all round, approx. 120 candles

600 ft

1500 ft   1500 ft   1500 ft

300 ft

Totem poles

450 ft

OUTER   MIDDLE   INNER

Runway lights (white)
150 ft between rows.
15 watts.
Visible 15° above horizontal &
just over 30° in azimuth

Funnels (white)
Two 60 watt lamps in
bulkhead fittings, visible
all round, approx. 120
candles

Lead out
lights

Angle of approach lights
On on each side of runway, close to
first pair of runway lights.
1000 candles yellow, 400 candles
red and green occulting.

Totem poles
Six white lights arranged as vertical bar.
Same lamps and cutoff as runway lights.

RAF Airfield Lighting Mark II.

made this system obsolete. A floodlight revealed the airfield to the enemy from great distances; a flarepath was needed that could be turned on and off. A hard-surfaced runway had too little texture for the pilot to judge his height; long runways could not be floodlit for their full length. Ground mist made this system useless.

The best of several extemporary installations was at RAF Drem in the autumn of 1940. Six white approach lights were arranged in a 90° V, 550 metres (1,800 feet) wide, 900 metres (3,000 feet) from the runway threshold. The runway was marked by lights at its four corners, three lights along the left-hand edge and a floodlight. The approach lights were visible from all directions, whereas the runway lights were visible only for 30°

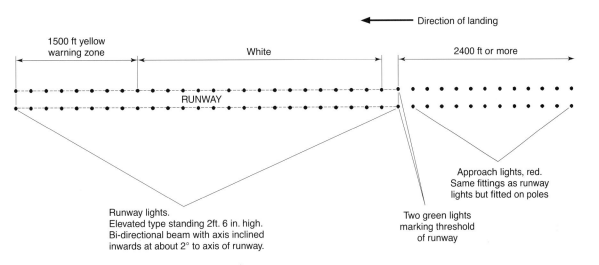

Direction of landing

1500 ft yellow warning zone

White

2400 ft or more

RUNWAY

Approach lights, red. Same fittings as runway lights but fitted on poles

Runway lights. Elevated type standing 2ft. 6 in. high. Bi-directional beam with axis inclined inwards at about 2° to axis of runway.

Two green lights marking threshold of runway

Notes:
Distance between lights in a row, 200 ft.
Distance between rows = width of runway + 20 ft.
Power consumed per fitting usually 200 watts (some later models 300 watts).
Approximate divergence of beam, 1° at maximum intensity; 4° at 1/10 maximum intensity.
Approximate maximum intensity, 35,000 candles, white; 7,000 candles, red and green.

US Army Air Corps Bartow airfield lighting system.

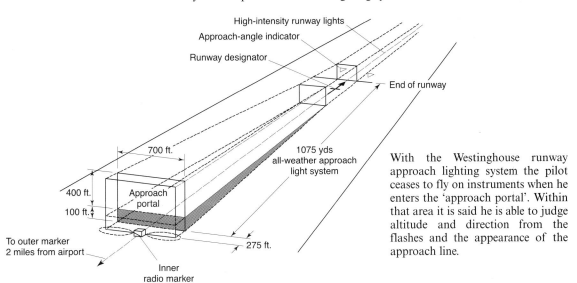

High-intensity runway lights

Approach-angle indicator

Runway designator

End of runway

700 ft.

1075 yds all-weather approach light system

400 ft.

100 ft.

Approach portal

To outer marker 2 miles from airport

275 ft.

Inner radio marker

With the Westinghouse runway approach lighting system the pilot ceases to fly on instruments when he enters the 'approach portal'. Within that area it is said he is able to judge altitude and direction from the flashes and the appearance of the approach line.

Westinghouse approach lighting system.

in azimuth and 15° in elevation. An approach slope indicator was so arranged that the pilot saw a yellow light if he was too high, a red light if he was too low and a green light if he was on the correct approach slope.

A circle of white lights passing through the approach lights was added to the Drem system, the result being known as Airfield Lighting Mark I. In 1941 the radius of the light circle was increased to one mile; lead-in lights were added from the circle to the approach lights; the number of approach lights was increased to three sets comprising six

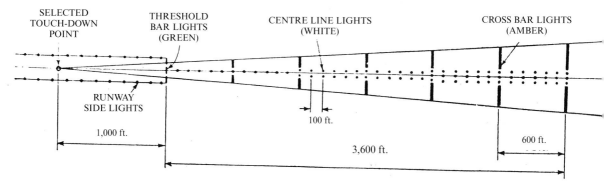

London Heathrow approach lighting system.

Diagrammatic plan of approach system proposed for London Airport. Coding is given by triple centre-line lights in the first sector, double lights in the middle sector and single lights in the final sector.

in a V, four in a V, and two side by side; the runway was marked by lights along both edges. An important discovery was that the lights along each side of the runway allowed a pilot to judge height accurately enough for a safe touchdown. The floodlights were eliminated. This system became standard, known as Airfield Lighting Mark II. It needed 2.9 km (1.8 miles) visibility or more, with no other lights nearby on the ground. It could not, therefore, be used by civil aviation when the black-out was lifted at the end of the war.

In 1942 RAF pilots discovered that the yellow sodium runway lights used in a training system to synthesize night conditions in daylight made a good landing aid in low visibility by day. The Sodium Flarepath Type F was the first use of runway lights as a landing aid in daylight and low visibility.

When breaking out of low cloud or flying an approach through fog, the pilot's view of the ground was often dangerously uncertain. The first blind approach experiments in the 1920s used aircraft capable of flying at only 110 km/h (60 knots) on final approach, but the new types of aircraft introduced in the 1930s and 1940s flew final approaches at progressively higher speeds. A DC-3, for example, flew at 165 km/h (90 knots) on final approach, a Lancaster at 195 km/h (105 knots) and a Stirling at 220 km/h (120 knots). This allowed the pilot less time to adapt from an instrument approach to a visual landing; in low ceilings or visibilities better lighting was needed to provide unambiguous references at the runway threshold.

The Americans were the first to use approach lights to help with this transition. A system devised by J. B. Bartow was tested in 1943 at a USAAF base in Newfoundland and was adopted for general use in 1944. Two parallel lines of red lights extended 730 metres (2,400 feet) or more back from the threshold, which was marked by two green lights. The runway was edged with white lights. The last 460 metres (1,500 feet) of the runway was marked with yellow warning lights.

Westinghouse Electric made an important contribution with a new lighting system which was tried at Cleveland, Ohio, in 1947.[11] The lights ran from the inner marker 975 metres (3,200 feet) to the threshold. Thirty-six krypton lights alternated with thirty-six neon lights. Each krypton light produced a 113-million-lumen (9-million-candle power) flash in a sequence giving the illusion of a light travelling along the ground towards the runway forty times a minute. This system, known as 'the rabbit', is still in use. A green arrow or a flashing red cross at the threshold showed whether the runway was clear for landing. The runway was edged with powerful lights at 60-metre (200-foot) intervals.

The days of landing into wind on a grass field, and of mobile radio approach aids that could be moved to suit the wind direction, were coming to an end. Apart from the need for paving to handle increasing aircraft weights, a runway fully equipped for blind approach was becoming a costly, static installation. This could only increase the incidence of crosswind landings and hasten the obsolescence of tailwheel aircraft; the ground looping hazard inherent in the tailwheel design was increasingly unacceptable.[12]

The leading British expert on airfield lighting

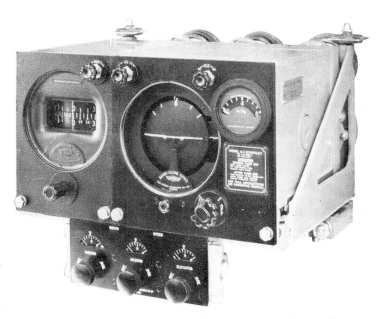

The Sperry A3 autopilot, gyroscopic instruments and controls.

was E. S. Calvert, in charge of the Illuminations Section, Electrical Engineering Department, RAE Farnborough,[13] where he had worked since 1928. Calvert designed a system of approach lighting which was installed experimentally at Farnborough in 1947. The approach lights extended 1,100 metres (3,600 feet) back from the threshold. White lights formed the centreline, three parallel rows for the first 365 metres (1,200 feet), two parallel rows for 365 metres (1,200 feet) and one row for the last 365 metres (1,200 feet) to the threshold. A cross-bar of amber lights was placed at every 183 metres (600 feet) as a horizon reference; the ends of each bar subtended an angle of 4° converging on the touchdown point 305 metres (1,000 feet) down the runway from the threshold. The threshold was marked with green lights; the runway was edged with white lights. This system resulted from studies with a purpose-built simulator and was scheduled for London Heathrow in 1948–9.[14] By 1948 more than 400 pilots had made more than 8,000 simulated landings in the course of this research.

In 1948 the British commented smugly[15] that in the USA, approximately two million dollars had been spent in 1947, conducting an investigation into the requirements of approach lighting. Nevertheless, the Americans had still not devised a system with which they were satisfied. The USAAF

had adopted the Bartow system as standard, while the airlines had adopted a variation using only a single line of approach lights extending from the left side of the runway. A system combining approach and glideslope guidance was scheduled for tests at New York Idlewild and twelve other American airports in 1949.[16] Standardization was important, as different systems could only produce confusion at a critical stage in the flight.

The problem of landing in dense fog would ultimately be solved by automatic flight control. The autopilots in service up to 1945, however, did not function properly over the whole speed range of the aircraft. They were complicated to use and needed frequent readjustment. The aircraft was sometimes briefly uncontrollable when the autopilot was engaged or disengaged. Malfunctions could cause terrifying manoeuvres. This last problem precluded autocoupled approaches other than experimentally.

By 1945 the American Sperry A-3 had become almost the standard automatic pilot in transport

11 *Flight*, 29 May 1947, 506
12 *Flight*, 21 February 1946, 181
13 Calvert, E. S. 1948; *Flight*, 22 April 1948, 450
14 *Flight*, 29 April 1948, 457
15 Ibid.
16 *Flight*, 17 March 1949, 310

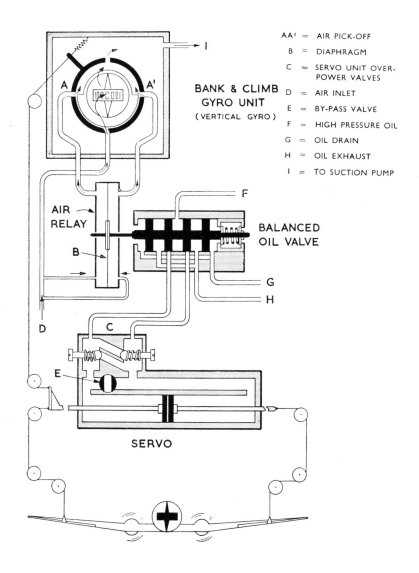

AA'	=	AIR PICK-OFF
B	=	DIAPHRAGM
C	=	SERVO UNIT OVER-POWER VALVES
D	=	AIR INLET
E	=	BY-PASS VALVE
F	=	HIGH PRESSURE OIL
G	=	OIL DRAIN
H	=	OIL EXHAUST
I	=	TO SUCTION PUMP

The Sperry A3 autopilot – schematic of aileron control.

aircraft.[17] New in that year was the Sperry A-12, driven by two gyroscopes, one for pitch and roll and one for direction, referenced to a Gyrosyn compass. Interlocks prevented engagement of the autopilot, or disengaged it automatically, if certain conditions such as live electric power were not met. The A-12 incorporated an independent automatic elevator trim that prevented the autopilot from fighting an out-of-trim condition. This had been a deficiency in earlier autopilots. The pilot's controls consisted of a turn control, elevator and aileron trim controls and an altitude-hold option. The complete unit weighed 54 kg (120 pounds).

Significant for the future, the A-12 could be coupled to the localizer and glideslope receivers of the new SCS-51 Instrument Landing System.

In Britain Smith's Aircraft Instruments Ltd had been active in autopilot development since the 1930s. The company's research organization was headed by F. W. Meredith, who had been connected with autopilot development since 1925, initially applied to pilotless aircraft for use as anti-aircraft gunnery targets. In 1947 the company brought out the SEP-1 autopilot, incorporating the best features of the latest German and American designs.[18] Like the Sperry A-12, the SEP-

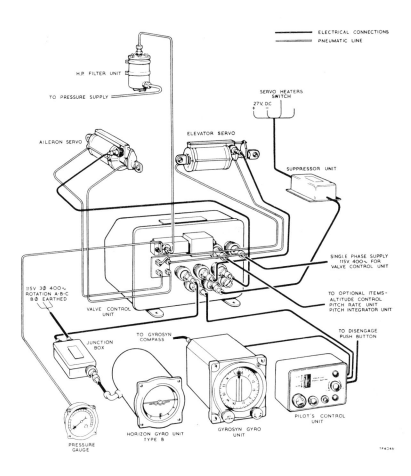

The Sperry AL30 autopilot – schematic.

1 was electrically powered. A significant innovation was that the servomotors moved the control surfaces at rates corresponding to the rate of rotation of the aircraft about its axes rather than by amounts corresponding to the amounts of displacement from the desired attitude of flight. The result was a rapid and sensitive response which, combined with the construction and mounting of the gyroscopes, one for each axis, allowed the autopilot, in laboratory conditions, to detect a rotation of less than 0.01°. The rudder gyroscope was monitored by a compass. The SEP-1 was 'officially regarded as the most advanced automatic pilot in the world'.[19]

The status and possibilities of automatic flight control, as they were in 1947, were spectacularly demonstrated by a fully automatic transatlantic flight by a C-54 of the USAAF Air Materiel Command All-Weather Flying Division based at

Wilmington, Ohio, on 22 September of that year.[20] The pilot, Captain Thomas J. Wells, positioned the aircraft for take-off at Stephenville, Newfoundland, and pressed a master switch; the aircraft then flew itself to touchdown at Brize Norton in England.

The autopilot was programmed with twelve sequences initiated by inputs from the radar altimeter, flux valve compass, air miles computer, pitot system, ADF and ILS. Automatic control of engine power was a significant innovation. The automatic landing was achieved by following the glideslope to touchdown. There was a device,

17 *Flight*, 31 October 1945, 463
18 *Flight*, 25 September 1947, 364
19 *Flight*, 9 October 1947, 415
20 *Flight*, 9 October 1947, 415; Taylor, M. J. H., Mondey, D. 1983

Boeing 247 with the RAF Telecommunications Flying Unit, used for blind landing trials, 1944.

sources are not specific, to flare the aircraft out immediately before touchdown.[21] The equipment weighed 204 kg (450 pounds), small in an aircraft the size of a C-54, but, even so, work was in progress to reduce the weight to less than 45 kg (100 pounds).

Automatic flare-out was planned, using a precise radar altimeter. One of the problems of radar altimetry was the variable reflectivity of the ground, but if the ILS could bring the aircraft over the runway, the radar altimeter had a surface of constant reflectivity by which to control the aircraft to touchdown.

It was foreseen, even in 1947, that automation would eliminate navigators, radio operators and flight engineers, but never the pilots, who would monitor the automatic equipment and take over if it failed. Even so, equipment failure on a blind final approach was a critical issue that will reappear in this narrative.

Britain was still making a difficult recovery from the war. The British attitude to this American achievement was: 'One of the tremendous advantages enjoyed by our friends in America is the – to our minds – seemingly limitless amount of money and manpower they can devote to any given task. We have sterner conditions to contend with over here.' Nevertheless, European weather would provide an incentive to develop fully automatic landing that would be lacking in America.

The question of who made the first fully automatic landing is not easily answered. Simple biplanes had made automatic landings whereby the pilot set up a glide with a small amount of power; a trailing weight closed the throttle automatically when it struck the ground. Semi-automatic landings from a glide to touchdown were made experimentally during the 1930s, notably in the USA, as mentioned earlier.

An interesting claim was made in a letter written

to *Flight International* in April 1964 by Group Captain J. A. McDonald.[22] He wrote that the first automatic landing was made in October 1944 by a Boeing 247 operated jointly by the RAF and USAAF at the Telecommunications Flying Unit at Defford, UK. The pilot was Squadron Leader J. Stewart, using a Minneapolis Honeywell autopilot. The aircraft was equipped with Rebecca and a DME set with automatic homing and orbiting designed and built by Flying Officer Barber. The landing system was SCS-51, which had been sent to Defford for demonstration to the US 8th Air Force. The autocoupling device was designed and built by Lieutenant Colonel F. Moseley. The aircraft flew about 300 hours on automatic approach and landing trials.

Group Captain McDonald wrote:

> The decision to equip this aircraft for autolanding trials followed the success of the SCS-51 ILS trials under Colonel Francis Moseley. Moseley is generally credited with designing the first military ILS. The concept of linking the autopilot with the ILS was entirely Moseley's. I well remember the first flights in a B-24, when Moseley carried the black-box equipment (breadboard fashion) on his knees: there were some dicey moments. At the time I was CO of the unit and co-ordinated the project and demonstrations.
>
> The designer of the first SEP autopilot (Moriarty) flew with us on one occasion. I remember his asking, 'Has my autopilot to do all this?' 'Yes, and more,' I replied. 'Give me a cup of tea, I'm not feeling very well,' he said …
>
> It all happened rather by accident. The war was ending. We had completed the ILS (SCS-51) trials and were rather bored. 'Let's put the whole system on the automatic pilot,' said Moseley, and off we went. Moseley, Stewart, and Barber were a rare combination of experts in instrument flying and electronics.

In January 1945 a completely blind automatic landing was made at night.[23]

In 1946 the RAF Blind Landing Experimental Unit was formed in the UK to continue these developments. Experiments were flown with Lancasters and Halifaxes, but tailwheel aircraft in general and these aircraft in particular were unsatisfactory for automatic landing because of their handling characteristics on final approach and touchdown. Prominent among the many problems facing the designers of automatic landing systems was the effect of crosswinds.[24] Not only was the wind likely to change in strength and direction as the aircraft flew down the glideslope but also, especially in strong, gusty crosswinds, a complicated series of rapid and delicate control movements and power adjustments was needed to land the aircraft safely. Paved runways, needed for increasing aircraft weights, meant that a high incidence of landings with at least some crosswind component was inevitable. Handling characteristics in crosswinds were therefore critical; tailwheel aircraft performed poorly in this regard. This aroused much controversy, both with the Air Ministry and with British aircraft manufacturers, because the British persisted with large tailwheel aircraft long after the Americans had gone over to nosewheel landing gear for all new aircraft types. McDonald wrote: 'The Ministry blew its top. Farnborough was furious and jealous of our results.'

The characteristics of localizer and glidescope signals had the results that a localizer could be tracked down to the runway and then along it, but a glideslope could not be followed to touchdown because of distortion just above the ground and it made no provision for flare-out. In the last seconds before touchdown, therefore, the aircraft had to relinquish the guidance of the glideslope and complete the landing by sensing the runway beneath it. This would depend on radar altimetry. The radar altimeters available in 1945 were accurate to only 3 metres (10 feet), but improvements were anticipated as microwave technology developed. The Germans had elaborated the mathematical relationship between altitude and time to touchdown. The FuG-101 radar altimeter was so designed that no current passed through a centre-zero ammeter when this relationship was achieved. Keeping the needle on zero theoretically provided the pilot with a glideslope. This device is mentioned as an example of German ingenuity rather than for any effect that it had on the development of automatic landing.

The most important advance in blind approach and landing during the 1940s was the widespread adoption of the SCS-51 Instrument Landing System which has been the worldwide standard ever since. Most subsequent developments in auto-

21 *Flight*, 12 April 1957, 488
22 *Flight International*, 30 April 1964, 737
23 Williams, J. E. D. 1992, 193
24 Pritchard, H. C. 1946

matic landing used the ILS as their basis. In early 1947 BOAC experimented with a Liberator, with its Sperry A-12 autopilot coupled to the SCS-51, to fly automatic approaches followed by manual landings. The test flying was done at Prestwick, with crosswinds up to 75 km/h (40 knots); sometimes the aircraft was flown automatically to 6–9 metres (20–30 feet) above the runway before the pilot took control. Automatic approach using SCS-51 and the Sperry A-12 spread rapidly in Europe.

Some pilots of exceptional skill did from time to time hand-fly completely blind landings using only the ILS and their blind-flying instruments. For the most part these were isolated emergency or experimental events. The aircrew of the French night airmail service, however, met the problem head-on and made routine manual landings at night in dense fog using only standard airline navigation aids, VOR/ILS and ADF, VHF communication and radar altimeters. This continued at least into the mid-1960s. La Postale de Nuit was set up in 1945 and operated entirely by night.[25] By 1964, after more than 110,000 flights, not one take-off had been cancelled or even delayed by weather. The regularity of service was 99.8%. In 1963, out of 11,698 night landings, only seven were diverted because of bad visibility and no more than 15% of arrivals were five or more minutes late. The aircraft fleet of the 1960s comprised fifteen DC-3s and five DC-4s. A Ju-52 of the service crashed fatally in 1948 and a DC-3 in 1953 but from then until 1964 more than 90,000 landings were achieved without injury.

Permanent three-man crews and the standardization of equipment and instrument layout were important factors. The crews achieved a high standard of proficiency by going through the complete procedure even in clear weather. As a result the night airmail flew when all other aircraft were grounded and road traffic was barely moving. An English aviation journalist was treated to a demonstration in 1964:

> We left Le Bourget … at 2315 hr. in a DC-4 operating Postale flight AF 1021 to Nice, with scheduled traffic stops at Lyons and Marseilles. It was a beautiful night without a breath of wind; but as we rumbled south on the first leg Lyons was steadily fogging itself in, and presently the tower announced an actual of 300 metres with 200 feet vertical, deteriorating fast. By the time we were overhead Lyons Ville, a faintly pale patch in the white blanket far below, a north-bound Postale DC-3 trying to get in for the second time reported that visibility was down to 100 metres and still falling.
>
> The captain decreed that we should start the ball rolling with a *présentation* at 100 feet. In front of us the DC-3 had turned around in 8 minutes flat and was taxiing out again for Paris, reporting barely 80 metres visibility in the process. But still, commented ATC hopefully, it might perhaps stir the fog up for us a bit … As the first tentacles of the odious white stuff started flickering over the windshield the radio altimeter steadied on 500 feet and the next second we were completely immersed.
>
> With the loss of precious height, the tint of the opaque wall changed from the colour of the night to a dirty, baleful yellow. But the voices intoning power commands and altimeter readings remained as impassive as ever – … *cent pieds* (100 feet) … *quatre-vingt-dix* (90 feet) … *quatre-vingt pieds* (80 feet) … *soixante-quinze* (75 feet) … *soixante-dix* (70 feet) … Then something dim flicked by under the port wing, the captain chimed in evenly with '*Remettez les gaz*,' and we overshot with a roar …
>
> A brief conference followed. The first officer thought he had identified a threshold light, but only through coming right down to 70 feet. This was a prime example of crew sympathy: they had planned a *présentation* at 100 feet, but when nobody spotted anything from that height no word was necessary to agree a change of plan. The captain had perceived one sodium, but decided we were too high to initiate an attitude change. The engineer had seen nothing at all, but his voice showed no trace of sharpening with anxiety as the aircraft sank below the predetermined height. He knew very well what the captain had in mind.

They flew a second *présentation* at 15 metres (50 feet) without seeing anything.

> It was obvious now that visibility had dropped right off to around 50 metres/50 feet, so for our third try the captain rearranged the workload. The first officer was to look after ILS only, while the skipper monitored the display, called the orders and watched for the lights.
>
> I shall never forget what followed. Listening to the altitude sinking to 20 feet with no variation in a blank opaqueness that one could almost

touch … was a horrible experience. Off came the power, and the enormous brute began floating blindly. Then there was a gentle squeal, the watery flare of sodiums swimming by each side with agonizing infrequency, and I knew that, somehow, we were down.

In visibilities such as this navigation on the ground was a problem.

One night last winter the base of the fog layer at one of the stops was just about six feet above the concrete. The airport vehicles were crawling about slowly, but the crew of the DC-4 that had just landed were completely blind at a height of 15 feet and could not even see to taxi. So the Post Office vans were driven onto the runway, the brown sacks were piled aboard and the aircraft took off downwind on the ILS localizer.

This would never become a normal operation in passenger service. The key to blind landing lay in automation. By 1950 autopilot development was so far advanced that an autopilot could fly an aircraft more accurately for longer than a human pilot. New logical connections were also becoming apparent. The safety and economics of turbine-powered airliners demanded an orderly traffic flow in all weather conditions;[26] automatic flight control was recognized as being essential to this process.[27] At the same time aircraft designers were realizing that automatic control would have be designed into future high-performance aircraft from the outset, not merely added on as before. These developments set the scene for the drive towards fully automatic blind landing in airline service that would follow during the next thirty years.

25 *Flight International*, 17 December 1964, 1041
26 *Flight*, 18 August 1949, 182
27 Nesbitt, F. G., article in *Sperryscope*, quoted in *Flight*, 18 August 1949, 182

CHAPTER 17

Airlines in the Post-war Era

Before the Second World War, commercial transport aircraft carried small volumes of mail and freight and small numbers of venturesome passengers over short distances. Few people had flown in an aeroplane. After the war, long-range, four-engined, pressurized airliners that had been in the design stage in the late 1930s transformed commercial aviation into a transport system linking the farthest points of the globe and with the potential for mass transport to rival surface means. Never again, however, would the airlines lead the way in all-weather flying. The Second World War was followed by the forty-year arms race of the Cold War. The airlines became the beneficiaries of military technology, the development of which could never have been financed privately. While some secret military all-weather flying aids, such as radar and hyperbolic navigation, were opened to civilian use as soon as war ended, others, such as Gee-H, remained secret, as did many military systems developed after 1945. Even if their existence was known, their details and capabilities were highly classified. The post-war progress of military all-weather flying is correspondingly more difficult to trace.

At the end of the 1930s, Europe-licensed commercial aircraft were slightly more numerous than their American counterparts, although many were of American manufacture. In 1938 British airlines operated 120 aircraft.[1] At the end of 1939 Lufthansa owned 145.[2] In 1941 US air carriers flew 322 aircraft, of which 80% were DC-3s,[3] a preponderance of one type never matched before or since.

The first of the American four-engined aircraft was the Boeing B-17, which flew for the first time on 28 July 1935, the same year as the prototype DC-3. A passenger derivative was the Boeing 307 Stratoliner with a fuselage pressurized at 17.24 kilopascals (2.5 psi) above ambient pressure. Pressurization allowed passengers to be flown without oxygen masks at altitudes above 3,000

metres (10,000 feet) and thus above the worst turbulence and icing. The 307's maximum gross weight of 19,050 kg (42,000 pounds) was almost double that of a DC-3. The prototype flew in 1938. Only ten were ever built. They flew for airlines in the last few years before the war and were then impressed into military service.[4]

The Douglas DC-4 first flew in 1942, militarized as the C-54. Although unpressurized, it carried a payload of 9,980 kg (22,000 pounds), almost the gross weight of a DC-3. Even as the C-54 was entering service in 1943, came the first flight of the pressurized Lockheed L-049 Constellation, militarized as the C-69. The design was stretched from the original L-049 at a maximum gross weight of 37,200 kg (82,000 pounds) to the L-1649 of the 1950s, weighing up to 70,760 kg (156,000 pounds) and cruising at more than 555 km/h (300 knots). The DC-4 was developed into the pressurized DC-6 of 1946 and the DC-7C of the 1950s, increasing in gross weight from the C-54's 23,590 kg (52,000 pounds) to 64,865 kg (143,000 pounds) in the DC-7C. The B-29 was developed into the 66,225 kg (146,000 pound) Boeing Stratocruiser.

The British developed the 30,845 kg (68,000 pound) Avro York from the Lancaster airframe as a military transport; it first flew in 1942 and remained in RAF and BOAC service until 1957. The Handley Page Halifax bomber appeared in a transport version as the Halton. More extensively redesigned, pressurized, but with a chequered career was the 32,205 kg (71,000 pound) Avro Tudor, based on the Lancaster/Lincoln airframe. Handley Page produced the 36,290 kg (80,000 pound) Hastings, an RAF transport which first flew in 1947, followed by the civilian Hermes. The

1 Cochrane, R., 1947
2 Davies, R. E. G. 1991, 64
3 *Flying*, April 1990, 104
4 Taylor, M. J. H. 1989, 173

Lockheed Constellation.

Boeing Stratocruiser.

De Havilland Comet.

twin-engined Bristol Freighter and Vickers Viking entered service in 1945–6.

The aircraft available for British civilian use in 1945 were a mixture of DC-3s and converted bombers; most new purpose-built transports were American. Initially the British had nothing to compare with the DC-4 and the Constellation, as their wartime effort had been devoted to combat aircraft, but in the late 1940s they established a sudden technical lead over the Americans with the turbojet de Havilland Comet and the turboprop Vickers Viscount, while the Americans were still building piston-engined airliners. The British suffered from being first in the jet airliner field; the structural failure of three Comet 1s in 1953–4 set the British back by four years. The Comet 4 flew in 1958 but by that time it had been made obsolete by the Boeing 707 (first flight 1954) and Douglas DC-8 (1958). The 707 benefited from the engineering that went into the B-47 and B-52, whereas the Comet had no military predecessor. Technical merit was unable to overcome an American dominance in transport aircraft based on a huge domestic market. After 1945 German aviation development was eclipsed for thirty years. The French aircraft industry recovered rapidly after the war but made little impact on an international scene dominated by the Americans and the British.

Civilian air transport in North America was not greatly disrupted by the war and indeed benefited from increased demand. In Europe commercial flying was progressively shut down as the war intensified. It was only gradually reactivated as the war ended with help from British and American military air transport, using a mixture of European and American navigation systems and IFR procedures, and underwent a difficult and dangerous resurrection. The British Isles, with their incessantly hostile weather, emerged as one of the hubs in the new global air traffic system.

One UK Ministry of Civil Aviation air traffic controller[5] stated in 1950: 'In the hope of an early ICAO agreement on aids and procedures only the most urgent problems were tackled. Procedures

Vickers Viscount.

had to be based on the inaccurate MF aids which were carried by most aircraft and were therefore far from ideal.' Post-war commercial flying in the UK was based on a pre-war outmoded organization, some pre-war outmoded navigation facilities, a mixture of communication systems, pre-war outmoded civil airports plus discarded military airfields in locations unplanned for civilian operations, non-existent procedures, and outmoded legislation. There were no mandatory weather minima for take-off or landing. As late as 1949 one British pilot[6] wrote: 'One of the ways to help the pilot and to ensure a common standard of operation and adequate safety margins, is to impose weather minima. Its value is a debatable point among pilots, but if applied and used intelligently, I consider it a definite requirement today.' Aircrew proficiency was uneven. Many inexperienced civilian operators went into business using converted military surplus equipment. The result was a dangerous situation, richly productive of fatal accidents, which did not stabilize until the 1950s.

In the autumn of 1942 the students at one RAF Operational Training Unit, equipped with ageing Wellingtons, faced night exercises with misgivings. Five aircraft had been lost on night cross-country flights within a week. One had crashed into the streets of Fishguard; another had vanished into the North Sea; the rear gunner of a third had thought conditions were extremely bumpy until he realized that the bumps were caused by a hilltop; the fourth and fifth were mysteries. Five aircraft were considered to be a heavier loss than the five crews.[7] By no stretch of the imagination could conditions where crashes were accepted as a normal aspect of aviation be converted overnight into a safe means of public transportation as soon as the war was over.

The viability of the postwar airlines depended

5 Young, M. A. 1950
6 James, J. W. G. 1949
7 Charlwood, D. 1956; 1984 ed, 27

on three interrelated issues: economy, reliability, and safety. Four-engined aircraft made air transport commercially viable; airlines had hitherto depended on government mail contracts and other subsidies. Before the DC-3, US domestic airlines covered less than two thirds of their costs from non-mail revenues. The DC-3 raised this to 80%. Four-engined aircraft allowed the airlines to become profitable without subsidy in about 1950.[8]

A USAAF study during the Berlin airlift, comparing the C-54 with the DC-3, showed the enormous economic advantages of large aircraft. To deliver 4,500 short tons of freight to Berlin each day for thirty days the C-54s used 74% less aircrew, 56% less maintenance crew and 40% less fuel.[9] A comparable RAF study showed that in 1945 a Transport Command squadron of twenty Yorks moved almost the same volume of passengers and freight as the 120 British airline aircraft of 1938.[10] These economies of scale enabled the airlines to become self-sustaining and resulted, ultimately, in the jumbo jets and giant airlines of today.

Air transport was becoming increasingly capital-intensive. A Ford or Fokker trimotor of the 1920s cost $US35,000–38,000. A DC-3 sold for $US90,000–115,000. A DC-4 cost $US300,000, while L-049s sold for $US1,000,000 each.[11] Such expensive equipment could not be allowed to sit idle, waiting for the weather to improve.

Regularity was essential to the credibility of air transport. In 1942 the average year-round regularity of US domestic airlines was 94% with a maximum of 98% in summer and a minimum of 88% in winter. Low visibility at airports accounted for 70% of all cancelled flights.[12] This remained constant; four major US airlines averaged 95.6% regularity in the twelve months to June 1946, and 94.8% in the twelve months to June 1947. Because of worse weather, the situation in Europe was less encouraging.

In October 1944, 147 Squadron, RAF Transport Command, was given the task of restarting civilian air services in Europe. It continued until August 1946, when British European Airways (BEA) took over. The squadron achieved a year-round regularity of 87.7%, with a minimum of 72.1% in the winter of 1944–5 and a maximum of 99.9% in the summer of 1946. Between April 1946 and January 1947, British military transport between the UK and Germany averaged 98.7% regularity.[13] Much depended on the radio and radar facilities at the terminal airfields; in 1947 BEA withdrew its night mail service to Prague because of the lack of radio navigation aids.[14] In 1948 a senior BEA official pointed out that a major criticism of air transport was its unreliability and warned that operators would never give good service and attract full potential traffic until the situation was greatly improved.[15] BEA cancelled 11% of its services because of weather in the autumn of 1946, increasing to 13% in the winter of 1946–7.

The problem of low visibility was not only in safe landings, but also in the reduction in traffic flow. At Washington and New York La Guardia a normal maximum of forty-six aircraft movements per hour in visual conditions was reduced to sixteen to twenty in instrument conditions; ILS and GCA increased this to only twenty-four.

Still uncertain were the ceiling and visibility minima needed by a pilot to land visually after a blind approach. Opinions differed because requirements varied from pilot to pilot, aircraft type to aircraft type, and in response to various other conditions. Weather data from London Northolt showed that if minima were reduced from 150 metres (500 feet) ceiling and 900 metres (3,000 feet) visibility to 45 metres (150 feet) ceiling and 450 metres (1,500 feet) visibility, cancellations due to weather would be halved. Efforts to define the ceiling and visibility minima needed for safe visual landings, and to reduce these minima, were just beginning.

Especially in Europe, a lack of standards and procedures and deficient, ill-assorted equipment resulted in an accident rate that threatened the credibility of air transport. Although the fatal accident rate decreased enormously over the years in relation to passenger numbers and distances flown, the volume of passenger traffic increased so much that the total number of fatalities increased year by year. The following table shows fatality rates in free-world scheduled air services from 1925 to 1958.[16] (This includes accidents from all causes, weather-related or not.)

The drastic reduction between 1925 and 1945 resulted from better aircraft construction and maintenance as well as from improved weather capability. Yet the ability to operate in bad weather drove aircrew beyond their limits; their equipment betrayed them; or they were deceived by a combination of weather and defects in the system. The weather-related air carrier accidents reported in the ICAO annual accident digests of the 1950s were so numerous that space permits only the briefest analysis.[17] The accidents notably involved large, modern aircraft flown by experienced crews.

Year or average of years	Passengers killed	Millions of passenger-kilometres flown	Passenger fatalities per 100 million passenger-km
1925–9	36	130	28
1930–34	80	445	18
1935–9	133	1,475	9
1940–44	114	3,795	3
1949	556	24,000	2.32
1954	447	53,000	0.84
1958	604	86,000	0.70

Surprisingly few accidents resulted from mechanical failure in IFR conditions; although fuel exhaustion while diverting to an alternate airport was a recurring problem and would remain so.

A small percentage of the accidents happened on departure, typically when night illusions caused the pilot to fly the aircraft back into the ground or water after take-off or when the aircraft hit high ground in cloud or darkness during the initial climb. Published instrument departure procedures helped to solve this problem.

A third of the accidents occurred *en route*. Icing was rarely the known cause, but was suspected in otherwise unexplained accidents. The aviation community went on learning the dangers of thunderstorms the hard way. Flying large aircraft visually in bad weather in high mountains caused several accidents. Most of the *en route* accidents, however, were caused by aircraft hitting high ground because of navigation failure while flying on instruments because of bad weather or darkness or both. This was an inevitable consequence of unpressurized aircraft cruising at altitudes below 3,000 metres (10,000 feet) among mountains with scattered, obsolete navaids. In such conditions, with sparse weather-reporting stations and localized weather conditions, strong winds could blow an aircraft off course without the crew being aware of it. Thunderstorms, mountains and dawn or dusk all interfered with NDB and radio range signals. Better coverage by better electronic navigation aids, including radar, and turbine-powered aircraft cruising above the highest mountains would bring this problem under control.

The greatest difficulty in bad weather lay in getting the aircraft safely back to the ground; approach and landing accounted for half the major accidents. Half of these occurred during the initial approach between starting the descent from cruising altitude and aligning the aircraft for final approach. Typically, the crew descended below a safe altitude in cloud or darkness without being sure of their position and hit high ground. A subsidiary cause was the pilot trying to keep within sight of the ground while flying towards an airfield in bad weather. In many cases the position of the crash showed that the crew were not following company or government approach procedures. None of these accidents occurred in areas covered by radar.

At many airports the approach aids sufficed only to bring the pilot to within sight of the airfield, but not necessarily aligned with the landing runway. The manoeuvring between catching sight of the airfield and aligning the aircraft to land was known as a circling approach. The circling approach sometimes placed the pilot in a confusing situation, flying partly by instruments and partly visually at low altitude over an unknown landscape that might be obscured by low cloud, fog, or darkness. In such a situation the pilot could easily become lost or disorientated. Flying large aircraft in tight turns close to the ground was dangerous in any event, especially if the airframe had collected ice during the descent. Circling approaches accounted for one in twenty of the major weather-related accidents reported in ten years. More and better instrument approach aids would reduce the need for circling approaches.

Half of the approach and landing accidents occurred on final approach, almost all associated with low cloud or fog, although one occurred on a clear night over empty country. Typically, the aircraft hit the ground or an obstruction short of the runway, wide of the localizer course and/or below the glideslope. Loss of control, icing and thunderstorms accounted for a third of the approach and

8 *Flight*, April 25, 1958, 581
9 Merer, J. W. F. 1950, 529
10 Cochrane, R. 1947
11 Brooks, P. W. 1958. Figures believed not to have been adjusted for inflation.
12 Pritchard, H. C. 1946, 953
13 Cochrane, R. 1947, 398
14 *Flight*, 25 September 1947, 369
15 Rowe, N. E. 1948
16 ICAO Circular #56, AN/51, 1959
17 ICAO Circulars #18, AN/15, 1951; #24, AN/22, 1952; #31, AN/26, 1953; #38, AN/33, 1954; #39, AN/34, 1955; #47, AN/42, 1956; #50, AN/45, 1957; #54, AN/49, 1958; #56, AN/51, 1959; #59, AN/54, 1961; #62, AN/57, 1961

landing accidents. The solution of the blind landing problem is the subject of the last three chapters of this book. Missed approaches were a minor cause, but the missed approach came to be recognized as a dangerous manoeuvre. The pilot, having realized that he was not going to be able to see to land, had to decide to miss the approach and at once arrest the aircraft's descent and go into a climb on instruments, retracting the landing gear and flaps as he did so. With large and not easily manoeuvrable aircraft, blind and close to the ground, this was a moment of great stress and potential confusion. Significantly, three of the five aircraft involved in missed-approach accidents in the 1950s were four-engined – a DC-4, a DC-6, and a Constellation.

When things went wrong, 'pilot error' was frequently the verdict; the question of what caused the pilot to err was often unasked. Small, under-financed, ill-managed companies employing inept, poorly trained and almost unpaid crews to fly dubiously maintained aircraft for inhuman duty periods has always been the dark side of commercial aviation and has contributed to the accident statistics over the years. Nevertheless, even the most experienced pilots in the world, flying the best equipment that money could buy, fell victim to the deceptive and merciless environment of all-weather flying.

In spite of these depressing events, aircraft of unprecedented performance extended airline routes all over the world, cruising above much of the turbulence and icing of the lower atmosphere. One outstanding feature of the new four-engined airliners was their enormous range. Flying at altitudes of 6,000 metres (20,000 feet), aircraft such as the Stratocruiser, DC-7C and Super Constellation could cruise at 460–550 km/h (250–300 knots) for 10–12 hours. The L-1649A Super Constellation, in particular, had a range of 8,700 km (5,400 miles),[18] permitting non-stop service between New York and London, Paris, Frankfurt or Amsterdam and such routings as Copenhagen to Tokyo, stopping only at Anchorage, Alaska. In 1949 300,000 passengers flew across the Atlantic and the airlines were threatening the shipping companies.[19] In the 1950s the airlines made long-distance passenger trains and ships obsolete. By 1954 transatlantic flights were so routine that one writer could only describe the BOAC London–New York Stratocruiser service as 'luxuriously uneventful'.[20] The same year a PanAm DC-6B used a known jet-stream[21] over the North Atlantic to fly from New York to Paris in 10.25 hours, equalling the world record at that time for a commercial aircraft.[22]

An aircraft closely associated with the North Atlantic, flying for several airlines for more than a decade, was the Lockheed Constellation. Designed as a transcontinental airliner, the prototype flew on 9 January 1943.[23] BOAC bought Constellations as soon as they became available; their first one flew non-stop from New York to London in June 1945, in record time.[24] TWA flew its first proving flight across the Atlantic from Washington to Paris via Gander and Shannon on 3–4 December 1945.

The BOAC Constellation L-049 crews comprised a pilot and copilot, navigator, two flight engineers and a radio operator, with forty-two passenger seats. The aircraft carried HF and VHF radio, a radio range receiver, an ADF, an ILS receiver, a radar altimeter and a Sperry autopilot. The navigator had a gyroscopic drift sight and a Loran set. Navigation over the US was by radio ranges, which were also in place in Ireland and parts of the UK. Over the Atlantic, ADF and radio DF were used, backed up by Loran and celestial. Loran suffered from a dead zone of about two hours' flying time in mid-Atlantic. Dead reckoning was still important, hence the drift sight. Hourly weather reports transmitted by aircraft over the Atlantic helped to keep dead reckoning track error within 50 km (30 miles), even with no fixes from other sources. By 1948[25] 130 Constellations were in service with thirteen airlines. Sixty were on the North Atlantic run, making 100 crossings each way each week.

Long east–west flights had effects on the human system never encountered before. Jet lag existed before jets came into service; they only made it worse. For the aircrews, such flights were interminable, monotonous work at all hours of the day and night, their circadian rhythms disrupted, which bad weather and equipment problems could make immeasurably worse. For some routes, the crew were on duty for more than twenty hours, to which travel to and from airports had to be added.

Jet lag was even more pronounced on flights over the High Arctic between Europe and the Orient. In 1957 Scandinavian Air Services began their Copenhagen–Tokyo service with DC-7Cs, followed by Air France with L-1649A Super Constellations.[26] Both of these ambitious airlines traded on speed; this was the quickest route from Europe to the Orient by any commercial means of transport. Air France passenger accommodation

Douglas DC-7C.

was thirty-four tourist-class seats, twelve first-class seats and eight 'Pullman berths'.

An Air France Super Constellation would leave Paris with 37,100 litres (9,800 US gallons) of fuel, sufficient for a still-air range of more than 9,650 km (6,000 miles). The heavily laden aircraft climbed to 2,750 metres (9,000 feet) at 445 km/h (240 knots), and then climbed to 7,300 metres (24,000 feet) as the fuel load lightened, and increased speed to 545 km/h (295 knots). How close each flight went to the pole depended on pressure patterns and winds aloft. The flight from Paris to Anchorage took 17 hours; from Anchorage to Tokyo a further 13. The flight crew changed at Anchorage, the Paris–Anchorage crew remaining there to await the return of the aircraft from Japan.

The aircraft carried a polarized-sky-light compass which allowed the navigator to determine the position of the sun during the long hours of Arctic twilight when it was below the horizon but no stars were visible.

With Air France you set off in evening darkness (if it's early April) at about 7.30 p.m. (1930 GMT), watch the following day's sun rise twice and set once, and lose a day in the calendar before arriving in Japan after about 30 hours' flying time: and, as the last dawn had cracked for you some 13 hours earlier, it's somewhat disturbing to find that you have reached Tokyo at 11.30 a.m.

The icy mass of Greenland was crossed, in darkness, diagonally from Jónsbú and over Kennedy Strait to Fort Conger on Ellesmere

18 Taylor, M. J. H. 1989, 185, 346, 607
19 *Flight*, 12 January 1950, 56
20 *Flight*, 6 August 1954, 169
21 Jetstream: a long but narrow zone of extremely high wind at high altitude; see Chapter 22.
22 *Flying*, 1954, 46
23 Taylor, M. J. H. 1989, 606
24 *Flight*, 11 July 1946, 29
25 *Flight*, 6 May 1948, 492
26 Barker, R. 1958

Controls and instrument panel of a typical light aircraft 1960–1980, a 1967 Cessna 182. Note dual VOR/ILS and VHF communication radios, ADF and single-axis autopilot.

Island. Now Friday's sun began to rise, from the southeast relative to our aircraft, so that we were able to pick out the forbidding peaks and glaciers of Grant Land in the twilight. [The aircraft landed at Anchorage at 1237 GMT, 2.37 a.m. local, and, at that time of year, just before dawn. Takeoff three hours later was in full daylight.]

On entering the area of the Pacific Ocean at the southwestern extremity of the Aleutians, one crosses the Date Line, and it becomes tomorrow … our arrival time in Tokyo was now expected to be lunchtime (1325 on Saturday, Japanese time). At Greenwich it was then 0425 on the same day, whereas at Anchorage it was still Friday, and only 1825 at that.

In America a set of economic, geographic and political conditions unmatched anywhere else in the world encouraged the growth of a huge fleet of small single- and twin-engined aircraft, operated both by private owners and by small air carriers. Transistorized radios gave these aircraft unprecedented instrument-flying capability. In 1954 a Piper Tri-Pacer could be bought with a full blind-flying panel plus VOR, VHF transceiver, LF range receiver and DF loop.[27] Although a full gyro panel had been required in commercial aircraft since the 1930s, this requirement did not become general for all IFR operations in the US until 1956.[28] Light aircraft and their operators remained on the fringes of a system designed for aircraft of higher performance and more comprehensive equipment.

Small size and low performance left them vulnerable to bad weather, and light aircraft reached a limit to their all-weather flying which has remained ever since. E. F. Flint of Rochester, New York, remarked:[29] 'Since receiving my instrument ticket in 1945, I have been practising instrument flying to a limited amount. My Cessna 140 is well equipped and I find you have to set up a definite pattern for scan. After practice I find flying in stratus or altostratus with rain not too difficult, but icing and thunderstorm conditions are definitely out. It is one thing to fly the aircraft on instruments, but another to fly instruments plus navigate on ATC clearance on a cross-country flight …'

A valid observation, made in 1954 and true today, was:[30] 'An airliner takes at least five separate radio sets to fly into a congested area such as New York. They have two pilots, one to fly the ship, and one to take down the current weather conditions and clearances. Those two men are busy from the time they start on an instrument flight to the time they come to a stop at the ramp. In (a light aircraft) one man is trying to do it alone with limited radio equipment.' More radio equipment, however, only increased the workload; flying a Cessna 182 IFR in the 1980s required the pilot's continual manipulation of forty-three knobs and switches for the avionics alone. Light aircraft and their pilots performed dismally in bad weather. In 1948 in the US alone 'continued VFR into instrument weather' was given as a cause of 113 accidents and 216 fatalities, whereas in 1949 total free-world airline crashes from all causes resulted in 556 deaths.[31]

Just as the wartime RAF had discovered that a bomber was useless if the crew could not navigate to their target and then return to their base, so the post-war airlines discovered that the economies of scale offered by bigger aircraft could not be realized if air travel was perceived as dangerous or unreliable. The danger of disastrous mechanical failure faded away with improvements in all aspects of aircraft engineering, but now pilot error and weather problems (increasingly interrelated) came to the fore, tragically highlighted by deficiencies in equipment and procedures in the immediate post-war years. The goal of all-weather operation had been desirable, yet elusive, from the earliest days of aviation; in the post-war world it became nothing less than the key to the future of air transportation.

27 *Flying*, November 1954, 9
28 *Flying*, May 1956, 82
29 *Flying*, December 1954, 8
30 *Flying*, February 1954, 56
31 *Flying*, April 1952, 20

CHAPTER 18

The Crisis of the Human Pilot

Over the years, aircraft became more complicated, and their on-board navigation devices more numerous. Gradually, but remorselessly, more and more tasks crowded in on the human pilot. Some of these could be delegated to additional crew members, but still the number of instruments and switches that the pilot had to read, interpret and operate, in addition to the basic task of flying the aircraft, grew. In particular, the task of electronic navigation devolved insidiously on the pilot. Aircraft came into service that could easily remain airborne for twelve hours or more. In jet aircraft, more things could go wrong faster than ever before. In the immediate post-war years the fact had to be faced that the human pilot had limits and that these limits were being approached. Unless the whole task of instrument flying could be made easier for pilots of normal ability, the future of aviation was bleak.

Wartime flying produced large numbers of highly skilled and experienced instrument pilots. Writing of the 'Hump' route between India and China, B. K. Thorne wrote:[1]

> Could there be a common denominator among men represented by these individuals? Only one really important one, and that hard to explain. Every one of the Hump pilots was able to learn to fly on instruments just as well as he could fly contact. Once a pilot had been checked out on the Hump and flew in the left seat, he had to be at home flying by the gauges just as well as if the whole route between India and China was completely in the clear ... Within months many pilots logged hundreds of hours on instruments. The faculty for having as much faith in the instrument panel as in actual vision was mandatory ... We acquired one other common characteristic – we were all loners.

These skills were, however, unevenly distributed; the fact that instrument flying was a part of all military flight training did not result in a uniformly high standard of instrument capability. One Air Canada Boeing 747 captain[2] remarked that, as a young pilot, he had assumed that ex-military pilots with wartime service were all highly proficient at instrument flying. He was surprised to find that their abilities varied widely. Only transport pilots gained the long experience needed for real proficiency. Bomber pilots began operational flying with 300–400 hours of flight training; many of those that survived finished their wartime service with less than 1,000 hours of flying. An RAF Bomber Command 'tour' of thirty operations amounted to less than 500 hours of flying time, including on-going training and incidental flying. One RAF bomber pilot completed his wartime service with just under 650 hours total time of which 160 were at night.[3]

The fighter pilot's attitude was:[4] 'I had little inclination for serious under-the-hood practice and generally avoided it. When the weather turned sour in those days, most fighter pilots looked for a hole, dropped to the deck, then hedgehopped home. The only trouble with this procedure was that it worked. Very well in fact. Most of the time. If occasionally someone flew into a mountain that was tough, but danger added zest to the business. We expected to take our chances.'

In January 1943, one pilot found himself at an ill-managed, demoralized training unit, flying obsolete, worn-out and poorly maintained aircraft in English winter weather.[5]

> It was bitterly cold but clear and starry ... We plugged in our oxygen and turned it on full, squeezing the tube to see if it was coming through.
>
> Mine seemed O.K. – his (navigator's) also. We taxied out – always a nightmare to me as I cannot reach the brake – and last night 40 mph cross

wind. The serviceability rate of these aircraft is so low that I always marvel whenever we leave the ground at all. Of course at any other unit we wouldn't – they would put every aeroplane unserviceable at once – this had been proved by aircraft from here – diverted to another aerodrome, being refused permission to take off again.

But anything goes here and off we went. As soon as we were off the ground I knew something was wrong. The old monster started plunging away to starboard. We flashed a torch through the filthy perspex to see if the gills had not shut, but they seemed O.K. so I continued. (I wonder if W. knows just how terrified I am at night? I hope not.) Then we started to climb. At 10,000 feet the pitch control of the port engine jammed. At 19,000 I was waffling about at 100 mph with the outside temperature 50° below. Then my R.T. packed up. (I could receive from the ground but not transmit.)

I told W. to get a homing. I listened to him calling up. His voice very drowsy. Oh God he's going to pass out. Down I pushed the nose, down until I thought my ears would crack – all the time hearing ground control giving us homing vectors and W. repeating them, slowly, happily and quite wrong.

I should of course have kept a mental note of the courses we were flying, but having so much else to do I had left it to W. What if the RT packs up altogether? A moment later it did so. A feeling oddly of resignation – not panic. Then I saw it, the flare path, way below us. We were all right. I came down slowly, feeling very sick (my own supply of oxyen cannot have been too good) and started to flash my navigation lights at 1,000 ft. Nothing happened. Why the Hell can't they answer? I glanced again at my instruments. 11,000 ft! What a fool – mustn't get drowsy. That might have led to disaster – a quick circuit at what I took to be 1,000 ft; turn on nicely over the East funnel of lights at 800 ft – wheels down, flaps down, throttle back, down to 100 ft. Why no Chance light? And then the stall. Too late I realise what has happened. We are not at 100 ft but at 10,000 ft and all the time the plane is spinning and spinning.

I lose more height and when I really am at 800 ft start flashing my navigation lights. A green lamp flashes back. I can land. I turn to W. and put up my thumb. He grins back, quite unaware that he was nearly out. (He has great confidence in me! If he did but know.)

Round the circuit and down with my wheels – a flood of light comes on where the ground crew have not put strips over the undercarriage position indicator lights. I am quite blinded, but W. gets down on his knees and holds his hand over the glare. We are coming in – Hell of a cross wind – we're drifting badly. I straighten up over the runway, throttle back, we're still going like a crab. Then the wheels touch and we are down. As I turn off the runway I can feel the sweat running down inside my Irving suit and my hands are trembling. Climbing out I put my foot gingerly to the ground. Oh how welcome it is. Solid earth beneath my feet.

The pilot and his radio operator were killed in an unexplained night flying accident soon afterwards.

Long-range aircraft of the 1940s carried a radio operator, a navigator and a flight engineer but, while all American large, multi-engined aircraft carried a copilot seated beside the pilot with a duplicate set of controls and instruments, most German and British bombers did not. The four-engined Stirlings, Halifaxes and Lancasters were single-pilot aircraft with no one fully trained to take over if the pilot was incapacitated; indeed it was impossible to take over the controls without removing the pilot from his seat. The flight engineer was the crew member who most directly assisted the pilot. The effect of this arrangement on the loss rate and, too, the long-term psychological effects on aircrew, are matters for speculation.

Instrument flying made demands for which the human system was ill equipped, and these continued from take-off to landing.[6] Flying in bad weather could be enormously stressful. B. K. Thorne wrote of the effects on pilots flying the Hump:[7] 'Although I had been wide awake when the orderly arrived, I hadn't been conscious of any noise in the *basha*. Now I was. There was mumbling – no, more than mumbling. There was mumbling, chatter, yells, words called into microphones, calls for help, curses damning the planes and the men that worked on them … I walked the length of

---

1 Thorne, B. K. 1965, 64
2 Personal communication, 1993
3 A. Foord, personal communication 1995
4 Reynolds, F. 1964
5 Burn, M. 1988, 213–220
6 *Flight*, 1 May 1947, 391–2
7 Thorne, B. K. 1965, viii

the dark hut, up and down ... Every one of the men in their beds, sleeping, was raving.'

One pilot commented, of post-war airline flying:[8]

> There is more mental strain in flying in bad weather than most (pilots) would care to admit.
>
> You rush off the end of the flare-path into that awful wall of gloom, and there, leering back at you from the windscreen, is the reflection of two frightened faces.
>
> [Without an autopilot:] Having settled down in cloud, steering a nice steady course, all goes well for the first half hour or so ... Then, for no apparent reason, you start to lose height, gradually and annoyingly. Impatiently, you tweak the elevator trim, though you are well aware that it really requires no adjustment. The loss of altitude is arrested, and as the needle creeps back to the cruising level you return the trim to normal. But you go on climbing, almost as fast as before, and, suddenly, as you are sorting things out, the engines desynchronize with that aggravating beat which destroys the rhythm of your soul. By the time you have fiddled the revs back to their best behaviour you find that you have wandered off course, and while bending down to reset the gyro you accumulate an alarming amount of bank. But it's all so silly, you decide, and lo, in a moment everything is all right again, and you are humming along motionless in the void, alone with your thoughts.
>
> Have you ever found yourself in a clear elevated cave near a warm front, between two oddly sloping layers, one sweeping on the other, and seen, a hundred yards away, another aircraft – just for a moment, before you are both swathed again in the cloud?

Instrument approaches in bad weather were particularly stressful, coming as they often did at the end of a long, tiring flight. This became worse as the endurance of long-range aircraft increased and the equipment and procedures for instrument approaches became more numerous and more complex.

> After a long plug in the overcast you eventually make the beam at the far end, and start your letdown and final approach. By now, perhaps, it's raining and bumpy ... Nobody really likes to be still in cloud at 300 feet, one hand on the throttle, the other feeling the slipstream beating on the elevator, one eye on the air speed, the other on the gyro, the altimeter almost audible, both feet firmly on the quivering rudder, and across your subconscious the sole link with the outside, the little model (aircraft) ludicrously gummed on the glass like a fly against the horizon, waiting while time stands still for the cloud to break and reveal the blessed Earth.

The aircraft could go on functioning tirelessly, whereas its human crew could not. Commercial demands and inefficient organization resulted in excessive duty hours, especially as the effects of fatigue on the human brain varied in response to a wide variety of factors. The investigation of one airline accident in the US in the late 1940s revealed that the pilots had been in the cockpit for 32 out of the previous 37 hours. This was not an isolated case. At 6.09 p.m. on 16 April 1952, a C-46 left New York, bound for California.[9] After a scheduled stop at Chicago, it reached Kansas City, Missouri, at 2.08 a.m. The crew were delayed there for eleven hours to replace an oil cooler, departing at 1.38 p.m. on 17 April, VFR, for Amarillo, Texas. They made a precautionary landing at Wichita at 3.00 p.m., departing IFR at 3.54. After encountering a thunderstorm near Tucumcari, New Mexico, they landed at Amarillo at 6.14 p.m. At 9.02 p.m. they departed IFR for Phoenix, arriving at 12.30 a.m. on 18 April. At 1.43 a.m. they departed, DVFR, for Burbank, California. As Burbank was closed by fog, they diverted to Los Angeles where the ceiling was 200 metres (700 feet) overcast and the visibility 4 kilometres (2.5 miles) in haze and smoke. The aircraft crashed on final approach. The pilot had had a heart attack a year previously and it was suspected that this recurred. The crew had been on duty for 36 hours.

On 17 December 1954, at 9.30 p.m., a Constellation landed 18 km (11 miles) short of the runway during a night instrument approach to Toronto.[10] The crew had been on duty for 16 hours, of which 12 had been spent flying from Montreal to Toronto to Tampa, Florida, and back to Toronto. The ceiling at Toronto was 90 metres (300 feet). The company approach procedure was to fly from the Toronto radio range to the outer marker and NDB, fly a procedure turn not below 600 metres (2,000 feet), intercept the localizer, and track it inbound until intercepting the glideslope. The captain swung wide of the outer marker in a slow descent, completed the procedure turn, and intercepted the localizer. He never stopped the descent, even though passing through 600 metres (2,000 feet) outside the outer marker, and continued to descend until the aircraft flew into some trees. The next day a DC-6 crashed at New York on the fourth attempt at a daylight ILS approach with a 60-metre (200-foot) ceiling and a visibility of 4 kilometres (2.5 miles) in light rain and fog. The crew had been 22½ hours *en route* from Rome, including 2½ hours of holds and approaches.[11]

On 5 November 1956, a Hermes crashed on final approach to London Blackbushe at night in low visibility.[12] The crew had been on duty for 30 hours, evacuating civilians from the Suez crisis, including a nominal rest in chaotic conditions which did little for them. A logbook entry left by the captain, who was killed in the crash, indicated other frustrations. 'We have spent six and a half hours at Malta with this blasted magneto, and we now face a duty day of 21½ hours which includes a complete night.'

The return to normal civil aviation after the war was, indeed, marred by so many accidents that the credibility of air transport suffered on both sides of the Atlantic. Many of these were caused by human error in bad weather. In 1946, as in 1919, the hazards of military flying in war were unacceptable to peacetime civilian passengers. In 1947: 'There have been far too many avoidable accidents lately – many in bad weather, too many funeral pyres on too many hillsides … (The passenger) is beginning to rebel. He won't go by air – the windy little rat – not until he's convinced that it's a lot safer than it is, and all this Passenger-mile per Prang stuff leaves him cold.'[13] The same British writer commented:[14] 'There is a general feeling that something, somewhere in the Battle against the Weather is impeding the advance – nobody seems to know just what … The art of bad weather flying has not progressed a whit since 1939 – some say it's even gone back a bit.'

On the afternoon of 7 August 1946, a BEA DC-3 crashed into a mountain in cloud during a radio range approach at Oslo, Norway.[15] The aircraft swung wide on the procedure turn. The radio range receiver in the aircraft was found switched to the radio compass mode, giving a beam width of 20° instead of 4°, something BEA neglected to find out from the US manufacturer. A fan marker was a part of the approach procedure; the BEA aircraft did not have a marker beacon receiver. An RAF Transport Command instructor commented on this accident:[16] 'I have found that in both service

and civil flying there seems to be an attitude of complete indifference towards radio beam flying that is positively dangerous. Air training in this form of flying is almost non-existent with the result that faulty execution of procedures in emergency is inevitable.' The writer commented on the lack of radio range training given to BEA pilots and the lack of thorough briefing. Pilots were unwilling to use Standard Beam Approach because of lack of confidence caused by lack of practice. SBA instructors could use the beam under the most appalling conditions without a second thought. But, to the inexperienced pilot the beam was a snare and a delusion. All the approach aids in the world were useless if pilots could not or would not use them.

On 27 September 1946, a Scottish Airways de Havilland Rapide crashed at Renfrew[17] in daylight with scattered cloud at 300 metres (1,000 feet), overcast at 350 metres (1,200 feet), visibility 3 km (2 miles) in drizzle and fog. The aircraft hit a hill while being given DF headings to the airport; the pilot seemed to have been following DF bearings given to another aircraft.

On 6 November 1946, a KLM DC-3 crashed into a hill near Croydon during an instrument approach using the Croydon NDB.[18] The Croydon ceiling was at 300 metres (1,000 feet) with lower cloud on the nearby hills. Whereas the pilot had intended to set his altimeter to QFE, to read zero on landing, he had set it to QNH, giving altitude above sea level; consequently the aircraft was 70 metres (230 feet) lower than he thought. The pilot also descended below a safe height, trying to break out of cloud. On 3 October 1947, the pilot of a Lancastrian freighter lost control during take-off at Belfast and crashed.[19] Visibility was only 45–90 metres (150–300 feet). Both pilots escaped.

On 2 March 1948, a Sabena DC-3 stalled 12 metres (40 feet) above the runway and crashed at London Heathrow at night in a visibility of 180

8 *Flight*, 1 May 1947, 391–2
9 ICAO Circular #31, AN/26, 1953
10 ICAO Circular #47, AN/42, 1956
11 Ibid.
12 *Flight*, 29 March 1957
13 *Flight*, 1 May 1947, 391–2
14 *Flight*, 1 May 1947, 391
15 *Flight*, 23 January 1947, 96
16 G. Percival letter in *Flight*, 6 February 1947, 151
17 *Flight*, 8 May 1947, 423
18 *Flight*, 17 July 1947, 65
19 *Flight*, 22 April 1948, 437

metres (600 feet) in fog after a GCA.[20] The pilot was believed to have become disoriented. GCA visibility minima were thenceforth established at 45 metres (150 feet) air-to-ground and 730 metres (2,400 feet) horizontally along the ground.

On 21 April 1948, a BEA Viking crashed during an SBA at Renfrew,[21] apparently because the aircraft's marker beacon receiver failed. The flight crew did not hear the outer marker signal while outbound on the approach and delayed the procedure turn too long. Because of this and a strong wind the aircraft hit a hill.

On 15 April 1948, a Pan American Airways Constellation crashed 550 metres (1,800 feet) short of the runway at 2.15 a.m. on the second attempt at an ILS approach at Shannon, Ireland, *en route* from Karachi to New York.[22] The ceiling was 120 metres (400 feet); visibility was 3–5 km (2–3 miles) but as little as 75 metres (250 feet) in fog patches. Exhausted crews and bad-weather arrivals in the early morning would remain a deadly combination.

On 6 January 1948, the pilot of a BEA Viking made two or three unsuccessful attempts to land using the SBA at London Northolt[23] at night in low visibility and then tried to make a visual approach during which the aircraft crashed into trees. The captain had held a licence since 1935 and had 6,520 hours of flying time. On 20 May 1948, a DC-3 freighter crashed while trying to land at Bovingdon under a 90–metre (300–foot) cloud base at night.[24] On 28 September 1948, a civilian-operated Halifax crashed on the Isle of Man while flying at 450 metres (1,500 feet) in daylight, supposedly in visual conditions.[25] On 22 November 1948, a civilian Lancaster crashed on the approach to Hurn airport.[26] The pilot was ex-RAF Transport Command with 2,350 hours of flying time; the suspected cause was homing onto the wrong Eureka beacon which put the aircraft 39 km (24 miles) off track.

Subtle defects in the IFR system could play hideous tricks on aircrew. Forty minutes after midnight on 21 October 1948,[27] Captain Parmentier, chief pilot of KLM, was killed approaching Prestwick in a Constellation; he had been flying with KLM since 1929 and had 20,000 flying hours. Visibility was 4 km (2.5 miles) under a 90-metre (300-foot) ceiling. Captain Parmentier made a successful GCA but circled to land on a runway more into wind. The aircraft struck high-tension cables on high ground in dense fog about 5.5 km (3.5 miles) from the airport and crashed 3 km (2 miles) farther on. Approach charts found in the wreckage

marked a 140-metre (450-foot) spot height misprinted as 14 metres (45 feet).

Shortly before two o'clock in the morning of 30 June 1951, a DC-6 on the initial approach to Denver flew into a mountain 29 km (18 miles) southwest of Fort Collins at an altitude of 2,600 metres (8,500 feet).[28] The crew had reported over the Cheyenne radio range at 1.47 a.m. at 4,600 metres (15,000 feet), reported level at 2,600 metres (8,500 feet) at 1.56 a.m., and did not reply to a call from Denver air traffic control at 2.00 a.m.

The normal approach procedure was to cross the Cheyenne radio range and turn onto a heading of 210° to intercept the north leg of the Denver radio range. Instead of turning onto the Denver range leg, the crew held the heading of 210° which took them into the mountains.

The investigation revealed an appallingly subtle ambiguity. At that time, Denver had both a radio range and a VAR; both had the same Morse code identifier and transmitted indistinguishable aural signals. The radio range north 'A' quadrant was on the east side of the equisignal, while the VAR transmitted an 'A' on the west side of its north course. The accident investigators hypothesized that, by an act as simple as pressing the wrong pair of neighbouring switches, the captain had silenced the radio range and VAR voice signals and had selected the VAR aural signals instead. The crew, it was believed, had held their course in anticipation of the radio range equisignal, unaware that they had already crossed it, until they hit the mountain. The ICAO investigation report commented: '... no logical explanation can be found for the length of time the aircraft was held on a heading which the crew should have known would lead to the mountains west of the airway.' Only a few minutes elapsed between the time when the aircraft should have intercepted the Denver range leg and the crash, perhaps just enough time for the crew to realize that events were not as planned and to start to wonder why. The ICAO comment seems to place unfair blame on the crew that fell victim to this hideous deception.

Experience was not a sure protector. In April 1958, a Viscount crashed in Scotland because the pilot, who had over 10,000 hours of flying experience, misread the altimeter by 3,000 metres (10,000 feet).[29] On February 3, 1959, a pilot with 29,000 hours crashed in an Electra flying an ILS approach to New York La Guardia on a foggy night.[30] Airline safety was better in the US because of more predictable weather and an IFR system which had already been more effective than the European system in 1939 and which had not been disrupted by war. Consequently the accident pattern differed from that in Europe. In 1949 it was reported[31] that all fatalities on American domestic airlines in the past fourteen months had been due to collisions. American Airlines had flown for three years without a fatal accident.[32]

The war was accompanied by a significant innovation in the way in which instrument flying was taught. Originally, instrument flying was by needle, ball and airspeed and was taught accordingly, known in North America as '1-2-3,' 'needle-ball-and-airspeed' or 'primary-secondary.' The three 'primary' instruments were the airspeed indicator, turn-and-bank indicator and vertical speed indicator because the pilot kept control of the aircraft by means of these instruments. The altimeter, compass, artificial horizon and directional gyro were 'secondary' instruments. The artificial horizon was known to have built-in errors; the gyroscope was liable to topple and, once toppled, was slow to re-erect. Vacuum pumps were liable to fail, which disabled the artificial horizon and the heading indicator. Consequently, these two instruments were at first regarded as luxuries rather than essentials.

The vital knowledge lost to the pilot in blind conditions was the aircraft's attitude. Attitude could only be deduced from the three primary instruments, indirectly and through lagging indications. Consequently a different and unnatural set of mental processes had to be substituted for those used in visual flight. Without an artificial horizon, this was extremely tiring if continued for any great length of time. Precise manoeuvring was difficult. Blind flying by needle, ball and airspeed was possible in slow, stable aircraft with benign behaviour in the event of loss of control. The faster and aerodynamically cleaner aircraft of the 1940s could rapidly reach dangerous airspeeds if control were lost, and could not be flown blind safely without an artificial horizon.

In the early 1940s a new training system came into use, known as the attitude system, based on the artificial horizon and heading indicator, which displayed the aircraft's attitude continuously in all three axes. The performance resulting from its attitude could be read from the peripheral instruments – altimeter, vertical speed indicator, airspeed indicator and turn-and-bank indicator. One of the chief proponents of this method was Colonel Joseph Duckworth of the USAAC, whose doctrine

began to spread in 1943.[33] Similar changes were also taking place in the RAF; the method of instruction set forth in a 1943 RAF manual is clearly the attitude system, although not referred to as such.[34] In spite of this change in teaching, in the late 1940s the artificial horizon and heading indicator were still regarded as unreliable and the US instrument flight test had to be flown without using them.[35] Needle-ball-and-airspeed are still taught today as a back-up method should the artificial horizon fail.

Fixation on a failed instrument could have serious consequences, as one instructor and student found out in a TF-9J jet trainer in the mid 1960s, when the instructor deliberately failed the attitude indicator while the student was flying instrument training under the hood.[36]

> We were at 25,000 feet when he lost control, entering a descending spiral to the left. At first, the rate of climb indicator buried itself at 6,000 feet per minute down with the altimeter unwinding at a horrendous rate, yet the attitude gyro showed nothing more exciting than a gentle left bank. Rationally, he knew what had happened and recognized the need to get off the gyro and recover from the 'unusual attitude' on the basic instruments, … but for at least half a minute he stayed glued to the gyro, pulling completely through a manoeuvre known as a split S (the bottom side of a loop in which we went supersonic) before pressing up into a steep nose-high climb. Only then, with the airspeed needle plunging to the 'zero' peg did he effect the transfer of scan and begin recovery. He brought it under control once, and then lost it, plunging us through a second set of octaflugerons to 8,000 feet, where

20 *Flight*, 11 March 1948, 280; 23 December 1948, 745
21 *Flight*, 1948, 596
22 *Flight*, 22 April 1948, 437
23 *Flight*, 8 July 1947, 47
24 *Flight*, 14 July 1949, 39
25 *Flight*, 5 May 1949, 535
26 *Flight*, 13 October 1949, 501
27 *Flight*, 28 October 1948, 520; 1 December 1949, 704
28 ICAO Circular #31, AN/26, 1953
29 ICAO Circular #59, AN/54, 1961
30 ICAO Circular #62, AN/57, 1961
31 *Flight*, 17 November 1949, 651
32 *Flight*, 7 April 1949, 398
33 Fuchs, A. S. 1951
34 Air Ministry Publication 1732b
35 *Flying*, May 1957, 38
36 Trotti, J. 1987, 127

again he seemed to regain control. After several seconds of straight-and-level, the left wing started down again until we were once again on our back with the nose steeply down. For the third time we pulled through a split S, this time bottoming at 1,500 feet and by the time that he had it completely under control, we were at less than 300 feet. 'Pop your hood,' I told him, just to let him see what a close thing it had been.

Other instances have occurred where the outcome was far less amusing.

Instrument flying had to be acknowledged as a complex, demanding activity in no way assisted by the ill-considered and unstandardized layout of an ever increasing number of instruments and controls. In 1947 the Psychological Branch of the American Aero Medical Laboratory, Engineering Division, at Wright Field carried out a major study to find out which instrumentation displays and control arrangements led to the greatest accuracy and fewest errors. The study also pointed to the need for the better selection and training of pilots.[37]

Increases in aircraft performance demanded quicker and more precise control. New blind navigation and approach aids added to the information that the pilot had to process, all of which was presented by an imperfect analogue never before encountered by the human mind. This demanded enormous mental agility. In the late 1940s and early 1950s the aviation community was forced to realize that the human pilot had certain limits and that those limits had been reached. Although the performance of the human pilot could be optimized through intensive psychological and physiological study and the resulting improvements in training, the 'design limits' remained. Henceforth, advances in the quest for all-weather flight would follow the paths of better instrumentation, more extensive and better-designed ground facilities and extraordinary advances in automatic flight control.

---

37 *Flight*, 14 August 1947, 170

CHAPTER 19

Technology to the Rescue

In spite of enormous increases in aircraft perform-ance during the war, the blind-flying instruments of 1945 had remained unchanged for fifteen years and more. Post-war, high-performance aircraft demanded not only better instruments capable of functioning in increasingly extreme environments, but a reconsideration of the whole blind-flying analogue. Helicopters were a whole new, post-war technology, posing new blind-flying problems.

The war had a negative influence on instrument design. When the needs of production were para-mount and the life of equipment destined for operational service was measurable in weeks or even days, it was not feasible to spend time and effort on refining instrument design.[1] Quality suf-fered from the demand for production, especially in Britain.[2] 'The British manufacturers had to lower the standards of performance in the panic for increased production during the war. As a test pilot I remember one period when my department had to turn down something like 25% of the gyro-scopic instruments fitted to our production aircraft because they did not even come up to the lowered standards.' Wartime production left large stocks of surplus instruments, some of which had suffered from abusive service. A flooded market provided little incentive to manufacturers to bring in new products.

The Sperry artificial horizon of 1929 remained the only instrument of its kind until 1945 and con-tinues in use in low-performance aircraft with minor modifications to the present day. It suffered, however, from inherent deficiencies and was no longer adequate for high-performance aircraft. The instruments available in the 1940s were limited to ±60° in pitch and ±90–100° in roll,[3] beyond which the gyroscope toppled and the instrument became temporarily useless. After the aircraft resumed level flight, it would read in error by 45–50° and would re-erect at only 4° per minute.[4] Because repeated toppling damaged the gyroscope,

the pilot could 'cage' it with a mechanical lock if violent manoeuvres were planned, although this disabled the instrument.

If the aircraft exceeded the limiting attitudes in blind conditions because of turbulence, combat manoeuvres or loss of control, the pilot was left with only needle, ball and airspeed; the artificial horizon became useless just when it was most urgently needed. Memoirs of wartime fighter pilots report disorientation, either when flying in cloud or after entering cloud with a gyroscope top-pled by combat manoeuvres, from which they recovered only after breaking out into clear air.[5] With faster and aerodynamically cleaner aircraft, pilot disorientation became both more likely and more dangerous, intensifying the demand for an instrument to indicate attitude reliably through 360° of pitch and roll.

In 1945 Sperry brought out its 'attitude indica-tor.'[6] The gyroscope rotor was an armature housed in a spherical casing, gimbal-mounted for 360° of rotation in pitch and roll, and erected by a pendu-lous magnet. The face of the spherical housing presented to the pilot was divided into a dark top half and a light bottom half, marked with latitudi-nal lines. In bank the instrument was true to life; the reference line on the gyroscope casing repre-sented the natural horizon while the lubber line represented the aircraft's transverse axis. In pitch, however, it was inverted; the 'horizon line' moved towards the top of the instrument as the aircraft pitched up, whereas the natural horizon would appear to do the opposite. In the existing artificial

---

1 Cochrane, R. 1947, 402
2 Neilan, J. C. 1950, 44
3 *Flight*, 29 March 1945, 334; Air Ministry Publication 1732b 1943, 111
4 Jordanoff, A. 1938, 178
5 Johnson, J. E. 1956; Clostermann, C. 1951
6 *Flight*, 29 March 1945, 334

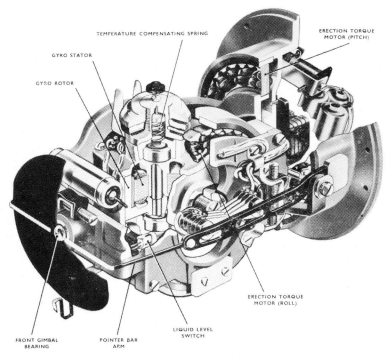

The Sperry electric artificial horizon.

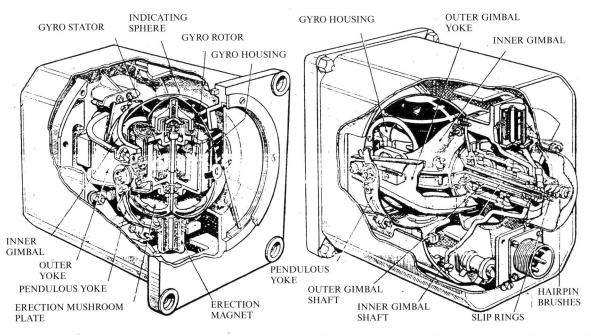

Above can be seen the interior arrangement of the gyro mechanism, erection mechanism and the relationship of gyro to sphere.

This view shows the co-axial arrangement of the inner and outer gimbal shafts together with the brush and slip ring assembly for power feed.

The Sperry attitude indicator.

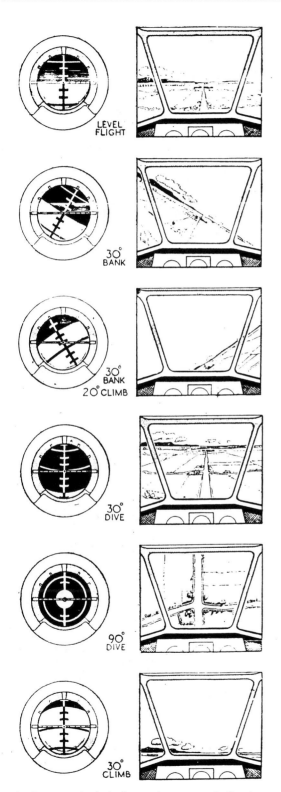

LEVEL
FLIGHT

30°
BANK

30°
BANK
20° CLIMB

30°
DIVE

90°
DIVE

30°
CLIMB

The Sperry attitude indicator, instrument indications.

horizons a mechanical linkage made the inversion to a true representation of the natural horizon, but at the expense of 360° pitch and roll capability. Because of its unnatural horizon representation, the Sperry attitude indicator of 1945 did not replace the artificial horizon.

In 1948 Sperry brought out a new electric artificial horizon[7] with several advantages over the older, vacuum-driven version. The rotor speed was 23,000 rpm compared to 12,000. The electric instrument read reliably through 360° of roll and at pitch angles up to ±85°. Natural re-erection after toppling, actuated by mercury switches, remained at 3–5° per minute, but an optional attachment allowed rapid re-erection at 180° per minute. Insensitive to low atmospheric pressures at high altitudes and to dirt in the air, the instrument found a wide market in Europe and the USA.

The conventional artificial horizon had two defects specific to jet aircraft. Acceleration caused false indications of pitch-up; the rapid acceleration of a jet fighter taking off could cause enough error to delude a pilot into flying back into the ground at night. This error compounded a physiological illusion of climb also produced by acceleration. The second defect appeared in early experience with the Comet.[8] In a prolonged turn the artificial horizon tended to re-erect itself in response to the false gravity produced by the turn. Because rate of turn decreases as airspeed increases for any given bank angle, jets had to bank more steeply than piston-engined aircraft to achieve a required rate of turn. A Comet, flying at 740 km/h (400 knots), for example, had to bank at 29° to achieve a half-rate turn (180° per 2 minutes), compared with 9° for an aircraft flying at 185 km/h (100 knots). This accentuated the tendency of the artificial horizon to re-erect itself to a false vertical; both the turn and the roll-out therefore had to be monitored with the turn-and-bank indicator. These inherent problems of the conventional artificial horizon hastened the introduction of instruments driven by precise master gyroscopes.

A significant innovation was an attitude indicator telling the pilot, not merely what the aircraft's attitude was, but what it should be in order to fulfil his wishes. In 1949 Sperry brought out the Zero Reader,[9] the forerunner of instruments now known

7 *Flight*, 21 October 1948, 479
8 *Flight*, 1 May 1953, 537
9 *Flight*, 18 August 1949, 182

as flight directors, an instrument that told the pilot what change of attitude was needed to follow a selected heading, altitude, or ILS. The Zero Reader was independent of the other instruments. Signals from an attitude gyroscope, a Gyrosyn compass, an altitude control,[10] a manual heading selector and a radio range or ILS were combined and presented on a crossed-pointer indicator. When the needles crossed in the centre of the instrument, the attitude was correct. By keeping the needles crossed, a pilot could, for example, fly a smooth curve to intercept a localizer and then track it more

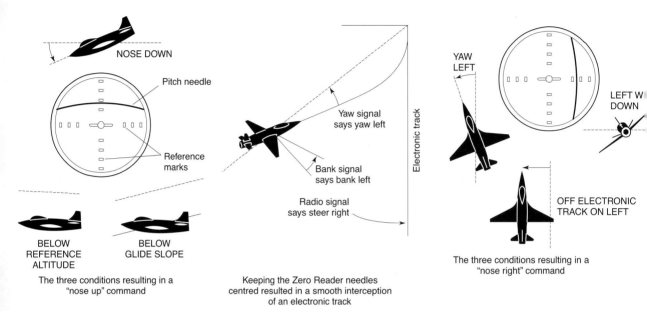

The Sperry Zero Reader, instruments and indications.

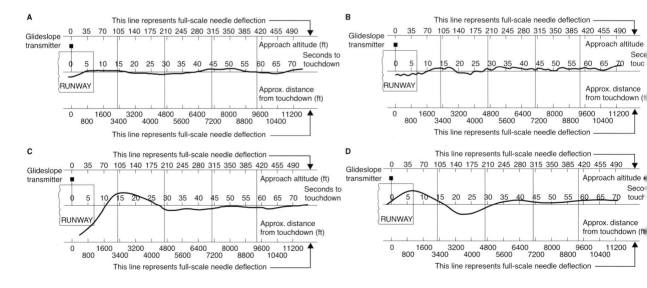

Comparison of localizer track errors using manual, automatic and Sperry Zero Reader control.

Bristol Britannia.

accurately than was otherwise possible. In cruise a pilot using the Zero Reader could fly manually to within ±2° of heading and ±20 feet of altitude. Its use required training but, once understood, it made the pilot's task easier. Most important, however, was the fact that it enabled manual instrument flying to be carried out with a degree of accuracy that was previously beyond the ability of even the most experienced of pilots. Preset limits prevented the instrument from directing the pilot into an unsafe attitude.

In the middle 1950s the Collins Radio Co. of Cedar Rapids, Iowa, produced a system[11] which presented attitude commands and attitude and navigation information on two instruments. One of these – the Course Indicator – would be recognizable today as a Horizontal Situation Indicator (HSI). It showed the aircraft's compass heading and its position and orientation relative to a VOR radial or an ILS localizer selected by the pilot. This made it easier to intercept and follow such electronic tracks. The other – the Approach Horizon –

a forerunner of the flight director, would be less recognizable. It provided steering commands in azimuth only to help the pilot to fly ILS approaches; it was not a substitute for the artificial horizon. The Collins Integrated Flight System was produced in four versions, FD-101 to FD-104. The smallest version, the FD-103, weighed 28 pounds; it needed 63 watts of electric power at 27.5 volts DC, 115 volts AC at 400 Hz and 26 volts AC at 400 Hz, entailing a relatively complicated electrical system on board the aircraft. The FD-104 could be coupled to the Collins AP-101 autopilot for automatic ILS approaches.

In 1955 Smith's Aircraft Instruments Ltd. of Britain unveiled its own flight director system, intended for use with a Smiths autopilot, which BOAC selected for its Bristol Britannias and which BEA was expected to select for its Vickers

---

10 Not described in the referenced article.

11 *Flight*, 11 February 1955, 167

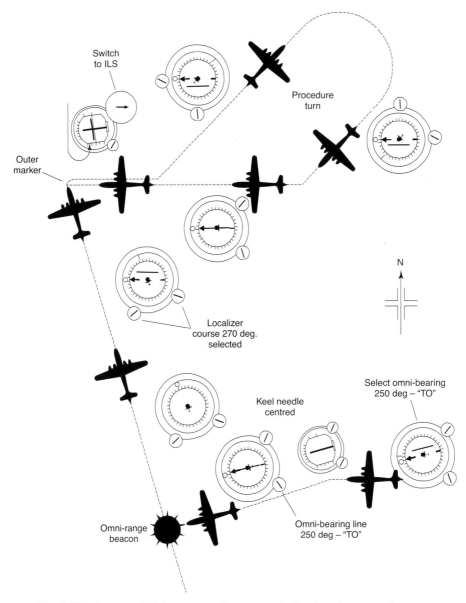

Switch
to ILS

Procedure
turn

Outer
marker

Localizer
course 270 deg.
selected

N

Select omni-bearing
250 deg – "TO"

Keel needle
centred

Omni-range
beacon

Omni-bearing line
250 deg – "TO"

The Collins integrated flight system – instrument indications in a procedure turn.

Viscounts.[12] The Smith's system resembled the Collins system in that information from several sources was displayed on an attitude director and a heading and track indicator, but the attitude director provided both information and commands and was self-sufficient as an artificial horizon. By 1957 Sperry, Smiths, Collins and Bendix were all producing flight directors for use with their proprietary autopilots.[13]

Until the 1950s gyroscopic instruments were self-contained with their own gyroscopes. Each gyroscope had its own errors and had to be small enough to fit inside the instrument. Advances in servo theory and design in the 1940s made it possible, by the mid 1950s,[14] to drive several instruments from a single, high-quality master gyroscope, also known as a stable platform. The new instruments in high-performance aircraft were parts of instrument systems driven by master gyroscopes and air data computers. These systems were heavy, costly

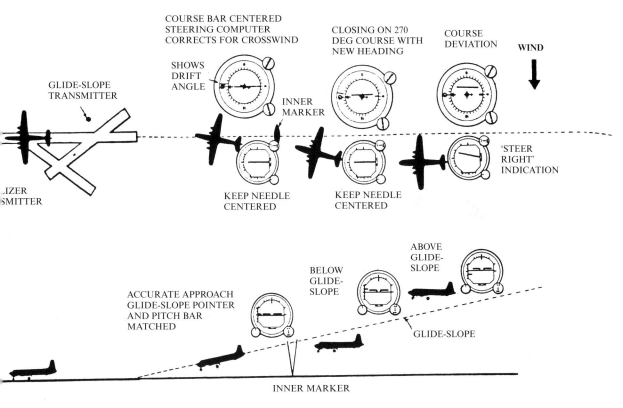

This chart of a hypothetical ILS approach to a localizer beam bearing 270 deg shows the instrument reactons during *en route* nagivation and final approach. It has been assumed that the pilot wishes to approach the VOR beacon along the 250 deg radial bearing.

The Collins integrated flight system – instrument indications in an ILS approach.

and demanding in electrical power; conventional instruments continued to suffice for low-performance aircraft.

Master gyroscopes were manufactured on both sides of the Atlantic. An American example, the Eclipse-Pioneer stable platform, manufactured by Bendix Aviation Corporation in 1957, weighed 13 kg (28 pounds) unmounted and consumed 75 watts of 3-phase AC power at 115 volts, 400 Hz and 26 watts at 26 volts DC. It would erect to within 1° of true vertical within two minutes of being switched on; maximum drift rates were 1° per hour in azimuth and 2° per hour in elevation. It provided a continuous attitude reference throughout 360° in any axis and could follow continuous loops by the aircraft in excess of 30° per second. Even this was improved upon. In 1958 the random drift of the Sperry Rotorace gyroscope was only 0.25° per hour; it was hoped that further development would reduce this to 0.05° per hour. This compared with 15° per hour in the simpler and less-expensive heading indicators installed in low-performance aircraft.[15] Master gyroscopes eventually made possible the ultimate attitude indicator, an instrument in which the artificial horizon was replaced by a sphere with a light top half and a dark bottom half, graduated in pitch and azimuth, free to rotate in 360° of pitch, roll and yaw and in which the horizon indication was true to life.[16]

As with gyroscopic instruments, the other instruments that told the pilot about the air

12 *Flight*, 19 August 1955, 254

13 *Flight*, 22 February 1957, 246

14 *Flight*, 12 April 1957, 484

15 *Flight*, 20 May 1958, 681

16 US Air Force Instrument Flying Manual, 51–37(C2), 1982, Fig. 1–8

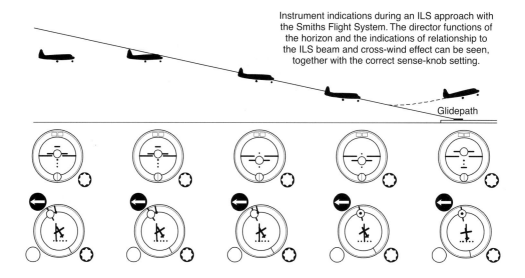

Instrument indications during an ILS approach with the Smiths Flight System. The director functions of the horizon and the indications of relationship to the ILS beam and cross-wind effect can be seen, together with the correct sense-knob setting.

Glidepath

The Smith's flight director system – instrument indications.

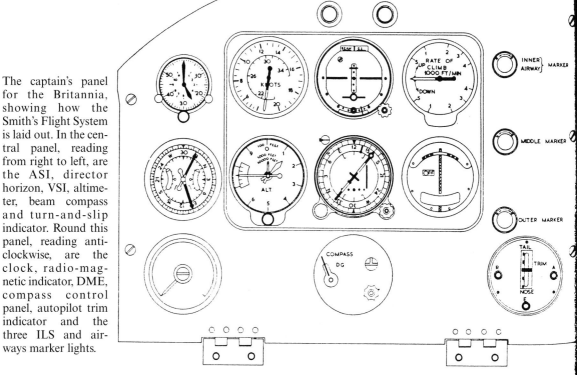

The captain's panel for the Britannia, showing how the Smith's Flight System is laid out. In the central panel, reading from right to left, are the ASI, director horizon, VSI, altimeter, beam compass and turn-and-slip indicator. Round this panel, reading anti-clockwise, are the clock, radio-magnetic indicator, DME, compass control panel, autopilot trim indicator and the three ILS and airways marker lights.

The Smith's flight director system in the Bristol Britannia instrument panel.

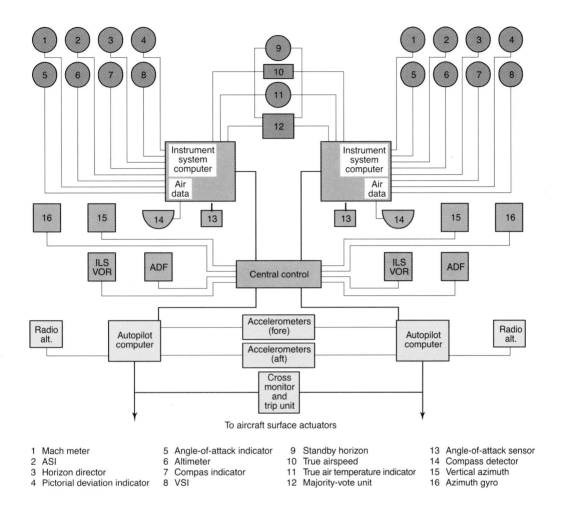

Integrated flight control and instrument system for airliners, 1958 – schematic.

1	Mach meter	5	Angle-of-attack indicator	9	Standby horizon	13	Angle-of-attack sensor
2	ASI	6	Altimeter	10	True airspeed	14	Compass detector
3	Horizon director	7	Compas indicator	11	True air temperature indicator	15	Vertical azimuth
4	Pictorial deviation indicator	8	VSI	12	Majority-vote unit	16	Azimuth gyro

through which he was flying were self-contained until the 1950s. For example, a static port and a pitot tube connected by tubing drove the airspeed indicator, vertical speed indicator and altimeter; the pilot or navigator read an outside air thermometer and used the temperature to convert indicated airspeed (IAS) to true airspeed (TAS). This type of system no longer sufficed for the more extreme ranges of airspeed, altitude and temperature in which jet aircraft flew.

The new jets of the middle 1950s – the F-101, F-105, B-58, Boeing 707, DC-8 and CV-880 – carried air data computers.[17] Sensors measured the pressure, temperature and density of the air sur-

rounding the aircraft and supplied information to electro-mechanical computers which drove instruments reading IAS, TAS, Mach number, altitude and angle of attack. The Bendix air data system for the F-101, F-105 and B-58 weighed 23 kg (50 pounds). These heavy, costly systems were justified only in aircraft whose performance rendered the older systems inadequate. Thousands of aircraft of lower performance were manufactured each year with instruments similar to those used by Doolittle in 1929.

17 *Flight*, 12 April 1957, 483

Convair B-58.

The new jet fighters were capable of very rapid changes of attitude and continuous high G forces which could disorientate the pilot easily and with disastrous consequences. Researchers, therefore, continued to look for radically new ways to replace the artificial horizon with something closer to the pilot's perceptions of visual flight. The long-standing debate between inside-outside and outside-inside displays continued. An inside-outside display, such as an artificial horizon, consists of a moving horizon reference, equivalent to the pilot's view ahead in clear air. An outside-inside display consists of a moving aircraft symbol as if an exter-

nal observer were viewing the aircraft from astern.

Researchers at Convair in the 1950s concluded that the two types of display were not opposites but poles of a continuum along which the pilot's perceptions moved in response to his bodily sensations. The result was an experimental attitude indicator called the Kinalog[18] bearing a surprising resemblance to the device suggested by Ocker and Crane in 1932,[19] although immensely more complicated. A stylized landscape provided the ground reference while a system of mirrors and lenses provided an aircraft symbol and adjusted the display between outside-inside and inside-outside presen-

Republic F-105.

tation. The system was evaluated in a simulator but development work ceased in 1958 and funding was withdrawn before the system was ever installed in an aircraft. The Kinalog suffered from the fundamental defect that it did not provide a constant, unambiguous horizon reference.

In 1954 the US Navy Bureau of Aeronautics was working to simplify the layout of instruments in jet fighters to reduce the eighteen months and $US50,000 needed to train an all-weather pilot. The US Navy programme proposed an outside-inside attitude indicator driven by remote attitude and heading gyroscopes. The horizon line ran around the outside of a rotating vertical drum, marked in degrees of azimuth, which acted as a heading indicator; an aircraft symbol moved in front of the drum.

The inside-outside concept finally prevailed and attempts to synthesize a picture of the outside world ceased. Most instrument flying could be specified in numbers: degrees of pitch, bank or azimuth, feet of altitude, feet per minute of climb

18 *Flight*, 28 November 1958, 823
19 Ocker, W. C., Crane, C. J. 1932, 62

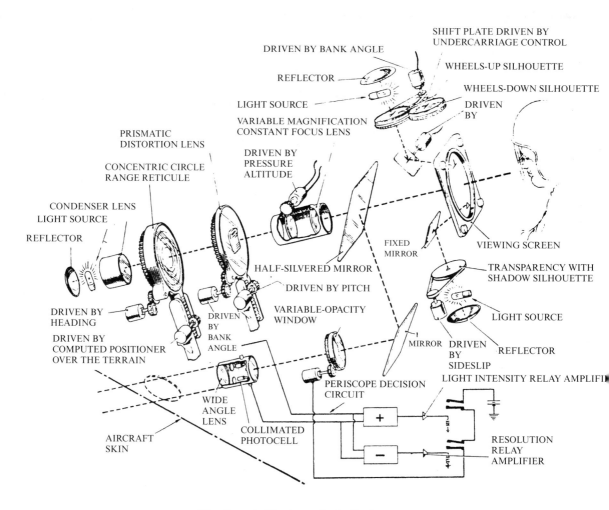

The Convair Kinalog attitude display system.

or descent. The problems of controlling high-performance aircraft in blind conditions would be solved by improvements to existing concepts of instrumentation and flight control rather than by elaborate and costly attempts to improve the attitude analogue. The specific needs of low-flying combat aircraft were eventually solved by an emerging group of technologies capable of penetrating darkness and obscurity: radar, infra-red and image intensification.

Work continued throughout the 1950s to improve the presentation of instrument indications to the pilot. The RAF used a standard instrument layout as early as 1937 (Basic Six); the US armed forces still had no equivalent system until 1955.[20]

The Basic T, derived from the RAF's Basic Six instrument layout began to appear in newly built US light aircraft in 1962.[21] A major American project was the Army-Navy Instrumentation Program (ANIP); Douglas was the prime contractor with 600 subcontractors. A small but significant ANIP concept was to enable the pilot to call up information, such as fuel remaining and course to base, when he wanted it, rather than calculating it or searching for it among an array of dials, all displaying their information continuously regardless of whether it was wanted or not. The results of the ANIP were released to civil aviation in 1957.[22]

By 1958 the USAAF had developed a simplified instrument panel for the F-102, F-105 and F-106.

Convair F-102.

Two large circular instruments occupied the centre of the panel: the flight director/attitude indicator above, the HSI beneath. Other important information was displayed on six vertical tape instruments, three on each side of the two main instruments.[23] Much of the remaining information needed by the pilot was displayed on a dozen small instruments.

It had been recognized for many years that the magnetic compass was incompatible with aircraft. In addition to the previously mentioned errors, it had to be placed where the pilot could see it, which tended to be in a part of the aircraft most affected by stray magnetism. Its torque was too slight to drive other devices, such as autopilots or remote-reading repeaters. The gyroscopic heading indicators of the 1930s and early 1940s suffered from the same limitation as the artificial horizon, becoming unusable due to toppling of the gyroscope if the aircraft's pitch or roll exceeded 55°.[24] A gyroscopic heading indicator with no north-seeking tendency, corrected manually from a magnetic compass, was both inconvenient and relatively inaccurate. Although this combination continues in use in low-performance aircraft to the present day, something better had to be found.

In Britain the Campbell-Bannerman aperiodic compass of 1918 was still in RAF service thirty years later,[25] but between 1925 and 1940 the RAE developed an improved compass system that was used during the Second World War. The motion of the compass card was damped by being clamped mechanically for 2.5 seconds at an interval related to its 14-second natural period of oscillation. If the card was not aligned with the clamping frame an electrical contact precessed a gyroscope. The system was thus damped, self-averaging and gyrostabilized. The gyroscope produced enough torque to drive other devices.[26]

The earth inductor compass (described earlier) was the first attempt to orientate to the earth's magnetic field other than by means of the compass needle. Improved electro-magnetic alloys developed during the 1930s (mu-metal and permalloy) led to the flux valve, also known as flux gate, compass, perfected in the Sperry Gyrosyn Compass

20 *Flight*, 9 July 1954, 45; 8 April 1955, 453
21 *Flying*, June 1962, 37; September 1962, 25
22 *Flight*, 20 December 1957, 951
23 *Flight*, 16 May 1958, 681
24 Air Ministry Publication 1732b 1943, 112; Jordanoff, A. 1938, 176
25 Williams, J. E. D. 1992, 140
26 Williams, J. E. D. 1992, 141

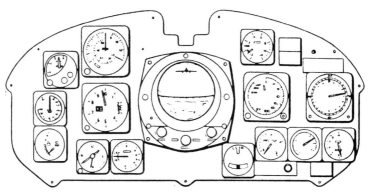

The experimental F9F-6 Cougar instrument panel. Anti-clockwise, round the heading/attitude dial, are combined Machmeter-A.S.I., veeder altimeter, V.S.I., turn and slip, fuel gauge and G-meter.

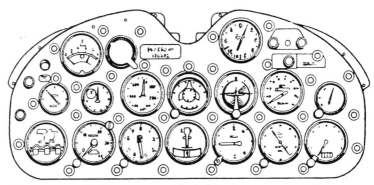

The present standard arrangement with six flying instruments centrally ranged and G-meter at top right.

US military instrument panel, mid 1950s.

developed during the Second World War. The principle of the flux valve is described by J. E. D. Williams:[27]

> The primary coil is wound in series in opposite directions around two identical parallel permalloy strips. The secondary coil is wound around the whole assembly. The primary AC excitation is sufficient to saturate the strips. In the absence of any other magnetic source, the total flux linked with the secondary will be zero. If, however, there is a component of the earth's magnetic field parallel to the strips, it will have no effect on the strip momentarily saturated in the same direction, but it will reduce the magnetization in the opposite direction of the other. The net result is that an electromotive force is induced in the secondary at twice the frequency of the primary excitation and of a magnitude that varies with the component of the earth's field parallel to the strips. Three such devices arranged as the sides of an equilateral triangle, or equidistant spokes, constitute a sensor of the earth's magnetic field.

In the Gyrosyn compass[28] the flux valve was sus-

27 Williams, J. E. D. 1992, 142
28 *Flight*, 31 October 1946, 464; 13 March 1947, 207

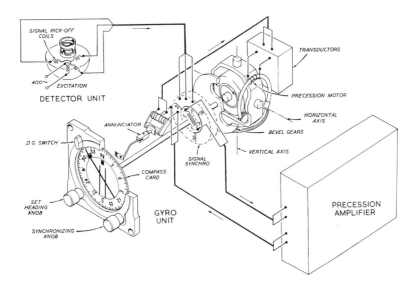

The Sperry Gyrosyn compass – Schematic (Type CL1).

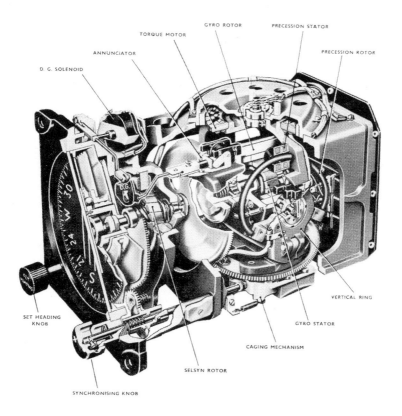

The Gyrosyn Compass, Type CL1 – sectional drawing of gyro unit and indicator.

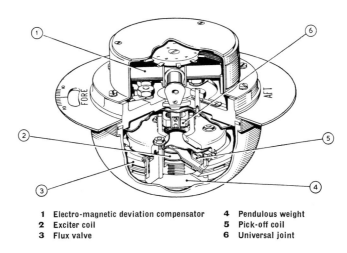

1 Electro-magnetic deviation compensator   4 Pendulous weight
2 Exciter coil   5 Pick-off coil
3 Flux valve   6 Universal joint

The Gyrosyn Compass, Type CL1, Flux Valve Detector Unit.

pended as nearly horizontally as possible. The exciter current alternating frequency was 400 Hz and the flux valve output precessed a gyroscope which drove a heading indicator. Because the flux valve was north-sensing rather than north-seeking, it was free of the acceleration and northerly turning errors of the magnetic compass. Because the gyroscope was slaved to the flux valve, continual readjustment of the heading indicator was unnecessary. A further benefit in long-range aircraft was that a repeater could be installed in the navigator's position. A feature as simple as clearly shaped reference marks resulted in pilots being able to hold a heading to 1°. The navigator's indicator could be read to 0.5°. The indicators could be set for magnetic variation by a mechanism like the barometric adjustment on a Kollsman altimeter; headings could be read directly in degrees true. The Gyrosyn compass was, clearly, a complex and costly device warranted only in long-range or high-performance aircraft. It consumed 90 watts of 400-Hz, 3-phase AC power at 115 volts and weighed 16 kg (35.5 pounds). A smaller version, without the navigator's indicator and weighing 7 kg (16 pounds), was manufactured for smaller aircraft.

Increasing Arctic flying entailed navigating in an area of large, closely spaced changes in magnetic variation,[29] making it difficult to navigate by reference to magnetic north. To solve this problem heading indicators were manufactured with precision gyroscopes that drifted so slowly that the gyroscope could replace the magnetic north pole as

the unchanging point of reference. The first of these was the Kearfott N1 compass of 1950 with a random error of less than 1° per hour,[30] followed during the 1950s by the Bendix Polar Path precision gyrostabilized compass system.

In North America all aviation altimetry was (and is) referenced to sea level. When a pilot set his altimeter with a barometric pressure, obtained from an altimeter on the ground and transmitted to him verbally by radio, the altimeter read the aircraft's altitude above sea level. A correctly set and calibrated altimeter read the airfield elevation when the aircraft was on the ground. If no altimeter setting was available before take-off, the pilot could set the altimeter by knowing the field elevation. Above 5,500 metres (18,000 feet) and in certain remote areas the standard pressure of 29.92 inches of mercury is used.

In Europe several different altimeter settings were used, referred to by the international Q code; confusion between them led to fatal accidents. QFE was the field-level barometric pressure measured for the highest point in the landing area. An altimeter set to QFE read 0 when the aircraft was on the ground. QNH was QFE corrected to sea level according to field elevation and the ICAO Standard Atmosphere. An altimeter set to QNH read approximately field elevation when the aircraft was on the ground. QFF was QNH corrected for local temperature.[31] Regional QNH or QFE were the lowest values forecast to occur within the region.

In the wartime RAF it was left to the pilot's discretion which setting to use.[32] '(The altimeter) should be set before take-off, either to read the height of the airfield above sea level (which is useful for cross-country flying), or to zero on the ground (for local flying).' Altimeter setting procedures were introduced after the war, but the debate between the American and British systems went on.

Shortly after midnight on 1 September 1966, a Bristol Britannia crashed 2 km (1.5 miles) short of the runway on the approach to Ljubljana, Yugoslavia, killing 97 of the 117 people on board.[33] Fog had formed over the airport, reducing visibility from 5 km (3 miles), as reported to the crew, to 760 metres (2,500 feet) at the time of the accident. The company operations manual required the captain to set his altimeter to QFE for the approach and landing 'at a convenient time', which he omitted to do. The investigation found both altimeters set to QNH. The approach had been flown about 380 metres (1,250 feet) below the minimum safe altitudes as if the captain's altimeter had been set to QFE.

On the night of 21 January 1967, a British-operated DC-4 freighter crashed at Frankfurt, Germany[34] in similar circumstances. Scattered low cloud overlay the area. The DC-4 crew were using the ILS but it was thought that they had tried to get below the low cloud to make the final approach visually. The company approach checklist required the captain to set his altimeter to QFE but, again, both altimeters were found still set to QNH, resulting in the crew believing that they were 113 metres (370 feet) higher than they were. The crew, who were killed, had never asked for, or been given a QFE. The aircraft hit the ground more than 2 km (1.5 miles) short of the runway.

At the time both the American and ICAO-standard approach procedures used QNH exclusively, yet the German accident investigation report recommended the continuing use of QFE. Captain D. H. Davison, chief pilot of Britannia Airways, operator of the Britannia that crashed at Ljubljana, commented on the difficulties of using QFE and advocated a change to the sole use of QNH,[35] which allowed the aircraft's altitude to be compared instantly with terrain and obstacle heights marked on charts that were referenced to sea level; and could not be otherwise. Using QNH, only one set of altitudes needed to be printed on approach charts. As similar values of QNH persisted over wide areas, gross errors in altimeter settings would be easier to spot. A missed approach and diversion, flown according to the British system, entailed setting QFE at the intended destination, resetting QNH on the missed approach when the crew were already busy, then setting a different QFE on the approach to the alternate airport, each setting offering opportunities for error in radio transmission from the ground, and reception and setting by the crew. Because of the danger inherent in using the wrong QFE, a pilot had to make a rough calculation of what the QFE should be, based on QNH and the airfield elevation, which added further to his workload. Captain Davison suspected that the Ljubljana and Frankfurt accidents were merely the tip of an iceberg of unreported altimeter setting errors that had not resulted in accidents because the aircraft had been in visual conditions for long enough before landing that the mistake made no difference, if it was even noticed. In Britain the optional use of QFE continues.[36]

As early as 1946 the Kollsman Instrument Division of the Square D Company brought out a self-correcting altimeter[37] using settings continuously broadcast by radio from the ground to a small receiver in the aircraft which corrected the altimeter. This idea never became current and to this day altimeter settings are still transmitted by voice and altimeters are set manually.

Flight at unprecedented altitudes caused new altimetry problems. Instruments had to measure altitudes of nearly 30,000 metres (100,000 feet) where the pressure change with each increment in altitude is only a fraction of what it is at sea level. An altimeter had to be readable to within a few feet, while having a range of many tens of thousands of feet. The high rates of climb and descent of which the new, high-performance aircraft were capable resulted in three-pointer altimeters being misread by 3,000 metres (10,000 feet). This caused

29 Magnetic variation: the difference between geographic north and magnetic north caused by the difference in location between the geographic and magnetic north poles.
30 Williams, J. E. D. 1992, 143
31 Wickson, M. 1992, 22
32 Air Ministry Publication 1732b 1943, 112
33 *Flight International*, 12 September 1968, 397
34 *Flight International*, 21 November 1968, 817
35 *Flight International*, 30 January 1969, 162
36 CAP 85: A guide to aviation law, flight rules and procedures for applicants for the Private Pilot's Licence, Appendix 11, June 1985.
37 *Flight*, 1 August 1946, 113

North American F-86D.

the crash of a Viscount in Scotland in April 1958,[38] and a Britannia in England that December.[39] In both cases the aircraft was descending blind and struck cloud-covered high ground. This resulted in an instrument being developed with a rolling counter displaying thousands and tens of thousands of feet in numbers and only a single needle to indicate hundreds of feet on a dial. The British Ministry of Civil Aviation required that the three-pointer altimeters be replaced in civilian aircraft capable of flying higher than 6,000 metres (20,000 feet) not later than 30 September 1959.[40]

The large, piston-engined airliners were the last new category of aircraft in which the pilot moved the control surfaces through direct mechanical linkages from the cockpit controls. In jets the air loads resisting deflection of the control surfaces were so great that powered controls were essential. Once powered controls were in place, putting an autopilot to drive them was a natural step.

From the late 1940s onwards the performance of certain new types of aircraft began for the first time to exceed the endurance, power of concentration and speed of response of the unaided human pilot.[41] In supersonic fighters too much happened too quickly for the pilot to handle without automation; the F-104, for example, could not be controlled in flight unless two out of the three axes

of its auto-stabilization system were functioning. In the B-58 supersonic bomber, which entered service in 1960 after ten years of development,[42] the pilot's stick commands were fed into a computer which deflected the control surfaces with no mechanical link between the pilot and the control surfaces.[43]

As early as 1952 an American automatic fire-control system allowed a pilot to fly an interceptor to the vicinity of a bomber, whereupon the fire control system would track the bomber and aim and fire missiles without the pilot ever seeing the bomber other than on radar. The first systems were retrofitted to F-94Cs, F-89Ds and F-86Ds but the F-102, which began to enter USAF service in 1955, was designed for automatic interception from the outset.[44]

In 1957 the leading free-world manufacturers of autopilots were Sperry on both sides of the

38 ICAO Circular #59, AN/54, 1961
39 *Flight*, 6 March 1959, 333
40 Ibid.
41 *Flight*, 12 April 1957, 485–8
42 Swanborough, F. G. 1963, 156
43 *Flight*, 16 May 1958, 665
44 *Flight*, 11 July 1952, 46; 29 April 1955, 548; 11 November 1955, 748; 16 May 1958, 665

Republic F-94C.

Lockheed F-104.

Atlantic, Smith's Aircraft Instruments and Elliott Brothers in the UK, and Bendix, Collins, Lear and Minneapolis-Honeywell in the US. These companies and two other smaller producers turned out some eighteen different models. Among the most sophisticated of these was the Minneapolis-Honeywell MB-3 which was standard equipment in the F-100D, weighing 44 kg (98 pounds). By 1957 orders for this autopilot alone (and its spare parts) had reached $38 million.

The Minneapolis-Honeywell MB-5 included a coupler that allowed the aircraft to be controlled, and its weapons launched, by direct radio control from the ground. A device of this kind had been used by the US Marines in Korea to attack ground targets at known positions at night. The referenced source[45] does not record how successful it was but, even so, considering the technology that was available in 1945, this represented an extraordinary advance in a few years.

The year 1945 saw the first use of helicopters. Helicopters were practically impossible to fly blind without extensive automation, and helicopter blind flying demanded all of the developments mentioned above, and more, to solve this problem. A fixed-wing aircraft flies because of its forward speed; its flight path is thus a function of its attitude. No such relationship exists for a helicopter. A helicopter is unstable in flight or, at best, neutrally stable and is therefore too demanding to fly blind without automatic help. A pitot-static air speed indicator is ineffective at low speeds. Some types of helicopter could be hand-flown on instruments in calm air, some not at all, but this was difficult in turbulence and impossible at low speeds or hovering.[46] These problems were acknowledged in the early 1950s and work began on automatic stabilization on both sides of the Atlantic. By the end of the decade auto-stabilizers and powered flight controls were standard in large helicopters.

By the mid-1960s two types of helicopter autopilots were in use: stability augmenters and auto-stabilizers.[47] Stability augmenters used a rate gyroscope which took the helicopter's current attitude as its datum and sought to return it to that attitude. Such a gyroscope would not detect slow changes in attitude but would accommodate itself to them; a stability-augmented helicopter would therefore tend gradually to diverge from its original attitude. Nevertheless, the short-term stability allowed the pilot to fly hands-off like a fixed-wing aircraft, which was not otherwise possible.

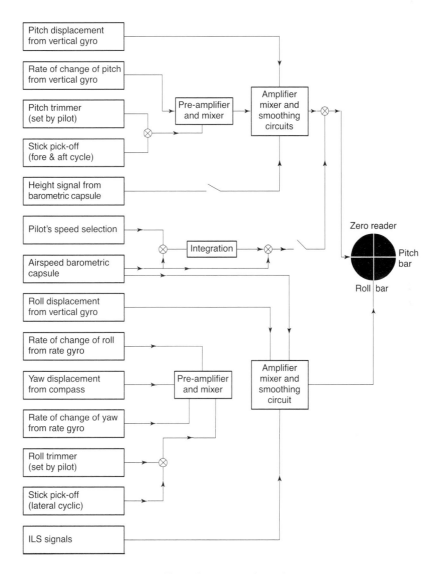

Helicopter flight director – schematic.

Schematic layout of the information and computation channels in the Zero Reader flight director tested in a BEA Whirlwind.

Stability augmenters were robust and simple. Auto-stabilizers used a gyroscope referenced to vertical but allowed the pilot to overcome the vertical gyroscope with stick position; the gyroscope would then reference itself to some new vertical established by the pilot. Auto-stabilization made instrument flight possible in the cruise but still offered no solution to blind flight at low forward speeds, or in the hover.

Flight directors for fixed-wing aircraft were adapted to helicopters, the first examples being made by Sperry and Ferranti in about 1960.[48] Helicopter flight directors gave directions for control position instead of attitude, so successfully that fixed-wing pilots were able to fly helicopters without prior experience and helicopter pilots were

45 *Flight*, 12 April 1957, 485–8
46 *Flight International*, 24 February 1961, 238
47 Curties, M. C. 1966
48 *Flight*, 24 February 1961, 244

Westland/Sikorsky Sea King helicopter hovering to a sonobuoy.

able to fly blind without auto-stabilization. A helicopter flight director, however, provided no information about the flight path; a separate navigation display was needed. The first of these used Decca and an enlarged-scale Flight Log but Doppler[49] was the natural source of precise information.

One of the first commercial helicopter operators was British European Airways; their Helicopter Experimental Unit was set up at London Gatwick in 1947.[50] BEA night mail flights in eastern England in 1949 were probably the first scheduled helicopter operations in blind conditions. They made the first helicopter blind landings in a Bristol Sycamore in 1954, using Decca with an extra-large-scale Flight Log. They tested a Bendix sonic altimeter and worked with Sperry to adapt the Zero Reader as a flight director. Blind approaches could be flown along straight approach tracks at 37 km/h (20 knots) and a descent rate of 230 metres per minute (750 feet per minute) with an autopilot and a flight director.[51] The low forward speed resulted in large angles of drift correction in crosswinds, consequently the landing ground often appeared in a different position to where the pilot expected to see it. Experience up to 1957 showed that blind approaches could be flown to minima of 60 metre (200 foot) ceiling and 180 metres (600 feet) visibility with a probable reduction to 45 metres (150 foot) ceiling and 140 metres (450 feet) visibility as experience grew.

Decca was found to be the best blind-approach aid for helicopters. GCA and ILS were less satisfactory because the glideslope corresponded to the natural flight of a fixed-wing aircraft but was difficult for a helicopter pilot to follow because of differing aerodynamics. Large drift correction angles made it similarly difficult to follow a GCA final approach track or an ILS localizer. A microwave ILS produced by Elliott Brothers in the UK offered good prospects, with the potential for auto-coupling. For military needs the Bell Helicopter Co. produced a portable Micro-Wave Remote Area Instrument Landing System (MWRAILS), based on a battery-operated transponder beacon on the ground with a range of 16 km (10 miles), weighing only 7 kg (15 pounds). Radar and a computer in the helicopter calculated range, bearing and elevation from the beacon. Touchdown accuracies of 6 metres (20 feet) were claimed. MWRAILS beacons could also be used for *en route* navigation.

Military helicopter users were particularly demanding in their requirements for operation in low visibility.[52] Anti-submarine helicopters were required to descend to a hover and lower a sonar buoy, in fog and darkness if need be. This manoeuvre could not be hand-flown blind. The inputs to the autopilot were provided by barometric or radar altimetry in the approach to the hover, Doppler and cable-angle once the sonar buoy was down. This application also required compensation for wave height. The US Navy progressively developed this system in their Sikorsky S-58 helicopters from the late 1950s onwards. By 1958 the HSS-1N had been flying with auto-stabilization for several years. The auto-stabilizer malfunctioned, on average, once every 800 hours, but the S-58 could be hand-flown on instruments to a landing if necessary. Helicopter autopilots differed from those of fixed-wing aircraft both in design and in the ways they could malfunction. Because the helicopter pilot depended on automatic control in blind conditions more than any fixed-wing pilot, autopilot failure modes and the pilot's capability after autopilot failure were studied intensively.

The highly developed military systems far outran anything available for civilian use. Restricted for security reasons, they also could not be coupled to civilian blind navigation aids. Not only were passenger safety and comfort of primary importance in civil aviation but, in 1960, there was no civilian pilot qualification for helicopter IFR.

In the 1970s helicopter IFR flight development went beyond the problems of retaining control in blind conditions to a more comprehensive investigation of helicopter all-weather operation.[53] Helicopters were more vulnerable to icing than fixed-wing aircraft. Engine air intakes, engines, windshields and pitot heads had to be designed for ice prevention; for the rotor blades, flexure and centrifugal force were thought to be sufficient to prevent ice from forming. Helicopter pilots had to be more cautious than fixed-wing pilots about flying in icing because flight trials in icing were potentially more dangerous. In the mid-1970s the effects of ice accretion on helicopters were still imperfectly known.

49 Doppler navigation radar: discussed in Chapter 24.
50 *Flight International*, 24 February 1961, 241
51 Hearne, P. A. 1957
52 *Flight*, 10 October 1958, 572
53 Moxam, L. R. 1974; Ginn, M. C. 1974; Locke, L. G. 1974;

IFR operation was so costly for a helicopter air carrier as to raise questions whether it was worthwhile. Irish Helicopters Ltd.[54] found that IFR operation increased crew cost by 100%, airframe capital cost by 20–35%, maintenance cost by 40% and crew training by 250%. IFR fuel reserves reduced passenger capacity. Specific training and a specific helicopter instrument rating were needed. The discovery of oil in the North Sea and the need to service drilling platforms by helicopter in all weathers was the real impetus behind civilian helicopter IFR. The American FAA rode on the shirttails of the British CAA in its regulation of this area.[55] Certification was type by type, depending on automatic capability, rather than for helicopters in general. By 1977, for example, the Aerospatiale Gazelle was certificated in the US for take-off and landing in Category 2 conditions of 30 metres (100 feet) ceiling and 1,200 metres visibility.[56]

The 1940s ended the days when a pilot could understand the construction and functioning of every component of his aircraft. 'Black boxes' proliferated.[57] Crew members controlled and used these devices, but understood little of their inner workings. Increased, and inescapable dependence on black boxes produced correspondingly intense arguments about their safety and reliability and about how much aircrew needed to understand of their internal functioning. The events of the 1940s

drove the development of all sorts of technologies directly and indirectly related to aviation; the Cold War forced developments at a pace that accelerated as one invention gave rise to another. Without the developments in instrumentation and flight control mentioned above, the new, high-performance aircraft would have become increasingly dangerous and ineffective, especially in blind conditions. Master gyroscopes, flight data computers, autopilots and radio navigation contributed logically to turning the aircraft into an autonomous vehicle capable of flying itself from one place to another under the supervision of its human crew, except for manoeuvres requiring interaction with human air traffic controllers. Cloud and darkness were immaterial. Automatic systems were, however, fallible and such an aircraft required more knowledge, and not less, on the part of the aircrew. Technology had come to the rescue but nevertheless remained the servant of the human pilot, never the master.

54 Ginn, M. C. 1974
55 *Flight International*, 23 November 1972, 742; 1 February 1973, 143
56 *Flight International*, 26 February 1977, 461
57 A 'black box' is a device (such as a television) for which the user understands how to manipulate the controls for desired results, but does not understand its internal working.

CHAPTER 20

Navigation and Politics

The new, global airline network needed internationally standard navigation aids. A decision on short-range navigation, however, was not reached until 1959 after a long dispute between the American proponents of VOR/DME and the British proponents of Decca. This dispute delayed the improvement of navigation aids in Europe. Meanwhile, the Americans pressed on with VOR/DME while the Europeans installed a mixture of British and American systems. Long-range navigation was less affected by the dispute.

VOR with DME was conceived as a common civilian and military system, providing complete range and bearing information, and was advocated as such to the PICAO[1] by the US State Department and the US Civil Aeronautics Board. The PICAO Radio Technical Division recommended them as the international standard for short-range navigation in November 1946.[2] The ICAO accepted this in 1947, but on the understanding that DME was an integral part of the system, that enough VOR beacons would be installed to cover wide areas and that area navigation computers would be developed to allow aircraft to fly tracks other than from beacon to beacon. These conditions had still not been met by the mid-1950s.

By 1950 the CAA had commissioned 300 VORs in the US[3] and planned for 415 by June 1951, with a final total of 466.[4] The sixty-four VARs would be converted to VORs. The first VOR airways approved for IFR connected such cities as Omaha, Denver, Kansas City, Albuquerque, Wichita, Tulsa, Oklahoma City, El Paso and Fort Worth. Continental was the first airline user, in October 1950. The CAA inaugurated the VOR-based Victor airways system on 1 June 1952, but the radio range airways remained in service for the time being. VOR coverage of the US was almost complete by early 1955[5] and by 1960 the American VOR airway system was in place in approximately its present form. Equipment has been improved

since then, but the VOR and the procedures for its use remain unchanged to the present day. The CAA began to decommission the radio range network, although eighty-eight ranges were left in place for aircraft not equipped for VOR.[6] The last radio range in the US, used for instrument approaches at Elkins, West Virginia, was decommissioned in 1969.[7]

Outside the US VOR coverage spread more slowly. In 1957 there was still only one civilian VOR in the UK, although some were built there by the USAF.[8] In spite of the ICAO recommendation, governments outside the US were less willing to use it. In particular, northwest Europe was covered by the two British hyperbolic systems, Gee and Decca.

The first DME beacons in the US, built by Federal Telecommunication Laboratories, were sited at radio range stations at Caldwell, New Jersey; Sellingsgrove and Phillipsburg, Pennsylvania; Youngstown, Cleveland and Toledo, Ohio; Millersburg, Indiana; and Chicago in 1951–2.[9] In 1953 the practice of pairing DME frequencies with those of VOR and ILS began so that, by tuning the VOR or ILS, the aircrew obtained signals from a collocated DME beacon automatically.[10] The first on-board DME receivers showed the distance to the beacon by means of a needle on a circular dial. Developments in microcomputer technology in the 1960s and 1970s allowed very small on-board

---

1 *Flying*, June 1955, 66; *Flight,* 6 September 1957, leading article.
2 *Flight*, 5 December 1946, 629; 20 March 1947, 243
3 Bailey-Watson, C. B. 1951
4 *Flight*, 11 January 1951, 53
5 *Flight*, 11 February 1955, 169
6 *Flying*, September 1957, 72
7 *Flying*, January 1995, 56
8 Greenhalgh, G. T. 1957
9 *Flying*, January 1952, 50
10 *Flight*, 6 March 1953, 292

receivers to be produced, giving numerical read-outs of distance, groundspeed (from which the pilot could easily calculate the windspeed component along track) and flight time. DME thus became a more powerful navigational tool than might be supposed from its original purpose.

The Australians made faster progress. In 1948, Amalgamated Wireless (Australia) Ltd. won a government contract to install ninety-five DME beacons on the Australian mainland and some nearby islands. The Australian system used 200 MHz with twelve channels.[11] In 1951 the British had a 1,000 MHz, 100 channel DME, manufactured by Ferranti, with a range of 320 km (200 miles), ready for installation at London, Rome and Cairo on the London–Cairo de Havilland Comet route. It was accurate to 800 metres (0.5 mile) and had a homing feature. DME was particularly useful in providing the crews of jet aircraft with a precise distance from destination at which to start their descent, minimizing inefficient fuel consumption at low altitudes.[12]

The studies for an international DME specification, however, took until 1951[13] and the implementation of DME lagged far behind VOR. By the mid-1950s DME was in extensive use in the US and Australia but the few beacons in Europe were still only experimental.[14] By 1957 there were still no 1,000 MHz beacons in use in the UK.[15] The introduction of DME in Europe was delayed by controversies between VOR/DME and Decca and between VOR/DME and TACAN.[16]

Although VOR/DME was at first promoted as a common civilian and military system, the US armed forces never converted from radio ranges and NDBs to VOR/DME because of the secret development of a new UHF range-and-bearing beacon called TACAN. This was developed by the US Navy in the early 1950s from a research programme begun in 1945,[17] using the 1,000 MHz band. In 1951 the USAF tested a similar device developed by Sperry, using the 5,000 MHz band.[18] A TACAN beacon transmits bearing information using the same principle, a reference signal and a rotating signal, as the VOR. Distance is provided by DME which is integral to the beacon. Both types of information are transmitted on the same channel. Maximum range is about 320 km (200 miles). Comparative tests by the CAA showed that TACAN was as vulnerable as VOR to siting errors caused by nearby obstructions, but was more complicated and less reliable. Airborne equipment weights in the mid 1950s were 38 kg (84 pounds)

for VOR/DME and 33 kg (72 pounds) for TACAN, but VOR receivers could also receive voice communications and ILS signals. Although the merits and demerits of VOR/DME and TACAN were roughly equal,[19] a TACAN beacon could be installed on a ship or even a large aircraft, such as a flying tanker, whereas a VOR beacon could not.

In 1955 the US armed forces publicly switched their allegiance to the newly unveiled TACAN, which pre-empted the DME frequencies, and they pressed for TACAN to replace VOR within ten years. The Departments of Defense and Commerce, the latter over-ruling its own aviation agency, the CAA, recommended to the Air Navigation Development Board that TACAN should replace VOR by 1965 and that DME be discontinued by 30 June 1955. This aroused a storm of protest from civil aviation which had already invested heavily in VOR/DME. The introduction of TACAN was, in any event, delayed by technical problems and it remained in only limited service until 1959. Until then the US armed forces relied on the civilian radio range airways and, as late as 1959, some military aircraft, especially fighters, had nothing more than an ADF for blind navigation.[20] By 1956 forty-five TACAN beacons were in service and a further 300 had been delivered to the armed forces.[21]

In 1956 the senior-level Air Coordinating Committee was appointed and reached a compromise for civilian purposes, known as a VORTAC. A VOR provided bearing while a TACAN beacon, situated nearby, provided distance. Paired frequencies allowed civilian aircrew to access the TACAN ranging information automatically. TACAN, VORTAC and VOR continue in use as, respectively, military and civilian short-range navaids to the present time. Not all VORs were converted to VORTACs.

Some of the original, pre-TACAN, civilian DME beacons remained in service into the 1960s (designated NSME – Non-Standard Distance-Measuring Equipment) for the benefit of aircraft with the original DME receivers.[22] The FAA required all aircraft flying above 7,300 metres (24,000 feet), and all jet aircraft, to be equipped with DME by 31 December 1965.[23] The Americans planned to install 1,300 VORTAC beacons by 1962 at a cost of $500–800 million,[24] but this was cut back and by 1965 352 VORTACs had been commissioned;[25] the programme was completed in 1967.

By 1959 all the NATO air forces were introducing TACAN into service. It was allocated 126 channels in the 962–1,024 MHz and 1,151–1,214 MHz bands; DME frequencies occupied the gap. The American armed forces intended to replace TACAN with other systems as they became available but, after such heavy investment, American civil aviation intended to retain VOR, DME and VORTAC as the standard short-range civilian navaids for as long as possible, a function which they retain to the present time, together with NDBs. This controversy induced a wait-and-see attitude on both sides of the Atlantic and delayed the introduction of the new systems.

The American dispute between VOR/DME and TACAN added uncertainty to a wider, international disagreement between the American trackline concept, represented by VOR/DME and TACAN, and the British area navigation concept, represented by Decca. This dispute harked back to pre-Second World War differences in blind navigation with commercial interests and national pride added as new factors. The controversy surfaced at the 1947 ICAO meeting and remained unresolved until 1959. Meanwhile, different countries pressed on with their own preferences. In particular, an American-type airway system, based on radio ranges and NDBs, went into service covering the UK in 1950 and was modified and improved with the addition of VORs in 1956–8 with similar coverage in Europe. The American system was thus already the *de facto* standard.

When first used in aircraft in the late 1940s, Decca had suffered from certain deficiencies. The Decca company worked hard and successfully to eliminate them so that, with the Mark 7 receiver and Flight Log, they had mostly been resolved by the end of 1950.[26] The Mark 7 airborne receiver reduced the effects of static and, whereas earlier receivers could become unreliable at speeds greater than 400 km/h (217 knots), the Mark 7 was designed to cater for all foreseeable speeds for passenger aircraft.[27] Flight Log was a paper chart on two rollers overlaid by a sliding cursor pen which marked the aircraft's track.[28] The Mark 7 equipment, including Flight Log, weighed 54 kg (120 pounds).[29]

The British pointed out that Decca was more accurate at greater range than VOR and that the ground system was cheaper to install and maintain because fewer beacons were needed to cover a given area. Decca was also a marine navaid, which VOR was not. The British commented on VOR in

1951:[30] 'Thus, it seems, there will eventually be in America a navaid system which, subject to some limitations, will do what a British system, Decca, already does with greater ease and accuracy.' The development of Decca continued apace; BEA began to use it in 1952.[31]

The fixing accuracy depended on the aircraft's distance from the four transmitters of the chain that it was using. At a maximum range of 480 km (300 miles), fixing accuracy was 1.6 km (1 mile) by day and 8 km (5 miles) by night, with no limitations imposed by altitude or terrain. Decca was so accurate within 80 km (50 miles) of the transmitters that it could be used as an approach aid. In 1953 three Decca chains were in service in the UK, one each in Denmark, Germany and France; others were planned for Sweden, Spain and Italy. Some 2,000 ships carried Decca receivers.[32]

In 1955 the UK Ministry of Transport and Civil Aviation issued a comprehensive report on Decca.[33] The tests, conducted in 1951–3, had shown a fixing accuracy of 5 km (3 miles) at 400 km (250 miles) range at night at the worst signal geometry. The Decca Mark 7 with Flight Log was accurate enough to allow increased traffic density; aircraft using Decca with another approach aid could be sequenced for landing at three-minute intervals without detailed guidance from ATC. Adding a pair of low-powered stations 8 km (5 miles) apart improved fixing accuracy to within 15 metres (50 feet) over an area of 50 square km

11 *Flight*, 21 September 1951, 394
12 *Flight*, 18 September 1953, 413
13 *Flight*, 31 August 1951, 258
14 *Flight*, 11 March 1955, 333
15 Grover, J. H. 1957
16 *Flight*, 25 October 1957, 635
17 *Flight*, 12 April 1957, 496
18 *Flight*, 6 April 1951, 409
19 *Flight*, 29 June 1956, 855
20 *Flying*, January 1962
21 *Flight*, 29 June 1956, 855
22 *Flying*, January 1962, 87
23 *Flight International*, 14 January 1965, 46
24 *Flight*, 20 February 1959, 263
25 Weeghman, R. B. 1965
26 Bailey-Watson, C. B. 1951
27 Bailey-Watson, C. B. 1951
28 *Flight*, 2 March 1950, 274; Bailey-Watson, C. B. 1951
29 *Flight*, 9 November 1951, 601
30 *Flight*, 11 January 1951, 53
31 *Flight*, 26 February 1970, 309
32 *Flight*, 30 October 1953, 601
33 *Flight*, 20 May 1955, 701

(20 square miles).[34] Tests were successful in aircraft of all types from low-flying helicopters to jets flying at 740 km/h (400 knots) at 12,200 metres (40,000 feet), including flight in heavy rain and hail. The two problems were limitation of range in some areas by signal ambiguity and the complexity of operating the airborne equipment, especially when changing from one chain to another.

The report stated that Decca was the only system sufficiently flexible and accurate for air traffic control over the UK.[35] Because of international airlines using VOR, a limited number of VOR beacons would be set up in the UK, but there were no plans to install DME, except for a small number of 200 MHz beacons for BOAC. The Ministry accepted the continued use of Gee. Some of the radio ranges and NDBs would be decommissioned, although NDBs would continue in use for the foreseeable future.[36]

In November 1955, within a month of this report, BEA announced that they would adopt Decca as their standard short-range navigation aid, regardless of international agreement, planning to equip nineteen Airspeed Elizabethans and twenty-four Vickers Viscounts.[37] The standard navigation package was to be a Mark 10 receiver and Flight Log, a VOR receiver and an ADF. Decca Mark 10 offered better airborne equipment, using a different signal pattern which, nevertheless, remained compatible with existing equipment.[38] Aircraft with Decca and Flight Log were allowed reduced traffic separation in UK controlled airspace and received special ATC expediting.[39] BEA was pessimistic that DME would probably never be provided in Europe, nor was it optimistic as to the future of a VOR-based system. At that time Decca signals covered the whole of northwest Europe, and in 1956 a new chain in northern Scotland extended coverage to the north. In 1957 four Decca chains went into service in eastern Canada[40] and one in Sweden.[41] In 1958 Decca achieved a triumph in penetrating the US when a chain was installed near New York, mainly for local helicopters.[42]

In 1957 the ICAO Jet Operations Requirements Panel, meeting in Montreal,[43] stated a requirement for an accurate and reliable short-range navigational aid based on the area coverage system and designed to provide pictorial presentation to the pilot in the cockpit. Decca fulfilled this requirement better than any other system. At a meeting of the ICAO Communications Division[44] in October 1957, the US delegation tried to insert the DME part of TACAN into the international DME specification, which dated back to 1952. This was opposed by the British and the Australians. The Australians had been using an extensive DME network for several years and considered it useful but not capable of meeting future needs. The British and Australians forced through a measure to convene a special meeting, attended by all participating countries, to decide finally on an ICAO standard short-range navigation system. The British position was reinforced by a Ministry of Transport and Civil Aviation circular published in 1958,[45] stating that any short-range blind navigation system had to be accurate enough to allow the maximum possible air traffic density over the UK. In this respect Decca was better than the combination of VORs, NDBs and radio ranges.

The ICAO meeting took place in Montreal in March 1959.[46] The British and Australian attempt to force a decision backfired and they were defeated overwhelmingly by twenty national votes to four (with fifteen abstentions). The four nations in favour of Decca were Britain, Canada, Australia and New Zealand. Even the international pilots' union, IFALPA, many of whose 30,000 members were Americans, supported Decca. The British, who had a Decca-equipped Comet standing by at Montreal Dorval airport for demonstrations, pointed out that the Americans, when comparing Decca with VORTAC, had used a Decca receiver which was eight years old, never used in civil airlines and not designed for that purpose. Many of the countries voting for VORTAC were small nations, susceptible to American influence but without significant aviation industries or air transport systems, such as Bolivia, Ecuador, Colombia, Nicaragua and South Korea. The Americans had previously secured the allegiance of the International Air Transport Association (IATA) at a separate meeting in Nice. By 1959 the Americans had so much invested in equipment and training for VORTAC that they said that they would continue with their programme regardless of any ICAO decision. In addition, more small private and commercial aircraft were flying in the US than in any other country and VOR/DME was better for them than Decca in its current state of development.[47] VOR/DME was therefore adopted as the international standard short-range navaid until 1975 at the earliest.

The American answer to the defects of VOR/DME for air traffic control was radar. Radar vectoring emerged as a navigation aid in its own right, combining collision avoidance with area navigation. The combination of radar with VOR, DME and NDB has continued to handle an increasing volume of air traffic ever since. It continues in use to the present time and shows signs of being replaced, if at all, only by the revolutionary possibilities of GPS.

The rejection of Decca as the world standard was a crushing defeat for the British who felt that a technically superior system had fallen victim to political and commercial interests. 'The greatest irony has been that those who most vehemently decried Decca also most clearly understood the need for what Decca had to offer. They spelled out word by word and figure by figure a specification which delineated Decca like a photographic portrait and yet they sealed their minds against it.'[48]

The 1959 decision by no means killed Decca; in that year the company brought out the Omnitrac computer which enabled the system to reach its full potential. Whereas Decca had hitherto needed geographically distorted charts to conform to the signal lattice, Omnitrac converted Decca signals directly into latitude and longitude. Omnitrac made possible a self-calibrating moving map using charts free of this distortion and eliminated the three cockpit Decometers. The Mark 2 Omnitrac of 1963[49] could be coupled to an autopilot and accepted additional input from Doppler and INS.[50] Omnitrac could also provide bearing and distance to a pair of coordinates (i.e. a waypoint), known as a Ghost Buoy. A waypoint could be located on a Flight Log chart to within 15 metres (50 feet) with a bearing accuracy better than 0.1°; Omnitrac could store up to thirty-two waypoints. Solid-state technology promised to eliminate the disadvantages of size, weight, complexity and poor reliability which had plagued Decca products hitherto. Even so, in 1964 neither Omnitrac nor the self-setting Flight Logs were in production and only the older Marks 7, 8 and 10 receivers were available, as used in BEA Viscounts, Comets, Argosies, Heralds and helicopters.

By the end of 1964 twenty Decca chains were in service worldwide, although most were sited for maritime coverage and 10,000 ship installations contrasted with only 1,000 receivers in aircraft. In 1963 the Russians tested Decca in Tu-104s and Tu-114s. More receivers were in use with the RAF than with BEA. The US Army bought a chain of transmitters and fifty receivers for helicopters in Germany. A chain for trial military use was set up in Georgia and in the early 1960s the US Army

11th Assault Group set up a transmitter chain and 116 receivers for tactical trials.[51] Experience in Vietnam influenced the US Army in favour of Decca. A Decca-equipped Fiat G-91 strike aircraft was demonstrated to the USAF in 1963.[52]

The Decca Flight Log provided a continuous, unambiguous fix of the aircraft's position which was not available from any other system. NDB, VOR and DME still required the pilot to calculate his position mentally and indirectly, using bearings and distances or, without DME, bearings only. This and the system of IFR clearances could give rise to errors and confusion, sometimes with fatal consequences when a Boeing 707 flew into Mont Blanc in 1966, even though under radar surveillance and in contact with Geneva ATC.[53]

Although few aircraft were equipped to the necessary standards, Decca was so accurate that fully equipped aircraft could safely fly in opposite directions on the same airway at the same altitude.[54] The pilot's initial contact with London ATC (the only area where this was done, and that after extensive trials) ended with the word 'Decca'. The clearance then included the words: 'Decca left' or 'Decca right', specifying which side of the airway the pilot was to follow. This procedure allowed a worthwhile increase in airway traffic.

A triumph for Decca was the sale of twenty-four receivers in 1967 to Seaboard World Airlines for their DC-8F freighters.[55] A further victory was the decision by the State of California the same year to

34 *Flight*, 6 April 1956, 384
35 *Flight*, 28 October 1955, 695
36 *Flight*, 18 November 1955, 789
37 *Flight*, 18 November 1955, 789
38 *Flight*, 12 October 1956, 603
39 *Flight*, 27 September 1957, 514
40 *Flight*, 23 August 1957, 242
41 *Flight*, 11 October 1957, 566
42 *Flight*, 31 January 1958, 158
43 *Flight*, 19 July 1957, 66
44 *Flight*, 25 October 1957, 634
45 *Flight*, 25 August 1958, 219
46 *Flight*, 16 January 1959, 113; 6 February 1959, leading article; 20 February 1959, 238; 6 March 1959, leading article
47 *Flight International*, 25 June 1964, 1053
48 *Flight International*, 22 October 1964, 705
49 *Flight International*, 11 April 1963, 502
50 INS: Inertial Navigation System, discussed in Chapter 24.
51 *Flight International*, 22 October 1964, 706
52 *Flight International*, 27 September 1963, 1002
53 Errington, G. 1966
54 *Flight International*, 25 June 1964, 1054
55 *Flight International*, 13 April 1967, 537

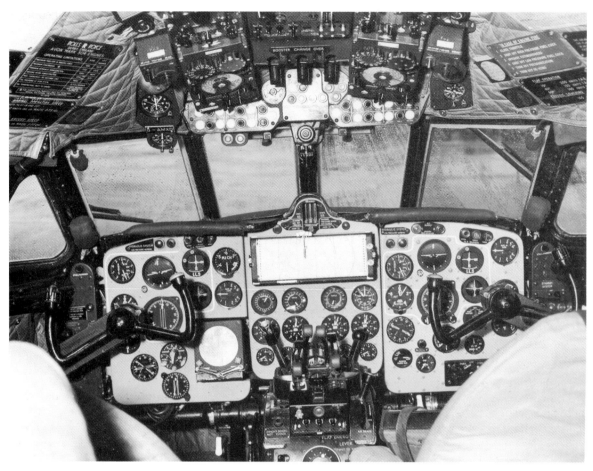

Controls and instrument panel of de Havilland Comet. Note ILS indicators with Sperry Zero Readers beneath. Decca Flight Log top centre with Decometers beneath.

install a Decca chain to cover the Los Angeles area;[56] the British felt that the effects of the Los Angeles decision were likely to be far-reaching and the general opposition to use of Decca in the USA was likely to be dropped. Decca coverage continued to expand. Complete coverage of the Norwegian coast was achieved on 14 May 1968, with chains at Skagerrak, Bergen, Trondheim, Lofoten and Finnmark.[57] Decca proposed to cover the whole of Italy with five chains.[58]

In spite of the ICAO 1959 decision, the debate between VOR/DME and Decca raged on[59] but the Americans had no intention of giving up their position.[60] In any case, the question of adopting a new aid of any kind seemed doubtful, because the new ICAO standard was protected until 1975 and little could be done to implement a non-standard European aid by 1965, as Eurocontrol appeared to

contemplate. Halaby, Administrator of the FAA, stated at the ICAO Communications Division meeting in Montreal that the USA would never support the adoption of a commercially proposed aid, which Decca was and VORTAC, apparently, was not, remarked the British sourly. Both systems continued in aviation use in Europe, but VOR/DME alone in North America, apart from local Decca coverage on the coasts. Although defeated in its bid to become the international standard short-range navigation aid for civil aviation, Decca was solidly established in Europe among both military and maritime users.

Long-range navigation aids were less affected by international disputes. From the late 1940s until the 1980s the main long-range radio navigation aids were Loran and Consol. The ten North Atlantic weather ships were an additional aid to navigation; each one carried radar with a 90-mile range, an NDB, and VHF radio for communication and DF. Loran-A was introduced in 1941, transmitting on 1,400 kHz. By 1955 coverage was available over much of the North Atlantic from stations in northeastern Canada and The Faeroes.[61] Loran-A, however, needed a navigator in the aircraft to operate the set, and the best accuracy obtainable was 9–18 km (5–10 nm). Towards the end of the 1950s, operational trials began with Low-Frequency Loran (Loran-C),[62] using 90–110 kHz. Transmitters were expected to need an output power up to 1 megawatt for maximum range. Using groundwave only, monitoring stations in the US reported fixing errors (averaged between day and night) of 45 metres (150 feet) at 640 km (348 nm), increasing to 300 metres (1,000 feet) at 2,250 km (1,215 nm). Loran-D was developed as a tactical military navaid using small, mobile transmitters with a range of about 650 km (350 nm).

Besides using a different frequency from Loran-A, Loran-C used a different signal pulse pattern which allowed its computations to be partly automated. At first, however, it still needed an on-board navigator and special charts at a time when the airlines were seeking to eliminate the navigator from flight crews. The continuity of transmissions needed by civilian users could not be guaranteed. The early Loran-C sets were adapted Loran-A sets which were less accurate when using Loran-C signals. For these reasons Loran-C remained a military system for many years and its acceptance by civilian users was slow.[63] Even so, the use of Loran spread during the 1960s and by the early 1970s a high proportion of large civilian aircraft carried receivers,[64] especially those flying outside North America. Although it was being overtaken by INS (Inertial Navigation System) for long-range navigation in large aircraft,[65] it retained a cost and weight advantage over INS which has assured its continuing use by ships and small aircraft to the present day.

Loran-A was phased out in the 1970s, replaced by Loran-C and Loran-D.[66] In 1975 eight Loran-C chains, comprising thirty-one stations, were maintained by the US Coast Guard and provided groundwave coverage to 460–1,850-metre (0.25–1 nm) accuracy over much of the North Atlantic, the Mediterranean and parts of the Pacific. Skywave provided fixes of 18–37 km (10–20 nm) accuracy at up to 4,600 km (2,500 nm) range over much of Europe, the eastern US, North Africa, Alaska, eastern Siberia and eastern Asia. Although sky-

wave was less accurate, the errors were well enough known for correction factors to be printed on Loran charts.

In 1975 the US Coast Guard planned to shut down Loran-A over the North Atlantic in 1977 as it was expected that all transatlantic aircraft would by then be equipped with INS.[67] Many IATA members, however, doubted this. The other contender was the still-untried VLF hyperbolic system, Omega, whose airborne equipment was cheaper than INS. The high cost of INS, the large volume of air traffic over the Atlantic and the uncertainty of a successor system all cast doubt on the wisdom of discontinuing Loran-A. In the 1970s the pressure on Loran-C development was to automate the on-board equipment; by mid-decade this could be done by feeding the information into a separate navigation computer such as Mona or the Decca TANS. Loran-C remained a military system until the airborne receiver could produce all the navigation information needed by pilots automatically. In the 1980s extremely small sets became available which could fit into the avionics racks of light aircraft and small helicopters and produce latitude, longitude, bearing, distance and flight time automatically.

Consol continued in use because the only airborne equipment needed was a radio receiver tunable to the Consol frequencies of 255–415 kHz. During the 1950s and 1960s a chain of five stations extending from Norway to Spain covered the eastern Atlantic;[68] two transmitters were installed in the US, at Nantucket and San Francisco.[69] Bearing accuracy was 0.25–0.5° by day. By night, skywave propagation could produce errors up to 2° in a zone 560–800 km (350–500 miles) from the stations.[70] Obtaining a fix took about a minute. The signal pattern generated repeated, ambiguous

56 *Flight International*, 21 September 1967, 474
57 *Flight International*, 23 May 1968, 778
58 *Flight International*, 13 June 1968, 877
59 *Flight International*, 25 June 1964, 1053
60 *Flight International*, 1 March 1962, 341
61 *Flight*, 11 March 1955, 334
62 *Flight*, 16 May 1958, 660
63 Stokes, P. 1976
64 *Flight International*, 26 August 1971, 335
65 *Flight International*, 13 March 1975, 401
66 *Flight International*, 21 August 1975, 271a
67 *Flight International*, 6 November 1975, 681
68 *Flight*, 11 March 1955, 334
69 *Flying*, January 1970, 57
70 Grover, J. H. 1956

patterns but the aircraft's ADF could resolve such ambiguities by obtaining an approximate bearing on a station.

In 1953 Decca introduced Dectra as a long-range version of Decca.[71] Dectra and another Decca development called Delrac were proposed for evaluation at the March 1954 ICAO Communications Division meeting. In 1956 the company planned to cover the North Atlantic from two stations in the UK and two in Newfoundland.[72] Dectra consisted of four stations generating a signal pattern to determine track, while the signal pattern from two master stations at opposite ends of the route provided distance information. The four Dectra stations were members of normal four-station Decca chains at each end of the route. Dectra would be usable through existing Decca Flight Logs with an extra receiver and special charts. The complete airborne installation weighed 64 kg (140 pounds). Accuracy was expected to be 16 km (8.6 nm) over the whole route from Prestwick to Gander, improving to 8 km (5 miles) in two lobate areas within 1,300 km (700 nm) of the two termini.[73]

Construction and initial tests took place in 1956–7 using an RAF Valiant bomber.[74] By the summer of 1958 BOAC, PanAm, SAS, Swissair and TCA were evaluating the system. Pan Am flew twenty-seven Atlantic crossings in a Dectra-equipped Stratocruiser between February and April 1958. On 1 June 1958, a BOAC DC-7C flew from London to New York, navigating by Decca and Dectra all the way.[75] With Dectra connecting Decca coverage in northeastern Canada and northwest Europe, the British felt that their system should be the one accepted by ICAO as an international standard[76] and extended to provide worldwide coverage.[77] By 1964, however, Dectra was still only in experimental service; it was made obsolete by INS, Loran-C and Omega.

Delrac (Decca Long-Range Area Coverage) was a long-range hyperbolic system using the VLF band. Twenty-one pairs of stations, transmitting between 10 and 14 kHz, were to provide worldwide coverage to 16-km (10-mile) accuracy for both ships and aircraft.[78] It competed unsuccessfully with Omega in the aviation field.

Increasing speeds and traffic volumes demanded ever more accurate navigation. Navigation errors were becoming more dangerous and costly than ever before. The maximum traffic density in an area was determined by the safety space needed around each aircraft. In turn this depended on how accurately the aircraft's position was known. The reliability of the equipment was as important as its accuracy. The new systems were indispensable, but the cost of equipment was colossal. Any new system entailed vast capital expenditure by airlines and governments, which neither was anxious to repeat at all frequently. The search for some ultimate system that would suffice for years to come, and the need for international standardization, made it very difficult to introduce new technology. Once a system was in place, it was becoming increasingly difficult and costly to change it.

The decisive selection of VOR/DME by the ICAO as the world standard for short-range navigation stabilized a new era of worldwide air transport following the confused aftermath of the Second World War. Even so, the effects of the diversity of navaids devised in the 1940s and 1950s was still being felt in the 1960s by a world airline industry that needed a single standard navigation system, or at least some minimal number of different ones. One writer commented that[79] 'no business is more fickle or beset with diverse and conflicting claims from all kinds of user and operator than is air navigation and control'. The cost of developing new navigation systems rose ever higher with the passage of time. For equipment manufacturers the capital investment and risks were terrifying.

71 *Flight*, 18 September 1953, 413
72 *Flight*, 6 April 1956, 384
73 Grover, J. H. 1956
74 *Flight*, 12 April 1957, 496
75 *Flight*, 20 June 1958, 829
76 *Flight*, 8 August 1958, leading article & 219
77 *Flight*, 23 January 1950, 121; 16 January 1959, 113
78 Grover, J. H. 1956
79 *Flight International*, 25 June 1964, 1054

CHAPTER 21

Traffic Jam in the Sky

It had been recognized from an early date that in blind conditions air traffic had to be co-ordinated from the ground, especially near airports, if excessive collision risks were to be avoided. The Americans already had an effective air traffic control system before the war and the new technologies of VOR, DME and radar were easily grafted onto it. The European pre-war ATC system was already inadequate; it was destroyed by the war and was then reconstructed in difficult conditions of technology, economics, politics and weather. The maximum permissible traffic density of any ATC system depended on how accurately each aircraft's position was known, and was thus a function of navigation standards. Radar on the ground was no cure-all because the line-of-sight characteristic of radar signals limited the range of each set; the spread of radar coverage was relatively slow because of the large number of sets required. Technology was also needed that would allow individual aircraft to be identified. A rapid increase in traffic density after 1945 made heavy demands on the American ATC system and threatened to swamp the European system. Jets added to the problem by increasing the differences in air traffic cruising speeds. The bigger the aircraft, the higher its operating cost, and the less its operator could afford traffic delays.

The most basic requirement for air traffic control was air-to-ground radio communication. The standard US ATC frequency of the 1930s was 3,023.5 kHz, but this frequency band suffered from a poor quality of voice transmission and from static interference. Because of the characteristics of the frequency band, signals spread much farther than necessary; US airline pilots in the 1930s were often confused by garbled, irrelevant transmissions from halfway across the continent.[1]

VHF radio made great advances in the 1940s.[2] VHF signals propagated to shorter distances, were less affected by static and provided clearer voice transmission. Shorter range allowed ground stations to use similar frequencies without interfering with one another. Even in the late 1950s air-to-ground radio was still a mixture of systems dating from the 1930s and the newer VHF. Some traffic clearances and weather information were still transmitted in the LF band from airport control towers, radio ranges and NDBs at 200–415 kHz; aircraft did not transmit in this band because of the length of antenna needed. The MF band was not used for air-to-ground radio, but ADFs could be tuned to commercial broadcast stations transmitting on 550–1,600 kHz for use as navigation beacons (sometimes as audio entertainment for the crew), provided the station could be identified. HF at 2,000–8,000 kHz was used for long-range communication over oceans and sparsely settled areas. A trailing antenna was reeled out from the aircraft in flight to produce the right antenna length.

The new VHF short-range communication systems used the 109–127 MHz band. These included ATC communications, VOR, VAR and ILS. Each facility had its own frequency; a directory or chart listing radio frequencies became an essential part of each pilot's equipment. In addition, certain frequencies were standard all over North America, such as the 121.5 MHz emergency frequency and 121.7 and 121.9 MHz for ground-to-ground communication at airports. UHF communication remains a preserve of the military, but TACAN, the ILS glideslope and DME all use the UHF band.

The limited range of VHF ground stations –

---

1 Gann, E. K. 1972, 44
2 Swanson, E. H. 1957. By the 1950s radio frequencies had been conventionally divided into five bands: 30 kHz to 300 kHz, Low Frequency (LF); 300kHz to 3 MHz, Medium Frequency (MF); 3 MHz to 30 MHz High Frequency (HF); 30 MHz to 300 MHz, Very High Frequency (VHF); 300 MHz to 3,000 MHz, Ultra-High Frequency (UHF).

65 km (40 miles) at 300 metres (1,000 feet) over flat land, increasing to 280 km (175 miles) at 6,000 metres (20,000 feet), reduced by mountains – was generally beneficial. To obtain uniform VHF coverage over large areas, however, repeater stations had to be built remote from air traffic control centres, accessed from them by land lines. By 1960[3] the American FAA was operating remote stations as far as 480 km (300 miles) from ATC centres; VHF voice communication was available down to minimum *en route* altitudes over 99% of the airways. By 1953 VHF communication coverage was continuous over most of northwest Europe but discontinuous in southern and eastern Europe.[4] For that reason, BEA Viscounts still had to carry an HF set for Morse telegraphy, with a specialist operator, but BEA was developing the STR.18 HF set for voice communication in order to dispense with the radio operator.

Aircraft VHF radio sets were channel-tuned, using separate quartz crystals or groups of crystals for each frequency. Increasing air-to-ground traffic demanded more and more frequencies. This increased the number of channels needed in aircraft radio sets from as few as six in some wartime military sets to 720 at the present time. As a fixed frequency band was allocated to aviation, an increase in the number of frequencies in use entailed a closer spacing of frequencies. This made increasing technical demands on the design and construction of the sets. By the end of the 1950s a 90-channel set was the minimum for IFR in the US;[5] 360-channel sets were available. Transistor technology introduced in the 1950s and 1960s resulted in smaller, lighter and more-capable aircraft radios. A new form of ground-to-air communication, introduced in 1956, was the airborne teleprinter for receiving weather information, although other uses were foreseen.[6]

Satellites for long-range VHF communication were a significant innovation of the 1960s. A geosynchronous satellite, SYNCOM 3, was first used by PanAm over the Pacific in 1965 and COMSAT went into service over the Atlantic in 1967.[7] Satellites offered a forty-fold increase in VHF range[8] and in 1967 eight airlines were experimenting with this form of communication over the Pacific.

Radar of the early 1950s was still immature for air traffic control purposes.[9] A surprising number of problems stemmed from the simple fact that the radar screens of those days had to be viewed in darkness, whereas ATC controllers needed light to write down information. Surveillance radar was difficult to use for air traffic control unless an aircraft's echo could be tagged with its identification. This entailed a transponder in the aircraft transmitting codes that would show up on a radar screen; otherwise the radar operator had to tell a pilot to fly a specified heading for identification, which was impractical. The wartime military Identification Friend or Foe (IFF) was a crude transponder but, until ATC radar became widespread, there was no need for transponders in civilian aircraft and, consequently, none was available.

In 1956 Decca produced a transponder called Aster, which transmitted through the aircraft's VHF radio. When activated by the pilot, Aster turned the aircraft's primary echo on the radar screen into a short line. Clutter attenuation and transponders were essential to convert primary radar, displaying undifferentiated echoes from aircraft and other objects, into secondary radar displaying coded echoes usable for ATC.

Altitude measurement by radar was also a problem; range and elevation were not accurate enough. The solution was to use an attachment to the aircraft's altimeter to transmit altitude with the transponder return but in 1951 the problem was still under review; a successful solution did not appear likely in the near future.[10] The first altitude-reporting transponders (Mode C) were installed in PanAm Boeing 707s in 1967.[11] Secondary radar and Mode-C transponders greatly reduced the amount of air-to-ground voice communication because of the reduced numbers of position and altitude reports required.

A direct approach to collision avoidance was the airborne proximity warning indicator. In 1956 the Hughes Aircraft Company and the Collins Radio Company were both working on their own versions of such a device.[12] The Collins unit was expected to weigh 30 kg (68 pounds) without cables and antennas. However, self-contained airborne collision avoidance systems did not begin to enter service until 40 years later; radar surveillance from the ground and track and altitude separation are still the primary methods of collision avoidance in blind conditions.

Although the American air traffic control system was undisturbed by the war, increasing volumes of traffic revealed fundamental problems. The airway system, in spite of its advantages for traffic control, concentrated aircraft on specified tracks and over navigation fixes, increasing the collision risk. Only verbal position reports radioed

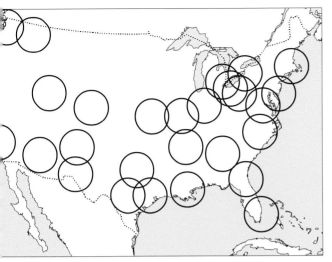
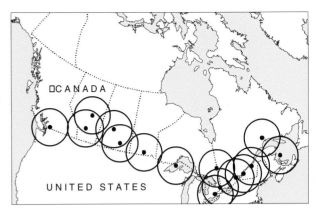

Map of North American radar coverage, 1957.

from aircraft and handwritten flight slips in ATC centres told controllers where each aircraft was. Pilots flying in cloud could, obviously, not see other aircraft; but even in clear conditions the cockpits of large aircraft offered limited vision in any direction other than straight ahead. Higher speeds gave pilots less time to see other traffic.

Energetic efforts were made to solve these problems. A major study of the future needs of the American ATC system resulted in the SC-31 report, issued in 1948.[13] SC-31 was the work of eighty-five people and cost $1 million. Relying heavily on automation, full implementation of its recommendations would have cost $1.1 billion. It was realized, however, that the air transport industry could not afford such a system, especially in the light of the cost of Cold War rearmament, therefore more limited goals were accepted.

Because of the time needed for a blind approach, inbound aircraft had often to be held over navigation fixes, each successive aircraft being stacked above its predecessor, the whole stack moving down through the holding pattern as each aircraft landed. Uncertain transit times from stack to final approach caused cumulative delays. A computer system for calculating the time from stack to final approach installed at New York La Guardia in 1950 was abandoned when it was found to increase delays rather than reducing them.[14]

The deficiencies of traffic separation in the 1950s were brought under public scrutiny by a collision, in daylight but in broken cloud, between a Constellation and a DC-7 near the Grand Canyon on 30 June 1956. This event unleashed a large allocation of public funds to expand radar coverage. The US Federal Airways Plan for 1957–61 budgeted $246 million, of which $57 million was for radar alone.

Several technological solutions to the air traffic control problem were in sight by 1960. The most pressing need was for expanded secondary surveillance radar coverage and better transponders in more aircraft. The UHF military navaid, TACAN, seemed to offer the possibility of automatic transmission of range, bearing, heading, altitude and ground speed from an aircraft to ATC. Computers would resolve conflicts between concurrent IFR flight plans. Routine information would be transmitted from the ground to airborne teleprinters, reducing the number of voice transmissions. Airborne navigation computers, Doppler, inertial and hyperbolic navigation aids would allow precise navigation off airways. Improvements in HF radio would reduce the periodic loss of long-range

3 Deltour, B. V. 1960, 44
4 *Flight*, 20 March 1953, 374
5 Ibid.
6 *Flight*, 21 September 1956, 512
7 IATA Bulletin, 1966, 87
8 IATA Bulletin, December 1967, 88
9 *Flight*, 21 September 1956, 511
10 *Flight*, 23 February 1950, 277; Stallibrass, G. W. 1952
11 *Flight International*, 6 April 1967, 504
12 *Flight*, 30 November 1956, 845
13 Stallibrass, G. W. 1952, 192
14 *Flight*, 23 February 1950, 277; Stallibrass, G. W. 1952

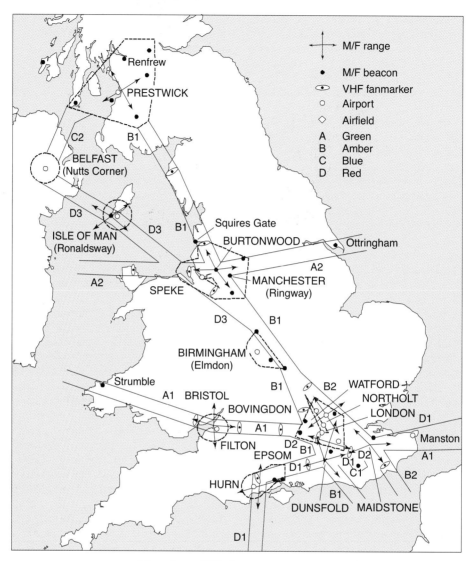

Map of new UK airways system, 1950.

communication over the Atlantic. These solutions succeeded in varying degrees over the next twenty years.

By the early 1960s the present-day US domestic airway structure was in place, both as an all-weather navigation system and as a system for air traffic control, in which function it was supported by air-to-ground VHF communication and an increasingly continuous radar coverage. US domestic airspace was divided into three layers: Low-Level, from surface to 4,400 metres (14,500 feet) above sea level; Intermediate-Level, from 4,400 metres (14,500 feet) to 7,300 metres (24,000 feet); and

High-Level, above 7,300 metres (24,000 feet).[15] The US Coast and Geodetic Survey issued charts for each of these levels. The low and intermediate level airways were designated by the letter V with a two- or three-digit number in the low-level airspace and a four-digit number in the intermediate-level airspace. High-level airways were termed Jet Routes. The route number was prefixed with the letter J and suffixed with V, L, or T, indicating whether the route was based on VOR, radio range, or TACAN signals. Radio ranges were still used to mark jet routes ten years after being declared obsolete.

By 1950 an American-type blind navigation and ATC system was in place in Europe. An airway system covering the UK went into service in that year, defined by nine radio ranges, seventeen NDBs and sixteen VHF fan markers. The fan markers divided the airways into sections within which no two aircraft were allowed at the same altitude at the same time. The system was upgraded between 1956 and 1958[16] with additional airways and a total of three radio ranges, ten VORs, twenty-five NDBs and ten fan markers, but still no DME beacons.[17]

On 22 February 1950, a long-range radar station went into service at London Heathrow, the first of its kind in the world. A four-engined aircraft at 6,000 metres (20,000 feet) could be detected 210 km (132 miles) away. Inbound aircraft were to be handed off to the GCA radar sites at Heathrow and Northolt. Communication was by VHF radio on 118.3, 119.1, and 119.9 MHz. The radar operators obtained positive identification by instructing pilots to turn onto specified headings.

In most traffic conditions, as in the US, inbound aircraft were instructed to hold over a navigation fix, stacked at increasing altitudes. This posed a number of problems. The holds were typically based on two NDBs or a radio range and two fan markers; the pilot therefore knew his exact position only twice in each passage around the hold. The time at which an aircraft left the hold could vary by as much as 1.5 minutes from the time assigned by ATC, adding to the uncertainty of the time from stack to final approach. Radar checks showed that descending aircraft were overshooting their assigned altitudes by several hundred feet and this became worse with higher descent rates. As a result, the minimum safe altitude separation in the stack had to be increased to 300 metres (1,000 feet), instead of 150 metres (500 feet) as hitherto. For reasons of passenger comfort the maximum acceptable descent rate in unpressurized aircraft was 150 metres (500 feet) per minute, so a minimum of two minutes was needed to move an aircraft from one altitude to the next, and this delay spread all through the stack. One solution was to feed aircraft to the approach from two stacks, but this increased the uncertainty of times from stack to final approach.

This was one aspect of a bigger problem.[18] The average error in position reports from aircraft over southeast England in IFR conditions, when checked by radar, was about 10 km (6 miles). Aircraft entering the London control zone reported over the entry beacons with an average

error of 1.6 km (1 mile), but an average error of five minutes in estimated time of arrival. Fifteen per cent of aircraft were more than 150 metres (500 feet) from their assigned altitude; the average error in straight and level flight was 67 metres (220 feet). When aircraft changed altitude, overshoots of several hundred feet were common and flying accuracy declined near airports with an average height loss of 120 metres (400 feet) in turns. All of this restricted the acceptable traffic density if collision risk was to be avoided. Radar coverage was still restricted to terminal areas and its use was limited until better transponders could be developed and more aircraft carried them.

On 4 July 1948, a DC-6 collided with a York at Northolt, London,[19] in instrument conditions. The DC-6 was holding at 760 metres (2,500 feet). The York was cleared to hold at 900 metres (3,000 feet). Because of weather conditions the captain of the DC-6 obtained a clearance to divert to Amsterdam. The collision took place as the DC-6 was leaving the area and the York was descending. The cause was never conclusively determined, but it is reasonable to suppose that, if ATC radar had been available and the holding altitude interval had been 300 metres (1,000 feet) at the time instead of 150 metres (500 feet), the accident would not have occurred.

A defect of the American concept was that it provided position fixes only when an aircraft passed over a range station, NDB, VOR, or marker. Therefore traffic separation was based on time intervals, such as five and ten minutes, between aircraft reporting over specified fixes. Gee and Decca were more accurate but the airborne equipment did not provide a continuous fix and not all aircraft were equipped. The exception to this was the Decca Flight Log which showed a pilot exactly where he was.

Any system relying on pilot position reports for separation was limited in the traffic density that it could accept. Cockpit work load, frequency congestion, and communication difficulties meant position reports missed, inaccurate, or late. Air traffic controllers were limited in their ability to visualize the positions of all aircraft within their zones and issue appropriate instructions.

15 *Flying*, January 1962, 87
16 *Flight*, 28 December 1956, 1006
17 Grover, J. H. 1957
18 Bell, G. E. 1950
19 *Flight*, 8 July 1948, 30, 37; 3 February 1949, 129

The UK during the 1950s offered an unparalleled combination of bad weather and rapidly increasing traffic density. Lack of international agreement on standard navaids, economic difficulties and political tensions meant that radio facilities that were ready for replacement in 1947 were still in use ten years later. By 1957, most aircraft flying in UK controlled airspace were relying on outdated navaids of questionable accuracy and the British air traffic control system was saturated.[20,21]

Between 1949 and 1957 only two mid-air collisions occurred in the UK, but in the two years 1955 and 1956 324 near misses were reported. In 1956 the press gave unwholesome publicity to 'four near misses every day'.[22] Without internationally agreed standard navaids of greater accuracy, any reduction in traffic separation would pose a threat to safety.[23] A Guild of Air Traffic Control Officers' Convention in October 1956 stated that the system was dangerously close to breaking down.

The US ATC system covered a vast, politically and linguistically homogeneous area and one that had never seen air combat or invasion. In western Europe nine countries, all with different languages, occupied an area the size of the northeastern US. Russian armed forces waited on a hair trigger to launch an invasion. Eleven air forces operated in that region together with some of the highest civilian air traffic densities in the world. As if this were not enough, an American fighter pilot commented that in winter: 'The average ceiling and visibility of the best base in Europe is worse than the winter weather of Pittsburgh, which claims the distinction of having about the worst weather in America. For days at a time the entire continent is buried in less-than-300-foot ceilings and only [military aircraft] fly. After a long spell of this, pilots are going mad with inactivity and as soon as one area lifts a little, the clouds are filled with flying metal.'[24] One F-100 pilot diverted to his alternate after his destination weather had deteriorated to a 30-metre (100-foot) ceiling and 800 metres (0.5 miles) visibility. With ten minutes' fuel remaining, he received the unsympathetic response from ATC: 'Roger, you are number nine in the emergency fuel pattern.'

Areas of positive control were discontinuous; in Germany no positive control was provided above 7,900 metres (26,000 feet). Otherwise pilots could only fly a quadrantal altitude and hope, relying on the RAF theory that the sky is a big place. Over France quadrantal altitudes not only differed from the rest of Europe but also changed every few months. One pilot remarked: 'You haven't lived until you've flown through somebody else's jetwash on solid instruments.' At military airspeeds it was possible to cross three international boundaries in ten minutes, each of which required the pilot to report five minutes before crossing and on crossing to both of the national jurisdictions each time. American pilots had to cope with altimeter settings given as QFE or QNH in millibars. Airspace transgressors could be shot at.

The chief means of navigation was 335 NDBs operated by fifteen agencies in nine countries. Some commercial radio stations doubled as navigation beacons. The Heidelberg beacon, transmitting on 383 kHz at 75 kilowatts output power, was noted on charts as: 'Use with caution. Intermittently reliable at all distances due to interference from broadcast station Kharkov (Russia) on 386 kc, 150 kw power located due east of Heidelberg.' Russian interference was not always passive; pilots heard anonymous voices vectoring them into Russian airspace.

Following the ICAO 1959 decision on standard navaids, more VORs and the first DME beacons were installed in Europe. The ICAO plan for the UK called for thirty-six VORs and sixteen TACANs. In 1961 a network of beacons was to be installed at 380 sites in the ICAO European/Mediterranean region,[25] but the piecemeal introduction of the system was already causing problems. VORs were already in place on some airways and could not be moved; TACAN beacons could not be added to existing VORs if the frequency conflicted with that of another TACAN beacon already in place nearby. To work properly as VORTACs, collocated VOR and TACAN beacons had to be within 600 metres (2,000 feet) of each other on airways, 150 metres (500 feet) in terminal areas. The pessimistic opinion was expressed that, because of the navaids already installed in the UK, in no instance could a TACAN beacon be properly collocated with its related VOR. In Norway the Stavanger VOR was on the airfield but its related TACAN (for DME) was 35 km (22 miles) away. Airlines refused to use beacons that did not meet their collocation criteria. Some airlines, particularly KLM and BOAC, stated that they would not install DME in their aircraft. Forty-six air routes in Europe were over seas which could not be covered by VORTAC at all. This fostered the use of Gee, Decca, Loran, Consol and Omega.

In the course of time more airline operations and increasing amounts of airspace were designated IFR-only. With effect from 1 March 1961, for example, the whole of the London control zone and the whole of the British airways system was so designated. By 1964 all BOAC aircraft operated under IFR at all times.

Only thirty years after Lindbergh's flight from New York to Paris, air traffic density over the North Atlantic was a problem.[26] By 1957 150 aircraft were crossing the ocean each day, most using the great circle route between Gander and Shannon or Prestwick. Although the navigation aids were more than sufficient for safe crossings, position fixing *en route* was still imprecise and communications were unreliable. Consequently 30 minutes' flying time had to be allowed between successive aircraft using the same route at the same altitude to avoid collision risk. In 1956 more than half of all transatlantic flights had difficulties with communications or ATC services; 40% had to change their flight plan *en route*; 20% were delayed on the ground waiting for ATC clearance. Getting there was no longer enough; continuous precise *en route* position fixing was required. This would eventually be provided by new and highly sophisticated self-contained navigation devices.

The American concept of air navigation offered no alternative to tracking from beacon to beacon, other than radar vectoring, which was intended for traffic control near airports and not as a general navigation aid. This added significant distances to certain routes which might be further increased by ATC routings due to congested traffic.

A keystone of the American advocacy of VOR/DME as the ICAO standard was a navigation computer using VOR/DME signals to fly direct routes off airways. In 1951 such a device was expected to be available within two to three years, but fifteen years later this promise was still unfulfilled.[27] With increasing traffic density, the problems foreseen by the British advocates of Decca came true: too many aircraft in too little airspace with much vacant space off airways. When aircraft were radar-vectored off airways, they became dependent for navigation on radio contact with the ground.[28] In the US, with more small air carriers than anywhere else in the world, there was an increasing need for instrument approaches to airports too small to justify approach beacons of their own.

In June 1967, Eastern Airlines began flight testing a Decca Omnitrac computer and a Flight Log moving-map display[29] in a DC-9 on the New York–Boston shuttle service, using VOR/DME signals instead of Decca as input. Eastern equipped a

DC-8 similarly, using Loran, Doppler and Dectra as inputs to the Omnitrac. This equipment shortened each flight by 5–10 minutes; at 112 flights a day between Washington, New York and Boston[30] this was significant. Cockpit workload and radio transmissions were also reduced and, because of improved navigation capability, the crews needed less radar vectoring.[31] Towards the end of 1967 Eastern planned to evaluate the Collins course-line computer, which had similar functions to Omnitrac but no moving-map display. The aircrew could create a waypoint by setting a range and bearing from a VOR into the area navigation (RNAV) computer.

In 1970 Eastern ordered Omnitracs for all eleven DC-9s on the shuttle service. Vertical guidance was fed into the aircraft's flight director and the FAA approved the equipment for instrument approaches down to ceilings only 200 feet higher than VOR/ILS minima, enabling the crews to use additional runways not equipped for instrument approaches, wind and weather permitting. By 1970 the FAA had already published six RNAV (Area Navigation) approach charts with more to follow.

By the end of the 1960s Butler, Bendix, Collins, Narco and Computing Devices of Canada were all on the point of marketing area navigation computers of varying degrees of cost and complexity.[32] Some RNAV computers allowed a waypoint to be used as a phantom VOR, showing track guidance on the VOR cockpit instrument. As RNAV became more widely used, waypoints were published on charts and more RNAV approaches were developed, referenced to VORs up to 50 miles from the airports they served.

The moving-map display was an important adjunct to area navigation. One originator of the idea, perhaps the first, was J. Hargrave, in England, who was granted a patent in 1938.[33] The outbreak

20 Grover, J. H. 1957, 273
21 Stallibrass, G. W. 1952
22 Pugh, A. T., Lambert, C. M. 1957
23 Bach, R. 1962
24 Ibid.
25 *Flight International*, 17 February 1961, 209
26 Pugh, A. T., Lambert, C. M. 1957
27 *Flight*, 11 January 1951, 53
28 Wright, T. M. B. 1971
29 *Flight International*, 6 July 1967, 11
30 *Flight International*, June 1970
31 Weeghman, R. B. 1968
32 Ibid.
33 *Flight International*, 21 May 1970, 863

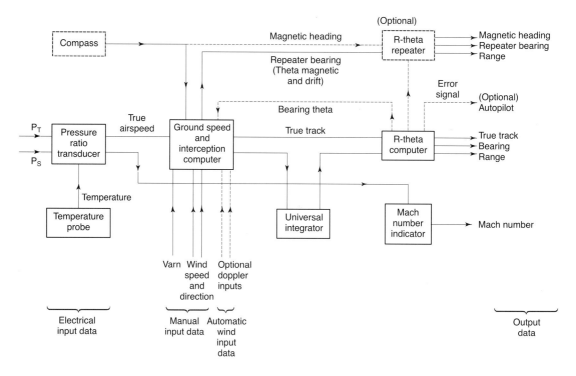

Navigation computer, 1957 – schematic.

of war interrupted development; by the time the war ended ground-mapping radar seemed to offer the greater promise and the patent was allowed to lapse. A moving map was not as simple as might be supposed because some device was needed to mark the aircraft's position in terms of navigation references and then to drive the display. The Decca Flight Log, where the map was driven by Decca signals, was the first post-war moving map. The next generation used micro-filmed charts projected onto a screen in the cockpit, as in the Convair F-106.[34]

Hughes Aircraft and Computing Devices of Canada both produced moving-map displays driven by area navigation computers. The Hughes Navigation Director, which incorporated steering commands, was flight tested in the spring of 1968 and by autumn was installed in a United Airlines Boeing 727 flying between New York and Chicago. The Computing Devices of Canada Topo-Map, also with steering commands, went into US Navy Corsair IIs. In Britain Marconi produced a similar display, without steering commands, taking navigation information from INS, Doppler, hyperbolic signals and VOR/DME.[35] A joint venture between Ambac Industries and Decca Navigator produced an RNAV computer with an electronic map display, known as Mona and installed in Delta Air Lines and Court Line Lockheed L-1011s.[36]

Butler National Corporation took the concept further to also provide descent guidance with their Vector Analog Computer (VAC). A study carried out for Butler showed that two major accidents between 1967 and 1970, involving 105 fatalities, caused by aircraft using an ILS when the glideslope was unserviceable, could have been prevented by RNAV vertical guidance. If an airport had a VOR approach, the minimum safe descent altitude was proportional to the distance from the VOR to the airport. With better descent guidance and a phantom VOR closer to the airport, approach minima could be lowered. American Airlines installed Butler equipment on two Boeing 727s flying between New York and Chicago after evaluating it against a Litton INS and a Decca Omnitrac. The Butler VAC cost $16,000 compared to $45,000 for the Omnitrac.

The need for RNAV was highlighted when the

FAA held a symposium on the subject in 1972.[37] An ever-growing volume of traffic confined to airways was saturating the system; the alternative, radar-vectoring off airways, was overloading the air traffic controllers, each of whom was, in effect, navigating several aircraft at the same time. Some airspace was saturated but many of the nearly 10,000 airports in the US were used at only 50% capacity because of ATC procedures. New FAA-approved routes were published for RNAV-equipped aircraft. The first four, between the US east and west coasts, were approved for use on 29 April 1971, and another ninety-six were scheduled for January 1972. The introduction of RNAV into Europe was slower; the British could not resist commenting that it was merely an attempt to achieve the navigation capability already offered by Decca in the 1950s.[38]

As in the 1920s, so in the early 1950s, awareness of the problems at first outran the technical means to solve them. Even so, there was no doubt that equipment and procedures then in use enabled regular services to be maintained as a routine in weather conditions that, before the war, would have confined operations to the occasional exploits of intrepid birdmen.

In the course of time the combination of NDB, VOR, DME and radar vectoring became the *de facto* standard for short-range blind navigation with the simple proviso that the vectoring phraseology gave the pilot the intent and destination of the vectoring and standard lost-communications procedures were put in place. This system has continued to handle an increasing volume of traffic ever since.

34 Weeghman, R. B. 1968
35 *Flight International*, 21 May 1970, 860
36 Cowin, H. 1973 (2); Hirst, M. 1978 (1)
37 Wansbrough-White, G. 1972
38 Cowin, H. 1973 (2)

Unsuspected Dimensions of the Weather

High-performance aircraft and wartime flying brought pilots into contact with weather conditions that were greeted with disbelief when reported on their return to the ground. The post-war years allowed time for these new dimensions of the weather to be probed and analysed, sometimes with surprising results.

Thunderstorms and icing remained serious and intractable problems. Airline flying in the 1930s brought pilots into contact with both, vividly described by E. K. Gann in *Fate is the Hunter*.[1] This experience was reinforced during the Second World War.

The worst aspect of the thunderstorm problem was its lack of definition. Because individual storm cells tend to be only a few miles across, typically completing their cycle of growth and decay in less than an hour and changing rapidly in that time, flying conditions in and around them have always been difficult to predict. One aircraft might go through a thunderstorm area undisturbed while another might encounter the most violent turbulence. In the war countless aircraft vanished without trace for all sorts of reasons but the means and manpower were not available to investigate their disappearance.

One British writer recorded in 1954:[2] 'During the war in the Far East, at least nineteen aircraft – mostly Dakotas, which probably flew in worse weather than the majority of operational aircraft – broke up in cu-nim.; and the number of unexplained losses was probably higher.' A more recent researcher, however, states[3] that no less than eighteen aircraft were lost in one storm over the Hump on 6–7 January 1945. Thunderstorm losses were greatly underestimated.

The tendency to underestimate the danger of thunderstorms was reinforced by a USAF study, flown by Northrop P-61 twin-engined fighters of the All-Weather Flying Division, and released in 1949. P-61s were chosen for their especially strong construction. The P-61s penetrated thunderstorms over the US roughly 1,300 times, measuring gust and draught velocities and durations and lightning strikes to determine the best procedures to follow and the best altitudes for penetration.

A British précis of the resulting report read:[4]

> During the war a number of unexplained crashes were attributed to flights through cu-nim. It is significant that, so far as is known, all these incidents occurred to Service pilots … The key to the puzzle as to why Service pilots and aircraft should be more susceptible to thunderstorms than their civilian counterparts is the essence of the information obtained by the American investigators. They have proved that, provided the pilot possesses a high degree of instrument-flying ability and has the necessary information as to how to fly his aircraft under such conditions, he can safely negotiate any cu-nim … Having by this time established that no conditions exist in a thunderstorm which of themselves can cause an aircraft to fail structurally …

The report went on to state that thunderstorm losses were due to the pilot losing control of the aircraft. Toppled gyroscopes and 20-ton aircraft being thrown about like leaves in a breeze do not appear to have figured in this calm assessment. The study drew caustic comment from pilots whose experiences had been less matter-of-fact.[5] '*Nice* Cu-Nbs! I wish the ones I meet had their bases above 6,000 feet. It's usually more like 1,600 feet in my experience; … Pilots who have been in a really super cu-nim, and lived to tell the tale, may feel that the Americans must have missed the really big ones, otherwise they would not advocate such a press-on-regardless policy.'[6]

Northrop P-61 used for USAAF thunderstorm research.

In the early 1950s the RAF 1301 Meteorological Flight, based in Ceylon, flew thunderstorm research using Bristol Brigand twin-engined fighters.[7] 'Pilots who flew through storms in India and the Bay of Bengal to collect data for the RAF cunim report are said to have been so badly shaken that they nearly decided to end their days in a monastery ...'[8]

The former pilot of an RAF Boston light bomber reported of a night sortie in October 1943:

Shortly after crossing the north coast of Sicily we entered the storm at 10,000 feet. After about 15 minutes – during which time all I could manage was to keep the aircraft right side up and within 90° of course – and with the rest of the crew violently sick, I decided to turn back. (This was my seventy-ninth bombing trip, and only once before, owing to flak damage over France, had I been forced to turn back.) ... Later, during

1946, I met a pilot, of about 45 years of age, who was flying Lancastrians for Qantas from Australia to Ceylon ... he said they flew through the inter-tropical front at night and at 10,000 feet, finding it very uncomfortable but quite safe ... About three weeks later I met him again. Now he was talking of retiring to a ranch; his best friend had just disappeared in a Lancastrian at night. The last position report had put the aircraft just entering the inter-tropical front at 10,000 feet.

1 Gann, E. K. 1961, Chapters 4 and 5
2 Anderson, M. 1954
3 C. M. Quinn, quoted in Spencer, O. C. 1992, 156
4 Brice, D. A. 1950
5 Neilan, J. C. 1950
6 Anderson, M. 1954
7 *Flight*, 21 March 1952, 312
8 Anderson, M. 1954

PHOTOGRAPHS SHOW CLOUDS AND THEIR CORRESPONDING P.P.I. PRESENTATION.

DATE 27. 6. 46
TIME 15.46
P.P.I. RANGE SCALE 20 MILES
RANGE 8 MILES: BEARING 340°

FIG I

PHOTOGRAPHS SHOW CLOUDS AND THEIR CORRESPONDING P.P.I. PRESENTATION.

DATE 29.6.46.
TIME. 16·15.
P.P.I. RANGE SCALE 20 MILES.
RANGE. 12 – 15 MILES; BEARING 340°

FIG. 2.

PHOTOGRAPHS SHOW CLOUDS AND THEIR CORRESPONDING P.P.I. PRESENTATION.

DATE 21.6.46.
TIME 15.22
P.P.I. RANGE SCALE 50 MILES.
RANGE 20 & 28 MILES RESPECTIVELY
BEARINGS 003° & 020°

FIG. 3.

PHOTOGRAPHS SHOW CLOUDS AND THEIR CORRESPONDING P.P.I. PRESENTATION.

DATE 27·6·46
TIME 17·16
P.P.I. RANGE SCALE 50 MILES
RANGE 30 MILES: BEARING 026°

FIG. 4.

Thunderstorm images on H2S. (*Royal Aeronautical Society Library*)

In December 1945 an RAF York had its middle tailfin torn away in a thunderstorm over France, while an RAF Liberator, only 30 minutes' flying time away, broke up in flight. A Viking landed at Nice, after a cumulonimbus encounter, with the captain unconscious and most of the passengers injured.

When magnetron-valve radar came into service in 1941 it was noticed that rain-clouds returned signals; tests were made to see if this interfered with the ability of the radar to detect aircraft.[9] RAF Catalina crews in the Far East found that their ASV radar would detect heavy rain and, hence, cumulonimbus clouds.[10] Radar, however, was secret throughout the Second World War; its existence was first revealed in August 1945. In 1946 a Lancaster equipped with a modified H2S set was sent to Singapore to test the effectiveness of radar in detecting cumulonimbus cells. Cells appeared on the screen up to 65 km (40 miles) away.

An association between heavy rain or hail and cumulonimbus clouds was clearly established; snow and drizzle were associated with harmless cloud types. This allowed the best radar frequency and beam shape to be designed. The best wavelength for detecting heavy rain was found to be 5–6 centimetres, but the equipment available at the time transmitted on either 3 centimetres or 10 centimetres. The set used in the RAF 1946 experiments transmitted on 3.2 centimetres. This equipment was too heavy and expensive for civilian use but in 1950 three 3-centimetre sets, reduced in weight to 70 kg (155 pounds), were installed in BOAC Hermes Mark IVs and were to be installed in the Comets.[11]

Radar suitable for civilian aircraft became more generally available in 1954. The American version was the RCA AVQ-10, transmitting on 5.5 centimetres and weighing 54 kg (120 pounds).[12] The British equivalent was the Ekco E-38, using the 3-centimetre band and weighing less than 82 kg (180 pounds).[13] The shorter wavelength of the British equipment allowed a smaller antenna to be used. Both companies realized that the antenna had to be mounted on a gyrostabilized platform to prevent interference from ground echoes during turbulence or manoeuvres.

United Airlines was the first airline to install weather radar because of its operations area in the American Mid-West and West which was much affected by thunderstorms. Their decision, taken in 1954, followed four months of tests using RCA radar in a DC-3 in the late summer of 1953. On one flight the DC-3 crew were able to use their radar to fly a smooth path between two cells of a storm that produced 76 millimetres (3 inches) of rain in 50 minutes. In 133 hours of tests near Denver the aircraft never ran into severe turbulence or hail without warning. United Airlines concluded that weather radar would allow aircraft to thread their way through thunderstorm areas by means of quite small detours. The radar would penetrate 24 km (15 miles) or more of heavy rain equivalent to 64 millimetres (2.5 inches) per hour or more, and would show the core of a storm. It warned of hail; skilled interpretation would enable aircrew to avoid tornadoes. It was also capable of terrain mapping. There was, however, no prospect that it would be usable for avoiding other aircraft. United planned to spend $4 million to equip 150 aircraft of their fleet of 176 CV-340s, DC-3s, DC-4s, DC-6Bs, DC-7s and Stratocruisers. They estimated the payback period at 10–12 years in terms of improved efficiency, reduced aircraft damage and customer goodwill.

In 1956 PanAm ordered $1 million worth of RCA AVQ-10 sets for its forty-five Boeing 707s and DC-8s and spent another $2 million to retrofit seventy-four Douglas piston-engined airliners. This decision followed 5,000 flying hours of evaluation in the winter of 1954–5.[14] Weather radar was standard equipment in the Lockheed Electra.[15]

One significant piece of knowledge to emerge from experimental work on both sides of the Atlantic was the association between severe turbulence and sharp rainfall intensity gradients as well as with the heavy rain itself.[16] The RCA set had circuitry to identify such areas. In some cases air traffic controllers could use their radar to vector aircraft around areas of heavy rain.

Once the early problems of cost and weight had been overcome and experience had built up, weather radar spread quickly. By early 1957 six models were available from RCA, Sperry, Bendix and Collins in the US and Ekco in the UK.[17] Typical weights were 68 kg (150 pounds). Power

9 Jones, F. E. 1949
10 *Flight*, 23 February 1950, 269
11 *Flight*, 3 August 1950, 154
12 *Flight*, 21 January 1955, 77
13 *Flight*, 8 October 1954, 565; 26 November 1954, 779
14 *Flight*, 13 January 1956, 61
15 *Flight*, 4 November 1955, 714
16 *Flight*, 21 January 1955, 77
17 *Flight*, 12 April 1957, 495

demand was typically 115-volt AC power at two different frequencies, plus 28-volt power, totalling 1 kilowatt. The RCA AVQ-10 was in service with six US and thirteen foreign airlines.

The enormous vertical extent of cumulonimbus clouds continued to astonish the aviation fraternity as aircraft flew ever higher and found cells extending to even greater heights. Such a cell, and the turbulence above it, could be dangerous to a jet aircraft flying close to its service ceiling, where its stalling speed and critical Mach number were close to each other. One jet pilot wrote:[18]

> It is a remarkable fact that, before the Comets started operating nobody thought that turbulent clouds ever extended higher than 20,000–25,000 feet, [although during the USAF study aircraft had entered storms as high as 29,000 feet].[19] People simply did not believe us when we reported going through the top of the inter-tropical front at 42,000 feet with active tops even higher.
>
> Since then, however, it has been recognized that there are occasions when it is not possible to go above the weather. I have myself seen one very active cu-nim, the top of which I estimated at 55,000–60,000 feet. (I went through this one at altitudes between 35,000 and 43,000 feet.) Most pilots probably share my intense dislike for this sort of activity, but in spite of this, and even when using airborne radar, one cannot always keep out.

The tropopause forms a cap to most weather. Even so, a proportion of thunderstorms, especially in the US and northeastern India, contain enough energy to penetrate 3,000–6,000 metres (10,000–20,000 feet) into the stratosphere and on one occasion a U-2 pilot reported a thunderstorm over India that he reckoned to reach 30,000 metres (100,000 feet).

Every increase in the understanding of thunderstorms indicated avoidance rather than penetration.[20] In addition to severe turbulence, thunderstorms were found to contain large local temperature variations. Because the speed of sound is proportional to temperature, such variations caused changes in the local speed of sound, altering the Mach number and, in transonic or supersonic flight, affecting the airflow and shock wave patterns around wings and engine inlets. Intense thunderstorm rain could, on occasion, douse jet engines. Hail caused severe   damage to leading surfaces, but without damaging the airframe itself.

Lightning strikes on aircraft in flight, the most obvious hazard of thunderstorm flying and at first thought to be the most dangerous, turned out to be relatively innocuous, although frightening to the occupants of the aircraft. The pilot of a Liberator

> Once, south of Greenland, I was struck by lightning. Suddenly there was an enormous magnesium flash and a noise like a land-mine going off. The whole aircraft became momentarily luminous. Every metal plate in the aircraft clanged like a hundred cymbals, the noise echoing and echoing in our ears. I could smell an acrid whiff of burning, as though we had been hit by anti-aircraft fire. Going out of synchronization, the four propellers began to scream their heads off. Then just as suddenly, silence except for the engines as the aircraft – unruffled, undamaged – chugged on its way.[21]

Although lightning strikes were less dangerous than had once been believed, their effects on increasingly complex avionics and control systems came into question.

The hazards of squalls, turbulence and low-level wind shear, all associated with thunderstorms, became worse with the passage of time because large jet aircraft with high inertia and slow throttle response proved vulnerable to low-level wind shear during take-off or landing. As far as was known in the 1960s: 'Apart … from a few particularly troublesome airfields, this is likely to be one of the many weather problems which is bad enough to be complained about but not bad enough for a worthwhile solution to be organized.'[22] A series of fatal jet airliner crashes would cause this appraisal to be drastically revised.

The aviation industry came to acknowledge that thunderstorms are so unpredictable and potentially so dangerous that avoidance is the only sure antidote. While weather radar has done much to alleviate this danger, thunderstorms have continued to take a toll of aircraft, although increasingly those of low performance, limited equipment and unwary crew. In addition, over the years air traffic authorities have become more and more willing to close an airport while it is affected by thunderstorms rather than risk accidents to arriving and departing aircraft.

The problem of ice accretion was already known in the mid-1930s. The American solution was to use inflatable rubber 'boots' along the leading edges of flying surfaces to break up the ice after it had formed. The British, in particular the RAF during the Second World War, favoured a de-icing paste that prevented ice from adhering to the wing. Early in the war, the Wellington bombers of 214 Squadron were fitted experimentally with equipment to dispense de-icing fluid along the leading edges of the wings. This equipment was not put into service because it would have disrupted production and was considered less effective than de-icing paste. British anti-icing research was deferred for the duration of the war.[23] In spite of the advanced state of aeronautical engineering in the early 1940s, ice protection remained uneven in both design and application. There is little doubt that many otherwise unexplained aircraft losses during the war resulted from this problem.

The Germans were the first to use wing heat extensively. Their most important discovery was that, contrary to earlier belief, only the leading edge of the wing needed to be heated, and not the whole wing. This was achieved easily enough using engine exhaust, a heat exchanger and ducting. The anticipated problem of moisture re-freezing on the rearward, unheated surface of the wing was found to have no effect. The equipment needed for a 22,600 kg (50,000-pound) aircraft weighed 226 kg (500 pounds); the weight did not increase in direct proportion to the aircraft's size. In the US, the NACA developed thermal de-icing using Lockheed 12As, B-17s, B-24s and C-46s and this became accepted as the standard for large aircraft. The B-29, for example, was fitted with de-icing boots, whereas its design derivative, the Stratocruiser, was thermally de-iced.[24]

Even so, complete ice protection was impossible and de-icing was intended to give a pilot time to escape from icing conditions, rather than continue to fly in them. On one Stratocruiser delivery flight:

We were flying at 19,000 feet ... riding in and out of cloud and picking up some ice ... With the wing-inspection lights on and thermal de-icers working we watched the ice disperse from the hot parts and heard small lumps fly off the airscrews.[25] More built up, however, on spinners, parts of the nacelles, and around the aileron hinges. Some slight tail buffeting could be felt on the controls, and the speed dropped by about 20 knots; so, the crew having little experience of icing with this new aircraft, it was thought prudent to lose height over Spokane and call up for clearance on track at a new height. The ice had nearly gone when the new clearance came

through as we circled the city at about 11,000 feet.

While iced up we noted a loud, continuous hooting noise above the cockpit, and came to the conclusion it was caused by ice forming on the short radio-aerial masts.

A pilot flying a Constellation over the Atlantic reported:[26]

At 18,000 feet I encountered light ice, which covered a long antenna that went from a mast up front to a fin at the back. The antenna vibrated and finally broke near the fin. The long wire, with a big anti-static insulator on the end, whipped around beating the fuselage. I tried different air speeds in the hope that the wire would 'fly' out straight and stop beating the fuselage. Nothing helped and finally the insulator gave a sound whack to a window and broke the outer pane; fortunately there were two. But this meant I had to reduce the cabin pressure and descend. I descended into a worse icing condition. It was a moment of relief when we finally landed at Gander, Newfoundland ... It is important to realize that de-icing equipment does not allow one to fly indefinitely in ice.

After the war ice protection became an integral part of aircraft design, not an optional extra, and not only for flying surfaces but also for propellers, induction systems, throttles and turbine inlets. Several problems made icing research particularly difficult. Icing conditions were not always easy to find; if they were found, research flying in such conditions, deliberately and for extended periods, could endanger the aircraft and its crew. Flights were cancelled because of the risk of severe icing, yet this justifiable caution prevented the gathering of information and the probing of the conditions feared. The elusiveness of the problem hindered the investigation of its cure. Simulation of icing, whether by wind tunnels or by spraying water onto

18 *Flight*, 23 January 1959, 125
19 Brice, D. A. 1950
20 O'Hara, F., Burnham, J. 1968; Patrick, K. B. 1968
21 Beaty, D. 1976, 198
22 O'Hara, F., Burnham, J. 1968, 478
23 Hardy, J. K. 1947
24 *Flight*, 15 December 1949, 775
25 The narrator was British. 'Airscrew' = Propeller
26 Buck, R. N. 1970; 1978 ed., 216

aerofoils in flight, was an approximation to actual conditions and not necessarily reliable. Icing research during the 1950s focused almost as much on developing valid simulations as on icing itself.[27]

Simple empirical facts concealed complex processes. Ambient air temperature, airframe temperature, and the size, size distribution and concentration of moisture droplets all played a part as did the latent heats of freezing and evaporation on the airframe. Kinetic heating became significant at airspeeds above 220 km/h (120 knots). Like thunderstorms, icing remained a hazard that would strike down the ill-equipped and the unwary in the course of time. The 1940s and 1950s brought increased awareness of the hazards of these two phenomena. The palliatives for both alike were intended for avoidance and escape, not as encouragement to reckless penetration.

The following narrative may qualify as 'reckless penetration'.

> I was supposed to take this C-54 westbound out of Calgary. They were calling for all kinds of icing, but I was young and full of piss and vinegar and I thought I could hack it. We'd just got over the mountains when I realized we weren't going to make it. It took 54 inches of manifold pressure to drag that thing back to Calgary and they spent three days chipping the ice off it. Maybe that's why I stayed a Flight Lieutenant for so long![28]

In theory, higher cruising speeds meant that navigation was less affected by wind, but in practice windspeeds increased with altitude and were still significant. The physics of the different types of aero engine determined optimum cruising altitudes: below 7,600 metres (25,000 feet) for piston engines; 6,000–9,000 metres (20,000–30,000 feet) for turboprops, and 9,000–13,700 metres (30,000–45,000 feet) for jets. From time to time during the war, aircraft encountered windspeeds at high altitudes which were greeted with disbelief. As evidence accumulated, however, it became clear that long, narrow channels of extremely fast-moving air were associated with the tropopause at middle latitudes where the tropopause height is of the order of 10,700 metres (35,000 feet). These came to be known as jetstreams and were found to be thousands of miles long, but less than 320 km (200 miles) wide and blowing in an easterly direction. Wind speeds of 280 km/h (150 knots) are common, up to extremes of 460 km/h (250 knots). In one

case jet airliners could not fly from Hong Kong to Bangkok because of forecast 370 km/h (200 knot) headwinds persisting for several days. The jets could not overtop the jetstream. They did not have enough fuel to complete the journey flying into wind in the jetstream, to avoid it, or to fly beneath it at lower altitudes where their engines were less efficient. Piston-engined and turboprop aircraft, cruising at lower altitudes, were unaffected.[29]

Flight operations during the 1950s were supported by broad-ranging weather reconnaissance flights. One example was the USAF 53rd Weather Reconnaissance Squadron, stationed in the UK in 1959.[30] One of seven USAF weather reconnaissance squadrons stationed in various parts of the world, the 53rd was equipped with B-50s. A typical weather mission, covering a 6,000 km (3,700 mile) track, flew from England to a point 400 km (250 miles) north of the Azores, followed the 30th meridian north to a point 675 km (420 miles) southeast of Greenland, returning thence to England. Other routes ran to Madeira and the Azores or up the Norwegian coast towards the north pole. Altitudes varied from 3,000 to 9,000 metres (10,000 to 30,000 feet); missions lasted up to 15 hours. The crew comprised a weatherman, two pilots, a flight engineer, two navigators, two radio operators and a dropsonde operator. A dropsonde was an expendable radiosonde which fell at 450 metres (1,500 feet) per minute when released, transmitting temperature, pressure and humidity measurements every hundred feet until it fell into the sea. Five dropsondes were released on every mission. Weather observations were taken at points 240 km (150 miles) apart and radioed to England. Navigation was by dead reckoning and celestial, backed up by Loran, mapping radar and Doppler.

Enormous advances had taken place in aviation meteorology since the days of Vilhelm and Jakob Bjerknes. Not only had the quality of synoptic weather observations increased with improved telecommunications and a denser and more worldwide observation network, but a great volume of data had accumulated on the behaviour of aircraft and pilots in response to weather phenomena. This burgeoning of information would have been useless without electronic computers to store and analyse it. Until the 1930s experienced human forecasters could still assemble all the synoptic observations and draw weather charts. This impressive combination of experience, skill, and judgment was developed to a fine degree by many forecasters of that era. This work, however, retained a subjective element, besides which the rate of data collection was increasing faster than the ability of unaided human minds to assimilate it.

Vilhelm Bjerknes approached the study of the atmosphere as a physicist applying the principles of hydrodynamics. His work influenced a British mathematician, L. F. Richardson, who published *Weather Prediction by Numerical Process* in 1922, proposing a new, objective approach, numerical rather than synoptic. The computing power needed to make this concept work, even with the volume of data available in 1922, did not exist at the time. Richardson's concept entailed the simultaneous work of 64,000 people with mechanical calculators. The first electronic computers were built during the 1940s to meet military needs. The first successful meteorological forecast by numerical means was made in 1950. Numerical weather forecasting at once demanded the most powerful computers in existence and continues to do so today.

In 1935 the US Weather Bureau and the Massachusetts Institute of Technology began a concerted effort, led by C. G. Rossby, to produce long-range forecasts. After years of analysis and experimentation, 30-day forecasts were first published in the US in 1948. In Russia, at the St Petersburg Central Geophysical Observatory, B. P. Multanovsky began work on a synoptic method of long-range forecasting; the first was made in 1922. The Germans made their own attempts in this direction with the work of F. Baur in 1929. The UK Meteorological Office did not begin to issue long-range forecasts until 1963; even then, because of the rapidly changing influences on British weather, this programme met with only limited success.

An entirely new source of weather information became available when the Americans launched the first weather satellite, Tiros I. In 1961 President Kennedy proposed an international weather prediction system. Sponsored by the World Meteorological Organization, it started in 1963 as World Weather Watch. This grew into a network of simultaneous observations by 9,200 land stations and 7,000 ships; 850 stations made upper air obser-

vations. Five geostationary and five polar-orbiting satellites made global observations from space.

Because few flights lasted more than twelve hours, forecasts longer than 24 hours were not needed for the average flight. By the mid-1960s radar, computers and photographs transmitted from satellites all allowed bad weather to be detected and predicted within that time-frame as never before. Nevertheless, fog, icing, thunderstorms and clear-air turbulence in the stratosphere (CAT) remained easier to report when they occurred than to forecast.

An ever growing volume of information on turbulence, gust-loading and airframe fatigue, processed by increasingly powerful analytical techniques, influenced both design and operating procedures. A big airframe designed to withstand extreme turbulence would be so heavy as to carry little fuel or payload. A balance had, therefore, to be struck between designing strength into the airframe and avoiding turbulence, a balance in which government certification authorities played a part. The information revolution allowed designs, costs and procedures to be more and more highly refined. This type of information and techniques made it possible to design gust-damping into autopilots; this became both more advantageous and more complex as larger and more elastic airframes came into service.[31]

In spite of all the technical advances, and no matter how accurate the reports and forecasts might be, the human pilot still had to make his own assessment of the weather risks to be faced, in the light of his training, mission and equipment, not least the possibility and consequences of a wrong forecast. The same decisions faced the same fallible human pilots: penetrate or avoid, go on, go around, or go back. The improvement in air transport safety resulted not only from better aircraft and better information, but also from an increasingly vast body of piloting experience.

27 Cheverton, B. T. 1959
28 J. F. Kaiser: personal communication.
29 Cheverton, B. T. 1959
30 Roberts, B. 1959
31 O'Hara, F., Burnham, J., 1968, 475

CHAPTER 2 3

The Jet Age

The jet aircraft brought the quest for all-weather flight to maturity. It could cruise in clear air above most weather phenomena, climbing and descending rapidly through the lower atmosphere and thus spending relatively little time in cloud, turbulence and icing. Its capital cost and operating economics justified the enormous investment of effort and money that went into fully automatic blind landing. The big jets revolutionized airline economics, demanded a new order of piloting skills and hastened the development of the aircraft as an autonomous vehicle capable of functioning in almost any weather conditions.

The first of the big jets was the Boeing B-47 bomber. Flying for the first time in 1947, it was one of the most astonishing and radical advances over contemporary aircraft in the history of aviation, considering that the first jet aircraft had entered service only three years earlier. Within ten years the USAF had 1,800 B-47s in service. With a maximum take-off weight of 83,900 kg (185,000 pounds) in early versions, it was also one of the biggest aircraft in the world. The operating characteristics of the B-47 set the conditions for subsequent heavy jet operations which were radically different from anything that had gone before

The Boeing B-47, first of the big jets.

and had profound implications for all-weather flying.[1]

Fuel consumption on the ground was high; (150–200 pounds per minute). This and high cruising speeds meant that take-off delays were costly in range; a 15-minute delay on take-off would reduce a B-47's range by 160 km (100 miles).

Once airborne, even a heavily loaded B-47 climbed initially at 600 metres per minute (2,000 fpm) and averaged 400 metres per minute (1,300 fpm) to cruising altitude, compared to 200 metres per minute (700 fpm) for a Stratocruiser.[2] A turbojet engine could operate continuously at 96–100% power in the climb, whereas take-off power in piston engines had to be reduced by as much as 33% in the climb to avoid overheating. The thermodynamics of the turbojet engine demanded a rapid climb to the thin, cold air at 9,000–12,000 metres (30,000–40,000 feet), a drift upward as fuel load lightened and a rapid descent at a constant Mach number to a landing. Any deviation from this bore a heavy cost in fuel.[3] The best cruising altitude depended on the weight of the aircraft. On reaching the calculated best altitude, the power setting had to be calculated by reference to the outside-air thermometer and the Machmeter. Jets typically cruised in clear air, penetrating adverse weather only during departure and arrival. At such altitudes, however, wind speeds of 90 km/h (50 knots) were normal, 185 km/h (100 knots) frequent and 280 km/h (150 knots) occasional. Winds aloft were therefore still significant to jets in spite of their high cruising speeds.

As the air became thinner with increasing altitude, an aircraft's stalling speed increased but the speed of sound decreased. Therefore, at any given aircraft weight an altitude existed where the stalling speed equalled the maximum permissible Mach number. For the B-47 this ranged from 10,700 metres (35,000 feet) at 90,700 kg (200,000 pounds) to 15,250 metres (50,000 feet) at 45,350 kg (100,000 pounds). As the aircraft approached this critical altitude it became vulnerable to being gust-stalled by turbulence, which could cause disastrous loss of control. Best cruising altitudes, also dependent on aircraft weight, were several thousand feet lower than critical altitudes.

The enormous power of the B-47's six engines, together with the effects of its aerodynamically clean exterior, demanded the pilot's continuous attention, otherwise control could be lost. A pilot flying a B-47 at a gross weight of 150,000 pounds with the throttles set to climb power, levelled off at 3,000 metres (10,000 feet) in order to pick his way through broken clouds during a VFR climb. The aircraft had been climbing at 670 metres per minute (2,200 fpm) at an indicated airspeed of 650 km/h (350 knots), equivalent to a true airspeed of 778 km/h (420 knots). In level flight with no power adjustment, the aircraft's speed increased at the rate of 1.9 km/h (1 knot) per second. The aircraft would reach its critical speed in about 60 seconds. The pilot passed control of the aircraft to the copilot while he tuned the ADF. He said later that he was distracted for no more than 30 seconds. When he looked up, the aircraft was in a dive of about 20° and a bank of 25–30° at an indicated airspeed of 84 km/h (450 knots). He immediately applied full right aileron. In certain conditions, aileron application could cause the B-47's long, elastic wing to twist in the opposite direction to the applied aileron, causing an effect known as aileron reversal. This probably occurred here because the aircraft continued to steepen its spiral dive until it hit the ground. Automatic flight control would become increasingly important in keeping such aircraft under control and within performance and structural limits.

Better information on destination weather became more important because of the fuel cost of a descent, missed approach and climb back to altitude. A typical letdown began 110 km (70 miles) from base. Two letdown procedures were used. In one the bomber descended to 6,000 metres (20,000 feet) over the approach fix and then flew a teardrop turn outbound and back to the fix, descending at 1,200 metres (4,000 feet) per minute. The other option was a straight-in approach using surveillance radar. Either of these could be completed with GCA or GCA-monitored ILS. Using the teardrop procedure, a wing of forty-five aircraft could be landed in instrument conditions at four-minute intervals, or at one-minute intervals using the straight-in approach.

The jets demanded more precise control during final approach than piston-engined aircraft. The jet engine did not have the immediate throttle response of a piston engine. Because of its clean exterior, the B-47 decelerated slowly; it had no dive brakes, spoilers, or thrust reversers, although these would be incorporated in subsequent types of aircraft.

1 Evans, R. E. 1957
2 *Flight*, 15 December 1949, 774
3 *Flight*, 5 April 1957, 437

Boeing 707.

Because the aeroplane is streamlined and has no windmilling propellers, it does not want to stop flying, and, once on the runway, it does not want to stop rolling. Ten knots excessive speed at flare-out will increase the required runway length by 1,700 feet. On a wet runway, at 3,000 feet elevation and 80°F, a 120,000-pound B-47 will stop, using drag chute and brakes, in 5,400 feet. With a GCA touchdown point 2,000 feet down the runway and 15 knots excess speed on final approach, it will stop just 50 feet short at the end of a 10,000-foot strip. If the chute had failed under these circumstances, the aircraft would have required 14,200 feet on the wet runway, 11,000 feet on a dry runway.

For these reasons, final approach speeds had to be pushed closer to the stalling speed than for piston-engined aircraft and the freedom to manoeuvre was much reduced. The stall speed of a B-47 at 45,360 kg (100,000 pounds) was 211 km/h (114 knots); the recommended approach speed was 237 km/h (128 knots). An additional G loading of only 0.25G would stall the aircraft. A crosswind component above 46 km/h (25 knots) made landing unduly risky. Yawing the aircraft on final approach just above stall speed could stall one of the long, swept wings with disastrous results. In 1950–2 inclusive the USAAF B-29 accident rate was 17 per 100,000 hours; 36% were landing accidents. In 1952–4 inclusive the B-47 accident rate was the same, except that 48% were landing accidents.[4] The implication for bad-weather approaches was that the whole approach system, ATC, electronic aids, approach lights, had to be designed to deliver the aircraft to the runway threshold ready for touchdown.

Big aircraft, and especially the jets, demanded 'flying by the numbers' and rigorous adherence to exact procedures established by testing.[5] With the Comet it was noticed, and this would be true of all jets, that attitude changes too small to be detected on the instruments, and certainly not by reference to the vague outside world of the high altitudes,

Controls and instrument panel of Boeing B-52. Note duplicate attitude indicator flight directors and horizontal situation indicators top left and top right and beginnings of the glass cockpit.

caused rapid changes in speed and altitude. Speed could easily increase to the limiting Mach number. The Sperry Zero Reader was especially useful in this regard. Even so, pilots were still trained to fly the Comet 'partial panel', using air speed indicator, vertical speed indicator, altimeter and turn-and-bank, should the need arise.

Stacking inbound aircraft over a holding fix at low altitudes, normal practice with piston-engined aircraft, was unacceptable for jets with their high fuel consumption below 6,000 metres (20,000 feet). At descent rates of 900–1,500 metres (3,000–5,000 feet) per minute, however, a jet could descend quickly from a hold at 6,000 metres (20,000 feet) to final approach. A typical Comet descent began 240 km (150 miles) from destination.

Thirty US gallons of jet fuel weighed as much as one passenger but sufficed to fly a big jet for only one minute.[6] This added to the demands of jet operations on weather and traffic services. Navigation had to be quicker and more precise to economize on fuel and maximize the use of airspace.

The Boeing 707 was as revolutionary as anything Boeing had produced before. The airframe

---

4 For comparison, the 1993 US general aviation accident rate was 8.79 per 100,000 hours (*Flying*, May 1994, 27); in 1991 US military 'serious mishaps', excluding the Gulf War, were 1.11 per 100,000 hours (*Flying*, February 1992, 27)

5 *Flight*, 1 May 1953, 535

6 *Flight*, 5 April 1957, 437

Boeing 747.

Lockheed L-1011 TriStar.

first flew in 1954 as the prototype KC-135 tanker. The first airliner version, the 707-120, flew in December 1957[7] and entered airline service the following year. At a gross weight of 112,000 kg (247,000 pounds) it was 2.5 times heavier than the Comet 1. Design improvements had increased the limiting Mach number from 0.75 for the B-47 and Comet 1 to 0.82,[8] allowing the Boeing 707 to cruise at true airspeeds of nearly 965 km/h (600 mph). On 21 October 1958, a PanAm 707 flew from London to New York in 9½ hours against strong headwinds, including a fuel stop at Keflavik. Two pilots, a navigator and a flight engineer occupied the flight deck. The Boeing 707 was the beginning of mass air travel as we know it today. Because of its relatively enormous speed and payload, the cost per seat-mile came down to where airlines could offer seats at a price within the average person's means. The 707 was soon followed in service by the Douglas DC-8 and the Convair CV-880; the medium-range Boeing 727 and 737 and the Douglas DC-9 followed in the 1960s; the jumbo-jet Boeing 747, the Douglas DC-10 and the Lockheed L-1011 followed in the 1970s, establishing size limits which remain unsurpassed.

Flight operations became routine that had been infrequent and hazardous only thirty years before. By 1970 up to two hundred aircraft were flying across the Atlantic at any one time. Civilian jet flights across the Atlantic had taken on most of their present-day features; as an example we will look at a DC-8 charter flight from McGuire Air Force Base, New Jersey, to Frankfurt.[9]

Regularity and uniformity had their less agreeable aspects:

> There is an appalling sameness about flight operations offices anywhere in the world … clacking teleprinters, ringing phones, and crowded ashtrays, all under that universal, hard, stale, fluorescent light. The altar of the proceedings is a huge 24-hour clock on one wall, while beneath it are clips of yellow notams, a well-fingered map of Europe, pigeonholes filled with papers their owners are thus advised to read. There are containers of coffee, mountains of crew baggage everywhere, dog-eared magazines on the table.

Drab surroundings, endless transience, and long, abnormal, irregular working hours had emerged as the dominant features of the pilot's life.

The charter company obtained computer-gener-ated flight plans from a flight-planning service contractor. The flight plan comprised lists of tracks and coordinates, times, distances and fuel weights. ATC would assign an altitude and cruise Mach number. The flight from McGuire to Frankfurt was scheduled for 7 hours 30 minutes with a fuel consumption of 41,087 kg (90,580 pounds). The captain was supplied with forecasts of departure and destination weather and prognostic weather charts for the Atlantic at 5,500 and 9,000 metres (18,000 and 30,000 feet). The most significant items of *en route* weather were winds aloft, especially jetstreams, and temperatures which would affect fuel consumption. The captain also received a departure briefing and the procedure to be followed if he needed to turn back immediately after take-off. The crew consisted of pilot, copilot, flight engineer and navigator. They calculated the critical speeds and distances for take-off, based on the gross weight of the aircraft which in this case was 142,430 kg (314,000 pounds).

Departure was at night in wind, rain, sleet and low cloud. Almost immediately after take-off the aircraft entered cloud which persisted to 900 metres (3,000 feet). ATC issued successive clearances to a cruising altitude of 9,500 metres (31,000 feet), reached after burning 6.7 tonnes (7.5 tons) of fuel. The crew navigated by VOR/DME as far northeast as Gander, where they were assigned a standard track, an altitude, a cruise Mach number and a transponder code for the flight over the Atlantic. A navigator was not needed over land but was essential when the aircraft was over the ocean.

Doppler provided ground speed and drift; a tailwind of 145 km/h (78 knots) approaching Gander increased to 260 km/h (140 knots) over the Atlantic. Doppler automatic navigation did not live up to its earlier promise; navigation computers were available using Doppler to keep a continuous position fix but the airlines found them so unreliable that they reverted to using Doppler to provide a human navigator with ground speed and drift angle. In 1970 neither Doppler nor inertial were reliable enough to use alone. Loran and Consol were the chief methods of long-range position-fixing; both needed a human navigator. Weather ships were an additional source of position fixes. Each

7 Taylor, M. J. H. 1989, 187
8 *Flight*, 31 October 1958
9 *Flying*, January 1970, 57

McDonnell Douglas Phantom.

ship carried radar and an NDB, although in bad weather the ships sometimes had trouble fixing their own positions. The aircraft carried HF radio; because of interference from static and neighbouring frequencies 'it had a quite different quality from VHF communications, for the background consists of weird, unearthly whistlings and rustlings, and it comes and goes in strength, and is loaded with high-speed Morse, and a babel of position reports, and "frying", and strange warblings'.

Dawn greeted the crew over the Atlantic as it has so many aircrew before and since.

'Soon the sky begins to lighten ahead. In the fading darkness, I can see that the wind has stretched little lines of cumulus cloud across the ocean.

For the first time, as the blackness dissipates, I begin to get an impression of tremendous height and speed. Dawn begins – green at first, then orange where you can see the sun appearing over the top layer of cloud. The sky is the palest blue above, while the land below is the deepest violet.'

After descending through cloud to an ILS

approach, the aircraft landed at Frankfurt at 8.22 a.m., 6 hours 47 minutes after leaving McGuire, with 19,960 kg (44,000 pounds) of fuel still on board.

Whether the return trip to McGuire could be made non-stop depended on the winds aloft. The aircraft was allocated a northerly track which would minimize their effect.

> Britain is gone in a trice, invisible beneath the clouds, except that they clear enough to allow a glimpse of the Isle of Skye, its seaward coastline etched in white Atlantic foam, and lenticular clouds piled over its hills like a stack of mother-of-pearl plates in the weak winter sun. Greenland, too, is sunk in cloud; were it not for the ADF proudly pointing to its several NDBs, I could easily believe Greenland did not exist, for not a single glimpse of it did we get.
>
> Approaching Labrador, the clouds clear, revealing a landscape savagely held in the grip of winter, for a huge sheet of ice covers everything on land and extends as pack ice for twenty miles out to sea. It is a landscape as desolate as the moon's. There are lakes in a million shapes, each covered with a crust of ice, with a thin series of moss-like trees lining their edges. Snow showers trail icy skirts across the frozen landscape and the pack ice. Nowhere is there any sign of life.

The return to McGuire Air Force Base was uneventful.

Long-range aircraft had the capacity for a variety of navigation equipment and a human navigator, which allowed them to fly blind over areas devoid of ground-based navaids. The new jet fighters, however, were designed primarily to intercept bombers, relying on ground beacons and radar vectoring for blind navigation. Although fighters had been extensively used to attack surface targets during the Second World War, this concept had to some extent lapsed and the problem of navigating such aircraft in blind conditions outside beacon or radar coverage was not effectively addressed. As a result, many tactical aircraft of the 1960s, such as the Phantom, carried only ADF and TACAN.[10] With the escalation of warfare in Vietnam, an NDB and TACAN network was installed in South Vietnam, but outside signal coverage pilots navigated supersonic aircraft using methods that their predecessors had used in the First World War.

You learned to use every clue, so that even though

I couldn't see the ground beneath me, I was not totally in the dark. The tops of the mountains to the west were clear, allowing me to estimate how far north I'd come. Though not quite as reliable, there were often patterns in the clouds that allowed you to discern features such as the coastline or boundaries between topographic regions. The main thing was to develop as many options as possible so that the loss of one set of clues didn't leave you in the lurch. When all else failed, you fell back on dead reckoning.[11]

Navigation capability differed widely from one aircraft type to another; F-105s carried a Doppler-inertial navigation system, albeit far from infallible.[12]

Unlike many of their predecessors in the Second World War, tactical aircraft of the 1960s were equipped, and their pilots trained, to operate at night and in all weathers.

> On February first (1966), we arrived over Xepon at two-thirty in the morning – a four-plane flight armed with twelve 500-pound bombs apiece. We had departed Da Nang in a driving rainstorm with no assurance that the weather would improve enough for us to return there to land – a routine but nonetheless nettlesome situation. But when we cleared the angry deck of clouds, we were greeted by a fairy tale night – a world studded with visual jewels of such beauty that for a moment I lost all thought of the task at hand. The weather was clear in Laos, where flickering fires – remnants of previous raids – created the powerful illusion of a world turned upside down. The moonless sky was ablaze with stars, and in successive bouts of vertigo, I saw them as the lights of a faraway city, the misconception accentuated by the reflection of the instrument lights above the canopy bow. From time to time a searing flash of lightning erased the black, presenting with stark radiance a row of boiling thunderheads towering like sentinels above the jutting Assam. Magically, the crossroads leapt into view, an arc-lit tableau crafted in the cozy detail of a miniature railroad scene. It was a glorious mirage – one of such stunning clarity that I was almost beguiled into forgetting

10 Trotti, J. 1984; Bach, R. 1963
11 Trotti, J. 1984, 68
12 Broughton, J. 1985

that this was the most heavily defended point on the Ho Chi Minh Trail.[13]

Instrument flying of a different order was required during air-to-air refuelling in bad weather, seen here from the cockpit of an F-105.[14]

We had huge thunderstorms on all of our refueling tracks and they started on the ground and went up above 35,000 feet, even in the early morning hours. There was simply no possible way to avoid them, and though I tried desperately to keep the heaving, bouncing mass of fighters and tankers under control, it got pretty well messed up from the start. All of the flight leaders managed to locate their tankers in the rain and clouds, which in itself was quite a feat. It gets real spooky probing through a thick cloud trying to locate another moving object, and neither the tankers nor the fighters are manoeuvrable enough in the refueling posture to salvage the situation if somebody goofs.

In bad weather two hookups are plenty demanding, but this day I had to accomplish eight separate hookups ... I don't care if I never have to do that again. The further north we went, the worse the bumps became. We had people falling off refuelling booms and sinking into the murk, separated from their flights, and we had entire flights slung off their tankers. There was just no place to go where conditions would be any better and it looked for a while like I would not be able to hold my troops together safely, and that I might have to scrub the mission that I wanted so badly to complete. We all had to stay on the same radio channel so that we could try to keep track of each other, and since every pilot was having problems, the radio turned into a screaming mess. I was trying to fly instruments, navigate the force, keep track of my tanker, and mentally picture the other tankers and fighters while attempting to figure out how I was going to maintain control of this mess. I had vertigo so many times I lost track of the number, and I repeatedly had to revert to straight instruments to convince myself that I was or was not in some degree of upside-down condition. The tankers were trying to give us all the help they could, but they became confused, and their turns became spastic as they bumped out of unison with us and exceeded the capabilities of our birds heavy with bombs and fuel. The entire situation approached the impossible.

But he succeeded nonetheless by finding a small patch of clear air and noting its coordinates for the guidance of other aircraft inbound to the rendezvous. Both the memoirs quoted here mention bad weather as a factor in the tactics of a mission and as affecting the ability of pilots to attack targets on the ground, but not as an absolute barrier or as a noteworthy source of accidents.

GCA and TACAN were the blind-approach procedures used to return to base. The first step was to establish radar contact:[15]

'Da Nang Approach, Boilerplate One, two-zero thousand,' from the inbound pilot, reporting the aircraft's altitude as 20,000 feet.

'Boilerplate One, Da Nang Approach, squawk[16] zero-two zero-zero, say position,' from approach control, instructing the pilot to activate his transponder with 0200 as its response code.

'Roger, Boilerplate One squawking zero-two-hundred, presently the zero-four-five for forty-eight Da Nang TACAN, a single Fox-four at minimum fuel.' The pilot reported the aircraft's position as 48 miles from the Da Nang TACAN beacon on the 045° radial.

The approach began: 'Radar contact, Boilerplate, turn left to one-six-five, descend at pilot's discretion to 5,000 feet. This will be a radar vector to the GCA final approach course landing runway three-five. Da Nang weather is presently 800 feet broken, one and one half miles in rain. The winds are zero-three-zero at eighteen gusting twenty-five. Altimeter setting is two-niner point eight-six. The morest gear is down.'

The pilot of the Phantom continues the story. 'Crossing the 075-degree radial at twelve miles, I reduced the power to idle, lowering the nose to maintain airspeed. The feeling is like driving a car from the roadway off onto sand. You press forward into the shoulder straps, conscious that without the might of the two J-79s, you are flying in something very much akin to a lead safe ...'

'Boilerplate One, continue descent to two thousand five hundred, turn right to two-six-zero. Lost communications procedures follow. In the event of no transmissions for one minute in the pattern or five seconds on final, proceed in accordance with TACAN One procedures, landing runway three-five. Copy?'

GCA minima were 200 feet ceiling and 1.5

mile visibility. If communication was lost the pilot was to revert to the TACAN One approach for which minima were 400 feet ceiling and one mile visibility.

'At nine miles south of the field we arrived at the extended runway centerline, descending through 4,000 feet on our way to 2,500. With my speed at 300 knots, I planned to be established inbound to the field and on altitude at about six miles and by then it would be time to lower the landing gear.

'Boilerplate One, turn right to three-five-zero, perform landing cockpit checks and reduce to approach speed. You are now seven and one half miles from touchdown approaching glide path.'

'At 220 knots I slammed the gear handle down, watching all of the indicators flip and flop as they confirmed the transition. At 170 knots, I selected full flaps and advanced the power, first to 88% and then to 92% as the speed decayed to 145 knots.

'Boilerplate One, gear down and locked, flaps down.'

'Roger, Boilerplate One. No need to acknowledge further transmissions. You are five miles from touchdown, slightly left of course approaching glideslope. Come right to three-five-five.'

The aircraft was still in thick cloud. The GCA controller went on.

'Still left of course heading three-five-five..up to and on glideslope ... You're correcting nicely to course four miles to touchdown, come left to three-five-three ... Now going slightly above glideslope. Adjust your rate of descent.'...

'You're now on course line, at three and one half miles; come left to three-five-one. You're very slightly above glideslope.'...

'Two miles, on course. Coming down to and on glideslope. Tower has you in sight. You're cleared to land.'

'At first I saw nothing, but gradually the threshold lights emerged from the gloom ... then the perimeter fence line ... Dogpatch ... the mirror datum lights ... and the runway with its black scrub marks where thousands of tyres had screeched, each adding its contribution to the growing smudge ...

'Even when you squeak the Phantom on, you know that you've arrived on the ground with all the rumbling and shaking.'

By the 1960s flying had taken on an unprece-dented diversity. Military jets, civilian jet airliners and the first 'bizjets' shared the sky with turbo-props, older piston-engined airliners, helicopters, and small, piston-engined private aircraft. Their ability to handle weather conditions was equally diverse. High-performance aircraft flown by highly trained and experienced crews were now seldom obstructed or endangered by bad weather. At the opposite end of the scale, the pilots of small, low-performance aircraft had to accept the same kinds of weather restrictions as their predecessors twenty and thirty years before, and the weather could often be a subtle adversary, dangerous to the unwise.

Airline safety continued as a major concern. In 1960 air carrier crashes worldwide killed 1,226 passengers and crew;[17] airline fatalities were running at 200–300 per 100 million passenger-hours. The corresponding figure for US road deaths was 75.[18] Contributing to these disasters were seven DC-8 crashes in two years, some of them weather-related.[19] The fatality rate per 100 million passenger miles flown declined from 0.95 in 1962 to 0.48 in 1968, apart from an increase to 0.69 in 1966, but so rapid was the increase in passenger-miles flown that the actual numbers of deaths increased worldwide.[20] In the reporting countries Australia, Belgium, Brazil, Canada, France, West Germany, India, Italy, Japan, Netherlands, Scandinavia, the UK and the USA air carrier fatalities increased from about 400 a year in 1954–5 to more than 1,300 in 1966. Between 1961 and 1969 twenty-eight Boeing 707 and DC-8 crashes contributed largely to this gloomy total.

The accident record for 1961 was as bad as 1960. In the first eight months of 1961 twenty-seven airline accidents caused 834 fatalities.[21] September 1961 was the worst month in the history of civilian air transport with seven airline accidents and 311 fatalities in the first twenty-three days of the

13 Trotti, J. 1984, 8
14 Broughton, J. 1985, 250
15 Adapted from Trotti, J. 1984, 93
16 Squawk: transmit a code on the aircraft's transponder, in this case 0200.
17 *Flight*, 13 January 1961, 57 (Total number recorded; may exclude unpublished Communist bloc accidents.)
18 *Flight International,* 10 February 1961, 189
19 *Flight International,* 20 July 1961; 6 September 1962
20 *Flight International,* 30 May 1963, 776; 2 January 1964, 5; 7 January 1965, 5; 6 January 1966, 6; 5 January 1967, 7; 16 January 1969, 99
21 *Flight International,* 14 September 1961, 415

month.[22] Three aircraft hit mountains; one crashed in a storm after a night take-off.[23] Worse was to come, with 331 fatalities in seven accidents in two weeks in early 1962.[24] In June 1962, *Flight International* predicted that at the current loss rate six jet airliners would be lost in six months; immediately thereafter three were lost in a month.[25] By no means all of these crashes were weather-related, although weather was suspected in some cases when an aircraft disappeared. The civilian aircraft landing accident rate in all conditions was two in each million landings, but night IFR approach accidents were more than one in 100,000 landings, twenty times the overall rate.[26] In particular, it was noted in 1962 that of twenty-three fatal accidents involving jet airliners since jet services began, ten had been in the approach phase of flight.[27]

The proportion of weather-related accidents increased during the 1960s from about a quarter at the beginning of the decade to a half or more towards the end. The four most common types involved thunderstorms and squalls *en route*, hitting high ground *en route*, hitting the ground on initial descent and crashes on final approach or missed approach during bad weather. The available information lists some accidents as 'crashed after take-off' although with no indication of the prevailing conditions of light or weather or if mechanical problems were involved. Jets crashed in bad weather for the same reasons as other types of aircraft, except that their higher speeds and descent rates allowed less margin for confusion and error. The approach phase of an instrument flight was the most critical. The hazards of a blind approach began as soon as the aircraft left its cruising altitude. If procedures were not followed precisely, or if there were no procedures, the risk of an accident was enormously increased. The boundary between 'weather' and 'human error' as accident causes became less and less distinct.

On 19 January 1960, a Sud Aviation Caravelle crashed at Esenboga, Turkey, after a premature descent for causes unknown. On 25 January 1961, a BOAC Comet brushed the tops of trees during a night approach to the newly opened Rome Fiumicino airport.[28] The aircraft was 95 km (60 miles) from where the crew thought it was. The captain had never flown the approach before, the initial segment of which was based on two NDBs, one of which was blanketed by the commercial radio station at Prague. At Junnar, India, on 6 July 1962, a DC-8 equipped with the most up-to-date navigational devices hit a hill because the crew made a premature descent for a straight-in approach at night. At Lima, Peru, on 22 December 1962, a Boeing 707 hit a mountain after the crew tuned the wrong beacon.

Thunderstorms, lethal in themselves, were additionally dangerous because they could affect VOR and NDB signals. The dangerous propensity of an ADF to point to thunderstorms rather than NDBs was legendary: 'more of a thunderstorm indicator than a navigation radio', as one pilot called it.[29] A thunderstorm destroyed a DC-8 at New Orleans on 25 February 1964. On 17 September 1965 a Boeing 707 crashed at Montserrat in the West Indies. The aircrew made a premature descent in thunderstorms while unsure of their position. It was thought, also, that the electrical storms might have caused false VOR readings.

As in the 1950s, final approach accidents continued as the biggest single group of weather-related accidents. At Boston on 24 September 1961, a Boeing 720 ran off the end of the runway following a PAR (Precision Approach Radar) approach. At New York on 7 April 1964, the pilot of a Boeing 707 lifted his aircraft over a fog bank on final approach but as a result landed long and ran off the far end of the runway. At Dhahran, Saudi Arabia, on the night of 14 April 1964, a Caravelle hit the sea during the procedure turn in a sandstorm. At Charlesville, Liberia, on 3 May 1965, a DC-8 reached the marker too high; the pilot increased his rate of descent but then failed to arrest it and crashed.

The terrible rate of accidents was gradually brought under control by a variety of factors. These included more widespread VHF navaids, expanded radar coverage, better radio communications, airborne weather radar, new approach procedures, better and more standardized runway lighting, better instrumentation, automation, better crew training (including improved simulators) and more stringent and standardized regulation of all aspects of safety.

The diversity of powered flying machines continued to increase in the 1960s from supersonic aircraft to helicopters that could hover or fly backwards. All of these tackled their own weather problems in different ways. In twenty years the jet airliner reached maturity in performance and general configuration. The Boeing 747 established new limits of size, range and payload which have not been surpassed since. The sound barrier became an economic barrier rather than a technical one. Within these limits airliner development continued apace as improved technology offered greater fuel efficiency, less noise, more effective automation, lower structural weight, better low-speed performance and more comfort for passengers and crew. Above all, the jet aircraft was the decisive and ultimate advance in all-weather flying because of its ability to fly above the weather. The jets spent only small portions of their flights climbing and descending through turbulence and icing, most of which occurred below 7,600 metres (25,000 feet), spending the cruise portion of their flights in smooth, clear air, an immense benefit to aircrew and passengers alike. Even if thunderstorm areas could not be overtopped, they could be flown around with only slight disruption to schedules. Hot air bled from jet engines offered new possibilities for preventing ice accretion. The economics of the jet airliner justified the enormous cost of fully automatic landing systems that would ultimately solve the problem of take-off and landing in dense fog. The jet aircraft finally achieved the quest for all-weather flight.

22 *Flight International*, 21 September 1961, 471; 28 September 1961
23 *Flight International*, 22 March 1962, 425
24 *Flight International*, 22 March 1962, 425
25 *Flight International*, 27 July 1962, 117
26 *Flight International*, 8 June 1972, 839
27 *Flight International*, 6 December 1962, 928
28 *Flight International*, 3 January 1963, 6
29 Bach, R. 1963, 1983 ed., 132

CHAPTER 24

The Autonomous Aeroplane

In eighty years the flimsy contraption on which the Wright brothers took to the air became an autonomous vehicle, flying itself from place to place, sensitive to weather but unimpeded by it, under the supervision of its human crew. All the blind navigation systems discussed hitherto, except H2S, depended on radio signals from the ground. They had limited range and could be jammed in war. In 1950, if radio navigation was not available, military flying was left with dead reckoning, celestial and ground-mapping radar, all of which were inadequate. Indeed, as indicated in the last chapter, this problem persisted into the 1960s in the conditions of the Vietnam war. Dead reckoning suffered from cumulative errors and was not self-checking. Celestial navigation was slow and inaccurate, even for propeller-driven aircraft. Ground-mapping radar was useless over water or featureless land.

Aircraft such as the B-47 demanded precise, self-contained navigation systems; in 1950 such systems were nothing more than speculation.

Increased Arctic flying in the 1950s posed new navigation problems. Mineral exploration and mine sites, weather stations, radar stations and military bases in the area could in some cases be maintained only by air. Bombers and reconnaissance aircraft crossed the Arctic on sinister and secret missions. Airliners began to use polar routes between Europe, America and the Orient. Within a thousand miles of the north magnetic pole compass readings were unreliable and magnetic variations were so closely spaced that use of a magnetic compass was inaccurate and error-prone. During the long periods of twilight, neither the sun nor the stars were visible for celestial shots. Conventional charts were of little use because for much of the

Boeing B-52.

year featureless, snow-covered land was indistinguishable from the frozen sea, both being often concealed by fog and darkness. An extremely sparse population resulted in an equally sparse network of radio beacons.

This accelerated the development of self-contained airborne navigation systems of a sophistication previously undreamed-of. The enormous size and military needs of such aircraft as the B-47 and B-52 allowed these devices to be developed with less regard for size, weight and cost than would have been the case with the civilian aircraft for which they eventually became available. Early B-52s, for example, carried three tons of electronics.[1]

The first of these devices was Doppler radar. First recognized by the Austrian mathematician and physicist, C. J. Doppler, in 1842, the Doppler effect is the frequency change at the receiver of a signal due to the relative movement of the emitter. The best-known example is the apparent drop in pitch of vehicle horns and engine noises as they pass a person standing still. Doppler air navigation was based on measuring the Doppler shift of radar signals transmitted from an aircraft and returned from the surface of the earth. This provided accurate measurements of groundspeed and drift which could be fed into a dead-reckoning computer and combined with a heading to calculate various types of navigation information.

As far back as 1933, the US Navy began experiments that led to Doppler radar.[2] During the war the Americans and the British both saw the urgent need for self-contained navigation and after 1945 the USAAF undertook a major study, assisted by General Precision Laboratory (GPL). Early Doppler aircraft radar projected two diverging beams towards the earth's surface; rotating the beams until the Doppler shift of each was equal gave the track and groundspeed of the aircraft.

Doppler began to emerge from military secrecy in 1956, when the USAF was using it, particularly for weather-reconnaissance flying. In 1957 four Doppler navigation radars were known to be in production, one in the UK by Marconi, three in the US by General Precision Laboratory and one in Canada by the Defence Research Telecommunications Establishment, called DAGMAR (Drift and Groundspeed Measuring Airborne Radar).[3] Of these the US AN/APN-81 military set weighed 172 kg (380 pounds), DAGMAR weighed 45 kg (100 pounds), and Radan – an American civilian set – 39 kg (85 pounds). The British Marconi AD.2000 had been in production since 1954 and

was in RAF service in 1957;[4] a new civilian set was planned for 1958. Doppler sets made by Decca in 1958 radiated on 8,900 MHz and drew 300 watts at voltages up to 950 volts for an output power of 20 watts. The unit, including the dead reckoning computer, weighed 36 kg (80 pounds).[5]

Once the secret was out, intense competition followed among avionics manufacturers to market civilian versions.[6] In 1957 Marconi, General Precision Laboratory, Bendix, Decca, English Electric and Ryan Aeronautical were all working on Doppler; RCA bought Marconi's technology for the US market. Commercial competition intensified as the 1950s drew to a close. In 1958 Ryan won a $20-million contract to supply Doppler to the US Navy.[7] In 1959 United Airlines ordered Bendix Doppler radars for their DC-8s.[8] The Russians were believed to have their own Doppler radar.[9] Various antenna arrays were developed, each with its own advantages and disadvantages; space does not permit them to be described here.

Doppler was not the solution to all problems. If the aircraft exceeded 10° of pitch or 20° of bank, the signal was lost unless the antenna was gyrostabilized, as it was in some American sets.[10] Even so, Doppler was best suited to straight-and-level flight; violent manoeuvres would result in intermittent or erroneous readings. The accuracy depended heavily on the setting accuracy of the reference compass. In particular, changes in variation had to be fed into the computer as they occurred; this problem became worse closer to the pole. Errors accumulated with time and the computer had to be periodically updated with position fixes from other sources. The RAF found that, if magnetic variation was updated hourly from star shots, Doppler would be accurate to within 27–32 km (17–20 miles) after 1,600 km (1,000 miles).[11] Better results could be obtained with more frequent updates. Reliability of the complete system was 77%.

PanAm started experimenting with GPL Radan

1 *Flight*, 15 November 1957, 775
2 *Flight*, 12 April 1957, 479
3 Ibid.
4 *Flight*, 21 June 1957, 822; 12 July 1957, 41
5 *Flight*, 16 May 1958, 662
6 *Flight*, 27 September 1957, 501
7 *Flight*, 28 November 1958, 826
8 *Flight*, 4 December 1959, 663
9 *Flight*, 29 November 1957, 844
10 *Flight*, 12 July 1957, 42
11 *Flight*, 29 November 1957, 844

Doppler in a DC-7C over the Atlantic in October 1957. The trials continued for three months, with the equipment coupled to the aircraft's autopilot for at least eighteen crossings. With the aircraft at 9,000 metres (30,000 feet), the signal was lost if it banked at more than 7–8°; at 300 metres (1,000 feet) this increased to 30°. Calm water, mountains, snow and ice were poor reflectors; the best reflector was a rough sea. In spite of this, Radan was accurate to within 1% of groundspeed and drift 98% of the time.

Decca combined Decca/Dectra with Doppler as DIAN (Decca Integrated Air Navigation), announced in 1957.[12] DIAN radiated four beams instead of the two used by other sets. This avoided the need to rotate the antenna. This antenna array provided groundspeed components along and across track, whereas the rotatable two-beam antennas provided groundspeed and drift angle. DIAN enhanced the accuracy of Decca/Dectra where signals could be received and provided navigation between areas of Decca coverage.[13] The Doppler output was displayed directly on the Decca Flight Log. DIAN was still at the trial stage in 1960.

After a brief ascendancy in the 1960s, Doppler was displaced by Inertial Navigation Systems (INS) and Omega in long-range airliners, although it continued in favour with military users. The European, joint-venture, Jaguar strike aircraft, the Westland Lynx helicopter, retro-fitted Avro Vulcans and the Saab Viggen were all new Doppler users in the 1970s.[14] Doppler was a part of the navigation package of the two prototype Concordes but was displaced from production aircraft by INS.[15] Manufacturers that had invested in Doppler brought out new, lighter, more accurate and more reliable sets in the attempt to keep their competitive position[16] and Doppler remained cheaper than INS. The Decca Series 80 weighed only 10 kg (22 pounds) and was accurate to 0.5% of the distance flown. By the late 1970s Doppler was flying in more than sixty-five types of fixed-wing aircraft and twenty-two types of helicopter; the Decca company alone had built 2,000 sets. The Decca Series 70 Doppler was selected for the new Panavia Tornado Multi-Role Combat Aircraft.

If an object's accelerations can be measured accurately enough, its velocity and position can be deduced relative to its starting point. This concept is the basis of inertial navigation. The possibility was recognized as early as the 1920s,[17] but the practical difficulties were enormous. Although the German V-2 missile of 1943–4 had a rudimentary inertial control system, the precision manufacturing and computing capability to turn theory into practice did not exist until the 1950s and needed the full force of US defence funding. Even in the 1960s inertial navigation devices were heavy, expensive, inaccurate and showed little promise for civilian use.

The enormous military value of INS, which justified almost unlimited expenditure on research and development, lay in its complete self-sufficiency; it was independent of all external references and emitted nothing by which the user might be detected. A subtle benefit was its automatic compensation for wind; the accelerations measured are absolute and not relative, hence, so are the derived velocities. If a hypothetical aircraft were to lift off the ground at 50 knots airspeed into a 50-knot headwind, it would rise vertically upwards; its horizontal acceleration, and hence groundspeed, would be zero. If the wind were then to abate, the aircraft would accelerate forward over the ground even though its airspeed remained constant; an inertial system would measure this acceleration and convert it into a velocity, the only limitation being the precision with which the measurements could be made. By feeding in the true airspeed and heading, the crew could even deduce the speed and direction of the wind.

Three accelerometers were needed, aligned for navigation purposes in the north–south, east–west and vertical directions. To ensure that the accelerometers did, in fact, measure accelerations in these three directions, they had to be mounted on a gyrostabilized platform that would maintain a constant attitude, regardless of the attitude and heading of the aircraft. This was not enough, however, because, to be usable for navigation, the three cardinal directions had to remain constant relative to the earth's surface, whereas the gyrostabilized platform would tend to maintain a constant attitude in space. An angular correction had therefore to be applied to the accelerometer mounts on the stable platform. This was done by feeding in a correction for latitude and longitude from the information which the east–west and north–south accelerometers had, themselves, supplied. A further, timed correction was needed to correct for the earth's rotation.[18] Space does not permit a discussion here of how this was achieved.

The technical challenges were enormous. The power supply to the gyroscopes had to be stable to within a fraction of a volt; temperatures had to be controlled to within 1°C; the early INS needed up to four hours to warm up and stabilize. Components had to be made so precisely that '… we are dealing with alterations in physical dimensions of the order of less than the wavelength of visible light or the crystal lattice of most of the materials we are using.'[19] The British had to concede enviously, that: 'rapid advances were made in America where financial backing was virtually unlimited'.[20] As errors accumulated with flight time, these costly devices were first applied to missile guidance, where their entire service life would be 30 minutes or less. They were also used in submarines where space and weight were less restrictive.

According to one source,[21] the first airborne unit was the Autonetics XN-1, flown for the first time in a C-47 in May 1950. Between then and 1959 more than 800 flights followed with various systems. In 1952 this was followed by the hybrid XN-2 stellar-inertial system; automatic star-tracking counteracted the accumulation of time-dependent errors in the INS. Another source[22] tells a different story. In 1946 Dr Charles S. Draper, director of the Instrumentation Laboratory at MIT, began research on inertial navigation at the request of the USAAF. Starting from existing gyroscope/accelerometer systems, such as the V-2 missile controls, he produced a prototype weighing 1,800 kg (4,000 pounds). The most notable innovation was to seal the gyroscope in a housing containing a viscous liquid which reduced the effects of accelerations and friction on the accuracy of the gyroscope. By 1953 Dr Draper's team had developed an airborne inertial navigator, although it still weighed 1,270 kg (2,800 pounds). On its first flight the INS navigated a B-29 on a twelve-hour flight from Boston to Los Angeles. Neither source mentions the other. The Russians may have been working on their own INS of which the West knew nothing.

In the early INS time-dependent errors accumulated too quickly for a sole navigation source. In 1955 a stellar-inertial hybrid navigated a USAF T-29 from Los Angeles to Patrick AFB, Florida. In 1957 a lightweight INS for US Navy fighters was reported to weigh 90 kg (200 pounds), and to be accurate to 1.6 km after an hour's flight.[23] For naval aircraft, start-up on a moving ship was a formidable problem.

The first production INS in a manned aircraft was the Doppler-inertial Sperry AN/ASQ-42 which was the primary means of navigating the B-58 supersonic bomber. INS was also planned for the F-105 and A-3J strike aircraft. In 1958:[24] 'It is probably true to say that a pure inertial system cannot yet be made to continue accurate position indications for longer than an hour.' In spite of the limited success achieved by the end of the 1950s, after immense expenditures of money and effort, the outlook for inertial navigation was optimistic.[25] The military justification had long been obvious; the commercial justification was different.

Airline navigation based on radio beacons depended on the willingness and ability of national governments to install, maintain and operate them. A system capable of functioning equally well over developed and undeveloped nations, oceans and uninhabited areas was needed urgently. Ever-more accurate position-fixing was needed to allow denser traffic over the North Atlantic. This in turn depended on precise navigation systems connected directly to aircraft autopilots.[26] Doppler was the first system to meet all these needs, but it depended on the heading input from a gyro-magnetic compass. By 1970 compasses had reached the limit of their potential accuracy, which was still insufficient for military and major airline purposes,[27] although magnetic and gyro-magnetic compasses remained adequate for lower-performance aircraft.

The first civilian aircraft to be certificated with automatic navigation was the Boeing 747. The core of its system was a pair of inertial platforms with a third as an option. The system, called Carousel IV and manufactured by AC Electronics, was derived in part from the inertial guidance and control system used in the Apollo space programme. The early life of Carousel IV was disappointing. Not only did it fail to meet its predicted performance, but it did not perform as well as the competing Litton LTN-51, which was already in service

12 *Flight*, 23 August 1957, 250
13 *Flight*, 27 September 1957, 515
14 Cowin, H. 1973 (4)
15 *Flight International*, 1 November 1973, 758
16 *Flight International*, 26 November 1977, 1593
17 Williams, J. E. D. 1992, 165
18 *Flight*, 12 April 1957, 475; Welch, J. F. 1981, 693
19 Cawood, W. 1958
20 *Flight*, 20 February 1959, 266
21 *Flight*, 20 February 1959, 266
22 Broadbent, S. 1976 (4), 1411
23 *Flight*, 12 April 1957, 478
24 *Flight*, 16 May 1958, 664
25 *Flight*, 12 April 1957, 474
26 Calvert, B. J. 1971
27 *Flight International*, 26 August 1971, 335

British Aerospace Harrier.

with American Airlines. The error of the first Carousel IV was 5.6 km/h (3.0 nm/h)[28] and its mean time before failure was only 140 hours. Nevertheless, AC Electronics had a contract with Boeing to equip the first 200 747s; this agreement came under severe pressure, especially from potential 747 customers already using Litton INS.[29]

By early 1971 the accuracy of Carousel IV had been improved to 3.7 km/h (2 nm/h) or less on 99.7% of flights by means of a self-correcting feature which compared the estimated position on shutdown with the position put in by the aircrew on the next start-up. The failure rate of the naviga-

tion system was 0.66 per 1,000 hours and of the attitude control system 0.22 per 1,000 hours. Already several airlines were using INS departures from Heathrow. Airways could be flown at least as precisely by INS as by VOR and ADF.

In military service inertial systems, such as the Ferranti Inertial Navigation and Attack System (INAS) installed in RAF Phantom and Harrier strike aircraft, had achieved astonishing robustness and accuracy. INAS was unaffected by the most violent manoeuvres and, at the push of a button, could redirect a pilot to his target after he had evaded a pursuer. This could make the difference

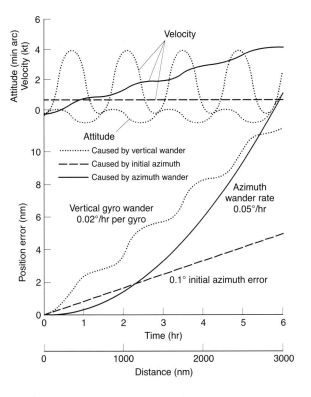

INS error accumulation.

The curves show typical errors which may be expected to occur in an inertial navigator for a 550kt aircraft.

between the aircraft reaching its target and failing to do so because of fuel shortage. INAS was accurate enough to aim weapons at ground targets with an average error of 0.3°[30] Increasingly, brush-fire wars required military aircraft to be self-suffi-cient for navigation anywhere in the world at any time.

By the mid-1970s INS was firmly established in long-range airline navigation and had achieved impressive accuracy and reliability. Even in 1972 Icelandair, using dual Litton LTN-51 sets in a DC-8, established an accuracy of 2.71 km (1.46 nm) per flight hour 95% of the time. Airlines found that INS saved several minutes on each long-haul flight,[31] adding up to significant fuel savings in the course of time. Further improvements in accuracy were in sight, but the major suppliers were waiting for the announcement of a new long-range airliner

before investing in new products. Less accurate (7.4 km/h (4 nm/h)) and cheaper INS were proposed for aircraft for US domestic service because they would never be out of range of ground-based navaids. Robustness was the prime military need, while the prime commercial need was reliability.

Large navigation errors with INS became excep-tionally rare but, ominously, they were not always due to equipment failure. INS navigation was based on waypoints, whose latitude and longitude the crew entered into the INS before the flight. The autopilot would then fly the aircraft from the point of departure, via a series of waypoints, to the des-tination. No matter what checks were used, gross errors did occur from time to time, the results of which depended on when and how they were detected. Input errors were the suspected cause of a Korean Airlines Boeing 747 straying into Russian airspace, where it was shot down.[32]

INS began to influence the crowded North Atlantic route. Less than fifty years after Lindbergh's flight more than 100,000 transatlantic flights were being made each year; the two-mil-lionth crossing was in September 1976.[33] The navi-gational capability of the existing fleet and the lack of continuous radar coverage still required aircraft separation of not less than 220 km (120 nm). In 1970, because of expanded radar coverage over Newfoundland, Ireland and the Hebrides, new tracks were introduced at only 110 km (60 nm) spacing, but the 220 km (120 nm) horizontal and 600 metres (2,000 feet) vertical separation between flights remained. In 1967, in the days of Loran-A and Doppler, ship-borne radar showed that about 600 of every 10,000 flights strayed more than 55 km (30 nm) from their assigned tracks. In 1975, when 70% of aircraft flying the North Atlantic car-ried INS and Omega, a sample of INS-equipped traffic showed no errors more than 55 km (30 nm). INS had also become extremely reliable. In 1967 Loran-A and Doppler sets had a mean time before failure of 500–600 hours; by 1976 the MTBF of INS in British Airways 747s was 9,000 hours.

28 The error of a dead-reckoning system was expressed in miles of error per hour of use with a 95% probability – 5% of errors could exceed the quoted figure.
29 Hirst, M. 1978 (3)
30 Summers, J. T. 1975
31 Broadbent, S. 1976 (4)
32 Suspected but unconfirmed; published works on this sinis-ter topic have expounded several theories.
33 *Flight International*, 25 September 1976, 962

As a result of these figures, an ICAO meeting in September 1976 implemented a minimum navigation performance specification with effect from 29 December 1977, which would, for practical purposes, require aircraft crossing the North Atlantic to use INS or Omega. The plan was to reduce lateral separation between flights to 110 km (60 nm). A further reduction in track separation to 55 km (30 nm) horizontally and 300 metres (1,000 feet) vertically was expected for 1981, although 15 minutes' separation would be retained for following aircraft on the same track at the same height. The adoption of Mach number rather than airspeed as a measure of cruising speed and improvements in automatic flight control offered the possibility of reduced longitudinal separation.

By the late 1970s the size and weight of inertial platforms had been reduced from 35–45 kg (80–100 pounds) to as little as 2.25 kg (5 pounds).[34] Even so, INS was challenged by the cheaper alternative, Omega, a hyperbolic navigation aid based on US Navy Very Low Frequency (VLF) signals.[35] Indeed, in the late 1970s, it was thought that Omega would displace INS completely and that it would eventually disappear. Omrega proved more problematic than anticipated, and this gloomy prognosis for INS has not been fulfilled.

By 1978 Litton and Delco had about half each of the 5,000 civilian INS in service.[36] Delco was producing sixty-five sets a month; two thirds were for military use. The improved Delco Carousel had Omega updating, a means of feeding in air data, such as airspeed, and connections for DME and RNAV. The Litton LTN-72 was selected for the DC-10 in 1971 and went into production in 1973. Declining INS costs and continuing propagation problems with Omega improved the competitive position of INS. In particular, Omega provided no attitude information, whereas INS lent itself naturally to a single integrated flight control and navigation system. Two significant developments were the 'strapped-down' INS and the ring-laser gyroscope. In a strapped-down INS the gyroscopes and accelerometers are mounted rigidly in the aircraft instead of on a gimballed platform. The corrections previously supplied through the gimballed system were delegated to a digital computer. This significantly reduced costs.

If any single device were to be singled out as the all-pervading essential of the quest for all-weather flight, it would be the gyroscope.[37] By the 1960s the highest-quality gyroscopes could detect rates of turn less than 0.005° per second. Even so, it was recognized that development of the conventional gyroscope might have reached its limits. The smaller the gyroscope, the higher the rotation speed needed and wear and tear on the rotor bearings became the limiting factor. This triggered the search for a device that would act as a gyroscope, but had no moving parts.

In 1940 the British experimented with a tuning fork gyroscope but the results were disappointing compared to existing gyroscopes.[38] Another attempt was a solid-state gyroscope using the piezoelectric effect.[39] Cryogenic and electrostatic gyroscopes were at the experimental stage in the 1960s, but the results were not encouraging. The device that succeeded was the ring-laser gyroscope. A ring-laser gyroscope consists of two laser beams projected in opposite directions around a (typically) triangular optical path. When the gyroscope is stationary, the time taken by each beam is the same. Rotation causes a time difference in the two paths, resulting in a measurable change in the interference pattern between the two beams.[40] A three-axis array of ring lasers is equivalent to a gyroscope. By 1967 a ring-laser gyroscope was being flight tested in the US.

In 1971 Honeywell's beryllium-sphere gyroscope[41] was under flight-test after eight years of development. A 38 millimetre (1.5 inch) diameter beryllium sphere was rotated at an extremely high speed in an electrostatic field in a vacuum chamber. Because there was no contact between the sphere and its container, many of the inaccuracies of conventional gyroscopes were eliminated. This device was the core of the USAF Gimballed Electrostatic Aircraft Navigation System (GEANS). Six years later the system was still under development but just over 900 hours of flight testing in C-135s, B-52s and C-141s gave results accurate to 110 metres (0.06 nm) per hour on flights longer than five hours.[42] By 1978 Litton, Sperry and Honeywell had test flown ring-laser INS; Ferranti and Marconi Avionics were also working towards a system with no moving parts and the first commercial ring-laser INS were on the point of being specified for the new airliners of the 1980s. A strapped-down ring-laser INS was expected to cost about half as much as a conventional set.[43] The ring-laser gyroscope, however, sensed only rotation and not attitude. As an aircraft would not necessarily be perfectly level on start-up, an independent attitude and heading reference was needed.

Even though conventional celestial navigation

with a hand-held sextant and manual computation was too slow and inaccurate for aviation, it persisted in long-range aircraft until the 1960s because nothing better was available. In the 1950s and 1960s automation gave celestial navigation a new lease of life. The earlier problem of obscuration by cloud disappeared when jets cruised above all but the highest and thinnest clouds.

In the 1950s the Kollsman Instrument Company developed the KS-85 automatic celestial navigation system which was installed in the B-52, B-57, B-58 and other US and British military aircraft.[44] The KS-85 comprised a star tracker, an amplifier and a computer. The human navigator used pre-calculated star azimuths and elevations and an approximate position from Doppler or INS to aim the tracker at the star selected for use. The tracker could be locked onto the star using the star's known brightness and spectrum. The system was designed to cope with thin cloud and to track the stars or moon at night or the sun or Venus by day. By comparing pre-calculated and observed values of azimuth and elevation, the KS-85 automatically calculated the aircraft's true heading to an accuracy of 0.3° and the navigator could use it to calculate a fix from lines of position from several stars. This information then corrected the Doppler or INS dead-reckoning position. Celestial navigation retained its former benefits of being independent of radio beacons and emitting no signals that could be detected by an enemy.

The long-range, hyperbolic navigation system, Omega, was mentioned earlier as both an adjunct and a competitor of INS. Work on Omega began in the 1950s; using a very low frequency of 10–14 kHz, hundred-kilowatt transmitters were expected to provide 8,000–9,650 km (4,320–5,111 nm) range and 1.6 km (0.8 nm) accuracy.[45] The characteristics of the frequency band allowed Omega to be received on land, by aircraft and ships, even by submerged submarines; eight stations could cover the globe. An aircraft could use its Omega receiver anywhere in the world to update and check a self-contained navigation system. Because of these advantages, the US Navy persisted with its development.[46] In the late 1960s the Navy contracted with Northrop to develop an airborne receiver. Whereas a ship moved slowly enough for manual reading and plotting, airborne use demanded a computer to plot the position automatically and read out latitude and longitude.

The low frequency entailed large, costly transmitters. By 1968 four had been built in Norway,

Trinidad, Hawaii and at Forestport, New York. In 1971 Litton Industries built a transmitter for installation at Lamoure, North Dakota.[47] Although full service was scheduled for 1973, the last transmitters to be built, in Reunion, Argentina and Liberia, did not go into service until 1976,[48] for a world total of eight. A ninth station in Australia was scheduled for service in 1979.

With 10 kilowatts output power from the transmitters, Omega was accurate to 1.9 km (1 nm) in daytime and 3.8 km (2 nm) at night at 14,800 km (8,000 nm) range, improving to 60–180 metres (200–600 feet) within 370 km (200 nm) of a transmitter. The two main sources of error were the diurnal effect of the sun on the ionosphere, which affected the skywave, and the variable conductivity of the earth's surface, which affected the groundwave.

Several factors delayed the use of Omega in aviation. No airborne receiver/processor giving direct read-outs was available.[49] The US Navy operated the transmitters and did not guarantee continuous transmission. The transmitter construction programme fell behind schedule; certification for civil aviation took time.[50] After two decades of development, Omega began to be used more widely in the early 1970s[51] and the first civilian airborne receivers began to appear, such as the Canadian Marconi AD.1800, at a quarter of the cost of INS. The US Navy delegated operation of the stations to the national civilian maritime authorities.

Airline trials began in 1974 (Laker[52]) and 1975 (PanAm[53]), but with mixed results. Omega was found to be as accurate as VOR and Loran but

34 Hirst, M. 1977
35 Hirst, M. 1978 (1)
36 Hirst, M. 1978 (3)
37 *Flight International*, 29 June 1967, 1069
38 Hunt, G. H., Hobbs, A. E. W. 1964–5
39 *Flight International*, 29 June 1967, 1071
40 *Flight International*, 16 December 1978, 2166
41 *Flight International*, 15 April 1971, 531
42 *Flight International*, 26 March 1977, 783
43 *Flight International*, 16 December 1978, 2166
44 Brown, A. A. 1962. See also Kayton, M., Fried, W. 1969
45 *Flight*, 16 May 1958, 660
46 *Flight International*, 11 July 1968, 65
47 Blake, B. H. L. 1971
48 *Flight International*, 11 December 1975, 863; Broadbent, S. 1976 (3)
49 Cowin, H. 1973 (3)
50 *Flight International*, 13 March 1975, 401
51 *Flight International*, 26 August 1971, 335
52 Broadbent, S. 1976 (1)
53 Ibid.

neither the airborne sets nor the transmitters were entirely reliable. Because of the long ranges involved, Omega signals might cross areas containing several thunderstorms at any one time,[54] resulting in distortion by lightning for as much as three seconds in every ten. One of PanAm's worst problems was signal distortion at airports by radio frequencies that were harmonics of the Omega frequencies. It was sometimes impossible to start up the equipment until the aircraft was airborne and the aircrew had to put their starting position into the computer which then navigated by dead reckoning until usable Omega signals could be received. Most new wide-body airliners were designed with INS as standard equipment, but retro-fitting with INS was difficult, which favoured Omega as a replacement for Loran-A. In early 1977 TWA ordered Omega for its Boeing 707 fleet, soon followed by PanAm.[55] Laker, however, chose dual INS because the Greenland ice cap caused unacceptable errors on transatlantic flights. At the end of the 1970s Omega was still not in widespread airline service.

The first flying machines were under the direct and continuous control of the pilot, at least that was the intention. In the course of time a succession of instruments, radios, specialist crew members and autopilots was grafted onto this combination of human and machine. This concept persisted until the early 1950s. The jet aircraft caused a radical change in concept. The speed and complexity of the aircraft outran the human brain and an increasing number of hours were flown routinely over oceans and featureless land surfaces at altitudes from which the earth's surface was obscured by cloud as often as not. Instrumentation, flight control and navigation were integrated into unified systems designed into the airframe at the outset. They displaced the human navigator and would displace the flight engineer; the two pilots became the supervisors of an autonomous vehicle capable of flying itself from place to place automatically and, ultimately, of landing itself.

54 Broadbent, S. 1976 (2)
55 *Flight International*, 5 March 1977, 533

CHAPTER 25

Manufactured by Unskilled Labour, Easily Maintained

'Man is not as good as a black box for doing certain specific things. However, he is more flexible and reliable. He is easily maintained and can be manufactured by relatively unskilled labour.' That remark, made in 1952,[1] raised several major questions as to the role of the human pilot in the aircraft of the future. By 1959 it was recognized that the human brain, although extremely efficient in almost all functions, had nevertheless serious limitations when it came, first, to speed of computation, and secondly, the number of functions it could compute at one time.[2] Until then the speed of operation of aircraft had been compatible with the speed of computation of the human brain that was governing the pilot's reactions. Also the size and complexity of the aircraft and its operation had been compatible with the number of functions the brain could compute at one time. By 1959 with aircraft such as the Boeing 707, a stage had been reached where the compatibility ended. The human pilot was approaching a stage beyond his design capabilities. That was especially true when the pilot was flying in blind conditions.

In the new types of aircraft the pilot was increasingly unable to function without the help of black boxes; indeed his performance was being measured against them. This trend raised several questions. How much did he need to understand their inner functioning? What happened when they failed? How much control should be given to the black boxes, especially if they were not perfectly reliable? The pilot still had to be given all possible help to perform the tasks he was good at, but the airliner cockpit became a place of quiet monotony where deadly errors and malfunctions could go unnoticed and where tired pilots might be faced with sudden demands on their most basic skills of airmanship. The more reliable systems

became, the more difficult it became to guard against their failure.

Efforts to alleviate the human problem were threefold. The development of automatic flight control in relation to all-weather flying is discussed in other chapters. The search continued for blind-flying instruments allowing faster comprehension and less ambiguity. Simulation became increasingly important, not only to train the pilot as an individual and as a member of a crew, but also as a research tool. Nevertheless, all-weather flying was left with the deadly, unpredictable human error which could be diminished but apparently never eliminated.

North America hosts the biggest population of small aircraft and private or small-time commercial pilots in the world. General aviation, as it is known, does not have the financial power of either the airlines or the armed forces and for this reason, and because of the low performance of their aircraft, most general aviation pilots have always remained on the fringes of all-weather flying.

In 1962 the FAA launched Project *Little Guy* to improve the IFR operation of small aircraft.[3] The title has a hollow ring to modern ears and nothing came of it. Ultra-modern instruments were planned for the cockpit. Many of them would be simplified versions of the latest military systems. The *Little Guy* cockpit probably would have included a large pictorial display combining the functions of compass, attitude indicator, turn-and-bank, altimeter, airspeed indicator; a central navigation display showing aircraft position in relation

1 *Flight*, 13 June 1952, 718
2 Prowse, B. O. 1959
3 *Flying*, May 1962, 101

SEPECAT Jaguar.

to charts projected on the screen; auxiliary displays for status and warning and simplified controls. The target price for the installation was $3,000, close to the price of a small aeroplane in those days. Light-plane pilots to this day still rely on instruments substantially the same as those used by Doolittle in 1929, a chart on a clipboard and an approach plate clipped to the yoke. Although the project came to nothing, its intentions represented the course of blind-flying instrument development.

All the private pilot's instrument flying problems seemed to be over with the Flite-Path FP-50 contact analogue developed for light aircraft from a military system by Kaiser Aerospace and Electronics, and scheduled for market launch in 1967.[4] A television screen with a fixed aircraft symbol displayed a computer-generated, stylized land surface. Symbols superimposed on the land surface provided navigation information and steering commands. A demonstration in a Cessna 210 drew the enthusiastic comment: 'This was no instrument panel with impersonal dials, but a real picture, so it seemed, a window into the world outside.' The unit weighed 4.5 kg (10 pounds), was small enough to fit into a light aircraft instrument panel and consumed 48 watts of 12-volt power. Certain types of aircraft, however, could be bought new for the projected unit price of $7,000. Neither the Flite-Path nor anything resembling it has been approved for use in light aircraft in the thirty years that have elapsed since.

Contact analogues were always a seductive but

abortive line of progress that was ultimately abandoned. Instead, the course of instrument development followed two parallel courses: the 'glass cockpit' and, specifically for low-flying combat aircraft, image-processing from the real world outside the aircraft.

With the flight director, mechanical instruments had reached their limits of complexity. Developments in computers and cathode-ray tube technology in the 1960s, however, allowed numbers and complex symbols to be generated electronically without the problems posed by mechanical instruments. The direct display of numbers – speed, altitude, heading, time, distance, fluid levels, temperatures – took up less space than a needle and dial and were easier to read. This also circumvented the problem that dial-type instruments became harder to design as the ranges that they had to display became more extreme. There were also limits to the accuracy with which a dial-type instrument could be read. A CRT-based device known as EFID (Electronic Flight Instrument Display) was developed at RAE Farnborough, but in 1965 had yet to be test-flown. In the early 1970s the Light-Emitting Diode (LED) and Liquid Crystal Display (LCD) offered a new means of displaying numbers in the cockpit.

The enormous improvement in performance and reduction in cost of electronic equipment began to

4 *Flying*, December 1966, 31

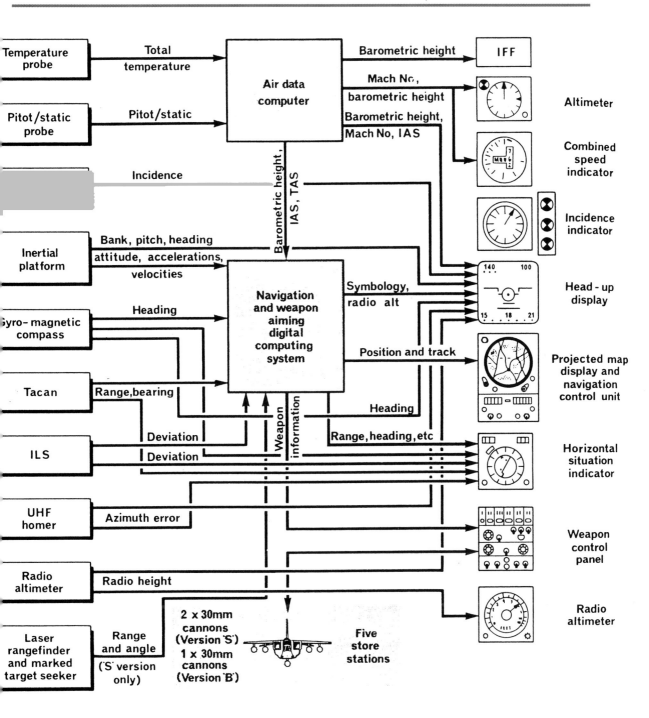

Integrated navigation, flight control and weapon-aiming system of Jaguar strike aircraft – schematic.

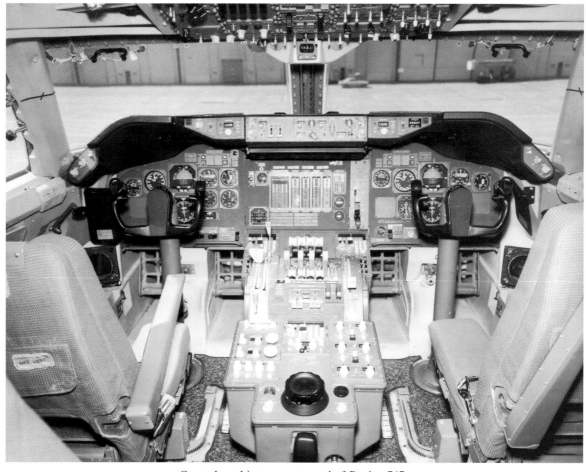

Controls and instrument panel of Boeing 747.

influence flight instruments in the mid 1970s. Until the 1950s each instrument had its own source of information and functioned independently. The new tendency was to feed information from all sources into a flight data computer which then disseminated information to the various instruments. The full scope and complexity of this concept can best be indicated by the accompanying diagram of the Jaguar strike aircraft navigation and weapon aiming system.[5] In such an aircraft the pilot did not have time to compute the required information mentally from indirect sources; everything that he needed had to be instantaneously available on demand.

Fertile minds then asked why instruments should be retained at all if there was some better way to impart the desired information. This concept was the origin of the so-called 'glass cockpit'. The substitution of CRTs for certain instruments,

in particular those for attitude and navigation, opened up options that were impossible with electro-mechanical instruments. Studies by McDonnell-Douglas[6], Lear Siegler and Smith's Industries indicated that this concept offered, in addition, substantial savings in weight, space, maintenance and spare parts with better reliability and reduced initial cost.

In 1976 Boeing was conducting trials with several CRT instruments in its 737 simulator at Seattle. The first trial installation consisted of an attitude director indicator screen, a navigation display and heading reference screen, a data entry screen and a keyboard. The control yoke was split into two side yokes to give the pilot an unobstructed view of the display. The second installation was an Advanced Systems Monitor consisting of a CRT and a keyboard which allowed the pilot to call up checklists, failure warnings, engine read-

Controls and instrument panel of General Dynamics F-16.

ings, fuel and oil quantities, flap positions and critical speeds, not only at will but in more detail than could be presented continuously on any electro-mechanical instrument.

Boeing was also working on an Integrated Strapdown Air Data System to integrate air data, attitude information, navigation, flight control and instrumentation into a single system. All this would contribute to the Boeing 757 and 767 which were still six or seven years in the future. In these and subsequent aircraft two pilots would perform all the functions that had previously required a captain, copilot, flight engineer, navigator and radio operator in smaller aircraft of lower per-

formance only twenty years before. In Britain Hawker Siddeley Aviation and the British Aircraft Corporation were active at the same time and along similar lines.[7]

The almost unlimited possibilities for symbolic display on the CRTs were themselves a problem. The symbols and their behaviour had to appear natural to pilots already trained on conventional instruments. Opinions were bound to differ as to

5 Keys, A. R. 1973
6 Belson, J. 1976
7 Belson, J. 1977

General Dynamics F-16.

HUD – head-up display – projects information into the pilot's line of sight. (*L.F.E. Coombs*)

the information to be displayed and the symbols to be used. After many experiments the result was an electronic display similar to existing flight directors and HSIs.

The glass cockpit was taken up more quickly by military aviation than by the airlines.[8] The first aircraft to present almost all information on CRTs was the F-18 Hornet. Multi-functional electronic displays were an efficient way of presenting the vast amount of diverse information needed by the military pilot and made economical use of limited cockpit space. Military pilots tended to be younger than airline pilots with fewer habits of instrument interpretation. Essential to the acceptance of CRT instruments were the rapid advances in CRT design that took place in the 1970s. High-resolution, colour, digital screens replaced the low-resolution, monochrome, analog screens with their problems of brightness, visibility and glare.

Aircraft are built today with all three types of instruments: conventional instruments that have changed little since 1929, flight director/HSI combinations originating in the 1950s, and CRT instruments originating in the 1970s. The performance and market price of the aircraft determines the type of instrumentation.

New technology developed in response to the military need for strike aircraft to fly low and fast in all weathers to escape detection and to attack targets in minimal visibility. By the 1970s such aircraft had acquired extraordinary capabilities, many of which were secret. Some aircraft, such as the F-111, had terrain-following radar connected to their autopilots, enabling them to fly at low altitude in cloud or darkness, in a way that no human pilot could imitate with any prospect of survival.

Another 1960s innovation was the Honick Topographical Navigation Display[9] which displayed a map on a 6 inch diameter screen showing the aircraft's track and position. The map was projected from microfilm and the problems of an electro-mechanical display remained. Moving maps could not reach their full potential until the display could be generated electronically. Moving maps became essential to low-flying strike aircraft because the pilot could not handle paper charts in the time and space available in the cockpit.[10] In the A-7 strike aircraft used in Vietnam in the early 1970s, forward-looking radar, Doppler, INS and a radar altimeter drove ground-mapping radar and moving-map screens side by side in the cockpit and a Head Up Display (HUD).[11] The moving map displayed full-colour aeronautical charts on 1:500,000 and 1:2,000,000 scales. This was essential for flying close to politically sensitive borders in low visibility.

In 1971 a Marconi automatic chart display was connected to the Carousel IV INS in BOAC's Boeing 747s[12] but, in general, civilian aircraft operators were less inclined than the military to accept the weight and cost of moving maps. Civilian aircrew flew repetitively on fixed routes definable in writing, or according to departure and approach procedures that could be depicted on small charts clipped to a control yoke.

Most new strike aircraft from the 1970s onwards were equipped with a Head Up Display (HUD), essential for high-speed, low-level flying in bad weather when the pilot could not safely make frequent transitions between instrument and visual flight.[13] The HUD originated in Second World War fighter gunsights, which projected a collimated light pattern onto a combining glass so that the pilot could see both it and the target in clear focus simultaneously. In 1943 an airborne interception radar picture was experimentally projected onto the windshield of a night fighter.[14] In the US the Autonetics Division of North American Aviation started to develop the HUD concept in 1954 as part of the ANIP with flight tests in 1958, using televised imagery and flight director symbols.[15] British work on the HUD began in 1956 with a suggestion from E. S. Calvert of the RAE to project an aiming bar, and later a Sperry Zero Reader image, into the pilot's line of sight. A Blind Landing Experimental Unit (BLEU) pilot using this device, both for approach and for ground roll guidance, landed safely at London airport in a runway visual range of 90 feet.[16] In 1964 an experimental HUD was installed in a BLEU Varsity. For strike aircraft the HUD retained its original function as a gun-, missile or bombsight, with computerized aiming and release information projected onto the screen.[17] In the middle 1970s HUDs were developed for strike aircraft that enabled pilots to see on the HUD what they could not see ahead of

8 Hurst, M. 1978
9 Naish, J. M. 1966, 667
10 Summers, J. T. 1973
11 *Flight International*, 10 January 1974, 34
12 *Flight International*, 26 August 1971, 335
13 Keys, A. R. 1973
14 *Flight International*, 25 December 1976, 1839
15 *Flight*, 16 May 1958, 679
16 Baxter, J. R. 1967, 408
17 *Flight International*, 30 October 1975, 665; 25 December 1976, 1839

1013
GUN

0.56

12,350

G 1.0

On fighter aircraft the HUD retains its original function as a gunsight, with computerized aiming information projected. *(Smith's Group)*

the aircraft; Low-Light Television (LLTV) and Forward-Looking Infra-Red (FLIR) showed the ground ahead of the aircraft when it was too dark for the human eye.

The research that went into these devices would have been practically impossible without thousands of hours of experiments in simulators. Now used both for research and training, simulation benefited as much as any other aspect of aviation

from the computer revolution.

The motion of the early Link trainers was far too crude to induce the correct sensory illusions of instrument flying and the Link trainer was never more than a step on the way to training in real aircraft. Descendants of the Link trainer are still in use with no motion at all, a generic cockpit and a pen recorder to show the track 'flown' across a chart. Their capital cost is about a quarter to a half

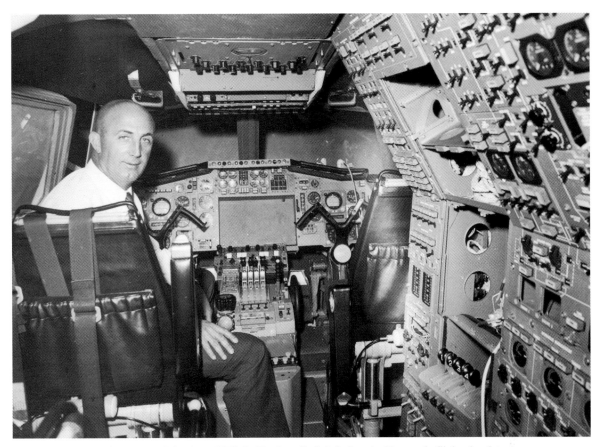

André Turcat, Director of Flight Testing, Sud-Aviation, in Concorde flight simulator.

that of a small training aircraft.

Larger aircraft and higher operating costs produced a demand for type-specific simulators; every hour that an aircraft was used for crew training was an hour of revenue service lost. The early simulators were generic in control response as well as cockpit layout. The first type-simulators were built for Pan American for the DC-6 and DC-7.[18] A type-simulator, however, demanded more than a mere duplication of the cockpit interior. To be a useful crew trainer, it had to duplicate faithfully the most subtle control responses and feel of the real aircraft, and preferably noises as well. If not, the discrepancies distracted the pilot, lowering his performance and causing frustration and resentment that negated its training value.[19]

Realistic simulation was expensive, but when a jet aircraft of the mid-1970s cost $25 million to buy and $2,000 per hour to fly, a simulator costing one tenth as much was a good investment. This justified investment by manufacturers in developing increasingly realistic simulators. Advanced simulators revealed interesting sidelights on the interaction between the human pilot and the flying machine.[20] Pilots flying on instruments were found to rely to a surprising extent on bodily sensations besides instrument indications. This, in turn, made further demands on simulation. Not only control response but also bodily sensations and noises had to be accurately reproduced if the full training value was to be obtained. It was also found that a visual approach to land was more difficult in a large aircraft than one guided by instruments, a fact with important safety implications in view of the unsatisfactory low-speed handling characteristics of big jets.

Muscular sensations could be reproduced by

18 Kelly, L. L., Parke, R. B. 1970, 123
19 *Flight International*, 30 January 1975, 139
20 Ibid.

Fog landing research using advanced simulation.

making the box in which the simulated cockpit was installed movable. However, not only was the movement of the box necessarily limited by space and by its mechanism, but the connection between a movement or attitude of the box and the illusions induced in its occupants was far from obvious. For example, a box that was stationary but pitched up could induce a sensation of acceleration, especially if other supporting cues were provided, such as sound and airspeed instrument readings. The new, full-motion simulators made subtle use of everything that was known about sensory illusions to delude the pilot into thinking that he was flying a real aircraft. Digital electronic computers were essential to these devices. Blind conditions could be simulated merely by presenting a blank windscreen to the pilot, but the simulation of the final approach to a runway in various weather condi-

tions was much more difficult. The first simulators to do this used film projection or closed-circuit TV cameras moving over a model landscape. The real breakthrough came in the 1970s with computer-generated imagery.

In 1975 the most that could be simulated was a crude night scene. The Singer Link-Miles Night Visual System used a computer programmed with up to 6,000 coloured lights and 30,000 combinations of location, colour, intensity and visible arc, which allowed the night view of any airport in the world to be simulated. Visibility and cloud base could be programmed in. This in itself was far from simple, as in foggy conditions, lights had to 'appear' out of the 'fog' gradually and in the right sequence as the simulated flight approached them. Realistic fog simulation was essential to the development of landings in progressively lower visibilities.

Advanced simulation for the F-18 Hornet strike fighter.

In 1970 British Airways took delivery of a four-axis Boeing 747 simulator, built by CAE of Montreal, followed by a second in 1975. It also received CAA approval to use the Singer Link-Miles Night Visual System.[21] The airline planned to spend £1.5 million on five of these; if one hour of type conversion training per pilot could be switched from an aircraft to a simulator it would save the airline £250,000 a year.

The first computer-generated daylight scene was the General Electric Compu-Scene, installed in Boeing's 707, 727, 737 and 747 simulators in

Seattle at a cost of $3 million, receiving FAA approval in 1976.[22] The company's 707 conversion course entailed sixteen days of groundschool, seven days in a cockpit simulator, twelve hours in a flight simulator and eighteen hours flying time. Compu-Scene allowed six hours of flying time to be switched to the simulator. Boeing foresaw the day when all training would take place in a

---

21 *Flight International*, 2 October 1976, 1009
22 *Flight International*, 23 October 1976, 1264

simulator. At $1,400 per hour to fly a Boeing 727, compared with $280 per hour for the simulator, this was very desirable. Simulator utilization as high as sixteen hours a day added to this economy.[23] Even so, in 1976 the computer-generated daylight imagery was crude compared with what has been achieved since; in particular the simulation of final approach below 150 feet and touchdown remained problematical.

The safety benefits of simulator training became clear in the course of time. In the 1960s 30% of all accidents to first-generation jets occurred during crew training, often when a simulated emergency became a real one. Ten years later such accidents had become rare. Simulators that faithfully reproduced every aspect of performance and response allowed the simulation of emergencies that would be unacceptably dangerous in a real aircraft. They also enabled flight crews to experiment with non-standard emergency procedures, thereby gaining experience that they never could in flight. This type of experience saved a DC-10 near Windsor, Ontario, on 12 June 1972, when the aircraft became partly uncontrollable after an accidental depressurization.[24]

Simulation became an important industry in its own right; in 1977 worldwide flight simulator production exceeded $200 million in sales. Each full-motion Boeing 777 simulator built by CAE in Montreal in the early 1990s took eighteen months to build and was sold for about $15 million. Since then simulation has taken on the broader definition of virtual reality and has expanded into such fields as public entertainment and operator training for large equipment such as ships and dragline excavators. Computer simulation has so increased in capability and decreased in cost that visual flight simulators are now being built for *ab initio* flight training.

During the 1970s the digital computer became the pilot's permanent, indispensable partner in high-performance aircraft. Although it would take another decade to implement these developments fully, by 1980 the advanced airliners of today were on the drawing board, except that the drawing board itself had become obsolete, replaced by a computer screen.

The hazard of aircraft flying blindly into high ground refused to disappear. In spite of expanding radar coverage, altitude-encoding transponders and ILS, accidents caused by aircraft hitting high ground were so persistent that some additional precaution was seen to be desperately needed. In

1967 Scandinavian Air Service and Boeing sought proposals for a ground proximity warning system (GPWS). Sundstrand Data Control of Seattle replied, having started work on just such a system the year before.[25] Flight testing began in 1969; in 1970 SAS flight-tested the device in a DC-9 and adopted it forthwith.

In 1973 the FAA began to evaluate GPWS, approved it the same year and made it mandatory in all US-registered transport aircraft over 12,500 kg (27,500 pounds) gross weight, with effect from 1 December 1975. All new Boeing aircraft had GPWS from 1973 onwards. In September 1975 Sundstrand stated at an FAA hearing that a radar-based GPWS would have given a warning in sixty-four out of eighty free-world fatal air transport accidents in 1969–74. In 1975 a USAF C-141 crashed into a mountain during a night descent to McChord AFB, Seattle; it was misidentified during radar-vectoring and was given a premature descent clearance. The British CAA flight-tested the Sundstrand GPWS in early 1975[26] and made GPWS mandatory in all UK-registered turbojet transport aircraft from mid-1976 onwards and all UK-registered aircraft of more than 15,000 kg (33,000 pounds) gross weight after mid-1977.[27] Manufacturing problems delayed the introduction of GPWS into American airliners until January 1977, which gave other US manufacturers (Bendix, Collins and Litton) a chance to start work on their own systems.[28] The worst problem was false alarms which frustrated aircrew and undermined the credibility of the system.

The Sundstrand GPWS gave visual and aural warnings in the cockpit in one or more of five conditions, deduced from the air data computer, a radar altimeter, the ILS receiver and flap and landing gear switches. These were: excessive sink rate at less than 745 metres (2,450 feet) above ground level; excessive terrain closure rate at less than 450 metres (1,500 feet) above ground level (rising ground beneath the aircraft); descent after take-off between 15 and 230 metres (50 and 750 feet) above ground level; aircraft less than 150 metres (500 feet) above ground level with landing gear retracted; aircraft significantly below glideslope between 200 and 15 metres (650 and 50 feet) above ground level. The first GPWS would have given 3.3 seconds warning to the crew of an aircraft about to fly into a sheer cliff; the Sundstrand Mark 2, which recovered the company's competitive position, improved this to 117 seconds, starting at a range of more than 12 km (6.5nm). By the summer of 1978 about 3,500 aircraft had been equipped with GPWS.[29] The introduction of this relatively inexpensive system was followed by a significant reduction in the fatal accident rate.

The dismal record of weather-related accidents in the late 1950s and early 1960s showed, time after time, that all-weather flying remained complex, demanding and unforgiving.[30] As aircraft design, construction and maintenance improved over the years, the proportion of accidents attributable to human error in bad weather increased. On 27 February 1958, a Bristol Freighter hit a hill in England; the crew had tuned the wrong NDB. At Lima, Peru, on 22 December 1962, the crew of a Boeing 707 did the same thing. They mistook their position, believed that they were on the ILS front course when they were on the back course, deviated too far from the localizer and hit a mountain. On 25 January 1961, a BOAC Comet brushed the tops of some trees during a night approach to the newly opened Rome Fiumicino airport,[31] 95 km (51 nm) from where the crew thought they were. Sometimes the navigation errors were more subtle. On 30 October 1959, a DC-3 hit high ground on the initial approach to Charlottesville, Virginia. It was surmised that the crew had missed a turn defined by VOR radials and had turned onto a track parallel to the correct one, but offset from it. A significant number of accidents occurred when aircraft hit hills in obscured conditions after take-off. On 2 June 1958, a Constellation hit a hill after take-off from Guadalajara, Mexico. The procedure for aircraft taking off to the southwest required a teardrop left turn to gain altitude; the crew flew straight southwest for 3 km (1.6 nm) and then turned right.

A high proportion of all accidents in the 1950s and 1960s happened at night to crews that had been on duty for more than ten hours. On 9 August 1958, a Viscount hit a hill during a night approach to Benina, North Africa, with a 150 metre (500 foot) ceiling and 10 km (5.4 nm) visibility. The crash occurred at 1.15 a.m. when the crew had been awake for 19 hours, on duty for nearly 13 hours and flying for 9½ hours. On 12 December 1963, a DC-4 crashed in the mountains of Afghanistan, 68 km (37 nm) off track; the crew had been on duty for 16 hours and had been flying for 2½ hours in an unpressurized aircraft at 4,600 metres (15,000 feet) with a low oxygen supply. Night illusions were deadly. On 28 August 1958, a DC-4 took off from Minneapolis at 3.30 a.m. and flew back into the ground, as did a DC-7 in France

on 24 September 1959. On 15 May 1959, in Argentina, a DC-3 crashed into the sea during a turn after a night take-off. The same happened to a CV-240 in India on 12 May 1958. On 16 January 1959, a C-46 in Argentina missed the approach and descended gradually into the sea.

The free-world fatal accident rate in scheduled airline service in 1973 was only one-tenth of what it had been in 1950 but traffic increased so fast that annual passenger fatalities doubled and almost tripled in the same period from 551 in 1950 to 1,402 in 1972, 939 in 1973, 1,382 in 1974.[32] Non-scheduled operations acquired a bad reputation with an accident rate four times that of scheduled operations.[33] Between 1958 and 1970 nine British independent airliners flew into high ground, killing 403 passengers and 44 crew.[34] Four of these accidents occurred in Spain. This record understandably resulted in public protest. South American airlines, with their ancient aircraft and sometimes cavalier maintenance and operating procedures, facing vicious weather in high terrain, also had a poor safety record, but the worst accident of the decade was caused by human error and weather when two Boeing 747s collided on the runway in fog at Tenerife on 27 March 1977, killing 581 people.[35]

A task for which the human system is ill suited is to stay continuously alert for unlikely events, especially when tired and when its diurnal rhythms are disturbed. The more infrequent the event, the less the human being is able to deal with it. Yet these were precisely the risks to which airline pilots were constantly exposed. Long flights in highly automated aircraft accentuated these conditions to the extreme. The quiet, orderly jet airliner cockpit, with its array of reliable, high-quality instruments, could become a dangerous place if any of the

23 Hirst, M. 1976
24 Ibid.
25 *Flight International*, 20 February 1975, 306
26 Broadbent, S. 1975 (1)
27 *Flight International*, 27 March 1976, 767
28 *Flight International*, 11 December 1975, 863
29 Hirst, M. 1978 (2)
30 ICAO Circulars #59, AN/54, 1961; #62, AN/57, 1961; #64, AN/58, 1963; #69, AN/61, 1964; #71, AN/63, 1965; #78, AN/66, 1966; #82, AN/64, 1968; #88, AN/74, 1968
31 *Flight International*, 3 January 1963, 6
32 *Flight International*, 22 January 1977, 180
33 *Flight International*, 21 January 1978, 183
34 *Flight International*, 16 July 1970, 67
35 *Flight International*, 2 April 1977, 806

instruments malfunctioned, a remote eventuality, often complicated when it occurred, which some crews, understandably, failed to notice until too late. On 1 January 1978, a Boeing 747 crashed into the sea after a night take-off from Bombay; the presumed cause was that the captain's flight director instrument failed.[36]

A senior British airline official recognized in 1959[37] that anxiety and emotions caused by external events degraded the brain's performance but, curiously, made no mention of the effects of fatigue or circadian rhythms. These came under increasing scrutiny. In 1973[38] the subject of in-flight fatigue was news.

> There is a virtual break in communication between those who do the mass of the flying in civil aviation – the line crews – and those who meet around tables on numerous committees in their functions as legislator, manager, doctor, union official or professional pontificator. The plain fact to be recognized is that power to settle or even recognize the flight-duty fatigue problem will usually lie in hands that are swayed in all directions by the forces of commerce and expediency ... let me finish by quoting what, on the face of it, is an easy, single-sector, long-distance (approximately 7hr duration) flight. This flight leaves at 1800 local time and arrives at 0500 local time. The crew goes to bed at about 0630 and sleeps until 1430 local time. Now 21 hr is the required time from going off duty until going back on duty again. So the crew gets up at 0130, after about 2hr of fitful sleep, ready for take-off at 0330 local time. Arrival time is 0630 local. Two complete nights have been spent out of bed, one period of 8hr sleep by day has been achieved, and 2hr by night. On arrival back at base after this trip, the duty times are so short that you can be used on the same service that very night, without infringing any rule.
>
> What about feeding? This is all done when your body should be asleep. No wonder the eyeballs feel gritty and the lids heavy. On this simple flight, by the way, one requires to carry out the following activity: 130 position reports; 148 re-selections of tracking navigation aids, with associated steering of the aircraft along these short tracks; 95 selections of cross-track check aids; and on one flight I know of there were 22 changes of flight level, mostly of course on the climb and descent. You cross ten countries but make only two take-offs and landings. Volmet

broadcasts are noted down 21 times and you work three ATC authorities at once for some of the route, which is impossible, but is required by the rules. Oh, and keep a look out, and keep a watch on the weather radar and all those instruments that do not seem to be quite as automated as the designers, or commentators, imagine – and try to keep thinking.

That coveted left seat in the big aircraft was not always what was supposed either. This caustic commentary from 1977 reveals a gritty combination of mediocre living and working conditions, fatigue, monotony, frustration, cumulative annoyances and technical devices that did not work as well as might sometimes be supposed.[39] It also refers to the aircraft in terms that would not delight the manufacturer's PR staff. Even this presupposes a stable and satisfactory personal life.

> Let's pick one of those bosses from Iran Air's public relations office and strap him down in the left-hand seat of our magic truth-finding simulator. By pushing the 'Instant SP Pilot' button I'll transform him into another me: a well qualified senior 747SP captain with 25 years' flying experience. To complete the simulation we'll cut his fat salary down to what a newly hired expatriate 727 flight engineer gets in this company, take away his mansion on the hills overlooking Tehran, and make him rent a flat by the airport which will cost him half his monthly pay. We'll then protect our training investment by making him sign a bond for $40,000 in case another airline grabs him or if someday he decides to jump ship.
>
> Now he's ready for his check ride – New York-Tehran non-stop. He will have a brand new SP with a dozen carry-forward items in the tech log, and equal number of exhausted cabin staff, a full load of intoxicated Yankee fortune-hunters on the way to their new goldmine, and a single cockpit crew.
>
> Departure is set for 2100hr, just about his bedtime. We don't give a damn if this is his fourth non-stop flight back to Tehran this month, he only has to cope with 17hr of time change each round-trip, so we'll cut his lay-overs so short that his body won't know its a*** from its elbow. Flying eastbound he takes off at night, goes through a short day and lands the following night – so he'd better not complain about a long day's work. This peasant won't understand bio-

logical clocks, changes in body temperature, and high-frequency stomach vibrations. After all, he's had a nice long sleep in his safe, quiet, peaceful hotel in the heart of Manhattan today.

Don't you worry about the authorities either. He'll still be awake on departure from JFK, so the FAA doesn't consider him a navigational hazard within US airspace. And if he prangs outside the US it becomes the Iranian DCA's problem. Besides Boeing can always sell the Iranians another SP – good for the US balance of payments ...

Let's not give him any problems *en route*, apart from some occasional light-to-moderate turbulence to keep him awake. And let's not forget the coffee every half hour either, just in case the No Doze pills lose their effect. Whoops, mind the INS, we're turning back to waypoint one. Will someone wake the engineer to untie the first officer so that he can input the new waypoints. We keep him strapped because we don't want him falling on the stick in his sleep and waking the passengers.

We're all getting sleepy now, so will you push the 'fast forward' button and put this bucket on finals for 29L. We'll have the usual winter weather at Tehran for the purposes of this exercise; 1,200m visibility in blowing snow and smoke, ILS and radar out of action of course. VASI? You must be joking! Approach lights? I prefer flare pots. No overshoots, please – the weather at the alternate is going down, and with all the big boys diverting there, hotel rooms will be as scarce as fertile SP pilots.

Message from dispatch: 'Will the captain of the 747SP now arriving please go to the office right after landing to explain about his noise violation at Kennedy last week.

There was a gradual, legislated reduction in duty hours for different kinds of operator and operation over the course of the years, but regulations varied from one jurisdiction to another and, when all was said and done, the supply of pilots has always exceeded demand.

The goal of perfect airline safety remained elusive. At the 1976 IATA AGM in Singapore it was said,[40] verbosely, that most accidents were caused by human error; baffling and unpredictable limitations, interactions and misperceptions. In 1979 twenty fatal air carrier accidents killed 1,267 passengers and 149 crew members[41] and the decade ended on a note of frustration with no break-

through in eradicating what appeared to be an irreducible minimum. In 1982:[42]

> It is all very well to rejoice over the fact that deaths are well down, but the reason for this is that there were not many people in the aeroplanes that crashed. The number of fatal accidents is marginally up. Smaller airliners crash for the same reasons that widebodies do – structural failure, equipment failure, fire, aircrew error, or administrative and engineering mistakes. The statistics show that airlines and manufacturers are having no success eradicating these basic crash-causers. It is unfair, though, to tar all airlines with the same brush: almost all the fatal accidents involved Third World operators, most of them Latin or South American second-line carriers ... as usual we have virtually no information on what actually happened to the biggest airliner operator in the world – Aeroflot.

The same writer went on:

> Arguably the most horrible statistic of the year is that seven of the twenty-nine fatal accidents were caused by aircraft running into high ground the pilot did not see; and 303 people died because of this – nearly half 1981's total fatalities ... In our report on the previous year we remarked that a quarter of all the crashes were collisions with high ground. We have argued in the past that, unless structural or engine failure precedes the impact, a large proportion of the blame must attach to the crew; it is their job to know exactly where they are and where the hills are, even if ATC feeds them erroneous information ... Is increased flight deck automation making aircrew complacent, and causing them to forget the basic rules of airmanship?

The question remains unanswered to this day

---

36 *Flight International*, 4 August 1979, 312; Learmount, D. 1979
37 Prowse, B. O. 1959
38 *Flight International*, 22 March 1973, 417
39 *Flight International*, 12 February 1977, 368
40 Quoted in IATA Annual Report from 20th IATA Technical Conference, Instanbul, 1975.
41 *Flight International*, 26 January 1980, 247
42 *Flight International*, 23 January 1982, 183

CHAPTER 26

The Final Challenge: The Blind-Landing Dilemma

The instrument approach systems developed up to 1950 sufficed to guide an aircraft to a point from which the pilot could catch sight of the airport in most weather conditions and land visually. All these systems, however, required a ceiling and visibility not less than 60–90 metres (200–300 feet) and 800–1,600 metres (0.5–1 mile) for the pilot to land safely. The problem of landing an aircraft safely in dense fog remained unsolved.

Instrument approach procedures became formalized in the 1950s as precision and non-precision. A precision approach was based on the SCS-51 ILS. A non-precision approach was one based on one or more NDB or VOR beacons and lacking an electronic glideslope. Pre-war procedures based on DF steers lingered on in Europe, known as VDF (VHF DF) approaches. Radar became an approach aid in itself, both in the form of GCA and, less rigorously, as a series of vectors and descent altitudes organized into an approach procedure.

The procedure for orientation to the ILS was derived from the radio range approach. Typically, a crew navigated to an NDB, sited at the ILS outer marker and known as a locator, and used it as a holding fix if necessary. From there they tracked the localizer outbound and flew a procedure turn to bring the aircraft back onto the localizer at a safe height above the ground, outside the outer marker and below the glideslope. Aircraft were not intended to intercept the glideslope from above because of the high rate of descent needed to do so and the consequent risk of flying into the ground, indeed some operators specifically forbade it. The pilot tracked the localizer inbound until the aircraft intercepted the glideslope, which was then followed to the decision height published for the airport, usually 60–90 metres (200–300 feet) above

the ground. If the pilot could not see the runway threshold from that point, he climbed away, following a missed approach procedure specific to the airport and the layout of the surrounding navaids and terrain. As early as 1951 radar allowed ATC to vector aircraft to a straight-in ILS approach, eliminating the procedure turn with great savings in time.[1]

Radio range approaches were augmented during the 1950s, and finally superseded, by similar procedures using VORs and NDBs. Such approaches required higher weather minima than ILS, but were better than nothing for an airport where traffic did not justify an ILS. During the 1950s more and more airports throughout the world acquired government- or government/company-approved instrument approach procedures. In 1961 the FAA began to incorporate DME into IFR navigation. DME with ILS provided continuous ranging information in contrast to the marker beacons previously available. The first ILS approach with DME as a part of the procedure was commissioned at New York John F. Kennedy in 1964.[2] DME also provided a new method of navigating from the initial approach fix to the final approach by means of an arc flown at a constant distance from the DME beacon.[3] For this purpose a DME arc could be referenced either to a DME beacon collocated with an ILS or to the DME component of a nearby VORTAC. DME with VOR or NDB[4] made it possible to fly straight-in approaches, reducing height at specified DME-indicated distances from the airport, known as step-down fixes.

1 ICAO Circular #21, AN/18, 1951
2 *Flight International*, 10 December 1964, 991
3 Weeghman, R. B. 1965
4 *Flight International*, 29 June 1961, 897

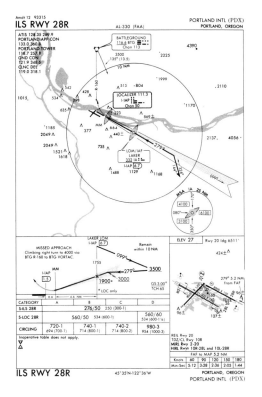

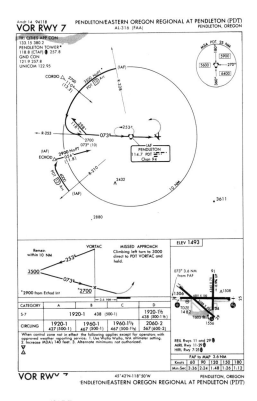

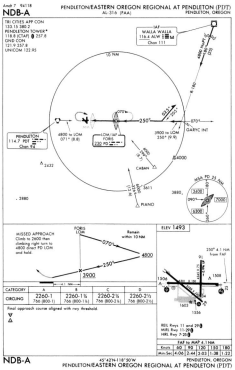

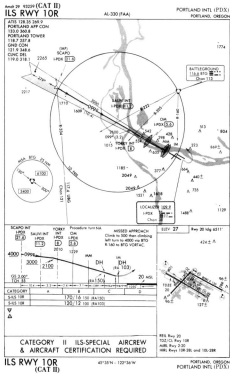

American instrument approach charts. *Flying*, March, 1965, 34.

Over most of North America a system allowing blind approaches down to 60–90 metres (200–300 feet) above ground level provided an acceptable compromise between reliability of service and cost that continues to the present time. Even in 1949, United Airlines completed 98% of their scheduled mileage.[5] Although the 2% missed included cancellations and delays of all kinds, the 98% figure was attributed to the increasing use of electronic navigation aids and to the design of routes according to weather patterns. Persistent, dense fog was not a serious problem for most of the continent. The same was far from true in northwest Europe.

In May 1952, the delegates to the IATA technical conference at Copenhagen spent 17,000 man-hours discussing a phase of flight lasting two minutes.[6] The minimum decision height in an ILS approach was determined by the time the average airline pilot needed to convert from instrument to visual flight; the conference agreed that this was not less than 15 seconds; the pilot also needed 3–5 seconds to react to what he could see as he landed the aircraft; the minimum acceptable visibility was thus the distance the aircraft would travel in that time. The increasing final approach speeds of new types of aircraft pushed the decision point farther and higher from the runway, whereas jet airliner economics demanded the opposite.

Too many aircraft crashed trying to land in fog, while adherence to safe landing minima often caused serious financial loss. In particular, fog, by day or by night, frequently disorganized scheduled flying and, as demonstrated in the winter of 1952–3, might suspend air traffic for long indefinite periods.[7] The proverbial density of British fog had to be seen to be believed. During one test flight in southeast England the pilot saw nothing outside his aircraft on final approach until reaching a height of 20 metres (70 feet) above the ground. Horizontal visibility on the ground at that time was 50 metres (165 feet) and the nearest available alternate airport was Prestwick, 480 km (300 miles) away.[8] On 4 December 1958, a DC-3 used for fog research took off from Heathrow in visibility less than 90 metres (300 feet). No other aircraft were flying. On return the approach was continued down to 200 feet without sight of the wingtips, let alone the high-intensity approach lighting. The aircraft diverted to Guernsey, 240 km (150 miles) away.[9] This type of persistent dense fog drove the British effort to achieve completely blind landings.

The problem grew worse as passenger aircraft became bigger and more expensive to operate. The direct cost of diversions and delays increased, as did the cost and inconvenience of providing for the passengers, especially if diversion to an alternate airport meant landing in a different country, which could easily be the case in Europe. The ability to take off and land in blind conditions also had vital military implications.

As mentioned earlier, approach and runway lighting came to play an essential part in the transition from instrument to visual flight in low visibility. The manager at Amsterdam Schiphol reckoned that the new runway lights installed there in 1953 would reduce cancellations and diversions due to low visibility by 20%.[10] By 1955 better approach lighting and refined electronic aids had reduced the minimum visibility for safe landings after ILS approaches to about 450 metres (1,500 feet).[11] By 1960 it was found that, in visibilities of about 800 metres (0.5 mile), horizon-bar approach lights reduced the percentage of missed approaches from 30% to 2%.[12]

The present-day Visual Approach Slope Indicator System (VASIS), developed in the UK by the RAE, provided both a visual glideslope and a horizon reference. A VASIS consists of two bars of two lights each, sited beside the left-hand side of the runway at the ILS touchdown point. If the aircraft is too high, both bars show white to the pilot; if too low, both bars show red; on the correct glideslope the pilot sees the far bar red, the near bar white. By 1959 VASIS had been installed at five UK airports[13] and was adopted as standard by both the FAA and the ICAO in 1960. The first US installation was at New York La Guardia in 1961. The equipment was manufactured by Sylvania Electric for $80,000, and was scheduled for installation at thirty-seven other airports.[14] Lighting systems were equally important in combating night visual illusions.[15] These were becoming increasingly dangerous with aircraft types that not only flew at higher approach speeds but also were less responsive in the landing configuration.

5 *Flight*, 9 February 1950, 201
6 *Flight*, 13 June 1952, 718
7 Makinson, W. 1953
8 Makinson, W. 1953
9 *Flight*, 19 December 1958, 947
10 *Flight*, 25 December 1953, 851
11 *Flight*, 25 February 1955, 247
12 Calvert, E. S. 1959
13 *Flight*, 20 February 1959, 268
14 *Flight International*, 21 September 1961, 489
15 Coombes, L. P. 1959; Calvert, E. S. 1959

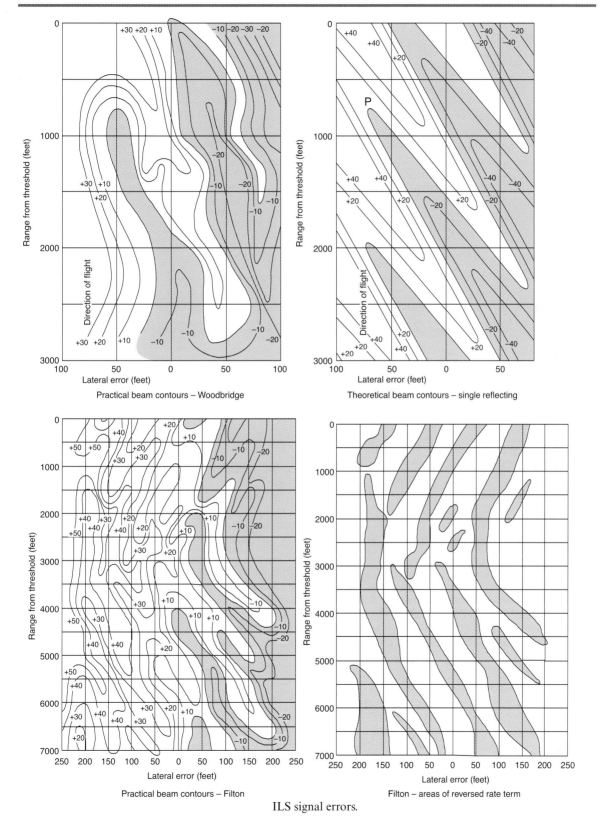

Practical beam contours – Woodbridge

Theoretical beam contours – single reflecting

Practical beam contours – Filton

Filton – areas of reversed rate term

ILS signal errors.

In the mid 1970s the RAE Bedford, UK, developed a better VASIS called the Precision Approach Path Indicator (PAPI).[16] The VASIS did not show a sharp enough change from red to white lights when indicating whether the aircraft was too high or too low. PAPI consisted of two bars, one each side of the runway (military) or one bar to the left of the runway (civilian), each of four lights. Each light changed sharply from a white light indicating too high to a red light indicating too low. Two red lights and two white lights indicated the correct glideslope. Three white lights and one red light indicated slightly high. Three red lights and one white light indicated slightly low. Four white lights indicated too high; four red lights indicated too low.

Visual approach slopes were bedevilled by the large size of modern aircraft. An apparent discrepancy between visual and electronic glideslopes could result merely from the difference in height between the pilot's eyes and the aircraft's glideslope antenna. With aircraft of various dimensions flying approaches in lower and lower visibility, the issue of approach lighting became increasingly complicated.

If blind approaches were to be continued below 60 metres (200 feet), the accuracy of the localizer and glideslope took on a sharply increased significance. Studies[17] showed that localizers were distorted by signal reflection from the airfield surroundings. As the beams narrowed towards the touchdown zone, the effects of distortion increased. Although an experienced human pilot could distinguish wind drift from signal distortion, the responsiveness and precision of an autopilot were a liability when intercepting and tracking a distorted beam. By 1958 it seemed certain that many, perhaps even the majority, of the existing ILS installations were unsuitable for automatic landing. At some sites there seemed to be little prospect that ILS would ever suffice for that purpose.[18] It was hoped that localizer distortions could be reduced by improved antenna design, but even the UHF glideslope was not reliable enough below 60 metres (200 feet) to be followed to touchdown, either manually or automatically[19] and this problem offered no prospect of solution.

In 1951 the US Weather Bureau began a programme of research, sponsored by the Air Navigation Development Board, to develop accurate, automatic methods of measuring ceiling and ground-level visibility for the information of inbound pilots. Ceiling was measured by light reflection from clouds; runway visual range (RVR) was measured by light transmission between a lamp and a photocell. The prototypes were tested at Washington National airport in 1954.[20] Research by the British BLEU, however, showed that there was no correlation between slant visibility along the glideslope and the horizontal visibility at ground level. Nevertheless, RVR was the best indicator of visibility that was available, and remains so to the present time.

The British effort to develop blind landing capability resulted from a military need. Crashes in fog when bombers were returning from wartime raids made blind landing an urgent priority for the efficiency of the RAF bomber force. This also applied to the V-Bombers[21] of the 1950s. The Blind Landing Experimental Unit[22] was formed in 1946 to meet this need, the latest of a series of specialist radio and blind-flying research units dating back before the Second World War. In 1957 the UK government released some of the results of BLEU work to civil aviation;[23] others remained secret.[24] Some of its work took place at the Woodbridge wartime emergency airfield with its runway 230 metres (750 feet) wide and 2,750 metres (9,000 feet) long. Because fully automatic landings had been made as early as 1944, it was felt that they should be attainable in normal service in the near future. By 1949 the BLEU had made about 500 landings in a specially equipped aircraft, with the pilot working only such devices as throttles, flaps and brakes. Some of the experiments were flown in dense fog and the pilots could, and sometimes did, make completely blind manual landings with the help of a radar altimeter.

By 1958 a BLEU Canberra was making fully automatic approaches and landings.[25] On initial approach the aircraft was set to fly level on autopilot at 300 metres (1,000 feet) above the ground and was turned to intercept the localizer. The pilot extended the landing gear and flaps and engaged automatic glideslope tracking. On the glideslope

16 *Flight International*, 6 November 1975, 676
17 Mercer, J. F. W. 1954; *Flight*, 6 November 1953, 623
18 *Flight*, 1958, 308
19 *Flight*, 20 February 1959, 268
20 *Flight*, 23 April 1954, 512
21 V-Bombers: collective name for the Vickers Valiant, Handley Page Victor and Avro Vulcan, British 4-jet bombers introduced in the early 1950s.
22 Makinson, W. 1953
23 *Flight International*, 9 March 1967, 361
24 *Flight International*, 22 February 1962, 296
25 *Flight*, 17 October 1958, 614

Avro Vulcan.

Handley Page Victor.

Vickers Valiant.

automatic throttles held a preselected air speed with the aircraft in the landing configuration. The radar altimeter began to read at 150 metres (500 feet) above ground level. At 90 metres (300 feet) the leader cables automatically took over azimuth guidance from the localizer. At 30 metres (100 feet) the radar altimeter took over glideslope guidance, also automatically, while the autopilot maintained the aircraft's average attitude. At 15 metres (50 feet) the aircraft was over the runway and the radar altimeter controlled the flare-out and reduced

power. At 6 metres (20 feet) the autopilot discarded the leader cable signal and aligned the fuselage with the runway if the aircraft had been crabbing in a crosswind. As soon as the aircraft touched down, the pilot took control, following the runway by means of a leader-cable indicator in the cockpit, and applied the brakes. Leader cables later became obsolete, partly because of improved ILS and partly because of the problems of installing them outside airport boundaries.

In spite of this success, major challenges

Vickers Varsity of the RAF Blind Landing Experimental Unit.

remained to be overcome before experimental success could be converted into routine airline operation. The worst problem was the possibility of the autopilot malfunctioning just before touchdown. The BLEU reckoned that, if the autopilot failed at any altitude below 18 metres (60 feet), the pilot would be unlikely to avert disaster. The BLEU estimated this probability at 4 in 100,000 landings with their single-channel autopilot. A duplex autopilot, with automatic disengagement of both autopilots in the event of a discrepancy, would reduce this probability to 7 in one million landings, the same as a human pilot, although automatic disengagement could leave the pilot in a very difficult situation. A triplex autopilot, arranged so that a discrepancy in one would disengage it automatically, leaving the other two functioning, would reduce the probability of disastrous failure to three per billion landings. By early 1959 the BLEU system, first demonstrated publicly in October 1958, had completed some 2,000 automatic landings with Varsities, Devons and Canberras.[26] The Smith's Mk 10 (military) and SEP-5 (civilian) autopilots that went into service in

the 1960s progressively inhibited bank angle to 25° during the ILS approach, 10° while under leader cable guidance and 5° during flare-out. The airborne equipment weighed 450 kg (1,000 pounds)[27] of which half was the auto-throttle.

The BLEU's success led BEA to specify that automatic landing be designed into the new de Havilland DH-121 trijet airliner, later known as the Trident, scheduled for delivery in 1964.[28] This was regarded as essential to BEA's quest to operate in zero ceiling and zero visibility.

Others besides the BLEU were at work on automatic landing. In the US in 1957 the Bell Aircraft Corporation demonstrated an automatic carrier landing system which guided a Douglas F-3D from 3.2 km (1.7 nm) from touchdown to a full stop on a runway without the pilot's intervention.[29] A radar set on the ground or ship compared the aircraft's position with a predetermined glideslope. The radar echo was fed into a computer which transmitted radio commands to the aircraft's autopilot. As the system was intended to operate from an aircraft carrier, it incorporated an automatic missed

English Electric Canberra during automatic landing trials.

approach feature for use if the carrier's deck was pitching so much that a successful landing was impossible.

The aircraft entered a 'gate' 240 metres (800 feet) above surface level, 6.4 km (3.4 nm) from touchdown, within 1.6 km (0.38 nm) of centreline and within 60° of the inbound heading. The pilot was to use ILS to monitor the automatic system. If radar lock-on was lost during the approach, a missed approach would be signalled automatically. A missed approach would also be ordered automatically if pitch or bank commands exceeded limits that progressively decreased, the closer the aircraft was to touchdown. Just before flare-out, the autopilot aligned the aircraft with the runway, removing any crab correction for drift. At the flare-out point the height command path levelled off and the autopilot raised the aircraft's nose to a precomputed angle for a touchdown at a descent rate of 0.6 metres (2 feet) per second. As the aircraft went outside the radar scan, and lock-on was lost, the automatic missed-approach command was disabled. The pilot could take control from the autopilot at any time, using a cockpit instrument fed by the error signals transmitted by the computer. A human controller on the ground could take over the system and use it as a normal GCA.[30]

In the autumn of 1957 an F-3D made 100 automatic landings aboard the carrier *Antietam*. In 1959 the Bell system was demonstrated in a B-47. By early 1959 DC-3s, B-47s and the prototype Boeing 707 had made more than 2,000 automatic landings with this system. It was under evaluation by the US armed forces and by the RCAF, PanAm, KLM, BOAC and Lufthansa.[31]

The Autonetics division of North American Aviation developed an automatic landing device for the X-10 pilotless research aircraft which was in operation in 1958,[32] using radar altimeter and accelerometer signals for the flare-out. Although this device was tried out in various manned and unmanned aircraft, it was designed for aircraft landing on dry lake-beds where the centreline and touchdown point were practically immaterial.

The conventional ILS approach sufficed for most of the world's airlines. The enormous cost and technical difficulty of achieving fully automatic landing in zero-zero conditions were of marginal value, but with two important exceptions. First, the Cold War demanded that military aircraft operate in any weather conditions. Second, the British Isles and northwest Europe combined some of the worst flying weather with some of the highest traffic densities in the world. The ability to operate in zero-zero conditions was an urgent commercial need for airlines serving London. The most notable of these was BEA with its short-haul European routes.

One aspect of the blind-landing development effort was to define the problem. In the mid 1960s, the FAA defined ceiling and visibility categories, as follows:[33]

Category 3	60 metres (200 feet) ceiling	800 metres (0.5 mile) visibility
Category 2	30 metres (100 feet) ceiling	400 metres (1,300 feet) RVR
Category 1	0 feet ceiling	45 metres (150 feet) RVR

Standards of airborne and ground-based equipment and aircrew certification were more rigorous as minima diminished.

The FAA categories were superseded by a different system, proposed by the ICAO All-Weather Operations Panel in 1962 and adopted internationally in 1966.[34] The ICAO classification was intended to address the problem of all-weather landing in three phases, represented by three categories of ceiling and visibility minima:[35]

Category 1 Minimum decision height 60 metres (200 feet), 800 metres (2,600 feet) RVR.

Category 2 Minimum decision height below 60 metres (200 feet), 800 metres (2,600 feet) RVR, to as low as 30 metres (100 feet) decision height, 400 metres (1,200 feet) RVR.

In 1964 Category 3 was divided into three phases:

Category 3a Operation down to and along the surface of the runway with external visual reference during the final phase of the landing down to RVR minima of 200 metres (700 feet). (In other words zero ceiling.)

Category 3b Operation to and along the surface of the runways and taxiways with visibility sufficient only for visual taxying comparable to an RVR of 50 metres (150 feet).

Category 3c Operation to and along the surface of the runway and taxiways without external visual reference. (In other words zero-zero.)

The ICAO specified three categories of ILS. Category 1 ILS provided reliable guidance down the glideslope to 60 metres (200 feet) above the runway elevation. Category 2 ILS provided reliable guidance down to 15 metres (50 feet). Category 3 ILS provided guidance down to the runway and along it with the aid of ancillary equipment.

No automatic flight control was required for Category 1 and the upper limits of Category 2. Automatic flight control coupled to the ILS was considered necessary for any decision height below 60 metres (200 feet), although a manual touchdown could still follow an auto-coupled approach. An automatic landing system was needed for Category 3a, adding automatic crosswind compensation during touchdown for Category 3b. In Category 3c conditions, not only the aircraft but also ground service vehicles had to be guided on the ground.

The increasing numbers of jet airliners in the 1960s intensified the need for lower minima, but because of their higher approach speeds, slower throttle response and swept-wing aerodynamics, US landing minima were set higher for jets, at 90 metres (300 feet) ceiling and 1,200 metres (¾ mile) visibility, than for propeller-driven aircraft, at 60 metres (200 feet) ceiling and 800 metres (½ mile) visibility, adding further to the rising cost of diversions and delays. Jet minima could be lowered to 60 metres (200 feet) and 800 metres (½ mile) only for individual airlines if certain stringent equipment and crew-training requirements were met. Propeller-driven aircraft were thus landing in weather that caused jets to be delayed or diverted. In 1963 one pilot commented sourly[36] that minima at Newark were the same in 1963 as in 1937, 200 feet ceiling and ½ mile visibility. He added: 'We have jumped in speed during that twenty-six years from 170 mph to 600, increased our range from 700 miles to more than 5,000, passenger capacity from 14 to 140, but we have not gained one inch

26 *Flight*, 20 February 1959, 269
27 *Flight International*, 12 September 1963, 458
28 *Flight*, 28 November 1958, 842; 23 January 1959, 143
29 *Flight*, 8 March 1957, 294
30 *Flight*, 9 January 1959, 57
31 *Flight*, 20 February 1959, 269
32 *Flight*, 7 February 1958, 165; 16 May 1958, 676
33 *Flight International*, 1 April 1965, 480; Baxter, T. 1966
34 *Flight International*, 22 February 1962, 276; 9 March 1967, 362; IATA Bulletin, December 1966, 87
35 Baxter, J. R. 1967, 402
36 *Flying*, May 1963, 6

toward all-weather flying.'

Reductions in landing minima faced a range of interlocking problems. The cost of their solution rose disproportionately as the ultimate aim of zero-zero operation was approached.[37] Ragged, indefinite cloud ceilings became significant when the ceiling itself was only 30 or 60 metres (100 or 200 feet) above the ground. When fog lay on the ground, its density could vary locally and patches with almost zero visibility could exist on a runway without anyone being aware of them. Landing and departing aircraft could, of themselves, cause rapid changes in visibility within the fog. The limit of accuracy for barometric altimeters was ±12 metres (40 feet); this was no longer sufficient for blind approaches to less than 60 metres (200 feet) above ground level. At those altitudes wrong altimeter settings, even a QFE for the wrong end of a sloping runway, were even more dangerous. Radar altimeters were not widely available in the 1960s. The ILS distortion problem has already been mentioned; it could vary with weather conditions.

More alarmingly, autopilot, ILS and flight director systems were prone to unpredictable, transient errors that undermined aircrews' confidence in them. One of the traditional autopilot problems is the interaction between elevator control and trim. A human pilot solves this problem without thinking about it, but in some types of aircraft the autopilot could work against itself. Power surges, wind shear, configuration changes, or airspeed variation could trigger this conflict, resulting in an unstable cyclic divergence from the required flight path such that the pilot had to disconnect the autopilot.[38] Design defects or maintenance deficiencies were conducive to this problem which could be extremely dangerous during a blind approach, and some crashes were thought to be attributable to it.

The sheer size of a modern aircraft meant that the vertical distances between wheels, ILS antennas and windscreens were significant in terms of a 30–60-metre (100–200-foot) ceiling.

Although approach lighting had improved in quantity and quality, there was still no standardization between jurisdictions, and too often, on breaking out of cloud, a pilot was presented with a bewildering array of dazzle. The swept wings, large flaps and slow throttle response of jet airliners all increased the time needed to go into a go-around from the landing attitude and configuration. This raised further questions as to how far jet minima could safely be reduced.

The economic issues of blind landing were as complex as the technical ones and differed on opposite sides of the Atlantic. The differences in philosophy between the British and the Americans arose from three main causes.[39] First, the British had more to gain from zero-zero capability because of weather conditions in northwest Europe. The British, too, had more reservations about lower decision heights. Second, the Americans had a greater interest in retrofitting their existing airliner fleet. Third, by the early 1960s the British had a functioning military automatic landing system which they sought to convert to civilian standards. The Americans had no automatic landing systems ready for service, civilian or military, although much money and effort were being spent on both.[40]

The US, as a whole, had better weather than the world average; weather conditions were below existing instrument approach minima for less of the time. London Heathrow, surprisingly, had slightly better ceiling and visibility than the world average most years, but in bad years British airlines lost hundreds of thousands of pounds through cancelled and delayed flights over a period of a few days. Landing minima at 30 metres (100 feet) ceiling and 200 metres (650 feet) RVR would suffice for 98% of the world's airline flights.[41] The whole immense effort to develop automatic landing systems acceptable for civilian use was thus directed to solving a problem that occurred infrequently. In 1962 it was estimated that lowering the jet approach minimum ceiling from 90 metres (300 feet) to 30 metres (100 feet) would eliminate 60–70% of the increasingly expensive diversions then current.[42] In a three-year period between 1958 and 1960 visibility at Heathrow was below 400 metres (1,300 feet) RVR just 3.2% of the time.

Automatic landing generated a ferment of divergent opinion.[43] The Americans continued a massive FAA/USAF research programme aimed at manual blind landings; the British had long ago abandoned this idea as impractical and had concentrated on complete automation. The British continued to rely on ILS; the Americans were looking for a completely new ground-based approach aid. The Americans wanted systems that would allow them to operate in lower minima, but did not believe it worthwhile to aim for zero-zero capability; the British did not believe that the cost of designing and equipping new types of aircraft for automatic landing was worthwhile unless it did lead to zero-zero operation.[44] New aircraft designed for automatic landing from the outset gave better results at less cost than retrofitted older aircraft. Both in the US and Britain individual airlines had their own policies and beliefs. The American scene was dominated by large, private airlines, such as American, PanAm and United. In Britain the only two airlines with the financial means to pursue blind landing were the two public corporations, BEA and BOAC. Competitive advantage between airlines was as powerful a driving force as a straightforward economic analysis.

Government bodies and airlines on both sides of the Atlantic came to accept ILS in progressively refined forms as the primary means of approach guidance rather than incur the immense cost of converting to some completely new system. ILS is still the *status quo*, worldwide, sixty years after its invention because it provides an acceptable compromise between performance and cost. If it is ever superseded, it will be by GPS, leapfrogging its successor technology, the Microwave Landing System.

Because the Americans were not seeking to land civil aircraft in zero-zero conditions, a simplex autopilot monitored by the human aircrew was enough. Boeing believed that with their system an aircraft could be landed safely in an RVR of 228 metres (750 feet) provided the crosswind component was less than 18–27 kilometres per hour (10–15 knots) and provided the aircraft was correctly aligned at 21 metres (70 feet) above ground level.[45] The British, in their drive for zero-zero capability, took control of the aircraft out of the hands of the human pilot altogether. This was permissible in military service using only a simplex autopilot, but if civilian safety standards were to be achieved, no less than three autopilots had to be installed. This requirement exacted a heavy penalty in weight and cost compared with the American concept.

Different philosophies also applied to equipment certification.[46] In Britain both the Air Registration Board and the Board of Trade had a hand in approving systems and operations. These bodies did not specify the equipment but did specify the degree of safety which the equipment had to

demonstrate. The worldwide average of fatal landing accidents was one in 1 million; the ARB required that any automatic landing system should be ten times safer. The FAA specified the equipment but not the level of safety that it had to demonstrate. For political reasons the FAA could not admit that a finite risk existed; they were thus obliged to approve equipment without the statistical error analysis required of British manufacturers. The FAA, on the other hand, was able to regulate all aspects of low-visibility operations, including airborne equipment, crew-training and maintenance standards. In the interests of public safety, regulations of the most stringent description had to be devised; the regulators were often treading ground as unfamiliar as those responsible for the technical and operational developments.

The first automatic landings in passenger service took place during the 1960s, albeit in visual conditions. The goal of blind landings in commercial service remained elusive, not so much because the technical means were lacking, but because pilots and regulators had to be convinced that the systems worked reliably enough. This could be achieved only by building up a huge experience base of automatic landings in visual weather conditions, a process that went on throughout the 1960s. Innumerable unsuspected problems arose; indeed, as the full complexity of the task became clearer, doubts arose, especially in North America, as to whether it was all worthwhile. No such doubts assailed the British. Possessing one of the world's major air traffic hubs in an area renowned for its dense and persistent fogs, they persisted in the quest for landings in zero ceiling and visibility.

37 Lee, L. 1964
38 *Flight International*, 20 February 1969, 281
39 Smith, K. W. 1972
40 *Flight International*, 22 February 1962, 291
41 *Flight International*, 9 March 1967, 363
42 IATA Bulletin, December 1962, p.81
43 *Flight International*, 17 October 1963, 642
44 Baxter, J. R. 1967, 404
45 *Flight International*, 17 October 1963, 644
46 *Flight International*, 9 March 1967, 366

CHAPTER 27

American Pragmatism: The Low Approach

Dense fog or a low but definite ceiling with good visibility beneath were simple situations offering obvious choices to a pilot contemplating an instrument approach. These two conditions, however, were the ends of a spectrum of indefinite conditions of mist, snow, drizzle, low, ragged ceilings and darkness when the pilot's choices were less obvious. Final approach in low visibility went on causing the biggest single group of weather-related accidents. The American philosophy was to advance the limits of safe landing within this spectrum and to improve the safety of landings within those limits, while avoiding the enormous cost of fully automatic blind landing.

On 15 August 1958, at Nantucket, a patch of fog moved over the runway while a CV-240 was on final approach; the pilot flew into the fog, became disorientated and crashed. At Shemya, Alaska, on 21 July 1961, a DC-6 crashed short of the runway during a GCA to a 60 metre (200 foot) ceiling, sky obscured, visibility 1,200 metres (¾ mile) in fog. At Jacksonville, Florida, on 2 December 1961, a DC-7 crashed during an ASR approach[1] when the aircraft entered smoke on final approach. On 30 November 1962, a DC-7 hit the ground beside the runway while the pilot was trying to land in fog at New York after an ILS approach. A similar fate befell a CV-340 at Grand Island, Nebraska, on 21 December 1962, at night in fog. At New York on 7 April 1964, the pilot of a Boeing 707 lifted his aircraft over a fog bank on final approach but landed long and ran off the far end of the runway.

In America, with its huge domestic market and defence spending, more different organizations were working on low-visibility landing than in Britain; they produced a correspondingly wider variety of concepts and devices. The early 1960s were a period of particularly intense experimenta-tion by industry and the FAA. The Americans worked to improve the safety of low-visibility landing in three ways: electronic guidance from the ground, devices on board the aircraft and automatic landing.

At the end of the 1950s Bendix produced a device called Microvision as an aid to ILS, not a substitute. Lines of microwave beacons were placed beside the runway; a receiver in the aircraft displayed the beacon signals on a cockpit CRT so that they resembled the normal runway edge lights. In 1960–2 a USAF C-131 flight-tested this device at Patterson Field, Dayton, Ohio; one pilot made a blind landing.[2] By 1964 C-131, Beech D-18S and DC-3 fixed-wing aircraft and Bell UH-1 and Hiller H-23 helicopters had flown more than 1,000 successful approaches with Microvision at Baltimore Friendship, Detroit Metropolitan, Wright-Patterson AFB and Teterboro, New York. USAF and Bendix aircraft had landed with the pilot under a hood.[3] Attempts were also made to project the microwave dots onto a HUD. In spite of its initial promise, nothing more was heard of Microvision. It seems likely that the benefits did not warrant the cost of installation and the penalty in cockpit space.

Gilfillan Brothers developed a system called Regal, first tried out at Atlantic City in March 1960,[4] and intended to fill the gap between the bottom limit of the usable ILS glideslope and touchdown. A beacon radiated two signals whose interference null provided a beam 0.05° wide which was used as a glideslope combined with a DME-type ranging system. An existing ILS localizer was used for the tests but Regal could also provide a localizer by means of a second antenna set. Studies showed that a touchdown longitudinal spread of ±60 metres (200 feet) and a descent rate at touchdown of 0.6 metres (2 feet) per second ±0.3 metres (1 foot) per second were possible. By early 1962 two B-25s and a T-33 had made at least sixty successful automatic landings using Regal.

Also under evaluation at Atlantic City in 1962 was Flarescan-ILS[5] from the Airborne Instruments Laboratory of Cutler-Hammer Inc. Flarescan was intended to interact with a new precision ILS. The Flarescan antenna was set up beside the runway beyond the ILS glideslope antenna. It transmitted a coded, fan-shaped, microwave (16,000 MHz) signal which intersected the ILS glideslope, providing precise guidance from the point of intersection to touchdown. Flarescan signals could be fed into an autopilot or used to drive a third needle on an ILS cockpit display. Even though transistorized, the airborne receiver weighed 9 kg (20 pounds). Initial flight tests using a B-25 showed that the system was accurate to within 1.2 meters (4 feet) throughout the approach and 0.6 meters (2 feet) at touchdown.

In 1962 the FAA tested the Bell GSN-5(ST) USAF landing radar[6] which provided flare guidance and a decrab command. The Bell SPN-10 carrier automatic landing system was already fully developed to land aircraft on carriers in zero visibility. By early 1962 more than 3,000 automatic landings had been made, on land and at sea, and twelve sets of equipment were scheduled for delivery to the US Navy in 1962–4. The first operational installation was on the USS *Enterprise* and nine other carriers were to be equipped.[7]

By 1970 some 800 runways worldwide had been equipped with ILS.[8] The technology had not changed in thirty years, dating back to requirements drafted in the 1930s. Yet even when ILS was introduced, its limitations were already acknowledged. At ILS frequencies signal reflection from buildings and nearby terrain caused distortion. At some airports distortion was so bad that ILS was unusable; at others distortion could be brought within acceptable limits by improved antenna design. Vehicles and aircraft moving on the ground affected the signals. ILS offered only a single, straight approach path at a fixed glideslope angle.[9]

In the 1940s and 1950s microwave technology had come into being, offering frequencies at which sharply focused beams could be projected, free from reflection and distortion. At the end of the 1940s the French had developed an experimental microwave landing system transmitting localizer and glideslope on a single frequency of 1,300 MHz. It was tested in France in 1949 and by the BLEU in 1950.[10] In the second half of the 1950s

the British company Elliott Brothers Ltd were developing a microwave ILS from a marine harbour course beacon that they manufactured.[11]

By the late 1960s, new needs had arisen that ILS could not meet. VTOL and STOL aircraft needed guidance to fly steep, curved approaches to small airfields or unprepared sites.[12] The armed forces demanded a landing aid that was robust, easily portable and quick to set up. The civilian requirements were defined by the ICAO All-Weather Operations Panel (AWOP) and the US Government Radio Technical Committee for Aeronautics. The resulting report from Standing Committee 117 of the RTCA appeared in September 1969. In February 1972, the 7th ICAO Air Navigation Conference finalized an operational requirement for a new system to replace ILS.[13] The ICAO did not specify microwaves, but the requirements were best met by using the microwave band.[14] Intense political lobbying and commercial competition followed to dominate a market of which the civilian segment alone was expected to be worth $1–1.5 billion over twenty years. The commercial risks were enormous.

In the 1960s the Airborne Instrument Laboratories division of Cutler-Hammer developed and produced a microwave landing system which was used by Swedish air force J-37 Viggens. Combined with DME, this system offered the prospect of Category 3 operation with an infinite variety of tracks and glideslopes within the signal coverage, including curved approach paths. In 1968 three other systems were available, all military. The RAE Microwave Interferometer used ground equipment to interrogate an airborne transponder, compute the aircraft's track and position and radio the results. Ferranti Navigation and Approach Radar was an update of an older idea

1 ASR: Airfield Surveillance Radar, used as a sole non-precision approach aid by means of vectoring along known safe tracks.
2 *Flight International*, 1 November 1962, 713
3 *Flight International*, 27 August 1964, 333
4 *Flight International*, 22 February 1962, 298
5 Ibid.
6 Ibid.
7 *Flight International*, 11 May 1961, 644
8 *Flight International*, 21 May 1970, 861
9 *Flight International*, 6 April 1972, 470
10 ICAO Circular #19, AN/16, 1951
11 Hearne, P. A. 1957
12 Hirst, M. 1976
13 McIlwraith, J. 1973
14 Hirst, M. 1976

with a radar set in the aircraft and a transponder on the ground. General Precision Inc produced a small microwave landing system capable of transmitting the steep glideslopes needed by helicopters, known as TALAR (Tactical Landing Approach Radar).

In 1968 Boeing started work on its Landing Aid System[15] and in 1972 delivered six ground beacons and five airborne sets to Wien Consolidated Airlines for trials with Boeing 737s in Alaska before approaching the FAA for certification. A beacon beside the runway transmitted four overlapping signals in the 5 GHz band to form a localizer and glideslope. These were received in the aircraft and displayed on a conventional ILS instrument. The advantages were low cost and freedom from distortion.

In October 1971 the British MADGE (for Microwave Aircraft Digital Guidance Equipment), begun as a private venture, won a NATO competition against the German Setac, the French Sydac and the USAF TALAR IV.[16] The aircraft interrogated a ground beacon which responded with elevation and azimuth. Airborne equipment compared this information with an approach path pre-selected by the pilot and displayed the result on a standard ILS instrument. The transmission frequency was in the 5 GHz (C) band. MADGE provided approach guidance down to 30 metres (100 feet) decision height and 400 metres (1,300 feet) visibility. Signals covered a 90° arc to 28 km (15 nm), a 130° arc to 3.7 km (2 nm) and elevation from 1.5° to 25°. Missed-approach guidance was provided to 28 km (15 nm) range through 90°. Ranging was available to 28 km (15 nm) through 360°. Development was rapid. By late 1972 MADGE I had been joined by MADGE III, intended as a civilian and military landing aid with Category 3 capability and MADGE IV, an area navigation system.[17]

In the civilian field, however, warning voices were heard. In 1972:[18] 'MLS is not just around the corner.' As long as the complex and diverse MLS technology remained unverified by experience, there was no likelihood that ILS would suddenly disappear, especially after so much had been invested in it. Whereas the ICAO had envisioned a single MLS completely replacing ILS, a 'mushrooming family of interim MLS systems (which the FAA, embarrassed, had been compelled to recognize)' had appeared. Many of them appeared to satisfy adequately the needs of undeveloped strips and tactical warfare. The introduction of any

new civilian landing aid would entail colossal equipment and training costs. Major sectors of aviation, especially airlines flying between city airports, did not need anything that could not be achieved by improvements to existing ILS.

The unifying characteristic of all the microwave systems was the use of the 1–15 GHz band, 5 GHz being the most suitable.[19] Similarities ended there. Some systems were 'air-derived', using a ground beacon and a receiver set in the aircraft (ILS is thus an air-derived system); others were 'ground-derived', with the aircraft interrogating a transponder on the ground which sent guidance to the aircraft. The ICAO regarded the air-derived systems as the replacement for ILS.

In the early 1970s MLS were being developed in America, Europe and Australia. The world scene of MLS development was too diverse and complicated to describe here. It was even described as a 'fragmented series of individual programmes that almost by chance happened to be headed in the same general direction'.[20] The most ambitious of these programmes was directed by the FAA towards a universal MLS to replace ILS, capable of everything from Category 3b automatic landing to the approach procedures of light aircraft.

In 1973 five countries made initial submissions to the ICAO to supply the new international standard MLS:[21] Australia, France, West Germany, the UK and the US. Intensive technical development, accompanied by fierce and at times unscrupulous political wrangling, followed over the next five years.[22] Meanwhile the American FAA and various civilian and military users continued to develop and install their own preferences. On 19 April 1978, the ICAO AWOP finally voted the American MLS as the future world standard approach aid.[23] The vote effectively put an end to all MLS development in Britain. This was, however, an empty victory. Although the ICAO decision brightened the overall outlook for MLS, civilian MLS never became anything more than an approach aid used by small air carriers at isolated sites. The advantages of MLS over ILS in most situations were too few to justify the cost of installation, re-equipping and re-training. By the middle 1990s MLS had still not penetrated the airline world and had been leapfrogged by a technology which was barely foreseeable in 1978; the satellite-based Global Positioning System (GPS).

Other American developments were directed at extending the limits of manual landings by improving the existing airborne equipment, yet short of automatic landing. In 1962 Douglas and Sperry Phoenix were working together on a glideslope extension device which averaged the descent rate to the inner marker and kept the aircraft on that descent rate through the Sperry SP-30 autopilot.[24] This project was intended to lower landing minima to 30 metres (100 feet) ceiling and then to 15 metres (50 feet). Collins was working on radar altimeters and aerodynamic sensors to extend the glideslope, using its existing range of autopilots and flight directors.

Douglas believed that the automatic flight control package which they had designed into the DC-9 could be upgraded for approaches to 30 metres (100 feet) ceiling and 400 metres ($\frac{1}{4}$ miles) visibility.[25] The additions would include an autothrottle, a flight instrument monitor, an autopilot monitor, dual radar altimeters, dual overshoot computers and dual vertical speed references. The autopilot and autothrottle would not be duplicated. The upgraded equipment would smooth out irregularities in the ILS signals immediately short of touchdown and extend the glideslope by memory. The overshoot computer used angle of attack and horizontal accelerations to generate flight director commands.

The Contact Analog (ANIP) program, mentioned earlier, was further developed in the 1960s; a stylized analogue of the outside world, from ILS and other information, was displayed on a CRT. The problem was that jet aircraft were reaching the point where the safety of visual landings was only marginally acceptable (about one fatal accident in every 1–2 million landings). Safety was unlikely to be improved by visual landings based on a synthetic analogue.[26]

The major US airlines had their own projects. TWA spent more than three years working with Boeing, Safe Flight and Bendix. The result, fitted to three Boeing 707s and three CV-880s, was called Autoscan.[27] It incorporated an advanced autopilot, dual flight directors, a speed director and autothrottles. Initial FAA approval was to minima of 45 metres (150 feet) decision height and 490 metres (1,600 feet) RVR. Approval to 30 metres (100 feet) decision height and 365 metres (1,200 feet) RVR would require 300 demonstration approaches to three different ILS. In addition to the airborne equipment and crew training, a precision ILS, standard approach lights with sequenced flashers, high-intensity runway edge lights, touchdown zone and continuous centreline lights, all-weather runway markings and RVR-measuring equipment

were required. In 1965 only Washington Dulles and Oakland, California, met these requirements, but plans were afoot to bring twenty airports up to this standard, with a possible maximum of fifty. PanAm, American and United had projects of their own. At the beginning of 1967 the stretched DC-8 was approved for Category 2 down to 30 metres (100 feet) decision height and 400 metres (1,300 feet) RVR with a Sperry SP-30AL autopilot, a Collins radar altimeter and a Douglas/Sperry flight director.[28]

The transition from instrument to visual flight came to be recognized as the most critical phase of the approach. Non-precision approaches were known to be hazardous in this respect, especially for large aircraft and at night. A VASIS came to be considered essential for both precision and non-precision approaches. During the 1970s RVR and cloud ceiling measurement, VASIS and ILS were installed at more and more airports and the ILS itself was improved. The major airlines recognized the need for one pilot to fly solely by instruments while the other looked for the runway and landed visually if possible or, if not, called for a go-around.

The airlines benefited from a military requirement originating in the 1950s, resulting in the HUD.[29] The Americans were more optimistic than the British that a human pilot could take off and land in low visibility, given suitable help, and the HUD was seen as a potential aid. The civilian demand for a HUD was less urgent than the military one. The French shared the American philosophy of extending the limits of manual landings; competition between airlines for lower

15 *Flight International*, 14 September 1972, 376
16 Derwent, H. L. 1972
17 Cowin, H. 1972
18 McIlwraith, J. 1973
19 Flounders, J. G. 1975
20 McIlwraith, J. 1973
21 Hirst, M. 1976
22 Wright, T. M. B. 1975; *Flight International*, 10 July 1976, 102; 17 April 1975, 645; 20 November 1975, 773; 27 November 1976, 1543; 30 April 1977, 1196; 17 September 1977, 843; 19 November 1977, 1489; 24 December 1977, 1845; 1 April 1978, 915; 25 March 1978, 844; Hirst, M. 1976; Goodman, W. 1976; Hirst, M., Feldman, J. 1977; Hirst, M. 1978
23 *Flight International*, 29 April 1978, 1255
24 *Flight International*, 22 February 1962, 297
25 *Flight International*, 17 October 1963, 644
26 Baxter, J. R. 1967, 405
27 *Flight International*, 7 January 1965, 7
28 *Flight International*, 2 February 1967, 161
29 Naish, J. M. 1966

landing minima created a demand for any device that would further that aim. Civilian progress was slow, but the French persevered and in the late 1970s the only company in the world producing an airliner HUD was the French company Thomson-CSF. It was used in Dassault Mercures flown by Air Inter.[30] The HUD benefited from the development of electronic instrument displays and the Thomson-CSF display was fully electronic.

The HUD display was simple. For the approach to landing it projected a runway symbol and a touchdown point with three dashes on either side. The dashes moved up or down in relation to the touchdown point to show if the aircraft was above or below the glideslope. A triangle moved up or down in relation to the touchdown point as an air speed command, while a second triangle, moving along a line representing the distant horizon, provided lateral guidance relative to the runway centreline. ILS information was displayed in a projected box. The combination of HUD and an automatic landing system could be used at airports without ILS if the aircraft carried INS and an angle-of-attack sensor.

The Mercure was equipped with a simplex, fail-passive, automatic landing system and in the three years 1975–7 Air Inter made 250 landings in passenger service in Category 3a conditions with equipment costing far less than the duplex or triplex automatic landing systems being developed by the British. National air regulations were decisive in this regard. Thomson-CSF hoped that their

Dassault Mercure.

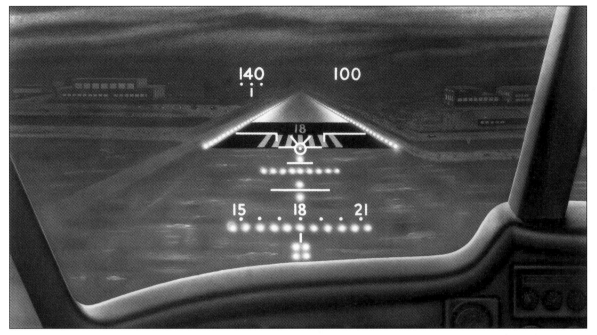

Early civilian HUD, *c*. 1970. (L. F. E. Coombs)

system would equip Swissair's DC-9-80s and the Airbus A-200. They were less optimistic about retrofitting older airliners.

In 1979 British Airways decided to equip their Boeing 737s with HUD,[31] as much for take-off guidance in low visibility as for landing. Swissair had decided to equip their DC-9-80s and thus, by the end of the decade, the HUD, standard in the military cockpit, was making a tentative entry into the airliner market.

As we will not return to the HUD in this narrative, we should look briefly at its subsequent impact.[32] Even in 1990 weather was still acknowledged as the biggest single cause of flight delays. Alaska Airlines, with frequent flights to and from Seattle, fitted a Flight Dynamics HGS-1000 HUD to twenty-four of its twenty-seven Boeing 727-200s and in 1991 was considering it for the company's other aircraft. The HGS-1000 was driven by master attitude, performance and navigation systems that did not exist when the HUD was first developed. It allowed Alaska Airlines to obtain FAA approval to lower its take-off minima from 183 metres (600 feet) RVR to 122 metres (400 feet) and to hand-fly ILS approaches in Category 3a weather. On 7 December 1990, an Alaska Airlines 727 took off from Seattle in early morning fog, the first jet airliner in scheduled commercial

service in US history to take off in an RVR less than 152 metres (500 feet). This was soon followed by a take-off in 121 metres (400 feet) RVR, which was causing other flights to be delayed or cancelled.

Although their philosophy differed from that of the British, the Americans ran a huge and diverse automatic landing programme of their own. In 1962 the FAA acknowledged the BLEU automatic landing system as 'probably the most advanced scheme for automatic landing in existence today'.[33] In 1961 the British company, Smith's Industries, supplied an automatic throttle control for an FAA-operated DC-7 with a Sperry autopilot, radar altimeter and leader cable receiver.[34] This aircraft flew successful trials, including 320 automatic landings, in 1961–2 at RAE Bedford, UK,[35] and at the FAA test facility at Atlantic City. Although leader cables had been installed at Atlantic City and the tests were carried out with and without using them, better localizers were expected to

30 *Flight International*, 25 February 1978, 495
31 *Flight International*, 24 March 1979, 892
32 *Flying*, March 1991, 10
33 *Flight International*, 7 June 1962, 919
34 *Flight International*, 20 April 1961, 540
35 *Flight International*, 7 June 1962, 919

make the leader cables unnecessary. By the summer of 1963 the DC-7 had completed 1,149 automatic landings at forty-seven airfields.[36] Twenty-five Category 2-standard ILS without leader cables were planned for the US in the next three years.[37]

In 1962 Sperry carried out several hundred automatic landings with its own aircraft using an SP-30 autopilot, a radar altimeter, a flare computer and the MacArthur Field ILS. Eclipse-Pioneer, a division of Bendix, was developing the PB-20 autopilot, as used in the Boeing 707 and 720, for lower approach minima and eventual automatic landing. Boeing was working on an automatic landing system for the 727, using the 707 prototype as a test-bed.[38] A Smith's Industries para-visual display,[39] a Lear flare director, a flare computer, a radar altimeter, an angle-of-attack sensor and a thrust command computer were to be added, feeding into the flight director.

Autonetics developed an automatic landing system, the APN-114. The pilot steered the aircraft manually towards the localizer at 450 metres (1,500 feet) above ground level below the glideslope. The APN-114 captured the localizer and, on intercepting the glideslope, reduced speed. When a radar altimeter sensed that the aircraft was 30 metres (100 feet) above the ground, a flare computer took over and further reduced speed. Any disturbance to the flight path caused a new flare to be computed, aimed at the original touchdown point. Bank angle was progressively limited from 33° to 15°. The localizer continued to supply azimuth guidance. At 2.1 metres (7 feet) above ground a light warned the pilot to decrab manually. The pilot retained the means to override the system by stick pressure. A test button allowed him to check the system for faults at any time. The APN-114 was first tested in 1960; it was delivered for USAF evaluation in January 1962, and was tested by the FAA the same year but was ultimately abandoned.[40]

The C-141 military freighter was the first American aircraft to be designed for automatic landing from the outset,[41] culminating in 1968 with approval for Category 3b landings.[42] The first automatic landing system to receive FAA approval was the Boeing-Bendix system developed for the Boeing 707 and 720.[43] Approval was granted on 18 March 1965, after a year-long evaluation, initially to minima of 60 metres (200 feet) ceiling and 800 metres (¼ mile) visibility. In 1966 the FAA certificated Boeing 707-320s equipped with this system to fly automatic approaches down to 30 metres

(100 feet) ceiling and 400 metres (1,300 feet) RVR. Aircraft thus approved were ordered by Air India, Varig and PanAm.[44] The long-term objective was to land in conditions down to zero ceiling and 150 metres (500 feet) RVR using an improved autopilot, dual radar altimeters, dual flare computers, autothrottles, an improved yaw damper and a system monitor to warn the aircrew of malfunctions. In 1965 the FAA contracted with Lear-Siegler for a fully automatic landing system for Category 3 minima. The equipment was to be tested in an FAA CV-880 at Atlantic City where Category 2-standard ILS was being installed.[45]

The first-ever fully automatic landing in passenger service was made by a PanAm Boeing 727, captained by William S. Ewing, at New York John F. Kennedy on the night of 28 February 1967, in good visibility.[46] British airliners were not allowed to do this at the time because of British regulations on back-up systems. On 7 July 1967, a PanAm Boeing 707 made the first fully automatic landing by a four-engined jet with passengers on board at Heathrow.[47] Regulatory differences gave PanAm a competitive edge over the British on its German internal routes where two Boeing 727s went into service in the winter of 1967–8.[48] On 26 June 1973, automatic landing saved a PanAm Boeing 747 from possible disaster when it landed at Heathrow with 200 passengers from Frankfurt.[49] Hail had broken two windshields and made the others opaque. The aircraft was equipped with a Bendix/Sperry automatic landing system certificated for Category 2 operation.

Under American regulations a single autopilot and a flight director sufficed for automatic approaches to Category 2 minima; an automatic touchdown was allowed, provided the airborne equipment had a monitor to alert the pilot to a malfunction and disconnect the autopilot. Aircraft operating under British regulations were allowed to continue to an automatic touchdown only if a second autopilot was available to take over if the first should fail. American manufacturers were to some extent forced to comply with British requirements in order to sell aircraft to British users.[50] With this in mind, Boeing planned eventually to equip 747s with triplex autopilots. This was required for Category 2 operations by British operators, but would be required in the future by the FAA for Category 3. The standard 747 automatic landing package in the late 1960s consisted of two autopilots and two flight directors, fed by three pitch and roll computers which obtained data from two sets of sensors. Monitoring remained the responsibility of the human pilot, although parts of the system had electronic self-monitoring.

By January 1968, Pan Am's fleet of 154 aircraft was qualified for Category 2 landings. By 1969 no less than 1,400 jets, 80% of the US fleet, were so equipped.[51] Most US airline jets had simplex automatic approach systems and dual flight directors; several hundred had duplex autopilots and about eighty-five had complete automatic landing capability. By mid-1969 PanAm, which had five Boeing 707s and two 727s equipped and FAA-approved for automatic landing, had made more than 1,000 automatic landings, 400 of them in scheduled passenger service. The major airlines had no doubts as to their own intentions to achieve Category 3 operations by whatever means possible.

Ingenious airline operators came up with their own ideas to meet their own needs.[52] Alaska Airlines Boeing 727 pilots approaching Ketchikan noticed that certain terrain features were distinctive on their RCA Primus-90 weather radar in the ground-mapping mode. Accordingly, in 1978, the airline obtained FAA approval for a reduction in minima at Ketchikan from 300 metres (1,000 feet) ceiling and 3.2 km (2 miles) visibility to 120 metres (400 feet) ceiling and 1,200 metres (0.75 mile) visibility.

The installation of ground equipment in the US lagged behind the advances in airborne equipment. In spite of grandiose plans,[53] in 1967 only one runway in the whole of the US (at Chicago O'Hare) was approved for Category 2 down to 366 metres (1,200 feet) RVR and another ten runways were certificated to Category 2 with various restrictions. The slow development of ground facilities remained a problem.[54] In 1973 the FAA awarded a $342,000 contract to Texas Instruments to install a Category 3 ILS at San Francisco. Two other Category 3 systems were being installed, one at the FAA centre at Atlantic City and one at Atlanta. The only operational Category 3 ILS in America at that time was at Washington Dulles and was a Plessey unit on loan from the British Department of Trade and Industry.[55] At the end of 1976 Washington was still the only US city with Category 3 capability. A year later three others had been added: Atlanta, Denver and San Francisco.[56] At the end of 1978 the FAA planned to increase the number of Category 3 ILS in the US from four to twelve and to approve thirty-seven airports with Category 2 ILS for limited Category 3 operations down to 213 metres (700 feet) RVR. The first

Category 3 operations in the US were flown at Atlanta in November 1977 in a 200–350 metre (650–1,150 foot) RVR. Of 113 landings scheduled in a 2½ hour period, only five were completed, all by Delta and Eastern TriStars. Two more approaches by autoland-equipped aircraft were missed.

Between 1970 and 1974 the proportion of airline crashes occurring during approach and landing increased to a half of the total. Although the crash rate in 1975 was only half what it had been ten years before,[57] eighty such accidents claimed 2,600 lives.[58] Intensive efforts went on, therefore, to improve all aspects of the low-visibility approach and landing. The Americans regarded automatic landing as a factor in improving safety as well as a part of the effort to lower the safe limits of ceiling and visibility. At the same time it was essential that automatic landing should not, of itself, contribute to the accident rate. The American pursuit of manual landings in low visibility delayed but did not prevent their ultimate acceptance of the need for fully automatic landing.

36 *Flight International*, 17 October 1963, 647
37 *Flight International*, 24 January 1963, 105
38 *Flight International*, 22 February 1962, 298
39 Para-visual display: roller mounted in the pilot's peripheral vision and marked with a spiral, giving steering commands when it rotated.
40 *Flight International*, 24 January 1963, 105
41 *Flight International*, 17 May 1962, 806
42 *Flight International*, 15 August 1968
43 *Flight International*, 1 April 1965, 480
44 *Flight International*, 24 November 1966, 866
45 *Flight International*, 25 November 1965, 882
46 *Flight International*, 9 March 1967, 345
47 *Flight International*, 13 July 1967, 42
48 *Flight International*, 7 March 1968, 341
49 *Flight International*, 5 July 1973, 3
50 *Flight International*, 7 March 1968, 344
51 *Flight International*, 30 October 1969, 674
52 *Flight International*, 27 May 1978, 1599
53 *Flight International*, 19 January 1967, 77
54 *Flight International*, 27 November 1976, 1544
55 *Flight International*, 11 January 1973, 51
56 *Flight International*, 21 January 1978, 169
57 *Flight International*, 26 June 1975, 989
58 Ramsden, J. M. 1975

CHAPTER 28

The British Go for Zero-Zero

The British were unrelenting in their pursuit of the ultimate in all-weather flight, automatic blind landing in airline service. The development of what had been achieved experimentally in 1944 into a routine airline operation took forty years.

As discussed earlier, the British effort was driven by a combination of military requirements and adverse weather and was led by the RAF Blind Landing Experimental Unit. Two British firms were closely associated with the BLEU, Smith's Industries and Elliott's. Although the BLEU's predecessor unit, the TRE, had achieved fully automatic landings in 1944–5, it took until 1962 to develop a military automatic landing system, based on the Smith's SEP-2 autopilot, clear it for use in a V-bomber at RAE Bedford and begin equipping the V-bomber force. The civilian version, the SEP-5, was conceived in 1957 as a new, multiplex flight control system. It was slated for the Trident airliner and the Belfast military transport after flight testing in the company's DC-3 and in a Comet 2E. By 1962 Smith's and the BLEU had completed more than 8,000 automatic landings, many of them in zero-zero conditions.

Short Belfast.

Vickers VC-10.

Far from being overawed by the complexity of landing big jets automatically, Smith's went so far as to say that landing 'cries out for automation', offering, so they said, safer landings, reduced runway requirements and reduced tyre and brake wear regardless of weather conditions. Even so, they realised that routine automatic landing in British airline service was not foreseeable before 1969–70 at the earliest.

The criterion guiding the British civilian automatic landing effort was the Air Registration Board requirement that the probability of a catastrophic system failure should not exceed one in ten million landings. Smith's and Elliott followed two different routes to this objective. Smith's applied the torque of three autopilots to the aircraft's control surfaces simultaneously. If the torque of one autopilot differed from that of the other two, it was disconnected automatically. If the two survivors disagreed, both would be disconnected.[1] Each subsystem could be checked before it was engaged. The Elliott system consisted of two self-monitoring autopilots with separate power supplies, only one being connected to the controls at any one time. If the monitors of one autopilot detected a fault, the other would replace it automatically. The Smith's system equipped the Trident and Belfast. The Elliott system equipped the VC-10.

The two British state corporations, BOAC and BEA, followed different policies, although both aimed at Category 3 operation. BEA aimed at fully automatic landing in Category 3b conditions (0 feet ceiling, 50 metres RVR) with Tridents using the Smith's triplex autopilots. BOAC aimed at automatic landing with manual decrab down to Category 3a conditions (0 feet ceiling, 100 metres RVR) with VC-10s using the Elliott twin self-monitoring autopilots.

The BLEU remained the chief proving ground for British blind landing, with impressive results.[2] One series of a hundred automatic landings in

1 Baxter, J. R. 1967, 405
2 *Flight International*, 8 March 1962, 378

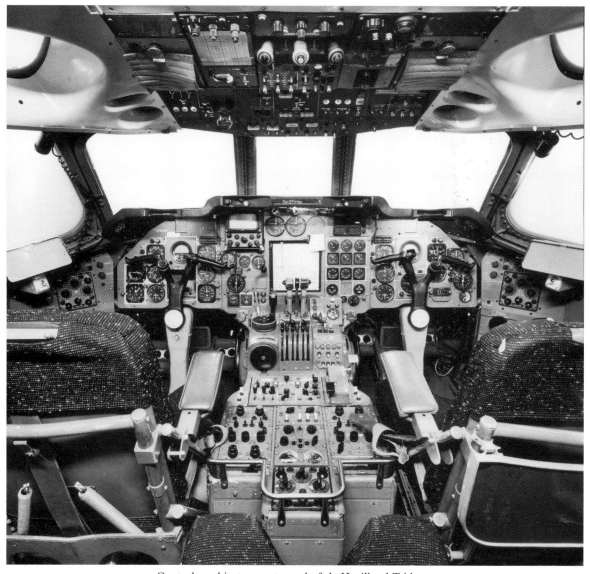

Controls and instrument panel of de Havilland Trident.

1961–2 with a Smith's-equipped V-bomber in turbulent conditions up to 37 km/h (20 knots) headwind, 28 km/h (15 knots) crosswind and 28 km/h (15 knots) tailwind gave an average rate of descent at touchdown of 0.55 metres (1.8 feet) per second (0.6 metres (2 feet) per second was acceptable), a longitudinal touchdown scatter of 113 metres (370 feet) and a lateral scatter of 0.6 metres (2 feet). Between 1959 and 1963 the BLEU made 230 landings in visibilities of less than 275 metres (900 feet). Sixty-six were at night; fifty-eight were in visibilities less than 300 feet, of which ten were

at night.[3] By 1965 Smith's-equipped aircraft had made more than 13,000 automatic landings.

As automatic landing became less an experiment conducted by test pilots and more a system to which airline pilots and passengers would have to trust their lives, it was essential to prove that the civilian version was safe in all weather conditions.[4] In 1961[5] BALPA[6] commented: 'Pilots tended to view with suspicion the introduction of any new device or procedure tending to undermine their powers of command.

'So far a pilot has never allowed any aid or

de Havilland Trident during automatic landing trials at Gatwick.

device to get his aeroplane into such a dangerous position that he was unable to extricate it from this situation by taking over manual control. Now for the first time he will be asked to allow a series of black boxes to manoeuvre his aircraft right down to the runway surface.' With this in mind Smith's demonstrated a modified Varsity with a triplex automatic landing system at the 1962 Farnborough airshow; the first aircraft in the world to be so equipped.[7]

The Trident entered service in April 1964, approved for normal jet minima of 90 metres (300 feet) ceiling and 1,200 metres (0.75 mile) visibility.[8] That November, however, based on experience and using an autothrottle, minima were reduced to 45 metres (150 feet) ceiling and 410 metres (1,350 feet) RVR, although these minima applied at London Heathrow only; elsewhere Trident minima were reduced only to 60–75 metres (200–250 feet) ceiling and 500 metres (1,650 feet) RVR. In 1965, however,

no airport in the world had Category 2-standard ILS, let alone Category 3. Triplex operation was preceded by a duplex phase in which the human pilot took control in the event of a discrepancy between the two autopilots.[9] Cockpit duties during the approach were divided between the two pilots, following a procedure developed at the BLEU in a simulator and flight trials.[10] One pilot concentrated on the instruments throughout the approach and landing or missed approach; the other looked for the runway and took control as soon as he saw it.

3 *Flight International*, 17 October 1963, 646
4 *Flight International*, 27 September 1962, 519
5 *Flight International*, 9 November 1961, 740
6 British Air Line Pilots Association
7 *Flight International*, 6 September 1962, 424
8 *Flight International*, 17 June 1965, 972
9 Bentley, J. 1966
10 Smith, K. W. 1972

If the aircraft strayed from the flight path needed for a successful landing, or if it reached decision height without the visual pilot taking control, the crew went into the missed approach without discussion.

On 12 November 1965, a Super VC-10 with Elliott Autoflare made a fully automatic landing at Gatwick.[11] Early on 4 November 1966, a Trident under test landed at Heathrow in fog which prevented all other flights.[12] 'Visibility from the flight deck varied between 50 yards and 100 yards during the landing. No approach lights could be seen, but the runway centreline lights became visible just before touchdown.' The Trident made three landings, using two of the runways, after which it returned to its fog-bound Hatfield base. On 24 November 1966, a Trident made six fully automatic landings at Heathrow in visibilities as low as 45 metres (150 feet).[13]

Between May 1965 and January 1967, flight-test Tridents made more than 2,000 automatic landings using duplex and triplex equipment,[14] proving that the Trident system could handle crosswinds up to

46 km/h (25 knots) and the turbulence associated with 65 km/h (35 knot) winds and could initiate a go around at any stage up to touchdown.

The procedure for an automatic landing is worth following in detail.[14A]

London radar vectored Papa Bravo, with Hawker Siddeley test pilots Mr. Jimmie Phillips, who is in charge of Autoland Development, as P1, and chief operations engineer Mr. John Wilson as P2, across London at 2,000 ft and 235 kt, well below a BEA Trident which was lining up for an approach to Heathrow's runway 28L as we crossed the Thames at Westminster. Six miles east of Epsom 20° flap and the undercarriage were lowered to drop the speed to 210 kt and soon we were turning in on a ten-mile final approach to Gatwick's runway 27.

The initial checks to ensure the aircraft was in the approach configuration – leading edge droop, flaps, undercarriage, airbrakes – were already complete. The landing weight of

VC-10 flight deck during automatic landing trials.

44,200 kg had been calculated and from it the approach speed of 137 kt was read off. In fact all approach speeds in the tests at this stage were being given a 5 kt margin so that the speed set on the autothrottle in the final approach phase was V_a + 5 kt, or 142 kt. The initial autothrottle setting, however, was V_a + 10 kt which, at 1,500 ft required very little throttle lever movement to maintain. At this stage the pilots were setting up and checking the ground aids for the landing runway on the radio input selectors situated centrally on the wide console between P1 and P2. The radio altimeters were switched on and the estimated drift set on the flight compasses together with the runway heading. The aircraft was by that time established on the localiser, flying level at 1,500 ft at a speed of 147 kt. The 'prime' switch on the flight controller was set to 'glide' and while we waited for the aircraft to intercept the glide-slope the radio altimeters were tested, together with the central and audio-warning system. The latter emits a varying pitched tweeting sound to indicate autopilot disengagement.

When the P2, who was monitoring the instruments, saw that the glide-slope bar on the flight compass was down to ½ dot from the centre he pressed the 'engage glide' button on the flight controller and the autopilot switched from constant altitude to following the the glide-slope. Full flap was selected and the speed command wheel turned to V_a + 5 kt – 142 kt. In preparation for a manual overshoot, if necessary, the flight compass drift index was zeroed and the runway heading was set on the steering index.

At 1,000 ft the 'prime' switch was turned to 'land' position; the radio altimeters were checked and runway wind velocity was re-checked to ensure that it was within limits.

At 220°/10 kt, the wind was 50° off the runway heading and producing slight turbulence below 1,000 ft. In particular there were two standing waves in the lee of the hangars and other buildings to the south of Gatwick's runway but despite these the speed never varied outside 5 kt of target on any of the approaches, neither were there any remarkable changes of either pitch or roll attitude.

The aircraft proceeded without any fuss down the glide-slope to 250 ft with the P2 resting his hands lightly on the control column and monitoring the ASI, flight compass, radio altimeter and mode indicator. P1 was engaged in the overall monitoring and at 250 ft put his hand on the throttle levers as a monitor for the autothrottle, to be ready to bring back the centre lever with the two outers when the flare started.

'Green light on,' called the P2 at 133 ft, easily identifiable on the large scale of the radio altimeter. The pitch attitude steadied, the drift was kicked off automatically and the wings levelled. At 62 ft, the call 'green light off' marked the start of smooth flare with the throttles coming right back. After 8½ secs the Smith's Autoland System touched Papa Bravo on Gatwick's concrete as smoothly as anyone could wish for. There was no jarring and both wheels touched at once, about ten yards to the left of centerline because of a slight kink in the localiser beam which persisted throughout all the morning's landings.

At touchdown the large autopilot cut-out button on the control column is pressed by P1 and the column pushed forward to destroy any residual lift on the wings and discourage any tendency for the aircraft to float. The autothrottle cut-out button is also pressed and reverse thrust selected as required. From touchdown, in fact, manual control is resumed.

The Short Belfast military transport was equipped from the outset for automatic landing, making its first such landing at RAE Bedford in June 1966.[15] Like the Trident, the Belfast was fitted with a triplex system, but differed in retaining the BLEU leader cable receiver. The pilot monitored the landing with an Elliott HUD. In 1965 the BAC-111 was certificated with the Elliott E-2000 autopilot. American Airlines owned the world's biggest BAC-111 fleet at the time and began a demonstration programme for Category 2 FAA certification. The programme was, however, abandoned for lack of US airports equipped to Category 2 standards.[16]

At the end of 1965[17] the British Ministry of

11   *Flight International*, 25 November 1965, 879
12   *Flight International*, 16 November 1966, 779
13   *Flight International*, 1 December 1966
14   *Flight International*, 26 January 1967, 114
14A Bentley, J. 1966, 980
15   *Flight International*, 16 June 1966, 1030
16   *Flight International*, 12 November 1970, 753
17   *Flight International*, 16 December 1965, 1034

Sud Aviation Caravelle.

Aviation announced that it would approve the Heathrow runway 10 Right ILS for Category 2 operations down to 30 metres (100 feet) ceiling and 400 metres (0.25 mile) visibility for suitably equipped aircraft, with effect from 13 January 1966. On 1 September 1966, however, the Civil Aviation Department of the Board of Trade imposed an arbitrary landing visibility minimum of 180 metres (600 feet) RVR on all British airlines.[18] This would not be relaxed until a vast body of statistical data from many thousands of automatic landings in all weather conditions proved the safety of automatic landing beyond doubt. In any event, Category 3 operations were not possible because of the lack of ILS to the required standards.

Because of its short-haul European routes, BEA needed blind-landing capability more urgently than BOAC. The latter, however, hoped for a competitive edge over American airlines which were

not able to land in zero ceiling. In January 1967 the Trident development programme for operations down to Category 3b minima was completed[19] after more than 2,000 automatic landings. During one week in May a BEA Trident logged 34.5 hours under automatic control with twenty-seven automatic landings at fifteen airports in nine European countries, controlled manually for an average of only 40 seconds in each flying hour.[20] On 16 May 1968, a Super VC-10 made BOAC's first automatic landing with passengers aboard at London Heathrow. The 146 passengers were told of this event after touchdown. BOAC planned to equip all seventeen of their Super VC-10s for automatic landing by 1970 at a cost of £2 million.[21]

British progress towards automatic blind landing with passengers inched forward. In 1967 government approval for Category 3b landings was expected for late 1970, but by the end of 1969 it was not anticipated that even Category 3a landings would be approved before 1971–2. In February 1969 the Board of Trade authorized BEA to land with passengers down to 45 metres (150 feet) decision height and 500 metres (1,650 feet) RVR, the middle of the Category 2 range. The same year the Super VC-10 was also approved for Category 2.[22] Of the Trident programme it was said:[23]

> … Hawker Siddeley,[24] which makes the Trident, Smith's Industries, which makes the automatic system, and BEA, the customer, have been leaders in a field where the pitfalls are many and the means to overcome them largely untried. It says a great deal for all three companies that they have persevered for so long without losing too much patience with the certificating authorities, even when progress abroad (under different rules) has brought superficially spectacular results. The process of certification in Britain of automatic landing devices is a much longer and more stringent procedure altogether than the US counterpart and when only a few aircraft are available it becomes a long drawn-out task.

The French were also active in automatic blind landing. In 1961 the French aircraft manufacturer, Sud Aviation, began to investigate automatic landing with a view to retrofitting the Caravelles which had entered service in the 1950s.[25] The French sided with the Americans in keeping the pilot in active control during the landing. Supported by the FAA and the French Air Ministry, Sud installed a Lear autopilot to certificate the Caravelle to minima of 30 metres (100 feet) with the ultimate aim of automatic landings. The Lear system used a barometric capsule, a vertical accelerometer and a radar altimeter to take over vertical guidance from the ILS glideslope immediately before touchdown. A flare computer started the flare-out at 15 metres (50 feet) as indicated by the radar altimeter.[26]

A Caravelle made the first-ever automatic landings by a jet airliner in 1962.[27] After 200 successful automatic landings at Toulouse, Sud Aviation and Lear announced that the system would be available for retrofitting Caravelles in late 1963. In that year Sud also experimented with a Caravelle fitted with the Smith's automatic landing system.[28] Sud Aviation's intention was to produce a system capable of Category 2 operation.[29] The French government imposed two requirements. The company had to prove that the system was accurate enough to allow nineteen successful landings out

of twenty regardless of weather; and the system had to provide the pilot with enough information and safety margin to allow him to take over manually at any time. Approval to Category 2 minima was granted in September 1964, but restricted to automatic approaches down to 15 metres (50 feet) above ground level followed by a manual touchdown.

Sud Aviation developed the system further for Category 3a by adding comprehensive monitoring and automatic disconnection in the event of a fault. Four components had to be added to the Lear 102 autopilot: an ILS auto-coupler with automatic decrab, a flare computer, an autothrottle computer, and a radar altimeter. This followed the American philosophy of a simplex autopilot monitored by a human pilot. The system was designed for retrofitting to the existing Caravelle fleet. In 1965 Alitalia equipped all twenty of its Caravelles with the Lear-Sud Aviation low-approach autopilot.[30] The Italian authorities required 200 recorded autoflare landings before approving the system for approaches to a 30 metre (100 foot) ceiling and 400 metre (1,300 foot) RVR. In spite of several thousand successful automatic landings the system did not have enough back-up to be approved for automatic landings in passenger service. Even so, the ILS at Rome, Venice and Milan Malpensa were cleared for automatic landing and those at Milan Linate and Turin were being upgraded. By 1967 Caravelles had made 10,000 automatic approaches at seventy-five airports with 3,500 automatic landings and 800 automatic overshoots.

The whole British effort to achieve blind landing was for a potential gain in reliability of just 1%.[31] BOAC estimated that a lowering of minima from Category 1 to Category 3b would improve regularity

18 *Flight International*, 15 December 1966, 1022
19 *Flight International*, 1 June 1967, 879
20 *Flight International*, 30 October 1969, 670
21 *Flight International*, 23 May 1968, 778
22 *Flight International*, 12 November 1970, 757
23 *Flight International*, 30 October 1969, 670
24 The British aerospace industry went through a series of mergers so that the Trident, first designed by de Havilland, was subsequently built by Hawker Siddeley.
25 *Flight International*, 20 April 1961, 540; 9 March 1967, 367
26 *Flight International*, 22 February 1962, 297; 3 January 1963
27 *Flight International*, 3 March 1964, 383
28 *Flight International*, 10 January 1964, 64
29 *Flight International*, 9 March 1967, 367
30 *Flight International*, 1 July 1965, 5
31 Andrew, J. 1970

of service due to weather from 98.67% to 99.95% at Heathrow and from 98.52% to 99.99% at John F. Kennedy. Small as this percentage was on an annual basis, fog could disrupt flights for days on end. More passengers and bigger aircraft meant that passengers had to be kept moving through the airports and nearby accommodation. Disruptions were costly to the airlines, inconvenient to passengers and caused chaos in and around the airports. The struggle to certificate zero-zero landing was focusing on Heathrow, one of the most heavily used air traffic hubs in the world and subject to some of the worst weather of any point of comparable traffic density.

Although automatic landing was normally associated with calm, foggy conditions, automatic landing systems were required to function equally well in strong crosswinds. The BAC-Elliott automatic landing system in BOAC's Super VC-10s was cleared for use in wind speeds up to 46 km/h (25 knots) which covered 98% of all wind conditions at Heathrow. Successful automatic landings had been made in 56 km/h (30 knot) headwinds, 52 km/h (28 knot) crosswinds and 22 km/h (12 knot) tailwinds.[32] During the final Category 3a Trident certification tests landings were made at Bedford in a gusty 46 km/h (25 knot) cross-tailwind. On one approach the turbulence caused such discrepancies between the three sensors feeding the gust comparator unit that the flight control system showed an unacceptable fault and the flight crew made a go-around from 3.7 metres (12 feet) above the runway.[33]

At the end of 1970 BEA was the only airline in the world with a fleet of aircraft, numbering thirty-six, fully equipped for automatic blind landing. Each crew member was trained, accredited and line-checked. Following BEA's standard procedure, the crew engaged the autopilot at 400 feet above ground level after take-off and continued the flight under automatic control until after touchdown. By the end of 1970 BEA had logged more than 15,000 automatic landings with some 500,000 passengers.

In the winter of 1970–1 BEA introduced routine Category 2 operations by its Trident fleet; delays due to fog were reduced.[34] Several factors, however, delayed progress towards complete regularity of service. New rules had to be devised, determining what equipment had to be working before an automatic landing could safely go ahead. Time was short for upgrading revenue-earning aircraft. Aircrew had to be trained. Simulator technology still lagged behind the needs of realistic blind landing practice. Simulation was essential to blind landing

development; real conditions occurred unpredictably and allowed no margin for error. The quality and availability of ground equipment, such as ILS, lagged behind both of these. Intensive study was needed on ILS interference, the structure of fog, weather reporting and safety heights. BEA helped the process by procuring improved versions of the Trident (Marks 1, 2 and 3) with improvements built into the aircraft as they were ordered. BOAC, however, found that individual VC-10s did not behave exactly the same; interchangeability of components took some time to achieve.

Unlike the Americans, the British were so unswervingly committed to completely automatic landing that no HUD was provided and flight directors were turned off at 300 metres (1,000 feet) above the ground during the approach. The pilot could, however, start an automatic missed approach procedure down to 3.7 metres (12 feet) above the ground by fully opening the throttles, even with an engine failure at the start of the go-around. Guidance was made independent of the ILS because its failure could be one of the problems dictating the go-around. Such complete dependence on automation required systems that would survive the failure of some of their components. Through multiplexing, the system had to monitor itself with a minimum of false alarms.

Blind conditions caused the additional problem of guidance during the landing roll. In the Trident 3 the para-visual display, concealed by shutters during an automatic approach, was exposed to view at or below 3.7 metres (12 feet) above ground if the automatic rudder control disconnected itself and when the autopilot was automatically disconnected at 150 km/h (80 knots) during the landing roll. The para-visual display (PVD) was a small device like a barber pole in the pilot's peripheral vision which issued a steering command by rotating one way or the other. Flight tests showed that the PVD enabled the average pilot to keep the aircraft within 15 metres (50 feet) of centreline in blind conditions, even if an engine failure caused asymmetric reverse thrust. Yet another device needed for blind operation on the ground was a speedometer. At speeds below 9 km/h (5 knots) the needle kicked at every quarter revolution of the main wheels to remind the crew that the aircraft was moving.

January 1972 marked the tenth anniversary of the first flight of the Trident prototype.[35] Since 1962 a million Trident passengers had been landed automatically. Airports other than Heathrow

Airbus 300.

equipped to automatic landing standards were Amsterdam, Cologne, Düsseldorf, Hamburg, Hanover, Paris Orly and Zurich. On 22 May 1972 BEA received CAA approval to land Trident 3Bs in Category 3a conditions.[36] The approval, however, was to a minimum RVR of 270 metres (885 feet), not to the Category 3a limit of 200 metres (655 feet). A 150 metre (500 foot) RVR was permitted for take-off. Part of the on-board ground guidance equipment was a Ground Roll Monitor giving ground speed and runway length remaining, the latter being subtracted from an initial figure put in by the flight crew. The PVD provided directional guidance.

BEA recorded its first operational automatic landing in Category 3 weather conditions on 30 December 1972, when anticyclonic conditions over the UK reduced visibility at a number of major airports and caused a large number of aircraft diversions. The landing was made when a Trident 3, under the command of Captain J. P. Robeson, operating the London Heathrow to Paris Orly service was forced by weather conditions to return to London. It landed at 1222 in a visibility of 270 metres (885 feet). Several other automatic landings were subsequently achieved over the next few days at London Heathrow on Runway 28L in Category 3 visibility, but reduced visibility at other airports prevented other aircraft from taking off for London.[37]

As important as the autopilots in lowering landing minima was ILS signal quality. A blind approach to Category 1 minima, followed by a

32 Brenchley, N. 1970
33 *Flight International*, 8 June 1972, 840
34 Wilson, J. W. 1970
35 *Flight International*, 20 January 1972, 84
36 *Flight International*, 8 June 1972, 838
37 *Flight International*, 4 January 1973, 5

visual landing, placed little reliance on ILS signal quality compared with the demands of Category 2 and Category 3 landings. By 1973 several types of airliner were capable of Category 3a landings, putting pressure on the British CAA to upgrade its ILS. It expected to spend £2.5 million by the end of 1974 to upgrade sixteen ILS to Category 3 standard, four of them at Heathrow.[38] The supplier was Plessey, which had bought Standard Telephone and Cable's ILS interests.

In 1973 RAE Farnborough made a thorough investigation of the Heathrow ILS.[39] The resulting report identified two sources of error, categorized as coherent and non-coherent. Coherent errors were distortions caused by the transmitter, by fixed objects nearby, and by aircraft and vehicles moving about on the airport. These errors could to some extent be controlled or guarded against. Non-coherent errors were from outside the airport, from sources that were not necessarily even identifiable. At Heathrow many such errors were observed during the working hours of nearby factories and contained harmonics of 50 Hz, the UK power grid frequency. It was even found that aircraft flying high overhead could reflect signals from other ILS. The new underground railway link to Heathrow was expected to cause interference to the Runway 28L ILS because the commutators of trains accelerating uphill towards London would modulate heavy direct currents at 90 and 150 Hz, the ILS modulation frequencies. Such effects, insignificant to Category 1 operations, could affect Category 2 and 3 operations if only because they were difficult to predict.

One of the ironies of the struggle for blind-landing was that, in the twenty-five years of its development, UK clean-air laws had reduced the incidence of the dense smog that automatic landing had been intended to deal with. As capability improved, the need declined, but by no means ceased.

In the autumn of 1973 British Airways[40] was certificated to operate its BAC-111s down to Category 2, which made an immediate valuable contribution to services between West Berlin and nine other West German destinations.[41] Category 2 weather covered Germany for the equivalent of ten whole days each year. The BAC-111's Elliott E.2200 autopilot included an autothrottle and was designed to accommodate the necessary additions for automatic landing and Category 3 operation. In 1974 British Airways and the French domestic Air Inter were the only airlines in the world operating routinely in Category 3 conditions.[42] At the end of 1976 France was the only country outside the UK with Category 3 airports. Category 2 runways were more numerous; British Airways used forty-nine, ten in the UK, sixteen on the European mainland and twenty-three in North America.

Cleaner air by no means ended the traditional foul weather of northwest Europe. In the last few months of 1975 British Airways Tridents made more than seventy Category 3a landings at Heathrow when other airlines were grounded.[43] Category 2 capability continued to prove its worth for BA's BAC-111s in Germany. In October 1975, nineteen Category 2 approaches were flown into Berlin Tegel one after another, and a total of sixty-two such approaches were flown in the month. In December 1976, Air Inter made twenty-three Category 3 landings at three French airports, involving sixteen Caravelles and A-300s, 2,456 passengers and seventy connecting flights.[44]

Operation in each category was not immediate after CAA certification because a working-up period was necessary. Thus, the Trident Category 3a flight trials were completed in January 1967. In February 1969, the CAA authorized British Airways to land in conditions down to the middle of Category 2. Category 3a clearance was granted in May 1972. By the end of 1975 the Trident fleet was ready for Category 3b operations, but complete Category 3b certification was not granted until 1979. Category 3b certification allowed an aircraft with a touchdown speed of 220–240 km/h (120–130 knots) to land in fog so dense (50 metres (165 feet) RVR) that one end of the aircraft would be invisible from the other – to all intents and purposes a blind landing. By means of multiplex, self-checking autopilots the probability of catastrophic failure was estimated at one in 100 million landings. The accident risk in the missed approach was estimated at three in 100 million.

BA needed Category 3 specifically for the London–Scotland shuttle; Glasgow and Edinburgh had therefore to be upgraded to the necessary standards. At Heathrow Runway 28L was preferred because visibility tended to be slightly better on that side of the field and because it had the best visual aids. High-intensity green centreline lights and a painted broken white line helped pilots to find their way off the runway. BA issued low-visibility taxi charts giving magnetic headings and Ground Roll Monitor read-outs; a vehicle checked the runway for obstructions before each low-visibility take-off or landing. Heathrow had a computer-aided taxiway lighting system unique in the world. Outside the UK, however, the rest of the world had little incentive to undertake the cost and effort required for Category 3 operations.

By mid-1976 300 BA captains had flown 40,000 automatic landings.[45] The human factor was a problem. Caution and professional pride made pilots reluctant to trust their lives to black boxes. Operating procedures had to be clear, simple and unambiguous. Crews had to be trained for a system that was, itself, evolving rapidly. It was essential that no doubt existed at any time as to who or what was controlling the aircraft. The most difficult problem was to avoid complacency when dealing with a system specifically designed for an extremely low probability of failure, and for the crews to stay alert during their repetitive, short-haul flights.

BEA, BOAC and their merged successor, British Airways, pioneered the development and certification of civilian aircraft for fully automatic blind landing, beginning in 1958 when the Trident was first ordered. In twenty years Trident automatic flight control evolved from fail-passive automatic approach to fail-operational automatic landing. Because of this work, progress with subsequent aircraft types worldwide was much quicker.

The first American airliner to be designed for automatic landing from the outset was the Lockheed L-1011 TriStar. The prototype flew for the first time on 16 November 1970; the first scheduled service followed on 26 April 1972.[46] TWA's first L-1011 made its inaugural flight on 25 June 1972, under automatic control from the time when it was lined up for take-off at St Louis until it turned off the landing runway at Los Angeles.[47] (This does not mean that the aircraft was pre-programmed, but the human crew did not directly control the flying surfaces.) The L-1011 was the first aircraft to receive FAA approval to land in Category 3a conditions.[48] The TriStar entered BA service in 1975. The first narrow-body US airliner to be approved for Category 3 was the Boeing 727 with a Sperry SP-50 fail-passive autopilot. Landings were allowed down to 15 metres (50 feet) decision height and 215 metres (700 feet) RVR.

Using Trident experience, Lockheed was able to deliver the first TriStars with Category 3b autoland already installed, although the aircraft was restricted to Category 1 until operating experience had been gained. UK Category 3b certification followed only two years later.[49] The TriStar's introduction into BA service, however, was delayed by labour disputes and a drop in passenger volume; after six months only 150 automatic landings had been made. Certification required 1,000 recorded automatic landings, but due to malfunctions in the recorder, not all of these were properly recorded. The programme received a further setback on 11 May 1975, when a TriStar landing at Heathrow pitched up on touchdown for no apparent reason and scraped the tail. The cause was believed to be a voltage fluctuation caused by a component failure in the aircraft's power supply, but the investigation took six months. False malfunction alarms wasted time in unnecessary maintenance. Category 3b certification was obtained in June 1977, but a BALPA directive banned the operation of any BA aircraft in conditions below Category 2.

The European Airbus consortium decided at an early date that automatic landing and Category 3 certification would be standard on all new Airbus aircraft. The consortium's first prototype, the A-300, flew for the first time on 28 October 1972; the production aircraft entered service with Air France on 30 May 1974.[50]

By the end of 1978 BA had still accepted only seven European airports for Category 3 although Milan, Munich and Venice were expected to join the list shortly.[51] At both Paris airports the French persisted with a fog-dispersal device called Turboclair, consisting of gas turbines mounted below ground, blowing their hot exhaust over the touchdown zone. This cleared only the touchdown zone so that a landing aircraft ran immediately into fog but, even so, it was well liked by pilots.

As the Americans veered towards fully automatic landing, so the British veered towards American concepts when it suited their purposes. In 1979 BA ordered Boeing 737s with Category 2-standard Sperry SP-177 automation and a Sundstrand HUD for certification down to 200 metres (650 feet) RVR and 15–18 metres (50–60 feet) decision height, with take-off minima at 75 metres (250 feet) RVR. Surprisingly, BA did not at first believe that Category 3 landing capability was necessary for its Boeing 747s, but the high cost of diverting hundreds of passengers at a time caused the management to change their minds. Swissair planned to certificate its DC-9s and DC-10s for Category 3, using a duplex, fail-passive system with a Sundstrand HUD. Lufthansa aimed for Category 3 with A-300s and A-310s, but was frustrated by the restriction of its main base at Frankfurt to Category 2.

BA's first winter with Category 3 certification was 1975–6, but the effect was small because of a lack of trained crews. The following winter saw real benefits with almost 160 take-offs and landings when other aircraft were grounded. Having obtained Category 3 certification for its Tridents and TriStars, BA was frustrated in 1977 by two problems. Fractures discovered on a soldered joint in the ILS transmitters reduced their reliability unacceptably; a year's delay on eleven of the twelve British Category 3 runways followed. The other frustration was the BALPA objection, aimed at extracting more pay for Category 3 flying. Having taken care to integrate its pilots with the introduction of automatic landing, and having heard their favourable comments, BA did not accept this demand lightly. These delays exposed the airline to competition by others, notably the French.

The first automatic Category 3 landing by Concorde took place in November 1978,[52] one of sixty-four fully automatic landings in Category 3 conditions on the BA network that month, fifty by Tridents, thirteen by TriStars, involving 8,000 passengers. Some aircraft made up to three automatic landings in one day down to 130 metres (425 feet) RVR. On 5 December 1978 alone BA crews made eighteen landings in RVRs of 200–300 metres (650–980 feet).

In May 1979,[53] BA Trident 2Es and 3Bs received CAA clearance to land in Category 3b conditions. This took the form of permission to continue an approach to a decision height of 3.7 metres (12 feet) under any RVR. In practice the airline imposed a limit of 75–100 metres (250–330 feet) RVR to allow visual taxying. This clearance was used within the year. In such conditions the slant visibility from the cockpit while the aircraft was on the ground became a significant factor. In Category 3b conditions ground vehicles had to be guided to the aircraft by ATC ground surveillance radar and radio.

By 1978 even the British were having doubts[54] that Category 3c capability would ever justify the cost. One writer stated categorically: 'experience in recent years has put paid to the prospects of ever seeing a Category 3c system, once the ultimate objective of the Trident programme. It has become clear that although the system integrity objectives could be achieved, the cost would be prohibitive in view of the few times that zero-zero visibility is encountered.' Category 3c operations would begin just four years later.

38 *Flight International*, 30 August 1973, 376
39 *Flight International*, 9 August 1973, 283
40 Formed by the merger of BEA and BOAC.
41 *Flight International*, 1 August 1974, 119
42 *Flight International*, 11 July 1974
43 Belson, J. 1976
44 *Flight International*, 18 November 1978, 1857
45 Owens, C. 197646 Taylor, M. J. H. 1989, 596
47 *Flight International*, 6 July 1972, 7
48 *Flight International*, 19 October 1972, 517
49 Tweed, J. 1978
50 Taylor, M. J. H. 44
51 *Flight International*, 18 November 1978, 1857
52 *Flight International*, 23 December 1978, 2252
53 *Flight International*, 5 June 1979, 910
54 *Flight International*, 18 November 1978, 1857

CHAPTER 29

The Quest Achieved

In March 1982, British Airways became the first airline in the world to obtain government approval for landings in zero-zero conditions – ICAO Category 3c.[1] The airline advised its pilots not to land if the RVR was less than 75 metres (250 feet) for ease of taxying and access for emergency services if needed. The RVR at Heathrow, however, had been below 75 metres only twice in the previous five years. The approval was granted to BA's TriStars only and the airline thought that Category 3c clearance would not be extended to other types, with the possible exception of the future Boeing 757.

Category 3c approval was put to use within weeks, but this ultimate event in the quest for all-weather flight, landing by an airliner carrying passengers in scheduled service in completely blind conditions, arrived and passed into history almost unnoticed. In the early hours of 5 May 1982, the fog at Heathrow was so dense that ceiling and visibility were to all intents and purposes zero.[2] The first aircraft to land was flight BA 131 from Jeddah, a TriStar commanded by Captain Geoffrey Clark; the second, soon after, was BA 032 from Bahrein, another TriStar with Captain Keith White in command. It was appropriate that this triumph was achieved by an American aircraft in British service.

In eighty years, within a human lifespan, the technology of controllable human flight sprang into being from nothing, acquired a pervasive influence on modern life and history, and matured to a *status quo*, accommodating itself to certain limits that are, for the time being, absolute. We are still so close to the convulsive efforts and political upheavals that nurtured and surrounded this technology that we have yet to become aware of it in either isolation or perspective.

Human flight has branched into an astonishing diversity of forms, from ultralights with no instruments or radio, and hence no practical capability of flying at night or in bad weather, to jet airliners capable of landing themselves in dense fog, and to military aircraft with secret powers to attack unseen targets.

The weather has always been among the most obvious but least considered of all the aspects of flying, yet the attention that it has received in the published history of aviation has been curiously slight. One measure of the maturing of human flight has been its ability to deal successfully with the weather. When aircraft can be flown from take-off to landing without the aircrew seeing anything outside the aircraft, when an aircraft can be navigated unerringly in time and space through or around weather of all kinds, in daylight and darkness at any season of the year and anywhere in the world, then the technology of flight has matured. The quest for all-weather flight has been achieved and those mariners called airmen have learned to sail their strange ocean in all its moods, or when to refrain from doing so.

For thousands of years humans looked wistfully at flying creatures and, indeed, attributed divine or magical properties to them. Myths are populated by gods and angels, dragons and devils whose divinity or magic lay in their ability to fly. As late as 1900 human flight in heavier-than-air machines was regarded by many as a figment of the imaginations of dreamers, cranks and lunatics. Reputable engineers said that it was impossible for an object of no natural buoyancy to make sustained and controllable flights through the air.

Yet on 13 May 1900, a Sunday, traditionally given to worship and quiet contemplation, a man named Wilbur Wright wrote a letter that must rank as one of the seminal documents of human history.[3] 'For some years,' he wrote, 'I have been afflicted with the belief that flight is possible to man. My disease has increased in severity and I feel that it will soon cost me an increased amount of money if not my life. I have been trying to arrange my affairs in such a way that I can devote my entire time for a few months to experiment in this field.' How little could he have known how those 'few months to experiment' would affect his own life and the lives of most of subsequent humanity. Such have been the astonishing consequences of that first flight at Kitty Hawk that cold, windy day in December 1903.

1 *Flight International*, 13 March 1982, 598
2 *British Airways News*, 14 May 1982, 1
3 Howard, F. 1987, 36–39

References

Abercromby, R. *Principles of forecasting*. London, UK. 1883.

Air Ministry (UK) *Instructor's handbook of advanced flying training*. Air Ministry Publication 1732b. London, UK: HM Government. 1st ed. May, 1943.

Alcock, J., Whitten-Brown, A. *Our transatlantic flight*. London, UK: William Kimber. 1969. Originally published: *Badminton Magazine*. September, 1919.

Anderson, M. Turbulence in cu-nim. *Flight*. 28 May 1954, 691–692.

Andrew, J. BOAC's programme. *Flight International*. 12 November 1970, 756.

Babington-Smith, C. *Evidence in camera: the story of photographic intelligence in World War II*. London, UK: Chatto & Windus. 1958.

Bach, R. Air traffic control in Europe. *Flying*. March 1962, 35, 74–76.

Bach, R. *Stranger to the ground*. New York: Harper & Row. 1963.

Bailey-Watson, C. B. International navigation aids. *Flight*. 11 January 1951, 44–47.

Baker, C. Night flying. *Aeronautical Journal*. December 1920, 627–649.

Baldwin, J. E. A. Training of pilots and instructors. *Journal of the Royal Aeronautical Society*. 1932.

Barker, R. Starliner to Tokyo. *Flight*. 25 April 1958, 564–566.

Baxter, J. R. Present trends in research towards all-weather landing for civil aircraft. *Journal of the Royal Aeronautical Society*. June 1967, 401–412.

Baxter, T. For love and money. *Flying*. March 1966, 34.

Beaty, D. *The Water Jump*. London: Secker & Warburg. 1976.

Bell, G. E. Paper to Institute of Navigation, 17 February 1950, abstracted in *Flight*. 2 March 1950, 276.

Belson, J. The real world of Cat 3a. *Flight International*. 3 January 1976, 8–9, 34.

Belson, J. Tomorrow's flight deck. *Flight International*. 6 March 1976, 536–538.

Belson, J. The twenty-first century flight deck. *Flight International*. 24 April 1977, 1118–1120.

Benkendorff, R. The organization of air routes for night flying. Abstracted in *Flight*. 12 February 1932, 134–136.

Bennett, D. C. T. *Pathfinder*. London, UK: Muller. 1958.

Bentley, J. Trident automatic landing progress. *Flight International*. 9 June 1966, 978–982.

Blackburn, R. J. Canberra night flight: to Bremen and back on Exercise 'Jungle King.' *Flight*. 3 April 1953, 430–433.

Blackburn, R. J. Ferry 604: the diary of a Viscount delivery flight to Montreal. *Flight*. 8 April 1955, 449–452.

Blake, B. H. L. Omega. *Flight International*. 7 October 1971, 571.

Blucke, R. S. The practical use of radio as a direct aid to the landing approach in conditions of low visibility. *Journal of the Royal Aeronautical Society*. 1938, 483–511.

Bowyer, C. *Air war over Europe 1939–1945*. London, UK: William Kimber. 1981.

Brackley, H. G. Piloting commercial aircraft. *Journal of the Royal Aeronautical Society*. 1936.

Brandon, L. *Night flyer*. London, UK: William Kimber. 1961.

Brenchley, N. BAC's automatic landing development. *Flight International*. 12 November 1970, 757–759.

Brent, F. Towards 100 per cent regularity. *Flight*. 27 April 1939, a–d; 4 May 1939, 461–464.

Brice, D. A. Cu-nim gusts. *Flight*. 12 January 1950, 32–34.

Brintzinger, W., Viehmann, H. Damage to aircraft by lightning. *Luftwissen*. 1, #2, 15 February 1934, 32–35. Abstracted in *Journal of the Royal Aeronautical Society*. 39, 1935, 176.

Broadbent, S. (1) Ground-proximity warnings. *Flight International*. 27 February 1975, 341–342.

Broadbent, S. (2) Ontrac II airborne. *Flight International*. 10 July 1975, 59–60.

Broadbent, S. (1) Omega first principles. No.1: theory. *Flight International*. 6 March 1976, 533–535.

Broadbent, S. (2) Omega first principles. No.2: in the marketplace. *Flight International*. 13 March 1976, 653–655.

Broadbent, S. (3) Omega first principles. No.3: in the air. *Flight International*. 10 April 1976, 889–891.

Broadbent, S. (4) Inertial navigation. *Flight*. 29 May 1976, 1411–1414.

Brooks, P. Transport airships, a short-lived dream: their economics examined. *Flight*. 25 December 1959, 780–781.

Brooks, P. W. Origins of the modern airliner. *Flight*. 11 April 1958, 490–493; 25 April 1958, 579–581; 9 May 1958, 632; 23 May 1958, 712–714.

Broughton, J. *Thud Ridge*. New York: Bantam. 1985. (1st ed. 1969.)

Brown, A. A. Automatic astro navigation. *Flight International*. 22 November 1962, 817–819.

Bryan, G. H. *Stability in aviation*. London, UK: Macmillan. 1911.

Buck, R. N. *Weather flying*. New York: Macmillan. 1970.

Burn, M. *Mary and Richard: The Story of Richard Hillary and Mary Booker*. London, UK: Andre Deutsch. 1988.

Calvert, B. J. Carousel IV in the 747. *Flight International*. 1 July 1971, 16–17.

Calvert, E. S. Visual aids for low visibility conditions. *Journal of the Royal Aeronautical Society*. 1948, 443–476.

Calvert, E. S. Takeoff and landing: safety and regularity in landing. *Journal of the Royal Aeronautical Society*. December 1959, 690–695.

Capper, N. J. Don't just sit there — worry. *Flight International*. 18 June 1964, 1012.

Casley, W. E. First double Atlantic crossing: the story of R34's remarkable voyage in 1919. *Flight*. 1 June 1961, 748–749, 778.

Castle, H. G. *Fire over England*. London, UK: Secker & Warburg. 1982.

Cawood, W. Some design problems in inertia navigation. *Journal of the Royal Aeronautical Society*. 1958, 704–722.

Charlwood, D. *No moon tonight*. Australia: Angus & Robertson. 1956.

Cheverton, B. T. Icing flight development. *Journal of the Royal Aeronautical Society*. 63, November 1959, 659–688.

Chinn, H. A. Radio range beacon free from night effects. *Proceedings of the Institute of Radio Engineers*. Vol. 21, #6, June 1933, 802–807.

Chïreïx, M. H. Blind approach system for horizontal and vertical guidance. *Revue de l'Armée de l'Air*. #82, May 1936, 589–594. Abstracted in *Journal of the Royal Aeronautical Society*. 1936, 733.

Chorley, R. A. Seventy years of flight instruments and displays. *Aeronautical Journal*. August 1976, 323–342.

Christie, C. A. *Ocean bridge: the history of RAF Ferry Command*. Toronto: University of Toronto Press. 1995.

Churchill, R. S. and Gilbert, M. *Winston S. Churchill*. London, UK: Heinemann. 8 vols. 1966–1988.

Clostermann, P. *The big show*. London, UK: Chatto & Windus. 1951.

Cochrane, R. The development of air transport during the war. *Journal of the Royal Aeronautical Society*. 1947, 384–416.

Coffey, T. M. *Iron eagle*. New York: Crown. 1986.

Collier, R. *Bridge across the sky: the Berlin blockade and airlift*. New York: McGraw-Hill. 1978.

Collinson, C., McDermott, F. *Through Atlantic clouds*. London, UK: Hutchinson. 1934.

Coombes, L. P. Takeoff and landing: the human engineering approach. *Journal of the Royal Aeronautical Society*. December 1959, 688–689.

Corkindale, K. G. A psychologist's point of view. *Journal of the Royal Aeronautical Society*. October 1965, 659–662.

Cowin, H. W. Madge in the market place. *Flight International*. 12 October 1972, 495

Cowin, H. (1) New TACAN from Marconi. *Flight International*. 4 January 1973, 37.

Cowin, H. (2) Anglo-US RNav. *Flight International*. 1 February 1973, 160.

Cowin, H. (3) Omega, rival to inertial nav? *Flight International*. 15 February 1973, 229, 232.

Cowin, H. (4) Decca's 70 series Doppler. *Flight International*. 22 February 1973, 270.

Crook, W. E. Telephony or .--- ? *Flight*. 8 July 1937, 62.

Curteis, M. C. Helicopter all-weather operation — equipment for the transport role. *Journal of the Royal Aeronautical Society*. March 1966, 229–236.

Davenport, W. W. *Gyro! The life and times of Lawrence Sperry*. New York: Charles Scribner's Sons. 1978.

Davies, R. E. G. *Lufthansa: an airline and its aircraft*. Rockville, Maryland: Paladwr Press. 1991.

Deltour, B. V. A guide to nav-com equipment. *Flying*. August 1960, 44–46, 88–92; September 1960, 44, 46, 82–89.

Denman, R. Radio air navigation: the trend of British development. *Flight*. 21 January 1937, 54–56.

Derwent, H. L. Madge, a tactical landing aid. *Flight International*. 16 March 1972, 382.

Diamond, H. Radio range beacon system – problem of night effects. *Proceedings of the Institute of Radio Engineers*. Vol.21, #6, June 1933, 808–832.

Diamond, H., Hinman, W. S., Dunmore, F. W. A method for the investigation of upper air phenomena and its application to radio meteorology. Abstracted in *Journal of the Royal Aeronautical Society*. 42, 1938, 1135.

Entwistle, F. The meteorological problem of the North Atlantic. *Journal of the Royal Aeronautical Society*. 1939, Vol.43, 69–104.

Errington, G. Towards automation in navigation. *Flight International*. 24 April 1966, 703.

Evans, R. E. Operational angles on the B-47. *Flight*. 25 January 1957, 115–118.

Feige, R. Measurement of upper limits of clouds and fog. Abstracted in *Journal of the Royal Aeronautical Society*. 39, 1935, 155.

de Ferranti, S. Instruments and electronics in aviation. *Journal of the Royal Aeronautical Society*. 1970.

du Feu, A. N. Evolution of the modern altimeter. *Flight International*. 26 December 1968, 1066–1067.

Florman, C. Night air mails. *Flight*. 20 March 1931, 255–259, 273–277.

Flounders, J. G. Which MLS? *Flight International*. 24 July 1975, 131–132.

Fredette, R. H. *The sky on fire*. Washington, DC: Smithsonian. 1991. Original edition: New York: Brace, Harcourt, & Jovanovich. 1976.

Ford, T. E. Doppler VOR. *Flight International*. 8 August 1974, 144.

Fowler, K. Flying in clouds. *Aeronautical Journal*. February 1918, 49–50.

Franck, P. Recent progress of aeronautical science in France. *Journal of the Royal Aeronautical Society*. October 1929, 915–934.

Friedman, R. M. *Appropriating the weather: Vilhelm Bjerknes and the construction of a modern meteorology*. Ithaca, New York: Cornell University Press. 1989.

Fuchs, A. S. Instrument rating – a new approach. *Flying*. May 1951, 38–39, 86.

Furnival, J. M. Wireless and its application to commercial aviation. *Journal of the Royal Aeronautical Society*. 1936, 159–197.

von Gablenz, C. A. Die Anforderungen an das Flugzeug und seine Ausrüstung auf Grund der Erfahrungen der Blindflugschulung. *Jahrbuch der Deutschen Akademie der Luftfahrtforschung*. 1941–2, 665–685.

Gann, E. K. IFR – Category 1930s. *Flying*. December 1962, 44–55.

Gann, E. K. *Fate is the Hunter*. New York: Simon & Schuster. 1961. Several editions.

Garratt, G. R. M. The automatic control of aircraft. *Flight*. 26 July 1934, 766a–d, 30 August 1934, 898a–g.

Genovese, J. G. *We flew without guns*. Philadelphia: John C. Winton. 1945.

Gibbs-Smith, C. H. Sir George Cayley; Father of aerial navigation (1773–1857). *Aeronautical Journal*. April 1974, 125–133.

Gilbert, J. The captain. *Flying*. January 1970, 56–61.

Gillman, R. E. Bright star from Burbank. *Flight International*. 13 January 1972, 61–64.

Gillman, R. E. Flying the flight deck of the future. *Flight International*. 11 September 1976, 799–802.

Ginn, M. C. The operation of the Bell 212 under instrument flight rules. *Aeronautical Journal*. May 1974, 194–197.

Goodman, W. US sells its MLS candidate. *Flight International*. 12 June 1976, 1567–1568.

Grahame-White, C. Commercial and pleasure flying. *Aeronautical Journal*. May 1919, 231–256.

Greenhalgh, G. T. Push-button pilotage: a Viscount captain's opinion of the 802 and its flying aids. *Flight*. 22 February 1957, 246.

Grover, J. H. Long-range navaids. *Flight*. 27 April 1956, 495–496; 4 May 1956, 540–541.

Grover, J. H. The air traffic control problem. *Flight*. 1 March 1957, 271–274.

H. M. Stationery Office. The measurement of upper winds by means of pilot balloons. Abstracted in *Journal of the Royal Aeronautical Society*. 41, 1937, 504.

Haddow, G. W., Grosz, P. M. *The German giants: the German R-planes 1914–1918*. London, UK: Putnam. 1962.

Hallion, R. P. *Legacy of flight*. Washington, DC: University of Washington Press. 1977.

Hallion, R. P. *Test pilots: the frontiersmen of flight*. Washington, DC: Smithsonian. 1988.

von Handel, P. Probleme und Stand der Blindlandung. *Jahrbuch der Deutschen Akademie der Luftfahrtforschung*. 1938–9, 259–279.

Handley Page, F. The military influence on civil aviation. *Flight*, 24 April 1953, 519.

Hann, J. *Lehrbuch der Meteorologie*. Leipzig, Germany. 1915.

Hardy, J. K. Protection of aircraft against ice. *Journal of the Royal Aeronautical Society*. 51, 1947, 271–305.

Hardy, R., Wright, P., Kington, J., Gribbin, J. *The weather book: a complete illustrated guide to meteorological phenomena, weather forecasting, and climate*. Toronto, Canada: Little, Brown. 1982.

Harper, H. *The romance of a modern airway*. London, UK: Sampson Low, Marston. (Undated, *c*.1930).

Harper, H. London to Manchester 1910. *Flight*. 20 April 1950, 491–495.

Hart, C. Burattini's flying dragon. *Aeronautical Journal*. July 1979, 269–273.

Harvey, W. J. *Rovers of the night sky*. Oceanside, California: Aeolus. 1984. Originally published UK, 1919.

Hastings, M. *Bomber Command*. London, UK: Michael Joseph. 1979.

de Havilland, G. *Sky Fever*. London, UK: Hamish Hamilton. 1961.

Hearne, P. A. Helicopter blind flying (abstract). *Flight*. 29 March 1957, 405–406.

Hecks, K. *Bombing 1939–1945: the air offensive against land targets in World War II*. London, UK: Robert Hale. 1990.

Hirst, M. Which microwave landing system? *Flight International*. 30 October 1976, 1322–1327.

Hirst, M. Simulation: better than real? *Flight International*. 4 December 1976, 1660–1661.

Hirst, M. The automatic navigator. *Flight International*. 8 January 1977, 67–70.

Hirst, M., Feldman, J. MLS — microwave landing systems on trial. *Flight International*. 17 September 1977, 844–846.

Hirst, M. (1) Airborne navigation systems. *Flight International*. 14 January 1978, 110–113.

Hirst, M. American MLS team confident of victory. *Flight International*. 11 February 1978, 354–355.

Hirst. M. (2) GPWS living up to its promise. *Flight International*. 15 July 1978, 201–203.

Hirst, M. (3) Ten years of airline INS. *Flight International*. 29 July 1978, 347–349.

Hirst, M. (4) Automatic flight control. *Flight International*. 5 August 1978, 411–414.

Hoffmann, K. O. *Ln-: Die Geschichte der Luftnachrichtentruppe*. Neckargemünd, Germany: Kurt Vowinkel. 1965.

Howard, F. *Wilbur and Orville: A biography of the Wright brothers*. New York: Alfred A. Knopf. 1987.

Howard, R. W. Automatic flight controls in fixed wing aircraft: the first hundred years. *Aeronautical Journal*. November 1973, 533–562.

Hoyt, E. P. *199 days: the battle for Stalingrad*. New York: Tor. 1993.

Hunt, G. H., Hobbs, A. E. W. in Development of an accurate tuning-fork gyroscope. *Proceedings of the Institute of Mechanical Engineers*. 179, 1964–5, Part 3E.

Hurst, M. The electronic flight deck. *Flight International*. 14 October 1978, 1405–1408.

Irving, D. *The rise and fall of the Luftwaffe: the life of Luftwaffe Marshal Erhard Milch*. London, UK: Weidenfeld & Nicholson, 1973.

James, J. W. G. Air safety from the pilot's point of view. *Journal of the Royal Aeronautical Society*. 1949, 949–965.

Jackson, W. E. Status of instrument landing systems. *Proceedings of the Institute of Radio Engineers*. Vol. 26, #6, June 1938, 681–691.

Johnson, B. *The secret war*. London, UK: Arrow. 1979.

Johnson, B., Cozens, H. I. *Bombers: the weapon of total war*. London, UK: Methuen. 1984.

Johnson, J. E. *Wing leader*. London, UK: Chatto & Windus. 1956.

Johnson, W. E. P. Blind-flying birthday. *Flight*. 23 November 1951, 646–648.

Johnson, W. E. P. Leaves from a log book. *Flight*. 2 August 1957, 169–171; 8 August 1957, 199–200; 16 August 1957, 229–230.

Jones, F. E. Radar as an aid to the study of the atmosphere. *Journal of the Royal Aeronautical Society*. 53, 1949.

Jordanoff, A. *Through the overcast: the weather and the art of instrument flying*. New York: Funk & Wagnalls. 1938.

Kayton, M., Fried, W. (eds.) *Avionics navigation systems*. New York: John Wiley. 1969.

Kelly, L. L., Parke, R. B. *The pilot maker*. New York: Dunlap. 1970.

Keys, A. R. Jaguar — a new look at combat effectiveness. *Flight International*. 22 February 1973, 257–258.

Kingsford, A. R. *Night raiders of the air*. London, UK: Greenhill. 1988. Original edition: London, UK: John Hamilton. 1930.

Lambert, C. M. Flying in the Valiant. *Flight*. 19 July 1957, 86.

Lambert, C. M. Bomex by Vulcan: a bomber exercise from Waddington. *Flight*. 18 July 1958, 66–67.

Lambert, M. Radio: why and wherefore. *Flight International*. 22 March 1962, 442–445.

Lawrence, T. E. *Seven pillars of wisdom*. New York: Doubleday. 1938.

Learmount, D. Captain, what's your attitude? *Flight International*. 1 December 1979, 1827–1828.

Lee, L. Lower landing limits. *Flight International*. 16 April 1964, 603–604.

Lewis, C. *Sagittarius Rising*. London, UK: Warner Books, 1994. Original edition, London, UK: Peter Davies, 1936.

Lindbergh, C. A. *The Spirit of St. Louis*. New York: Charles Scribner's Sons. 1953.

Van der Linden, F. R. *The Boeing 247*. Seattle, Washington: University of Washington Press. 1991.

Locke, L. G. The Bölkow BO-105D. *Aeronautical Journal*. May 1974, 197–199.

Lockspeiser, B. The prevention of ice accretion. *Journal of the Royal Aeronautical Society*. January 1936, 1.

Lovel, M. S. *The sound of wings: the life of Amelia Earhart*. New York: St. Martin's Press. 1989.

Ludlum, F. H. *The cyclone problem: a history of models of the cyclonic storm*. London, UK: 1966.

Macmillan, N. The history and growth of commercial air transport. *Flight*. 3 January 1930, 77–80.

Makinson, W. All-weather landings. *Flight*. 18 December 1953, 805–806.

McIlwraith, J. Towards microwave landings. *Flight International*. 26 July 1973, 131–138.

McKinlay, W. H. The Trident's flight control system. *Flight International*. 2 April 1964, 544.

Melvill Jones, B. Flying over clouds in relation to commercial aeronautics. *Aeronautical Journal*. May 1920, 220–249.

Melvill Jones, B. Cloud flying in the First World War. *Journal of the Royal Aeronautical Society*. January 1966, 207.

Mercer, J. F. W. A quantitative study of the instrument approach. *Journal of the Royal Aeronautical Society*. February 1954.

Meredith, F. W. Air transport in fog. *Flight*. 7 November 1930, 1226–1227.

Merer, J. W. F. The Berlin airlift. *Journal of the Royal Aeronautical Society*. 1950, 513–533.

Merrick, K. A. *Halifax*. London, UK: Ian Allen. 1980.

Middlebrook, M. *The Nuremberg raid*. London, UK: Allen Lane. 1973.

Middlebrook, M. *The battle of Hamburg*. London, UK: Allen Lane. 1980.

Middlebrook, M. *The Berlin raids*. London, UK: Viking. 1988.

Miller, E. M. How they flew the air mail. *Flying*. August 1966, feature article.

Mohler, S. R., Jackson, B. H. Wiley Post, his 'Winnie Mae,' and the world's first pressure suit. *Smithsonian Annals of Flight*, #8, 1971

Moulton, M. Technology for better all-weather landings. *Flight International*. 12 November 1970, 753–755.

Moxam, L. R. Westland design philosophy on the Lynx for instrument and all-weather flying. *Aeronautical Journal*. May 1974, 187–193.

NACA Hazards to aircraft due to electrical phenomena. NACA Technical Note #94, March 1934. Abstracted in *Journal of the Royal Aeronautical Society*. 39, 1935, 176.

Naish, J. M. Display research and its application to civil aircraft. *Journal of the Royal Aeronautical Society*. October 1966, 662–669.

Neilan, J. C. Cumulo-nimbular comments. *Flight*. 26 January 1950, 44.

Nelson, G. L. A partial panel — what's next? *Flying*. August 1972, 58, 98.

Norris, G. *The Royal Flying Corps: a history*. London, UK: Frederick Muller. 1965.

Noth, H., Polte, W. The formation of ice on aircraft. *Journal of the Royal Aeronautical Society*. 41, 1937, 595–608.

Ocker, W. C., Crane, C. J. *Blind flight in theory and practice*. San Antonio, Texas: Naylor. 1932.

O'Hara, F. Burnham, J. The atmospheric environment and aircraft — now and the future. *Aeronautical Journal*. June 1968, 467–480.

Olley, G. P. *A million miles in the air: personal experiences, impressions, and stories of travel by air*. London, UK: Hodder & Stoughton. 1934.

Oomen, P. In memory of MF and MF/DF. *Flight*. 5 August 1955, 199–200.

Ormonroyd, F. Visual aspects of cockpit management. *Journal of the Royal Aeronautical Society*. October 1965, 651–659.

Owen, K. Northern route — from Vancouver to Amsterdam. *Flight*. 24 August 1956, 293–295.

Owens, C. Operations. *Aeronautical Journal*. August 1976, 350–353.

Parton, J. *Air force spoken here: General Ira Eaker and the command of the air*. Bethesda, Maryland: Adler & Adler. 1986.

Patrick, K. B. Thunderstorm project. *Aeronautical Journal*. September 1968, 748–754.

Perry, W. H. Requirements for the helicopter instrument rating. *Aeronautical Journal*. May 1974, 200–203.

Piper R. E. *Point of no return: an aviator's story*. Ames, Iowa: Iowa State University Press. 1990.

Price, A. *Instruments of darkness: the history of electronic warfare*. London, UK: Macdonald & Jane's. 1977.

Pritchard, H. C. Problems of blind landing. *Journal of the Royal Aeronautical Society*. 1946, 935–973.

Pritchard, J. L. Sir George Cayley: The Man: His Work. *Flight* 12 November 1954, 701–703.

Prowse, B. O. Takeoffs and landings: the pilot's problems. *Journal of the Royal Aeronautical Society*. December 1959, 687–688.

Pugh, A. T., Lambert, C. M. Three-dimensional dilemma. Traffic control: civil aviation's big problem. *Flight*. 3 May 1957, 581–584.

Quill, J. K. *Spitfire*. London, UK: Arrow. 1985. Originally published London, UK: John Murray. 1983.

Ramsden, J. M. The last thousand feet. *Flight International*. 23 January 1975, 107–112.

Ramsden, J. M. Air navigation. *Flight International*. 18 September 1975, 406–409.

Rawnsley, C. F., Wright, R. *Night fighter*. London, UK: Collins. 1957.

Reynolds, F. Ordeal by thunderstorm. *Flying*. January 1964, 50.

Rimell, R. L. *Zeppelin!* Belleville, Ontario, Canada: Canada's Wings. 1984.

Roberts, B. Falcon Echo: the 53rd Weather Reconnaissance Squadron USAF. *Flight*. 5 June 1959, 769.

Rowe, N. E. Problems facing civil air operations. *Journal of the Royal Aeronautical Society*. 1948, 87–115.

Samuelson, H. M. The future of aircraft radio. *Flight*. 27 January 1938, 66–68.

Sarjeant, R. Panel games. *Flight International*. 30 April 1964, 721–723.

Sawyer, T. *Only owls and bloody fools fly at night*. London, UK: Goodall. 1982.

Scanlan, H. La postale de nuit. *Flight International*. 17 December 1964, 1041–1044.

Serling, R. J. *The only way to fly: the story of Western Airlines*. New York: Doubleday. 1976.

Shaw, W. N. *Forecasting weather*. London, UK. 1911.

Shaw, W. N. Meteorology: the society and its fellows. *Quarterly Journal of the Royal Meteorological Society*, 45, 1919, 97.

Shiner, J. F. *Foulois and the US Army Air Corps*. Washington, DC: Office of Air Force History. 1983.

Simpson, G. S. Ice accretion on aircraft — notes for pilots. Meteorological Office Professional Notes, #82, 1937. Abstracted in *Journal of the Royal Aeronautical Society*. 42, 1938, 102.

Sinclair, P. Long-range navigation aids. *Flight*. 2 March 1951, 257–258.

Smith, H. L. *Airways: a history of commercial aviation in the United States*. New York: Knopf. 1944.

Smith, K. W. All-weather Operations – present achievements and future prospects. *Aeronautical Journal*. 1972, 183–187.

Spencer, O. C. *Flying the Hump: memories of an air war*. College Station, Texas: Texas A & M University Press. 1992.

Stallibrass, G. W. Radio and air traffic control. Lecture to Institute of Radio Engineers, 1951 convention, abstracted in *Flight*. 8 February 1952, 160–161; 15 February 1952, 190–192.

Stein, E. P. *Flight of the Vin Fizz*. New York: Arbor House. 1985.

Stewart, C. J. Modern developments in aircraft instruments. *Aeronautical Journal*. 1928, 425–481.

Stewart, C. J. *Aircraft Instruments*. London, Chapman & Hall, 1930.

Stringer, F. S. Air navigation philosophy. *Flight International*. 21 October 1965, 702–705.

Stokes, P. Loran C – development prospects? *Flight International*. 24 January 1976, 165–167.

Stüssel, R. The problem of landing commercial aircraft in fog. *Journal of the Royal Aeronautical Society*. June 1934, 807–836.

Summers, J. T. Inas in service. Abstracted in *Flight International*. 18 October 1973, 678.

Summers, J. T. Instant orientation. *Flight International*. 27 March 1975, 542.

Swanborough, F. G. *United States military aircraft since 1909*. London, UK: Putnam. 1963.

Swanson, E. H. Radio frequencies. *Flying*. November 1957, 40–42, 72, 74, 76, 78.

Taylor, G. *The sky beyond*. Boston: Houghton Mifflin. 1963. Bantam ed. 1983.

Taylor, H. A. Blind into Tempelhof. *Flight*. 14 February 1935, 175–177.

Taylor, H. A. Instrument flying. *Flight*. 17 October 1935, 401–404.

Taylor, H. A. Radio and air traffic. *Flight*. 30 January 1936, 120–122.

Taylor, H. A. Switzerland non-stop. *Flight*. 20 February 1936, 192–194.

Taylor, H. A. (1936b) Down the beam. *Flight*. 18 June 1936, 648–649.

Taylor, H. A. Transatlantic experiment. *Flight*. 8 July 1938, 44.

Taylor, H. A. Scientifically to Sweden. *Flight*. 23 December 1937, 618–622.

Taylor, H. A. Organizing for safety. *Flight*. 20 January 1938, 52–55.

Taylor, H. A. Netherlands terminal. *Flight*. 10 February 1938, 134a–c.

Taylor, H. A. Atlantic overture. *Flight*. 12 January 1939, 30.

Taylor, M. J. H., Mondey, D. *Milestones of flight*. London, UK: Jane's. 1983.

Taylor, M. J. H. *Jane's Aviation Encyclopedia*. London, UK: Portland House. 1989.

Thomas, H. A. The determination of the meteorological conditions of the atmosphere by the use of radio sounding balloons. Abstracted in *Journal of the Royal Aeronautical Society*. 42, 1938, 89.

Thorne, B. K. *The Hump*. New York: J. B. Lippincott. 1965.

Trotti, J. *Phantom over Vietnam*. Novato, California: Presidio. 1984.

Tweed, J. British Airways TriStar autoland development. *Flight International*. 4 March 1978, 569–570.

Voss, V. *Flying minnows*. New York: Hippocrene. 1977. Original edition 1920s.

Vulliamy, A. T. New conceptions of aerodrome lighting. *Flight*. 2 February 1939, 102f–h, 103.

Wakefield, K. *The first pathfinders: the operational history of Kampfgruppe 100, 1939–1941*. London, UK: William Kimber. 1981.

Walker, E. G., Walls, R. J. Evolution of Doppler navigation systems. *Flight International*. 21 July 1966, 105–107.

Wansbrough-White, G. Off the beacon track. *Flight International*. 16 March 1972, 378–379.

Ward, C. E. Lighting the airport for night flying. *Flight*. 7 December 1933, 1224–1225.

Warwick, G. All-weather A-10. *Flight International*. 1 December 1979, 1844–1849.

Watson-Watt, R. Radio and civil aviation. *Flight*. 7 March 1946, 249–250.

Webster, C., Frankland, N. *The strategic air offensive against Germany 1939–1945*. London, UK: HM Stationery Office. 1961.

Weeghman, R. B. Navigation by Doppler. *Flying*. June 1963, 32–33, 59, 62.

Weeghman, R. B. For good measure: DME, promising child of technology … *Flying*. March 1965, 33–35.

Weeghman, R. B. Magic maps and mystery omnis. *Flying*. October 1968, 78–83.

Wein, T. The not so Rapide flight to Miami. *Flight International*. 15 October 1970, 599–602; 22 October 1970, 639–640.

Welch, J. F. (ed.) *Van Sickle's Modern Airmanship*. New York: Van Nostrand Reinhold, 5th ed. 1981.

West W. FIDO was no dog. *Flying*. August 1957, 26, 62, 74.

Westman, W. S. 'Nice flight, captain.' *Flying*. March 1974, 87–88.

Wickson, M. *Meteorology for Pilots*. Shrewsbury, UK: Airlife Publishing. 1992.

Williams, J. E. D. *From sails to satellites: the origin and development of navigational science*. Oxford, UK: Oxford University Press. 1992.

Williamson, G. W. Instrument planning. *Flight*. 19 August 1937, 193–195.

Williamson, G. W. Blind flying on the ground. *Flight*. 28 October 1937, 416–419.

Wilson, J. W. Autoland all-weather progress. *Flight International*. 12 November 1970, 750–752.

Woodforde, J. *The Diary of a Country Parson 1758–1802* Beresford, J. ed. Oxford, UK: Oxford University Press, 1978.

Wright, M. D. *Most probable position: a history of aerial navigation to 1941*. Wichita: University Press of Kansas. 1972.

Wright, T. M. B. Radio aids – what does the future hold? *Flight International*. 15 April 1971, 527–531.

Wright, T. M. B. Difficult MLS choice. *Flight International*. 9 January 1975, 39–40.

Wronsky, M. German commercial air transport. Abstracted in *Flight*. 21 March 1930, 328–331.

Young, M. A. The controller's viewpoint. Abstracted in *Flight*. 2 March 1950, 276.

Yuill, G. F. QBI and why. *Flight*. 16 March 1939, 270c–f.

Anonymous Authorship

– Fog flying experiments. *Flight*. 27 June 1930, 721.

– Kingsford-Smith's Atlantic flight. *Flight*. 4 July 1930, 757–761.

– The Brown aero turn indicator. *Flight*. 5 December 1930, 1413.

– Wireless and aircraft. *Flight*. 17 April 1931, 347

– On 'instrument flying.' *Flight*. 7 August 1931, 779–781

– Night flying at Croydon. *Flight*. 11 September 1931, 925–926.

– The Reid-Sigrist turn indicator. *Flight*. 18 September 1931, 953–954.

– The Braun relative altitude meter. *Flight*. 23 October 1931, 1063.

– New wireless beacon for Croydon. *Flight*. 27 November 1931, 1177.
– Night flying at Heston. *Flight*. 24 June 1932, 572–573.
– School house and school room. *Flight*. 6 October 1932, 934.
– Wireless equipment for the African air route. *Flight*. 22 December 1932, 1219.
– The Marconi 'homing' device. *Flight*. 18 May 1933, 482; 30 November 1933, 1205.
– For safe navigation. *Flight*. 29 June 1933, 652.
– The Emeraude disaster. *Flight*. 18 January 1934, 56; 1 February 1934, 100.
– Researches on lightning discharges striking aeroplanes. *Revue de l'Armée de l'Air*. #56, March 1934, 325–340. Abstracted in *Journal of the Royal Aeronautical Society*. 39, 1935, 176.
– The Douglas DC-1. *Flight*. 1 March 1934, 189–191.
– Wireless navigation at Hamble. *Flight*. 24 May 1934, 1219.
– Before dawn flight. *Flight*. 13 September 1934, 961.
– An acoustic altimeter. *Flight*. 20 December 1934, 1363.
– Six-thirty ex Paris. *Flight*. 20 December 1934, 1367.
– Blind landings in America. *Flight*. 20 December 1934, 1367.
– A German 'robot' pilot. *Flight*. 10 January 1935, 41–42.
– Night mail. *Flight*. 24 January 1935, 109.
– Modern aircraft radio equipment. *Flight*. 14 March 1935, 274–279.
– Some interesting instruments. *Flight*. 21 March 1935, 320.
– An American 'radio compass.' *Flight*. 11 April 1935, 400.
– Ex Heston. *Flight*. 3 October 1935, 370.
– A radio compass in action. *Flight*. 19 December 1935, 650.
– Behind the Gyorizon. *Flight*. 27 February 1936, 235–236.
– Blind approaches in England. *Flight*. 27 February 1936, 240.
– Light aircraft equipment. *Flight*. 23 April 1936, 432–433.
– Air traffic control. *Flight*. 21 May 1936, 540a–d.
– Another blind approach demonstration. *Flight*. 28 May 1936, 587.
– The technique and approach: some useful information on the recommended methods of using the Lorenz receiver: different indications and their meaning. *Flight*. 17 September 1936, 286–287.
– Radio meteorograph system. Abstracted in *Journal of the Royal Aeronautical Society*. 41, 1937, 504.
– An airline pilot thinks aloud. *Flight*. 25 March 1937, 310–311.
– The Lorenz blind landing system tested in USA. *Inter Avia*. #433/4, 22 May 1937, 9.
– Short wave direction finding. *Flight*. 8 July 1937, 61.
– Atlantic routine. *Flight*. 15 July 1937, 68–72.
– The modern touch: how the technique of flying is changing: Swissair as an example. *Flight*. 12 August 1937, 169–170.
– Full automatic blind landing system. The landing system developed by the US Army. *Inter Avia*. #484, 26 October 1937, 1–2.
– Specialized Training. *Flight*. 18 November 1937, 492–493.
– Berlin-New York-Berlin. *Flight*. 18 August 1938, 148.
– A new blind approach system. *Flight*. 15 September 1938, 233.
– Automatic fix. *Flight*. 27 October 1938, 377–378.
– More automatic D/F. *Flight*. 17 November 1938, 445.
– QBI contact. *Flight*, 26 January 1939, 89.
– Present trends in radio services. *Flight*. 2 February 1939, 106–109.
– Pan American preliminary. *Flight*. 13 April 1939, 371–373, 385.
– Another blind approach system. *Flight*. 27 July 1939, 86d.
– A little blind flying. *Flight*. 27 July 1939, 95–96.
– Sperry attitude gyro. *Flight*. 29 March 1945, 334–335.
– Towards complete automaticity: Sperry A12 electrically-operated automatic pilot described: the Gyrosyn compass. *Flight*. 31 October 1945, 463–465.
– Atlantic air conference ends. *Flight*. 4 April 1946, 347.
– Constellation proving flight to New York with BOAC. *Flight*. 11 July 1946, 29–32; 18 July 1946, 55–58.
– Approach by ground control. *Flight*. 11 July 1946, 47–49.
– Decca navigator. *Flight*. 1 August 1946, 113.
– Air traffic control. *Flight*. 19 September 1946, 313–316.
– Clearing the air: FIDO an expensive but effective expedient. *Flight*. 6 March 1947, 193–195.
– The Gyrosyn compass. *Flight*. 13 March 1947, 207–209.
– Stormy weather: are we overlooking that vital link between the dashboard and the controls – the pilot? *Flight*. 1 May 1947, 391–393.
– Radar in civil aviation. *Flight*. 20 March 1947, 242–245.
– A new autopilot. *Flight*. 25 September 1947, 364–367.
– Automatic control: operational sequence of the transatlantic flight. *Flight*. 9 October 1947, 415–418.
– On the level: a new electrically-actuated gyro horizon by Sperry. *Flight*. 21 October 1948, 479–480.
– Zero reader: air experience of Sperry's new flight instrument. *Flight*. 18 August 1949, 182–185.
– Collecting a Stratocruiser. *Flight*. 15 December 1949, 774–777.
– London radar. *Flight*. 16 February 1950, 208–209.
– Test flight navigation: practical experience with the Decca navigator system in the Ambassador. *Flight*. 2 March 1950, 274–275.
– Thermal fog-dispersion. *Flight*. 22 June 1950, 742.
– American navaid systems. *Flight*. 11 January 1951, 53.
– All-weather approach lighting. *Flight*. 3 August 1951, 139.

– Distance measuring equipment. *Flight*. 31 August 1951, 258–259.
– AntipoDME: DME now developed in Australia. *Flight*. 21 September 1951, 394–395.
– Answer to the pilot's prayer? Trying out the Decca flight log. *Flight*. 9 November 1951, 601.
– Finding the right approach. *Flight*. 13 June 1952, 718–719.
– London airport FIDO? *Flight*. 28 November 1952, 670–671.
– Airline avionics, *Flight*. 6 March 1953, 291–292.
– Viscount in the air: aids and instruments. *Flight*. 20 March 1953, 374–375.
– 'Jungle King': Bomber Command's big exercise. *Flight*. 27 March 1953, 390–391.
– Conversion to Comets. *Flight*. 1 May 1953, 535–539.
– Radio at Farnborough. *Flight*. 18 September 1953, 413–415.
– IFR without tears. *Flight*. 2 April 1954, 389–391.
– Airfield visibility assessment. *Flight*. 23 April 1954, 511–512.
– Instrument panel developments. *Flight*. 7 July 1954, 45.
– Across three oceans. *Flight*. 6 August 1954, 169–173.
– Civil airborne search radar. *Flight*. 25 November 1954, 779–780.
– Airborne radar discussed. *Flight*. 21 January 1955, 77.
– Integrated flight system: Collins two-instrument system for radio navigation and ILS approach. *Flight*. 11 February 1955, 167–170.
– Airline navigation. *Flight*. 11 March 1955, 332–335.
– Radically new cockpit design. *Flight*. 8 April 1955, 453.
– Automatic interception. *Flight*. 29 April 1955, 548–549.
– Decca evaluated. *Flight*. 2 May 1955, 701–702.
– More on VOR-DME/TACAN. *Flying*. June 1955, 66.
– Smith's flight system. *Flight*. 19 August 1955, 254–255.
– Lead-collision attack: America's development of automatic interception. *Flight*. 11 November 1955, 748–749.
– Developments in Decca. *Flight*. 6 April 1956, 384.
– TACAN evaluated. *Flight*. 29 June 1956, 855.
– New developments in radio and radar. *Flight*. 21 September 1956, 511–512.
– Decca Mark 10. *Flight*. 12 October 1956, 603.
– Airborne proximity indicator. *Flight*. 30 November 1956, 845–846.
– The new airways system. *Flight*. 28 December 1956, 1006.
– Jet transport operation problems. *Flight*. 5 April 1957, 437–438.
– Flying aids. *Flight*. 12 April 1957, 471–500.
– Marconi Doppler navigators. *Flight*. 12 July 1957, 41–42.
– Radio Mailles. *Flight*. 19 July 1957, 87.
– Fighter flight instrumentation. *Flight*. 16 August 1957, 212.
– DIAN. *Flight*. 23 August 1957, 250–251.
– Air radio developments. *Flight*. 27 September 1957, 514–516.
– Flying aids. *Flight*. 16 May 1958, 659–682.
– Automatic stabilization for helicopters. *Flight*. 10 October 1958, 572.
– British automatic landing system. *Flight*. 17 October 1958, 614.
– Jet clipper: riding Pan American's Boeing 707 to the USA. *Flight*. 31 October 1958.
– Kinalog: a new approach to blind-flying instrumentation. *Flight*. 28 November 1958, 823–825.
– Operation 'Smoke Plume.' *Flight*. 19 December 1958, 947.
– Bell automatic landing trials. *Flight*. 9 January 1959, 57.
– BEA and the DH 121. *Flight*. 23 January 1959, 143.
– Navigation. *Flight*. 20 February 1959, 262–272.
– Helicopters, all-weather. *Flight International*. 24 February 1961, 237–250.
– That one-eighty rating. *Flight International*. 8 June 1961, 808.
– Harco and Eurocontrol. *Flight International*. 2 November 1961, 689.
– Our amazing airways system. *Flying*. January 1962.
– Automatic landing: economics and timing. *Flight International*. 22 February 1962, 291–300.
– BLEU at work. *Flight International*. 8 March 1962, 378–379.
– Full triplex system flies. *Flight International*. 9 September 1962, 424–425.
– Stavanger accident report. *Flight International*. 4 October 1962, 557.
– TWA relies on Doppler. *Flight International*. 11 October 1962, 588.
– Caravelle automatic landing. *Flight International*. 3 January 1963.
– The Viterbo accident. *Flight International*. 3 January 1963, 6–7.
– World air safety. *Flight International*. 30 May 1963, 775–779.
– The FAA and all-weather landing. *Flight International*. 17 October 1963, 642–650.
– Air safety in 1963. *Flight International*. 2 January 1964.
– Navigation at the cross-roads. *Flight International*. 25 June 1964, 1053–1054.
– Pan Am goes inertial. *Flight International*. 30 July 1964, 171.
– Second sight for landing. *Flight International*. 27 August 1964, 333.
– Concord navigation. *Flight International*. 24 September 1964, 548–550.
– Aviation electronics. *Flight International*. 22 October 1964, 701–708.
– 1964's best ever safety record. *Flight International*. 7 January 1965, 5.

– Trident automatically. *Flight International*. 17 June 1965, 972–973.
– The Innsbruck accident finding. *Flight International*. 5 August 1965, 211.
– Elliott's new civil inertial system. *Flight International*. 30 September 1965, 571.
– Better 1965 accident record. *Flight International*. 6 January 1966, 6.
– Dead reckoning – 1966 style: the performance of inertial navigation equipment. *Flight International*. 17 February 1966, 254–257.
– Bad year for air safety. *Flight International*. 5 January 1967, 7.
– Automatic landings nearer. *Flight International*. 26 January 1967, 114.
– Automatic approach and landing. *Flight International*. 9 March 1967, 361–372.
– Air navigation survey. *Flight International*. 29 June 1967, 1057–1073.
– Shuttle test for Decca. *Flight International*. 6 July 1967, 11.
– Hyperbolic world-wide. *Flight International*. 11 July 1968, 65, 71.
– Altimeter setting in doubt at Ljubljana. *Flight International*. 12 September 1968, 397–398.
– Investigators recommend QFE approaches. *Flight International*. 21 November 1968, 817–818.
– 1968: the overall safety picture. *Flight International*. 16 January 1969, 99–100.
– QFE or QNH? *Flight International*. 30 January 1969, 162.
– Autocoupling problems. *Flight International*. 20 February 1969, 281.
– Gee chain closure. *Flight International*. 17 July 1969, 104.
– Automatic landing. *Flight International*. 30 October 1969, 670–675.
– Radio and navigation aids. *Flight*. 26 February 1970, 308–313.
– Decca details. *Flight International*. 19 March 1970, 430–431.
– Microwave arrival. *Flight International*. 21 May 1970, 861–862.
– Who started the map moving. *Flight International*. 21 May 1970, 863–864.
– Automatic landing. *Flight International*. 12 November 1970, 750–759.
– Honeywell on the ball. *Flight International*. 15 April 1971, 531.
– Trident 3 demonstrates reliability. *Flight International*. 20 January 1972, 84–85.
– Boeing's microwave ILS. *Flight International*. 14 September 1972, 376.
– Microwave landing aids. *Flight International*. 6 April 1972, 470.
– Green light for autoland. *Flight International*. 8 June 1972, 838–842.
– IFR certification for Bell 212. *Flight International*. 23 November 1972, 742.
– Tired out of your minds? *Flight International*. 22 March 1973, 417.
– Sources of ILS errors. *Flight International*. 9 August 1973, 283.
– Navigating Concorde. *Flight International*. 1 November 1973, 758–759.
– PMS in action. *Flight International*. 10 January 1974, 34.
– CAA's plans for Doppler. *Flight International*. 7 March 1974, 307.
– MRCA nav-attack system. *Flight International*. 28 March 1974, 400–402.
– Two accidents analyzed. *Flight International*. 1 August 1974, 102.
– Ontrac II. *Flight International*. 29 August 1974, 246.
– Speechless. *Flight International*. 21 November 1974, 728.
– Current instrument techniques. *Flight International*. 5 December 1974, 799.
– The simulation industry. *Flight International*. 30 January 1975, 138–141.
– Sundstrand pioneers in ground proximity warning systems. *Flight International*. 20 February 1975, 306–307.
– Pitot icing caused 727 accident. *Flight International*. 6 March 1975, 355.
– Navigation system choices. *Flight International*. 13 March 1975, 401–402.
– Ontrac II: versatile navigator. *Flight International*. 10 April 1975, 597.
– Nigerian MLS operation. *Flight International*. 17 April 1975, 645.
– Looking at Loran – the transmissions. *Flight International*. 21 August 1975, 271a.
– Raster head-up displays. *Flight International*. 30 October 1975, 665–666.
– America defers GPWS. *Flight International*. 11 December 1975, 863.
– Omega on trial. *Flight International*. 11 December 1975, 863–864.
– New VLF/Omega navigator from Global. *Flight International*. 31 January 1976, 237–238.
– MLS and flight systems research at RAE. *Flight International*. 10 July 1976, 102–104.
– ICAO introduces new navigation requirements. *Flight International*. 25 September 1976, 962.
– Where does MLS go from here? *Flight International*. 27 November 1976, 1543.
– Coming soon: no more diversions. *Flight International*. 27 November 1976, 1543–1544.
– Pilot's view of the first twelve months. (Concorde) *Flight International*. 21 February 1977, 363–365.
– SP stands for Sleepy Pilots? *Flight International*. 12 February 1977, 368.
– Helicopter IFR for the single pilot. *Flight International*. 26 February 1977, 461–462.
– Omega: two sides of the story. *Flight International*. 5 March 1977, 533.

– USAF tests 'world's most accurate navigation system.' *Flight International*. 26 March 1977, 783.
– 580 killed in Tenerife collision. *Flight International*. 2 April 1977, 806.
– Voting controversy at final MLS meeting. *Flight International*. 30 April 1977, 1196.
– PAIR: talkdown in the 1980s. *Flight International*. 28 May 1977, 1494.
– An MLS first. *Flight International*. 17 September 1977, 843.
– MLS trial sites agreed. *Flight International*. 19 November 1977, 1489.
– Doppler sales shift up and up. *Flight International*. 26 November 1977, 1593–1594.
– All-weather landings in the US. *Flight International*. 21 January 1978, 169.
– Flight safety 1977. *Flight International*. 21 January 1978, 182–187.
– The world of civil simulators. *Flight International*. 18 February 1978, 435–437, 447.
– Thomson-CSF looks ahead. *Flight International*. 25 February 1978, 495.
– Microwave landing system battle intensifies. *Flight International*. 25 March 1978, 844.
– Microwave decision clears the air. *Flight International*. 29 April 1978, 1255–1256.
– Raytheon updates the radar talkdown. *Flight International*. 23 September 1978, 1165–1166.
– Europe's airlines fear no fog. *Flight International*. 18 November 1978, 1857–1858.
– Laser navigators for Boeing 757/767. *Flight International*. 14 December 1978, 2166.
– First Concorde in-service blind landing. *Flight International*. 23 December 1978, 2252.
– Air-India 747 accident: inquiry calls for improved instrument training. *Flight International*. 4 August 1979, 312.
– NATO studies Navstar GPS. *Flight International*. 29 September 1979, 1034.
– BA beats fog with new Trident minima. *Flight International*. 1 December 1979, 1819.

Index